The My Lai massacre in American history and memory

MANCHESTER
1824

Manchester University Press

To Patricia

The My Lai massacre in American history and memory

Kendrick Oliver

Manchester University Press

Manchester and New York

distributed exclusively in the USA by Palgrave

Published by Manchester University Press
Oxford Road, Manchester M13 9NR, UK
and Room 400, 175 Fifth Avenue, New York, NY 10010, USA
www.manchesteruniversitypress.co.uk

Distributed exclusively in the USA by
Palgrave, 175 Fifth Avenue, New York,
NY 10010, USA

Distributed exclusively in Canada by
UBC Press, University of British Columbia, 2029 West Mall,
Vancouver, BC, Canada V6T 1Z2

British Library Cataloguing-in-Publication Data
A catalogue record for this book is available from the British Library

Library of Congress Cataloging-in-Publication Data applied for

ISBN   0 7 190 6890 8   *hardback*
EAN   978 0 7190 6890 4

ISBN   0 7190 6891 6   *paperback*
EAN   978 0 7190 6891 1

First published 2006

14 13 12 11 10 09 08 07 06   10 9 8 7 6 5 4 3 2 1

Typeset in 10/12pt Century Book
by Graphicraft Limited, Hong Kong
Printed in Great Britain
by CPI, Bath

Contents

List of illustrations

Preface

To speak or to write of the 'My Lai massacre' is to trade in a necessary, if unfortunate, fiction. The principal (but not the only) settlement in which the killings occurred was marked on US military maps as My Lai (4), signifying a sub-hamlet within the hamlet of My Lai, within the village of Son My. This was the name that subsequently came to represent the location of the massacre in American public discussion, and that designation has survived into written history, including this author's early publications on the subject. In fact, the settlement was known to its residents as Xom Lang, and it was a sub-hamlet within the hamlet of Tu Cung, not My Lai. One of the main themes of this study is the displacement or erasure of Vietnamese perspectives from the American story of the massacre. It would seem consistent with that critique, therefore, to use local Vietnamese nomenclature when discussing the experiences of the local Vietnamese, and especially the victims of the killings. It has been impossible, however, to avoid all reference to 'My Lai', either in describing the actions of American troops in the settlement they identified as My Lai (4) or in discussing the reception and memory of the massacre within US society at large. I have chosen not to bore readers with persistent textual corrections of this misnomer; in return, I ask only that the misnomer be acknowledged.

It is normally a melancholy business to contemplate one's debts, more melancholy still to publicize them. In this instance, however, I welcome the opportunity to record what I owe, and to present the meagre offering of my gratitude to those many individuals and institutions who afforded me assistance during the course of this project. In particular, I would like to thank the British Academy and the Arts and Humanities Research Board, in the case of the former, for funding my initial research investigations into the reception of the massacre and, in the case of the latter, for the award that allowed me to prolong my sabbatical and finish this book. Gareth Davies and Michael Heale served as referees for the AHRB award and were supportive of the project throughout. Cambridge University Press granted permission to include material in this book that previously appeared in the *Journal of American Studies*. I am grateful also to the staff at Manchester University Press, and especially Alison Welsby and Jonathan Bevan, for the enthusiasm with which they responded to the project when first approached, and for their guidance as it edged closer to completion.

I am bound, in addition, to acknowledge the help and advice provided by archivists at the following repositories: the National Archives (including the Nixon Presidential Materials) in College Park, Maryland; the Vanderbilt Television News Archive in Nashville, Tennessee; the US Army Military History Institute in Carlisle, Pennsylvania; and the Liddell Hart Centre for Military Archives at King's College, London. Whilst researching at the Military History Institute, I benefited greatly from discussions with Colonel Alan Cate, Alexander Cochran, Conrad Crane and David Perry. In Washington, General Charles Dyke kindly agreed to be interviewed about the army's response to the massacre.

However, I have not been entirely dependent upon the kindness of strangers. Colleagues and friends at the University of Southampton have provided a receptive sounding board as my ideas have developed, interested as many of them are in questions of memory. I think particularly of Peter Gray, Mike Hammond and Peter Middleton. John Oldfield and Neil Gregor read this work in draft and offered valuable suggestions as well as encouragement. During my visits to the United States, George and Elena Dryden, William and JoAnn Morandini, David Rosenberg and Kathleen Morandini, and Constantine and Roula Pagedas were generous in their offers of food, wine, accommodation and companionship.

As ever, my work on this book has been an attempt to justify the faith that my parents, Terence and Christine Oliver, have shown in me, and the love and support they have provided throughout my life. My greatest debt, however, is owed to my wife, Patricia Morandini, who has had to live with this project for as long as she has known me, enduring its lengthy passage towards completion with (mostly) patience and good humour. She probably will not thank me for dedicating this book to her, thus associating her name with one of the grimmest chapters of her country's past, but I have done so anyway, in recognition of her love and her partnership in the enterprise.

I remain, of course, entirely responsible for the views and judgements expressed in this work and for any errors and omissions.

List of abbreviations

ABC	American Broadcasting Company
ARVN	Army of the Republic of Vietnam
AWC	Art Workers Coalition
CBS	Columbia Broadcasting System
CCI	National Committee for a Citizens' Commission of Inquiry on US War Crimes in Vietnam
CGSC	US Army Command and General Staff College
CIA	Central Intelligence Agency
CID	Criminal Investigation Division (US Army)
KCL	King's College, London
LBJL	Lyndon Baines Johnson Presidential Library
LHCMA	Liddell Hart Centre for Military Archives
MACV	Military Assistance Command, Vietnam
NACP	National Archives (College Park, Maryland)
NBC	National Broadcasting Company
NCO	Non-commissioned officer
NPM	Nixon Presidential Materials
OCINFO	Office of the Chief of Information (US Army)
RAS	Records of the Army Staff
RCCPI	Records Created after the Completion of the Peers Inquiry
RPI	Records of the Peers Inquiry
USAMHI	US Army Military History Institute
VTNA	Vanderbilt Television News Archive
VVAW	Vietnam Veterans Against the War

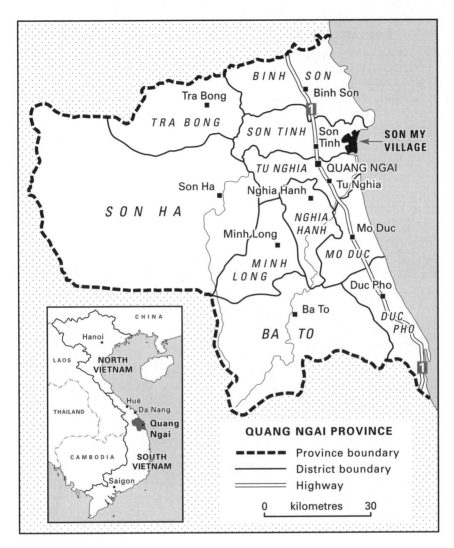

Map of Quang Ngai province

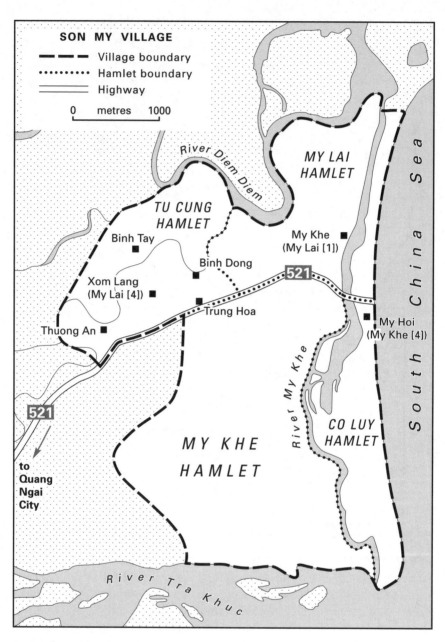

Map of Son My village

Introduction

On the morning of 16 March 1968, the men of Charlie Company, 11th Light Infantry Brigade, Americal Division, US Army, entered the hamlet of Tu Cung, in the village of Son My, on the coast of central Vietnam.[1] The company was assigned to a temporary battalion-sized unit named Task Force Barker, and it was led by Captain Ernest Medina. In charge of the company's 1st Platoon was Lieutenant William Calley. Inside Tu Cung, the company encountered no enemy forces, no opposing fire of any kind. Its only casualty was self-inflicted. Nevertheless, by early afternoon, well over 300 residents of the hamlet lay dead. Those killed were, predominantly, either women, old men or small children. For a number of the women, rape had preceded death. Other victims had been tortured and mutilated, then killed. Much of the killing, though not all, had occurred in the sub-hamlet of Xom Lang, known by the Americans as My Lai (4). Much of the killing, though not all, had been conducted by 1st Platoon. That same morning, a mile or so away, another Task Force Barker unit, Bravo Company, killed close to a hundred civilians in the sub-hamlet of My Hoi, Co Luy hamlet, known to the Americans as My Khe (4).

Through the 11th Brigade up to divisional headquarters, senior military officers were aware that a large number of civilians had been killed at My Lai (4). In contravention of army regulations, however, the divisional command allowed the 11th Brigade to investigate itself. In the subsequent report, to the extent that civilian casualties were acknowledged, they were asserted to have been small-scale and accidental, primarily the result of

---

[1] For comprehensive accounts of the massacre in Son My, see: M. Belknap, *The Vietnam War on Trial: The My Lai Massacre and the Court-Martial of Lieutenant Calley* (Lawrence: University Press of Kansas, 2002); M. Bilton and K. Sim, *Four Hours at My Lai* (London: Penguin, 1992); J. Goldstein, B. Marshall and J. Schwartz, *The My Lai Massacre and Its Cover-up: Beyond the Reach of Law? The Peers Commission Report with a Supplement and Introductory Essay on the Limits of Law* (New York: The Free Press, 1976); R. Hammer, *One Morning in the War: The Tragedy at Son My* (New York: Coward-McCann, Inc., 1970); S. Hersh, *My Lai 4: A Report on the Massacre and Its Aftermath* (New York: Random House, 1970); W. Peers, *The My Lai Inquiry* (New York: W.W. Norton and Company, 1979).

long-range artillery bombardment and the crossfires of battle. Rumours and allegations of deliberate massacre were dismissed as enemy propaganda.

For a year thereafter, the official record remained silent on the subject of the killings in Son My. In April 1969, however, Ronald Ridenhour – a young GI who had served in the 11th Brigade – wrote a letter to the President, the Secretary of Defense, the Chairman of the Joint Chiefs of Staff, and several Congressmen and Senators describing what had happened in My Lai (4) and requesting an investigation. Ridenhour himself had not been present at the massacre, but his account was compiled from detailed conversations with soldiers who had witnessed and, in some cases, participated in the killing. Quietly, the army's Office of the Inspector General began to investigate the allegations. In September, William Calley was charged with six specifications of murder, including the deliberate shooting of 109 Vietnamese civilians.

Although brief details of the charges against Calley were released to the press, it was only in November – following the appearance of a news story by Seymour Hersh – that the massacre began to attract serious media and public attention. In the same month, it was announced that Calley would be court-martialled, that other members of Charlie Company were also suspected of involvement in the massacre, and that there would be an official inquiry into the investigation conducted by the local command. Eventually, three officers and nine enlisted men were charged with major crimes relating to the massacre in Tu Cung; another officer was charged in relation to the killings in Co Luy. Fourteen officers – including the commander of the Americal Division – were charged with offences connected to the initial investigation. Many of the charges in both categories, however, were subsequently dismissed. Of the handful of cases that went to court martial, all but that of Calley resulted in acquittal. Convicted of murdering at least twenty-two villagers at My Lai (4), Calley was sentenced in late March 1971 to life imprisonment with hard labour. That sentence was swiftly commuted to twenty years, and then later to ten. In November 1974, he became eligible for parole and left military custody. In 1976, Calley married and took over the management of his father-in-law's jewellery store in Columbus, Georgia.

Throughout the period that the massacre in My Lai (4) featured prominently in American public discussion – from the initial media revelations to the immediate aftermath of Calley's court martial – commentators were rarely inclined to understate its historical significance. As evidence accumulated in November 1969, a *New York Times* editorial declared that the atrocities 'may turn out to have been one of this nation's most ignoble hours'.[2] After Calley was convicted, the theologian Reinhold Niebuhr suggested that the episode had caused a rupture in modern American consciousness: 'This is a moment of truth when we realize that we are not

---

[2] *New York Times* (22 November 1969), p. 36.

a virtuous nation.'[3] *Time* magazine agreed, asserting that 'the crisis of confidence caused by the Calley affair is a graver phenomenon than the horror following the assassination of President Kennedy. Historically it is far more crucial.'[4] In these renderings, the My Lai massacre (as it came to be known) was a pivotal event not just in the history of the Vietnam war, but also in the history of the American nation as a whole.

Nearly forty years on, however, the status of the massacre as historical pivot is unclear, not so much because it is explicitly contested, but because of the apparent muteness of its memory. Often, those who write about My Lai reflect upon the silence that seems otherwise to surround it in contemporary American discourse. According to the authors of one of the most detailed recent accounts of the killings, the massacre 'is now almost completely forgotten, erased almost entirely from the national conscious-ness. What was once an image of incandescent horror has become at most a vague recollection of something unpleasant that happened during the Vietnam War.'[5] In 1993, Christian Appy asserted that My Lai 'has virtu-ally disappeared from public debate or memory'. During the 1980s, very few of his students 'even recognized the name'.[6] In the view of David Anderson, meanwhile, 'Answers to disturbing questions about My Lai remained diffi-cult to fashion because the event itself was so painful to recall. For many years Americans sought to repress the entire Vietnam war experience in both their own minds and the nation's collective memory.'[7]

As Anderson's assertion indicates, the status of the My Lai massacre within American collective memory cannot be considered in isolation from the content of national memories of the Vietnam conflict as a whole, or from the political and cultural contexts in which those memories have been and continue to be produced. Over the course of the last two dec-ades, the practices of cultural representation and public commemoration, which are generally regarded as constituent of national memories of the war, have stimulated a succession of critical and historical studies.[8] In many of these studies, individual acts of memory are allocated an ideo-logical value on the basis of their compatibility with American tradition and myth; commonly thereafter, the authors chart the changes in the mean ideological coordinates of these memory acts over time, from the immediate aftermath of the war when responses to Vietnam existed in a condition of tension with long-standing cultural assumptions through progressive stages

[3] *New York Times* (4 April 1971), p. 56.

[4] *Time* (12 April 1971), p. 19.

[5] Bilton and Sim, p. 4.

[6] C. Appy, *Working Class War: American Combat Soldiers and Vietnam* (Chapel Hill: University of North Carolina Press, 1993), p. 277.

[7] D. Anderson, 'What really happened?', in Anderson (ed.), *Facing My Lai: Moving Beyond the Massacre* (Lawrence: University Press of Kansas, 1998), p. 12.

[8] For a fuller discussion of the conceptual issues surrounding 'collective memory', see 'Introduction', P. Gray and K. Oliver, *The Memory of Catastrophe* (Manchester: Manchester University Press, 2004).

of convergence as the nation's centre of political gravity shifted to the right during the late 1970s and 1980s.[9] In their assessment of ideological content, these studies frequently place particular emphasis on the way in which representations and commemorations of the conflict engage in attributions of victimhood and guilt. Evidence of the conservative drift of national memory is thus found in the silence that apparently surrounds the subject of American wartime atrocities and in the ethnocentricity with which politicians, film-makers and writers dwell upon the human costs of the war. Fred Turner states that representations of 'the American soldier as executioner', which he considers to have been pervasive in the national culture during the late 1960s and early 1970s, had entirely disappeared from public discourse twenty years later; various tropes of veteran as victim stood in their place.[10] Similarly, Andrew Martin argues that, in so far as the national conscience continues to be exercised by the conflict in Vietnam, its principal concern has been the treatment of US veterans, not the violence inflicted upon the Vietnamese.[11] According to Jim Neilson, even the war literature sanctioned by more progressive critical forces has tended to 'woefully misrepresent the heroism and the vast suffering of the Vietnamese and consistently view the war through the narrow prism of American history and culture'.[12] Philip Melling, meanwhile, asserts that the peripheral place of Vietnamese suffering in American representations of the war reflects a deeply-rooted cultural solipsism stretching back to the autobiographical conversion narratives offered up by the Puritans in colonial New England, a solipsism which encouraged Americans in the mid-twentieth century to see their activities in south-east Asia as another errand in the wilderness and which led them subsequently to adopt combat strategies and tactics unsuited to the conditions. It is no surprise, therefore, to find a similar self-absorption evident in post-war narratives, in which the tragedy of the war resonates primarily in its consequences for Americans, not for the people of Vietnam.[13]

---

[9] Examples include K. Beattie, *The Scar That Binds: American Culture and the Vietnam War* (London: New York University Press, 1998); W. Capps, *The Unfinished War: Vietnam and the American Conscience* (Boston: Beacon Press, 1990); M. Clark, 'Remembering Vietnam', in J. Rowe and R. Berg (eds), *The Vietnam War and American Culture* (New York: Columbia University Press, 1991), pp. 177–207; A. Martin, *Receptions of War: Vietnam in American Culture* (London: University of Oklahoma Press, 1993); R. McMahon, 'Contested memory: the Vietnam war and American society, 1975–2001', *Diplomatic History*, 26 (2002), 159–84; P. Melling, *Vietnam in American Literature* (Boston: Twayne Publishers, 1990); J. Neilson, *Warring Fictions: Cultural Politics and the Vietnam War Narrative* (Jackson: University Press of Mississippi, 1998); M. Sturken, *Tangled Memories: The Vietnam War, the Aids Epidemic, and the Politics of Remembering* (London: University of California Press, 1997); F. Turner, *Echoes of Combat: The Vietnam War in American Memory* (New York: Anchor Books, 1997).

[10] Turner, p. 11.

[11] Martin, pp. 157–8.

[12] Neilson, p. 7.

[13] Melling, pp. 17–33, 85–95.

It is not the case, however, that the sort of pathologies that characterized the killings in Son My have entirely disappeared from cultural representations of the Vietnam war. Even whilst they develop their overall
arguments about the conservatism and ethnocentricity evident in national
memories of Vietnam, many of these writers acknowledge that the ideological project of reincorporating the war within American tradition and
myth has not gone uncontested. Andrew Martin, for example, identifies in
a number of memoirs and novels a rejection of official political renditions
of the conflict as a 'tragedy without villains', of 'those contrivances that
would displace war and death onto historical myths of a politics of inadvertence, or that condense two decades of killing and maiming into the
metaphor of the quagmire'.[14] Indeed, in the view of some critics, the canon
of Vietnam war literature in particular has functioned very effectively as a
counter-hegemonic cultural force; both Thomas Myers and Tobey Herzog
contend that many of the most widely-read literary works on Vietnam
have sought to disrupt and challenge the erasure of the moral problematic
from the nation's memories of the war.[15] Myers considers the writings of
Vietnam veterans to have been an especially valuable resource in the
struggle against conservative revisionism: 'Mixtures of rage and regret,
guilt and expiation, their reports point steadfastly to the complexity and
to the continuing influence of the historical configuration in which the
American soldier was both brutal agent and endangered species.'[16]

Atrocity, it seems, is not quite the unspeakable and unspoken memory
of the Vietnam war; nor – as the final chapter of this book reveals – has
the My Lai massacre itself been entirely forgotten. Nevertheless, as that
chapter also reveals, instances of massacre remembrance tend to manifest
a somewhat incidental and accidental quality. They are not the product of
a culture intent on preserving a memory of the crime for future generations.
Furthermore, the stories of which they form a part are almost exclusively
stories about America and Americans, rarely dwelling for very long upon
the toll of lives, limbs, health, families, communities, resources and history
experienced by the massacre's actual victims.

The fragile, intermittent and partial character of the massacre's hold on
the nation's consciousness, once again, cannot be explained in isolation
from the process by which the memory of the Vietnam war as a whole has
been detoxified over the course of the last three decades. Students of that
process of detoxification, however, often disagree on the question of where
agency lies. Criticizing the failure of American films about the war to

[14] Martin, pp. 70–1.
[15] T. Myers, *Walking Point: American Narratives of Vietnam* (New York: Oxford University Press, 1988); T. Herzog, *Vietnam War Stories: Innocence Lost* (London: Routledge,
1992). See also P. Beidler, *American Literature and the Experience of Vietnam* (Athens:
The University of Georgia Press, 1982); and Beidler, *Re-Writing America: Vietnam Authors
in Their Generation* (Athens: The University of Georgia Press, 1991).
[16] Myers, p. 193.

engage seriously with the moral issues that it raised, Peter Marin abstains from more complex articulations of cultural authorship and simply blames the film-makers themselves.[17] Philip Melling attributes the indifference with which American memory regards the fate of the Vietnamese to the revitalized condition of evangelical Christianity in the late 1970s, when the literary testimonies of Vietnam veterans became subsumed within the popular but solipsistic genre of spiritual autobiography, the conversion narrative of Puritan New England revived for another troubled age.[18] He also ascribes a role to critical postmodernism, which has tended to commend to the attention of the culture texts that ultimately disarticulate the war experience for their readers, fracturing perspective, disrupting narrative and asserting all knowledge – even knowledge of violence and its consequences – to be local and thereby unreliable.[19] Fred Turner, meanwhile, argues that the responses of wider American society to the Vietnam war replicated those of the traumatized veteran, passing from a state of memory repression through spasms of recollection and denial to an attempt to reconcile the past with the national sense of self.[20] The originality of his study lies in the sustained development of that central metaphor, but it is in the nature of metaphors that the phenomena that they link are essentially distinct: the individual's struggle for recovery from trauma and the efforts of a complex capitalist society to adapt to the consequences of a lost war are surely charged from very different sources.

A more forceful explanation of the place of Vietnam in American cultural discourse is offered by Andrew Martin, who connects the operations of collective memory to 'the historically specific structures of power and production'.[21] In this respect, Martin declares allegiance to the British tradition of cultural studies, which he considers more sensitive to the work of hegemonic forces in the field of language and text than either the pluralist American studies movement of the 1950s or the more recent attempts by some postmodernists to reduce historical conflict and change to the self-referential play of signs and symbols across the surface of contemporary culture. In the case of Vietnam, he suggests, hegemonic interests have not been able to entirely sublimate the divisions that the war engendered in American society, but some strategic silences have been imposed upon cultural memory. In Martin's view, cinematic and televisual depictions of Vietnam consistently borrow from the generic conventions of domestic melodrama: in accordance with these conventions, the war becomes primarily a tale of sibling tensions within the American family. The devastation that it wrought upon the Vietnamese

---

[17] P. Marin, 'Coming to terms with Vietnam: settling our moral debts', *Harper's*, (December 1980), pp. 41–56.

[18] Melling, pp. 49–64.

[19] *Ibid.*, pp. 3–7.

[20] Turner, pp. 12–16.

[21] Martin, p. 8.

people are a marginal element in these renderings and, thus excluded from mainstream representations, issues of national morality are cast to the dark, unexplored recesses of American cultural memory.

Despite his emphasis upon the role of hegemonic structures in the creation of such silences in popular discourses, however, Martin's account of their operation in specific historical instances seems rather attenuated, limited largely to the observation that many publishers in the 1970s were unwilling to consider works about the war and to a brief discussion of conservative attempts to intimidate both Hollywood studios and television networks during the Reagan Presidency.[22] In Martin's analysis, the interplay of diffuse popular desires and hierarchical cultural forces in the erasure of images of national pathology from the American memory of Vietnam remains suppositional; it is not empirically demonstrated.

For Jim Neilson, as for Martin, the cavities that have developed in the nation's consciousness of what was done in its name during the war in Vietnam cannot be understood without reference to the role of material forces and the ideological alignments they have generated and sustained within hegemonic institutions. Neilson asserts that the increasing dominance of media conglomerates within the publishing industry, together with the emergence of a complacent liberal-pluralist paradigm within academic literary studies, has led to the marginalization of any text that engages in more than a very modest moral critique of American actions in Indochina, or that attempts to explain those actions in terms that could also implicate existing structures of power. Those literary works which have advanced radical condemnations of national conduct, Neilson suggests, have tended to be either ignored or castigated for their ostensible crudity, or else commended primarily for their aesthetic qualities, with their political content attributed little significance. Neilson's analysis, like Martin's, identifies few instances of direct institutional manipulation of literary discourses concerning Vietnam, but it is, of course, in the nature of hegemonic forces that they do not have to operate through such means. Instead, by examining the canonizing process, Neilson establishes on the part of the gatekeepers of literary culture a pattern of behaviour – in particular, a persistent reluctance to interrogate the relationship between the pathologies of the American war effort and the exploitative practices and counter-revolutionary logic of the capitalist system – which corroborates his argument about the investment of American political and economic elites in the ideological rewriting of national memories of Vietnam.

What the nation now remembers about the Vietnam war, however, cannot be entirely explained by the constellation of ideological interests within the sphere of cultural production, as Neilson himself acknowledges.[23] The readership of literary texts about Vietnam was often rather

---

[22] *Ibid.*, pp. 75–6, 121–3.
[23] Neilson, p. 6.

modest, whilst students of filmic and television representations of the war can rarely make wholly confident deductions about the capacity of these fleeting sensory experiences to permanently refashion the historical consciousness of their audience. Although cultural critics have often quite rigorously decoded the ideological assumptions of the Vietnam texts that they have studied and lucidly mapped the broader political world through which those texts passed, none of their analyses has yet provided a completely convincing historical explanation of the radical transformation in memory that they assert has occurred: the identified agents are either too diffuse for their activities to be effectively scrutinized, or else they operate in cultural arenas too local to produce the ecumenical effects for which they are said to be responsible. The problem may lie in an interpretative overstretch: they have magnified the dimensions of the phenomenon, and thus their analyses of its causes, seeking to explain too much, subsequently fall short by explaining too little.

Jim Neilson, for example, begins his investigation with the following enquiry: 'How, against the best efforts of so many, did a war once perceived as a nearly genocidal slaughter to perpetuate American neocolonialism come to be viewed as an American tragedy?'[24] In addition, reflecting upon the indifference of American public opinion to the violence perpetrated against the people of Iraq during the Gulf War, Neilson asks: 'How did a nation that had once had a mass antiwar movement and had once responded with outrage to US atrocities become oblivious to such horrors?'[25] There seems to be a paradox here: the departure point for the rightwards march of memory was a period of popular enlightenment which apparently occurred some time in the late 1960s, even though, at the very same moment, the nation was implicated in a collective moral catastrophe. It is an interpretation that exaggerates the contradictions existing between national policy and national conscience at the height of the war, and also, therefore, the distance travelled by that conscience in the years since.

Although collective memory is constantly subject to change, early conceptualizations of a particular experience must receive special attention from scholars seeking to comprehend the way in which it has subsequently been remembered. Indeed, to examine the manner in which Americans received and responded to the revelations about the massacre in My Lai (4), and to the prosecution of the soldiers most immediately responsible, is to be left largely unsurprised that the public memory of the incident has since taken the form and course that it has. This was not a society which really wanted to know about the violence of the war that its armed forces were waging in Vietnam. When they finally came to be confronted with that knowledge in the form of the massacre revelations, Americans felt keenly the absence of precedent and context, and diverged widely in the

[24] *Ibid.*, pp. 5–6.
[25] *Ibid.*, p. 4.

lessons that they drew from the affair. The massacre also intruded upon their world at a moment when the established centres of national political and cultural authority – which might usually have been expected to channel and guide public reaction – seemed somewhat diminished in competence and wisdom, and prone to fighting amongst themselves, especially with respect to the war in Vietnam. What Americans thought about the massacre, then, was never really to cohere into consensus, into the sort of stable and accepted 'truth' most easily converted into a usable past.

In addition, even as the massacre was dominating news headlines, the conditions for the ethnocentricity which later characterized its memory were already in place. The story of the massacre progressively evolved into a story about Americans, about the burden of blame carried by Calley, Medina and their men, and about the wider distribution of guilt upwards, through the ranks of those who had managed the war, and horizontally across American society as a whole. The actual victims of the massacre were displaced from the centre of debate and concern and thus rendered powerless to make their claims upon American memory and conscience stick.

This was not, however, an entirely deliberate design, expressive of a culture determined from the outset to drive those at the raw end of the atrocity to the margins of its consciousness. Certainly, the same asymmetries of language, culture and political allegiance that left Charlie Company confused about who in Vietnam, and Son My in particular, was an enemy and who was not worked in the wake of the massacre disclosures to confound and discourage the efforts of investigators and news reporters alike to learn from the survivors what had been perpetrated in their village. Certainly, many Americans perceived that they had more in common with William Calley than with any of his victims, to the point that they thought they might have done the same thing. Yet the displacement of the victims was also in part a function of the endeavour to bring the perpetrators to justice. It is in the nature of a court martial to focus on questions of causation and culpability, and, after the fact of the atrocity had been established in late 1969, it was this judicial process, the courtroom arguments about who was to blame and the ultimate legal fate of the American soldiers involved that provided the day-to-day news content of the story, not the bloody human mess they had left behind them in Son My and the struggles of the survivors to rebuild their lives amidst the ruins. Moreover, the outcomes of the judicial process, limited as they were to the conviction of one man – William Calley – helped foster the impression not just that the army had failed to bring all of those responsible to account, but that Calley himself had suffered an injustice: it was the lieutenant, subsequently, who became the object of public sympathy, not the inhabitants of My Lai (4) whom he had hastened to death, and the orphans and widows he made of many of the rest.

For most Americans, therefore, an empathetic identification with the war experiences of the Vietnamese was not easily achieved even at the moment when the human waste and suffering caused by the conflict were being most vividly exposed. Though American debates about the massacre in Son My were impassioned and inclusive of much of the national community, they were not sufficient to force the country to conscience. Most likely, they represented the first stage of forgetting. Even as the massacre dominated public discourse, the ordeals of its victims became neutralized as a source of national anxiety and remorse and their presence within the culture reduced to half-remembered images of what the first newspaper to print them called 'A clump of bodies on a road in South Vietnam'.[26] The cause was probably lost by the end of the massacre courts martial; that the murderer could be cast as victim, as William Calley was, indicated the extent of the displacement that had already occurred. This displacement continued through the 1970s and 1980s, as what remained of American empathy for the Vietnamese dissolved almost entirely in the wake of withdrawal and the fall of Saigon, as the plight of the boat-people revised the ethical indices that had earlier condemned the United States for its efforts to resist the revolution in the south, as American veterans claimed for themselves the status of victims of war, and as the country's ideological orientation took a conservative turn. Usually, the failures of national memory over Vietnam are perceived to have originated in the wake of these developments. With My Lai, however, we must look much earlier, in particular to the complex, diffuse operations of culture and politics at the time when the massacre first broke upon the American scene.

[26] *Cleveland Plain Dealer* (20 November 1969), p. 1.

1

Reporting atrocity

In Vietnam, horrors were often routine. Whilst the atrocities in Son My may have been exceptional in scale and whilst the personal conduct of most young Americans who fought in the conflict was probably conscientious and humane, the battlefield practices of the US military exaggerated the ordinary viciousness of a civil war to such an extent that the boundaries of ethical behaviour became obscure for many of those concerned.[1] By establishing the body count as the central index of operational success, the command created incentives towards the killing of anyone whose corpse might subsequently be reported as that of an enemy soldier. Meanwhile, even historians keen to rehabilitate the war as a necessary and noble cause have condemned as 'immoral' the reliance of American armed forces upon technology-intensive forms of war fighting, including long-distance artillery shelling and bombing from the air, which provided only limited scope for discriminating between legitimate enemy targets and the homes and bodies of South Vietnamese civilians.[2]

---

[1] Other known instances of large-scale face-to-face killings of Vietnamese noncombatants by US ground troops include the shooting of sixteen unarmed women and children in the hamlet of Son Thang, near Danang, in February 1970 by a team of five US Marines from Bravo Company, 1st Battalion, 7th Marine. In 2001, it was revealed that former US Senator Bob Kerrey, whilst serving in Vietnam as a Navy Seal, had – in February 1969 – led a raid upon the hamlet of Thanh Phong in the Mekong Delta, which resulted in the deaths of around 20 civilians. During a visit to Vietnam in late 1989, the British journalist Justin Wintle was told of a two-day massacre reportedly committed by troops of the Republic of Korea in December 1966: between four and five hundred inhabitants of the village of Binh Hoa, north of Quang Ngai, were said to have been killed. Most recently, an Ohio newspaper, the *Toledo Blade*, conducted an investigation into the conduct of a platoon of soldiers known as Tiger Force, from the army's 101st Airborne Division. Over a seven-month period from May to November 1967, the platoon committed a series of atrocities against civilians in the provinces of Quang Ngai and Quang Nam; it is likely that hundreds died. See G. Solis, *Son Thang: An American War Crime* (New York: Bantam Books, 1998); G. Vistica, 'One Awful Night in Thanh Phong', *New York Times Magazine* (25 April 2001); G. Vistica, *The Education of Lieutenant Kerrey* (New York: St Martin's Press, 2003); J. Wintle, *Romancing Vietnam: Inside the Boat Country* (London: Penguin, 1992), pp. 265–78; *Toledo Blade* (19–22 October 2003).

[2] M. Lind, *Vietnam: The Necessary War: A Reinterpretation of America's Most Disastrous Military Conflict* (New York: The Free Press, 1999), pp. 252–4.

They have also condemned the command's failure to effectively disseminate and enforce its own rules of engagement among junior officers and soldiers deployed in operations on the ground.[3] What senior US commanders offered to their men, it appears, was an aggregate imbalance of behavioural stimuli, encouraging indifference towards the fate of non-combatants rather than a solicitous interest in their protection from harm – an imbalance which a rather fitful series of directives from the Military Assistance Command, Vietnam (MACV) reasserting the necessity of care was unlikely to entirely redress.[4] To read the oral history testimonies and memoir accounts of American veterans, indeed, is to engage with a world upon which such directives seemingly had no traction at all, in which civilians were routinely killed, tortured or mutilated for no reason of military logic, in which the rape of women and the desecration of bodies were mundane, everyday occurrences, and in which atrocity was a banal and unremarkable fact of life in the field.[5]

Arresting though such narratives undoubtedly are, they invite a rather undifferentiated appreciation of the moral content of the US war in Vietnam. Variations in unit function, combat environment, quality of training and leadership, as well as in the value systems of individual soldiers, produced an unstable mosaic of ethical sub-cultures and practices across the American battle fronts, and sometimes within individual companies and platoons as well. The US Army Military History Institute (USAMHI) recently initiated a Vietnam War Era Service Survey which asks veterans for their opinion of the My Lai massacre and 'other incidents of this type', and also for descriptions of how they treated enemy prisoners. No clear pattern of experience emerges. One respondent notes that the consensus

---

[3] G. Lewy, *America in Vietnam* (Oxford: Oxford University Press, 1980), pp. 233–41.

[4] In July 1965, William Westmoreland, commander of US forces in Vietnam, wrote a letter to 'All Subordinate Units' in which he noted: 'The number of non-combatant casualties resulting from combat air and ground operations is a matter of concern.' This was a problem, he said, 'worthy of increased command emphasis, particularly with regard to the discriminate use of heavy weaponry in populated areas'. In November 1966, after observing a 'potentially serious trend reflected in recent reports', he was obliged to repeat the lesson, urging his commanders to place renewed emphasis on troop indoctrination 'to insure that newly arrive [*sic*] personnel in particular are thoroughly conversant with need for minimizing non-combatant battle casualties, and understand the rationale behind current instructions on the subject'. 'Summary of Remarks by COMUSMACV Emphasizing Troop Conduct', 23 December 1969, folder: My Lai 8/11, Papers of *Four Hours in My Lai*, Liddell Hart Centre for Military Archives (LHCMA), King's College London (KCL); Westmoreland, 'Relationship between US Military and Vietnamese', 18 November 1966, folder: 'MACV Directives [3]', Box 3, Administrative and Background Materials Files – Open Inventory, 1967–1970, Records of the Peers Inquiry (hereafter referred to as RPI), Records of the Army Staff (hereafter RAS), RG319, National Archives, College Park, Maryland (NACP).

[5] See, for example, M. Baker, *Nam: The Vietnam War in the Words of the Men and Women Who Fought There* (London: Abacus, 1982), pp. 131–53; M. McPherson, *Long Time Passing: Vietnam and the Haunted Generation* (London: Sceptre, 1988), pp. 567–603; and P. Caputo, *A Rumor of War* (New York: Ballantine Books, 1977), pp. 290–320.

within his unit 'was that there would be no enemy POWs, only KIAs'.[6] Another records his feelings of shame when he learnt of My Lai: 'But there were *many* in my unit that de-humanized the enemy.'[7]

A number of those surveyed asserted that, given the pressures of the combat situation in Vietnam, they could understand how the massacre might have happened, even if they had not witnessed any atrocities themselves.[8] Some, however, considered such acts entirely aberrant: 'I have never heard of *any* similar incidents in Vietnam.'[9] Of a group of forty Vietnam veterans in southern California studied in the early 1970s, all of those who had been involved in heavy combat reported that they had participated in atrocities, compared with 32 per cent of those involved in moderate combat, and 8 per cent of those whose combat experience was more limited.[10] In a survey of over one hundred general officers who had held command positions in Vietnam, meanwhile, a majority of respondents (61.1 per cent) took the view that before the massacre at My Lai (4) the rules of engagement had been 'fairly well adhered to throughout the chain of command'. Some 19.4 per cent of respondents considered that the rules had been 'carefully adhered to', while 14.8 per cent judged that they were 'not particularly considered in the day-to-day conduct of the war'.[11]

What might be witnessed in the way of the conflict's human costs, therefore, depended very much upon where one chose to look; whether to bear witness to those costs was another choice again. Before 1968, little of the casual, random violence which often characterized the US war effort in Vietnam was reported in the news media at home, certainly when compared with accounts that appeared in foreign newspapers or with the emphasis placed by American reporters upon atrocities committed by the other side.[12] The failure of the mainstream media to communicate the most unpalatable aspects of the military campaign embodied a wider complex of institutional practices and ideological alignments which, contrary to the popular image of an adversarial press in Vietnam, actually

[6] Dennis Bowen (503rd Airborne Infantry Regiment), Vietnam War Era Service Survey Questionnaire, USAMHI, Carlisle, Pennsylvania.

[7] Alan Gustafson (1st Aviation Brigade), *ibid.* (italics in original).

[8] See, for example, William Bedsole (1st Cavalry Division), Thomas Davies (1st Infantry Regiment), and Richard Ellis (MACV Armed Forces Vietnam Network TV), *ibid.*

[9] Marvin Mathiak (1st Cavalry Division), *ibid.* (italics in original).

[10] R. Strayer and L. Ellenhorn, 'Vietnam veterans: a study exploring adjustment patterns and attitudes', *Journal of Social Issues*, 31: 4 (1975), 81–93.

[11] D. Kinnard, 'Vietnam reconsidered: an attitudinal survey of US Army general officers', *Public Opinion Quarterly*, 39 (Winter 1975–76), 445–56. For a useful general discussion of American war crimes in Vietnam, see J. Bourke, *An Intimate History of Killing: Face-to-Face Killing in Twentieth Century Warfare* (London: Granta, 1999), pp. 171–214.

[12] W. Hammond, *Public Affairs: The Military and the Media, 1968–1973* (Washington, DC: US Army Center of Military History, 1996), p. 223; D. Hallin, *The 'Uncensored War': The Media and Vietnam* (Berkeley: University of California Press, 1989), pp. 156–8; P. Knightley, *The First Casualty: The War Correspondent as Hero and Myth-Maker from the Crimea to Kosovo* (London: Prion, 2000), pp. 423–6.

produced a reporting culture that was broadly sympathetic to the methods and objectives of the United States in the war, at least until the Tet Offensive in early 1968.[13]

There was nothing especially novel about such reticence. It had been evident too in coverage of US military campaigns during the Second World War. In many parts of the Pacific theatre, John Dower observes, the killing of Japanese prisoners became 'everyday practice'; yet, in his study of the output of war correspondents during the conflict, Phillip Knightley records that he could find no reports in wartime Allied newspapers of atrocities committed by Allied troops.[14] It was not just the processes of state censorship that prevented accounts of unwarranted American blood-letting from reaching the public sphere; neither US media outlets themselves nor their readers and listeners seemed particularly receptive to stories that disturbed, however faintly, the discursive nexus between war-making and national virtue.[15]

This was true also during the Korean War, when the confederates of Joseph McCarthy policed the boundaries between Americanism and communism, and discouraged editors from adopting too nuanced a position on the distribution of righteousness across that divide.[16] In addition, news organizations feared that the military authorities would refuse them logistical assistance – and access to the war zone – if they dwelt too long on the price in blood that UN operations were exacting from the civilian population. The Columbia Broadcasting System (CBS) network refused to broadcast a radio report by Ed Murrow in which he spoke of the 'dead valleys' being created by the American military in South Korea.[17] Correspondents from *Associated Press* and the *New York Times* were present in early August 1950 when a bridge carrying refugees away from the front was destroyed by American army engineers ordered to deny the crossing to advancing North Korean forces. The grim fate of the refugees on the bridge at the time was described in the stories that these correspondents

---

[13] See Hallin, *The 'Uncensored War'*; also Hallin, 'The media, the war in Vietnam, and political support: a critique of the thesis of an oppositional media', in Hallin, *We Keep America on Top of the World: Television Journalism and the Public Sphere* (London: Routledge, 1994), pp. 40–57. Other studies that question the adversarial media thesis include: M. Arlen, *Living-Room War* (Syracuse: Syracuse University Press, 1997); G. Comstock *et al.*, *Television and Human Behaviour* (New York: Columbia University Press, 1978), pp. 49–52; E. Herman and N. Chomsky, *Manufacturing Consent: The Political Economy of the Mass Media* (London: Vintage, 1994); and C. Wyatt, *Paper Soldiers: The American Press and the Vietnam War* (New York: Norton, 1993).

[14] J. Dower, *War Without Mercy: Race and Power in the Pacific War* (New York: Pantheon, 1986), p. 68; Knightley, p. 321.

[15] One Canadian journalist, reflecting on the role that correspondents had played during the war, commented: 'We were a propaganda arm of our governments. At the start the censors enforced that, but by the end we were our own censors. We were cheerleaders.' Knightley, p. 364.

[16] *Ibid.*, p. 379.

[17] C. Hanley, S. Choe and M. Mendoza, *The Bridge at No Gun Ri: A Hidden Nightmare from the Korean War* (New York: Henry Holt, 2001), p. 162.

submitted, but left out of the published versions.[18] When scores of civilians were being shot by soldiers of the 7th Cavalry at a railroad trestle near the village of No Gun Ri, journalists were visiting the regimental command post only two miles away from the scene.[19] What the history of American press in Korea suggests, however, is that even had they been aware of the slaughter, even had they dispatched authoritative witness accounts to the news outlets for which they worked, the story might well still have been buried – for the duration of the conflict, at least, if probably not for the next fifty years.

The United Nations command in Korea initially relied upon correspondents to judge for themselves what could and could not be reported from the war zone; full censorship was only imposed after the Chinese entered the conflict and UN forces had been driven into a hasty retreat.[20] The association of press censorship with conditions of acute military emergency had implications for the information strategy of the American mission in Vietnam, a decade or so later. Policy-makers in Washington wished to maintain the impression that US military assistance to the regime in Saigon was limited in size, function and duration.[21] To activate the censor's red pen would provoke more questions about the nature of that commitment than the pen could likely cross out. Instead, a system of accredited correspondents was adopted, along with voluntary codes concerning the reporting of planned and ongoing military operations and a forceful supply-side approach to news management.

In the early stages of the conflict, it would have been difficult for any censors to make the daily flow of news reports from Vietnam read much more benignly than it already did. At this time, the political convictions of most print and broadcast journalists, and of the media outlets that employed them, faithfully reflected those of the foreign policy establishment which had ordered American advisory and troop deployments. The view was that the Vietcong were the agents of an international communist movement organized and supported by the authorities in Moscow and Beijing; that if this movement was not stopped in South Vietnam, the rest of south-east Asia would eventually fall, allies elsewhere would begin to buckle, shrinking the contours of the democratic capitalist sphere to the point that the security of the United States itself would come under threat.[22] In early 1965, a number of American newspapers – most notably the *New York Times* – did express doubts about the wisdom of military escalation in their editorial columns, but they rarely challenged the ideological framework within which the issue was being discussed, nor did they show

[18] *Ibid.*, pp. 164–5.
[19] *Ibid.*, p. 162.
[20] Knightley, pp. 367, 376–7.
[21] *Ibid.*, pp. 412–13; Hallin, *The 'Uncensored War'*, pp. 29–36.
[22] Hallin, *The 'Uncensored War'*, pp. 48–53.

much enthusiasm for any of the policy alternatives. Once the decision to escalate had been made, moreover, these sceptics scuttled back behind the flag.[23]

Critical assessments of the military effort in Vietnam were also advanced on a number of occasions by American correspondents in Saigon. Once again, however, these were motivated not by ideological opposition to the US commitment, but derived rather from a concern that – for whatever reason, flawed tactics, the instability of South Vietnamese politics or the incompetence of the Army of the Republic of Vietnam (ARVN) – a fundamentally just war was not being won. Neither of the two correspondents who most closely interrogated official claims of battlefield progress in this period (David Halberstam of the *New York Times* and Charles Mohr of *Time*) doubted the ethical necessity of American military intervention in Vietnam.[24] Nor did the Saigon correspondents find their employers uniformly indulgent of even the limited reservations expressed in their reports. *Time* would regularly rewrite Mohr's submissions to lend a more favourable cast to his descriptions of the war, and in September 1963 the magazine published an article denouncing the press corps in South Vietnam (and implicitly its own correspondent) for their persistent cynicism about the prospects of victory.[25]

Overall, then, those responsible for assembling news of the war and conveying it to the American public remained convinced of the righteousness of their government's objectives in Vietnam; as a result, they were generally prepared to overlook what they regarded as incidental moral lapses that occurred on the road to success. Not long after he had arrived in Saigon to cover the conflict for CBS, John Laurence witnessed an interrogation session in which an American intelligence officer permitted his ARVN translator to slap an enemy prisoner repeatedly around the face. Informed later that the prisoner had eventually given details of the Vietcong's escape route from an ongoing battle, allowing US air and artillery fire to target the departing force, Laurence agreed not to report what he had seen.[26] At that stage, he notes, what he recorded in his dispatches was very much influenced by 'my personal loyalty to the American cause'.[27]

What ideological inclinations encouraged, professional practices reinforced. In accordance with the doctrine of 'objectivity', journalists envisaged their role to be that of unbiased and apolitical communicators

[23] F. Logevall, *Choosing War: The Lost Chance for Peace and the Escalation of War in Vietnam* (Berkeley: University of California Press, 1999), pp. xxvii–iii, 283, 287–8, 341–2; Hallin, *The 'Uncensored War'*, p. 61.

[24] W. Prochnau, *Once Upon a Distant War: Reporting from Vietnam* (Edinburgh: Mainstream Publishing, 1996), pp. 140–1, 259.

[25] *Ibid.*, pp. 408–11; D. Halberstam, *The Powers That Be* (New York: Knopf, 1979), pp. 461–7.

[26] J. Laurence, *The Cat from Hué: A Vietnam War Story* (New York: Public Affairs, 2002), pp. 128–32.

[27] *Ibid.*, p. 125.

of information about current affairs. Their professional routines, however, ensured that the information they communicated was far from politically neutral.[28] For most reporters writing about the Vietnam war, the principal ports of call in the search for stories were the departments and agencies of the American government: in Washington, the White House, the State Department and the Pentagon; in Saigon, the MACV Office of Information and the Joint US Public Affairs Office at the US mission. Such sources were considered 'objective' and credible in a way that anti-war or enemy information outlets were not.[29] Thus, journalistic routines privileged precisely the kinds of sources which had an investment in suppressing news that the American military would find embarrassing, including – most obviously – accounts of operations in which Vietnamese civilians were killed. Except on very rare occasions, John Laurence recalls, the public affairs officers who conducted media briefings in Saigon

> did *not* report such events as successful enemy ambushes, lost battles, lost outposts, casualties from friendly fire, battle fatigue, accidents, nervous breakdowns, atrocities by our side, mutiny, looting, rape, courts martial, rebellion, bombs dropped on our own troops, the shooting of ARVN allies, torture, theft, corruption, murder, fragging, suicide or anything that might reflect negatively on the public image of the US armed services. All that other activity was happening, of course, but the facts were not made readily available to the press.[30]

Although many correspondents in Saigon came eventually to recognize that the chaos and human carnage unleashed by the war was not to be captured by listening to the deathless summaries offered in military briefings, they also understood that the further a reporter travelled from the grain of official truth, the greater became the professional risks. At the end of 1966, Harrison Salisbury of the *New York Times* travelled to Hanoi, and used not just the evidence of his own eyes but also casualty statistics provided by the North Vietnamese authorities to call into question the care taken by American bombers to avoid civilian residential areas in the city and the surrounding region. His reports prompted the Pentagon to suggest that he had been the dupe of enemy propaganda, aspersions which

[28] Hallin, *The 'Uncensored War'*, pp. 24–5, pp. 65–74.

[29] Noam Chomsky observed that few mainstream American news organizations reported on the proceedings of the International War Crimes Tribunal founded by Bertrand Russell to enquire into the conduct of the US war in Vietnam. Chomsky, 'Foreword', in P. Limqueco and P. Weiss (eds), *Prevent the Crime of Silence* (London: Allen Lane, 1971), pp. 9–10.

[30] Laurence, p. 482. It is possible that the public affairs officers were themselves unaware of many of the atrocities committed out in the field. In the case of Tiger Force, the platoon's immediate commanders encouraged its mistreatment and killing of civilians, but the evidence suggests that knowledge of its activities reached battalion headquarters and no further. It was only in February 1971, more than three years after they had occurred, that army investigators learned about the atrocities. Their subsequent inquiry, which produced no criminal prosecutions, appears not to have been brought to the attention of the press. 'Inquiry ended without justice', *Toledo Blade* (20 October 2003); 'Hearsay account triggered the probe', *Toledo Blade* (22 October 2003).

were repeated by a number of his fellow journalists. When Salisbury was recommended for the Pulitzer Prize, the prize's advisory board – comprising publishers, editors and the president of Columbia University – took the virtually unprecedented step of rejecting the jury's decision, awarding the prize elsewhere.[31]

There were other professional reasons for not departing too abruptly from the combat narratives constructed by the military command and its public affairs officials. Correspondents whose reports radiated optimism about the war, and made little mention of those caught in its crossfire, were often favoured with early information about battlefield developments and logistical assistance in getting out to the story. They might benefit in addition from more frequent access to senior commanders and members of the US mission. John Laurence recalls that 'almost anything was possible as long as you were on the team and played by the rules'.[32] Conversely, of course, these privileges could be swiftly rescinded if the reporter went sour on the war, or drew attention to events that the military would rather have kept concealed. In such instances, sanctions might apply not just to the individual concerned, but also to the news organization they represented: a prospect that could work like a sobering draught upon the correspondent as he or she converted their observations into copy. In October 1965, Laurence and his camera crew were invited to fly with American pilots as they undertook a bombing mission over South Vietnam. The planes in which they were flying, however, struck a village in Cambodia by mistake, strafing and killing its inhabitants as they worked in their fields. Laurence did not mention the incident in his report, partly because he had no independent confirmation of the village's location, and partly because the revelation 'would cause a major rift between the Air Force and CBS News, and it might seriously affect future news coverage'.[33]

Away from Saigon, reporters cultivated relationships with junior officers and ordinary GIs, upon whom they relied for protection and technical assistance in the field. In addition, these soldiers might provide useful information and illuminating anecdotes about progress on the ground. Sometimes they were the source of perspectives that allowed reporters to question official interpretations.[34] Nevertheless, such relationships also operated to limit the scope for reports of American atrocities to percolate out into the public sphere, even when the journalist concerned witnessed them at first hand. Not only might atrocity stories adversely affect the careers of officers to whom the journalist had reason to be grateful, they might also make that journalist the object of resentment and suspicion

[31] *New York Times* (25 December 1966, 27–31 December 1966, 1–2 January 1967); Knightley, pp. 457–8; J. Aronson, *The Press and the Cold War* (New York: Monthly Review Press, 1990), pp. 253–9.

[32] Laurence, p. 205.

[33] *Ibid.*, pp. 223–33.

[34] Wyatt, pp. 93–8; Prochnau, p. 89.

whenever he or she chose to travel out into the field again. Soon after *CBS Evening News* had broadcast a report from its correspondent Morley Safer describing how, in response to sniper fire from its vicinity, US Marines had torched the hamlet of Cam Ne, one Marine officer informed John Laurence: 'If that sonofabitch comes up here again he better not turn his back.'[35]

The doctrine of journalistic objectivity, then, intercepted its practitioners before they told too independent a tale about what was happening; on those rare occasions, moreover, when the horrors of the conflict could not be entirely obscured by the blandishments offered by public affairs operatives in Saigon, the doctrine disqualified from use the sort of language that newsmen required to effectively communicate those horrors – and their causes – to audiences at home.[36] According to the classical conventions of 'objectivity', fact had to be kept separate from value; there was a necessary distinction to be maintained between the provision of information (the function of the news pages) and its analysis and interpretation (an activity confined to clearly identified editorial columns).[37] In practice, of course, there is no such thing as value-free information about death and injury in war. Thus, what 'objectivity' directed in instances when reporters could not help but address the fate of civilians exposed to US firepower was a response ideologically consistent with its procedural preference for the kind of sources which really did not want such matters addressed: the adoption of a diminutive tone, abbreviated in its descriptions of hurt and grief, empathetically reticient, and hesitant in its attribution of moral responsibility. When the enemy killed non-combatants, the 'objective' American reporter was often not quite so fastidious.[38]

John Laurence, once again, provides an instructive example. In late August 1965, he witnessed an American paratrooper 'casually' toss a grenade into the bomb shelter beneath a home in the village of Vinh Tranh; the body of a pregnant young woman was subsequently pulled from the shelter. He describes his reaction – in particular, his attempt to imagine what the victim must have experienced after the Americans entered the village:

> I pictured the young woman crouched by herself in the dark hole in the earth, worrying, the seconds passing slowly, waiting for the noise to stop, hearing the footsteps of the soldiers approaching, the squawking of their radios, conversation in a language she did not understand, then the shouts: 'Fire in the

[35] Laurence, pp. 139–40.

[36] John Laurence recalls: 'Even when we thought we *knew* what was going on – that the war, for example, had evolved from a limited program of military and political support for the South Vietnamese government into an uncontrolled campaign of violence and pain, a runaway rampage of murder and mayhem – there was no way to say it to the public. No one would print it or put it on the air. The language of our daily journalism was insufficient' (*Ibid.*, p. 405).

[37] Hallin, *The 'Uncensored War'*, pp. 65–74.

[38] *Ibid.*, p. 156.

hole!' and feeling the bump of the strange metal object falling into the bunker with her, hearing the hiss of the fuse burning in the moments before the consciousness-shattering blast. *God, how terrifying that must have been*, I thought.[39]

The empathetic reach of Laurence's personal response to the incident, however, was almost entirely absent from the report later broadcast on *CBS Evening News*. The killing of the woman became a minor detail in a broader account of the American operation in Vinh Tranh. Her body was shown for five seconds of the three-minute story, under Laurence's laconic narration: 'This woman is killed in the attack. She was hit by a grenade thrown into a bunker.' Where responsibility lay for her death, meanwhile, was left somewhat unclear; though the report indicated that the killing was not entirely accidental, it nevertheless fell shy of suggesting a culpable carelessness: 'The commander changes the order. Smoke, rather than fragment grenades, are to be thrown into suspected hideouts. The commander wants to make sure no more villagers are killed, and he tells his men to be careful with their grenades. "These Vietnamese bunkers – or bomb shelters," he explains, "are as common as garages back in the States."'[40]

The professional ethics and routines of American journalism, and the formal and informal networks of relations through which they were practised, were, therefore, key factors in the silences that prevailed on the issue of civilian casualties in the US news media before 1969.[41] The readiness of the print and broadcast media to report such casualties, and especially instances of American atrocities, was also circumscribed by their status as commercial enterprises, dependent for income upon advertisers attracted by the size and class profile of their readership or audience and by the extent to which their news content was compatible with the aesthetics of salesmanship. In general, the category of war coverage that those responsible for the editorial policy of American news outlets considered to be most consistent with their own commercial interests was known as 'bang-bang': exciting accounts of US military engagements with the enemy, ideally including unambiguous indications of battlefield success. Reports which described the lives of Vietnamese civilians, by contrast, were judged to have an enervating effect upon the attention of readers and viewers. Ron Steinman, NBC's bureau chief in Saigon, recalls that the network's news producers in New York 'had little interest in stories about the Vietnamese people and their struggles.' Only when a producer was 'in a weakened condition or desperate to fill two minutes of

[39] Laurence, pp. 116–18 (italics in original).

[40] *Ibid.*, pp. 120–1.

[41] The most detailed account of the relationship between the US military and journalists in Vietnam is provided by W. Hammond: see Hammond, *Public Affairs: The Military and the Media, 1962–1968* (Washington, DC: US Army Center of Military History, 1988), and Hammond, *Public Affairs: The Military and Media, 1968–1973*.

empty air time' could Steinman muscle such material onto the evening news.[42]

There was a commercial weightlessness, then, to Vietnamese civilians whilst they remained alive; when they were dead, either that weightlessness continued, or their bodies were judged to carry the kind of charge that might damage the company accounts. Although it was probably unlikely that a single set of pictures or graphic description of American atrocities would be judged so offensive that large numbers of readers and viewers would desert the journal or programme concerned for a sustained period of time, editorial perceptions of that threat differed from outlet to outlet. The first American newspaper to publish Ronald Haeberle's photographs of the massacre in My Lai (4), the *Cleveland Plain Dealer*, received 250 calls from readers in response to the images, 85 per cent of which asserted that they should not have been printed.[43] This reaction did not, in itself, represent a wave of public outrage likely to prove fatal to the *Dealer*'s future, but – as reporter Joe Eszterhas recalls – it nevertheless plunged members of the paper's editorial staff into 'prolonged stupors of melancholia'.[44]

Generally, however, if editors were concerned about the adverse impact of individual atrocity reports upon the commercial well-being of their institution, it would not have been because of the potential threat to overall readership or audience levels. It was only when a print outlet established a reputation for such stories that the composition of its readership would change, and with it the flow of advertising revenue. From 1967 onwards, for example, the *New Yorker* adopted a clear anti-war stance, publishing Jonathan Schell's famous essays on the brutal pacification of Ben Suc and the destruction caused by American bombing raids and ground operations in the provinces of Quang Ngai and Quang Tin, as well as Daniel Lang's account of the rape and murder of a Vietnamese peasant girl by four US soldiers.[45] As a result of this political repositioning, the *New Yorker* began to attract more young readers and its overall circulation increased; nevertheless, profits declined, for the periodical's demographic base was no longer as affluent as it had been and, therefore, no longer as attractive to its traditional advertisers.[46]

The impact of individual atrocity stories upon circulation or audience figures was thus unlikely to be so significant as to deter editors from publication or broadcast. Probably more troubling to the day-to-day commercial

[42] R. Steinman, *Inside Television's First War: A Saigon Journal* (Columbia: University of Missouri Press, 2002), p. 34.

[43] *Cleveland Plain Dealer* (21 November 1969), p. 12–A.

[44] J. Eszterhas, 'The Selling of the Mylai Massacre', in B. Rossett (ed.), *Evergreen Review Reader: An Anthology of Short Fiction, Plays, Poems, Essays, Cartoons, Photographs, and Graphics, 1967–1973* (London: Four Walls Eight Windows, 1998), p. 465.

[45] These reports were subsequently published in book form; see J. Schell, *The Real War* (London: Corgi, 1989), and D. Lang, *Casualties of War* (New York: McGraw-Hill, 1969).

[46] B. Bagdikian, *The Media Monopoly* (Boston: Beacon Press, 1997), pp. 106–10.

relationships between a media outlet and its advertisers would be the disruptions caused by such stories to what Ben Bagdikian calls the 'buying mood' of readers and viewers.[47] Any cosmetic company, for example, that found an advertisement for its lipstick juxtaposed with images of mutilated bodies was liable to experience fewer sales and greater dissatisfaction with the journal involved than the happy company whose advertisement shared page space with a profile of Raquel Welch.

These concerns are rarely acknowledged by professional journalists, but they are clearly present in, though partially disguised by, the discourse of 'taste' that was often invoked to justify the failure to report a particular atrocity story. 'Taste', indeed, was the explanation provided years later by Wes Gallagher, head of *Associated Press*, for his decision in December 1965 not to distribute pictures of American soldiers with a severed human head and to excise an account of the beheading from a report by Peter Arnett.[48] Richard Clurman, a senior correspondent for *Time* magazine in the late 1960s, recalls that he chose neither to report nor submit photographs of an incident he witnessed in which GIs set an attack dog upon an old Vietnamese man: 'Too grisly, we decided – and how to explain it?'[49] When Martha Gellhorn submitted an article to the *Ladies' Home Journal* in January 1967 describing the injuries suffered by Vietnamese children as a consequence of American bombing, she was conscious of the constraints that 'taste' imposed upon her candour. Gellhorn exercised a careful self-censorship, for if she had reported the true extent of the horrors she had witnessed, the article would not have been published: 'The sugar coating on the pill sickened me at the time and still does.' The discretion extended to the choice of accompanying image – a photograph not of one of the many children scorched and disfigured by napalm, but instead of a small boy with a single shrapnel wound in his back. Gellhorn comments: 'By Vietnamese standards the child was hardly wounded; the gash was not even infected. Few people have seen what napalm does and neither the *Ladies' Home Journal* nor any other American magazine could have published then (or now?) photographs of its effect on human flesh.'[50] In general,

---

[47] *Ibid.*, p. 133.

[48] P. Arnett, *Live from the Battlefield* (New York: Simon & Schuster, 1994), pp. 174–5. Carol Polsgrove records that, in 1968, *Esquire* elected not to publish a similar image: 'It was a question, really, of taste – a feeling that the picture was too gory for *Esquire*', Polsgrove, *It Wasn't Pretty, Folks, But Didn't We Have Fun? Esquire in the Sixties* (New York: Norton, 1995), pp. 178–80. That other media, not needing to be sensitive to the desires of advertisers, were more comfortable with images of atrocity was evidenced by the cover of *The New Face of War* – a book written in 1965 by Associated Press correspondent Malcolm Browne – which displayed, in William Prochnau's words, 'a bright-eyed American GI thrusting forward the decapitated head of a Viet Cong guerrilla' (Prochnau, p. 26); M. Browne, *The New Face of War* (New York: Bobbs-Merrill Co., 1965).

[49] R. Clurman, *Beyond Malice: The Media's Years of Reckoning* (New Brunswick: Transaction Books, 1988), pp. 213–14.

[50] M. Gellhorn, *The Face of War* (New York: Atlantic Monthly Press, 1988), pp. 261–3; Gellhorn, '"Suffer the little children . . ."', *Ladies' Home Journal* (January 1967).

graphic representations of combat – atrocity-related or not – were hardly as prevalent in press coverage of the Vietnam war as popular myth suggests, and the need of media institutions to supply a product conducive to successful advertising provides part of the explanation.[51] Images of the slaughterhouse don't sell toothpaste.

The ideological discomfort of correspondents with stories that were critical of the national military effort, their dependence upon less than candid government sources, the need to preserve workable relationships with officers out in the field, the empathetic continence and ethical agnosticism required by the 'objective' register of journalistic address, and the commercial constraints upon the broadcast and publication of graphic accounts of injury and death, however, do not entirely explain the silences within the US news media on the issue of civilian casualties before the late 1960s. One further factor was the difficulty seemingly faced by many journalists in delineating – for both themselves and their audiences – the boundary between morally acceptable and unacceptable behaviour in wartime. In Vietnam – as perhaps in most conflicts – the reporting culture was highly masculinized. Self-conscious displays of physical and mental fortitude were part of the courting ritual between journalists and their prospective sources out in the field.[52] Furthermore, if reporters possessed a reputation for tough-mindedness and resilience under fire, an increment of credibility was added to any criticism they chose to make of the military command; they could not be so easily stigmatized as unseasoned innocents.

However, this ethos of robust masculinity, with its suspicion of emotion and sentiment, also functioned to repress the articulation of outrage at the wanton pathologies of the American war effort. In addition, the terrible regularity with which civilians were killed and injured may have actually served to chloroform moral judgement, diminishing the capacity of reporters to regard such casualties as anything other than the inevitable wages of war. In September 1967, while covering an operation in the province of Quang Ngai, the British photo-journalist Philip Jones Griffiths witnessed American soldiers gather together a group of villagers and then leave them behind to be killed in an artillery strike. Asked later why he had not reported the incident, Griffiths replied: 'If I had gone back to Saigon and into one of the agencies and had said, "I've got a story about Americans killing Vietnamese civilians," they would have said, "So what's new?" It was horrible, but certainly not exceptional, and it just wasn't news.'[53]

[51] O. Patterson, 'Television's living room war in print: Vietnam in the news magazines', *Journalism Quarterly*, 61 (1984), 35–9, 136; Hallin, *The 'Uncensored War'*, pp. 129–31. In a comparative study, however, Michael Sherer argues that magazine photographs of the Vietnam war were more graphic than those that appeared during the conflict in Korea: Sherer, 'Comparing magazine photos of Vietnam and Korean wars', *Journalism Quarterly*, 65 (1988), 752–6.

[52] N. Sheehan, *A Bright Shining Lie: John Paul Vann and America in Vietnam* (London: Picador, 1990), p. 270.

[53] Knightley, p. 435.

Constantly exposed as they were – through formal briefings and informal contacts – to the attitudes and rationales of the military command, it was often difficult for American journalists in Vietnam to preserve the independence and integrity of their own value systems and to retain the self-confidence to denounce as reprehensible actions which all official comment cast as morally normative and militarily justified. Even those reports which did provide accounts of civilian casualties before 1968 tend to evidence a failure of moral compass. In late 1965, Neil Sheehan wrote a story for the *New York Times* describing the destruction of five fishing hamlets by naval and aerial shelling, as a result of which around 600 civilians may have been killed. As he noted later, however, 'it did not occur to me that I had discovered a possible war crime. The thought also does not seem to have occurred to my editors or to most readers of *The Times*.'[54]

In the absence of any objective, transcendent definitions of what constitutes news, the processes by which journalists decide what to report and media institutions select what to print or broadcast are essentially social ones. Although many reporters – and especially war reporters – have sought to cultivate an image of competitiveness and independence, the terrain within which they exercise that independence is circumscribed by the ideological assumptions of the day, by the caste interests of the contacts upon whom they rely for information and by the commercial imperatives of the organizations for whom they work. Over time, these forces have also become abstracted into a set of social group norms, which – through the pressure of peer expectation – function to police the process of writing the news. In a study of foreign policy correspondents, Bernard Cohen discovered that many were reluctant to write anything that might attract the disdain of professional colleagues: 'The correspondent fears being caught out on a limb by having written a story that is not admired or picked up by other reporters – that is, followed by a rush of validation.'[55]

Reputations were invested in news reporting that did not break with precedent. In Vietnam, such pressures meant that atrocity stories were not written because atrocity stories had not been written. With only a handful of exceptions, American journalists chose not to disturb the silence over the darkest aspects of the national war effort. In December 1969, *Time* magazine noted that the revelations about My Lai 'started a flood of other horror stories. Dozens of journalists, soldiers and visitors to Viet Nam have begun to recall other incidents of US brutality. Individual acts of senseless – sometimes gleeful – killing of civilians apparently happened often enough to be deeply disturbing.'[56] Even then, when it was clear just

[54] N. Sheehan, 'Should we have war crimes trials?', *New York Times Book Review* (28 March 1971), pp. 1–3, 30–4.

[55] B. Cohen, *The Press and Foreign Policy* (Westport: Greenwood Press, 1963), p. 82.

[56] *Time* (5 December 1969), p. 30.

how much had not been told, few commentators were inclined to draw causative connections between the earlier silence of the news media on the subject of atrocity and the recently exposed massacre, to entertain the notion that – comprehensible though each individual suppression might have been – collectively they amounted to a kind of licence.

In 1968, the capacity of establishment ideology, the doctrine of journalistic objectivity and concerns of 'taste' to police the way in which atrocities were communicated to the American public declined, principally as a result of the Tet offensive, which disrupted the complacent conventions of the mainstream reporting culture and excavated new space for critical perspectives to emerge and be expressed. Prior to the offensive, media doubts about the war policy and challenges to official constructions of battlefield progress had not been entirely unknown; during 1967, a number of commentators diagnosed stalemate and the *New York Times* called for a de-escalation of the American military effort.[57] 'I have a sense,' wrote David Halberstam in *Harper's* magazine, 'that we are once again coming to a dead end in Indochina.'[58] Nevertheless, as Peter Braestrup notes, the discourse of victory retained a broad political currency: 'Although they voiced misgivings, newsmen in Vietnam (or Washington) could not *prove* in 1967 that the Administration's professed optimism was overblown.'[59]

When General William Westmoreland, US commander in South Vietnam, and Ambassador Ellsworth Bunker visited Washington in November, many newspapers reported their assertions of steadily deteriorating enemy capabilities without critical comment.[60] The subsequent offensive – in which Vietcong guerrillas and North Vietnamese regulars launched assaults on cities and towns throughout the country, entering the US embassy compound in Saigon and briefly capturing the ancient imperial capital of Hué – made talk of a weakened foe seem deluded.[61] The impression was sustained even as American and ARVN forces successfully counter-attacked and finally inflicted the sort of severe damage upon the enemy's military resources that had often before been claimed but never really achieved.[62]

[57] Hammond, *Public Affairs: The Military and the Media, 1962–1968*, pp. 315–37. 'The tragedy of Vietnam', *New York Times* (2 January 1967).

[58] D. Halberstam, 'Return to Vietnam', *Harper's* (December 1967), p. 58.

[59] P. Braestrup, *Big Story: How the American Press and Television Reported and Interpreted the Crisis of Tet 1968 in Vietnam and Washington* (Boulder: Westview Press, 1977), p. 708 (italics in original).

[60] Hammond, *Public Affairs . . . 1962–1968*, pp. 333–6.

[61] In October and November 1967, the US embassy in Saigon had prepared a number of responses to be used whenever the press asked questions about military stalemate. These included the assertion that progress was signified by the recent failure of the enemy to mount a major military offensive. 'Measurement of Progress: Texts of Cables from Embassy Saigon (7,867 and 10,573)', 7 November 1967, doc. 30a, folder: 'Vietnam 7 E(2) 11/67 Public Relations Activities', Box 99, Country File, National Security Files, Lyndon Baines Johnson Presidential Library (LBJL).

[62] For an examination of American news reporting during and immediately following the Tet Offensive, see Braestrup, *Big Story*. For a critique of Braestrup's conclusions, see Herman and Chomsky, *Manufacturing Consent*, pp. 211–28.

As the Johnson administration rejected proposals for an enlarged US military presence in Indochina and embarked upon a new bid for a negotiated settlement, the discourse of victory did not disappear entirely from the public sphere, for the goal of preserving the non-communist status of South Vietnam survived into the early years of the Nixon presidency, together with the conviction that this still could be secured through the use of force.[63] The balance of popular opinion, however, shifted markedly in a dovish direction after the Tet offensive, with most members of the public – and probably most representatives of the press – now seeming to believe that negotiation and compromise represented the best available means of ending the conflict and effecting an American withdrawal.[64]

In the wake of the Tet offensive, therefore, national goals became more conditional and more mutable, and as they did so, the moral coordinates of the war changed. Neither the sacrifice of young American lives nor largescale civilian casualties were as easily justified by the pursuit of honourable withdrawal (the conditions for which remained open to debate) as they had been by the stable, concrete objective of a democratic non-communist South Vietnam. In the absence of such an objective, the language of national service and battlefield necessity could no longer be relied upon to sublimate and detoxify the raw facts of injury and death. The exhaustion of this broader logic, the inward turn of military rationales towards self-reflexive absurdity, was embodied most obviously in the famous assertion of a US Air Force officer, recorded by Peter Arnett in February 1968, that it had become necessary to destroy the town of Ben Tre in order 'to save it'.[65] The Tet offensive loosened the hold of command and establishment narratives upon the way in which the ongoing devastation of Vietnam was reported, and the story of the war as it appeared in the American news media could at last become the story that perhaps it really should have been all along: the story of injury and killing.

The battles of Tet further facilitated the emergence of that story by denaturalizing the incidence of civilian suffering, as the rate of devastation suddenly intensified and, in the more conventional military engagements of the period, the historical forces responsible could be viewed with greater clarity. Journalists who had become so accustomed to the attritional effects of Vietcong guerrilla warfare and the American strategy of search-and-destroy upon the population of South Vietnam that they no longer considered them worthy of comment in their reports, now found the bodies piling up in a way that they had not experienced before and could not rationalize according to any meaningful definitions of collateral damage.

[63] J. Kimball, *Nixon's Vietnam War* (Lawrence: University Press of Kansas, 1998), pp. 67, 239–40.

[64] J. Mueller, *War, Presidents and Public Opinion* (New York: John Wiley & Sons, 1973), p. 107.

[65] Hammond, *Public Affairs . . . 1962–1968*, p. 355.

In his novel *The Short-Timers*, Gustav Hasford – who served as a combat correspondent with the First Marine Division in Vietnam – describes the sensation of entering Hué during the US counter-offensive as 'a strange new experience. Our war has been in the paddies, in hamlets where the largest structure was a bamboo hut. Seeing the effects of war upon a Vietnamese city makes me feel like a New Guy.'[66] He provides an unsparing, visceral account of the fate of Hué's civilian inhabitants, 'buried alive, faces frozen in mid-scream, hands like claws, the fingernails bloody and caked with damp earth'.[67] On the second day of the offensive, Michael Herr – a writer for *Esquire* – served as a medic in the hospital compound at Can Tho; he was confronted with all the concentrated waste of war and traumatized for some time to come: 'For the next six years I saw them all, the ones I'd really seen and the ones I'd imagined, theirs and ours, friends I'd loved and strangers, motionless figures in a dance, the old dance.'[68] John Laurence – who covered the worst of the fighting in Hué – recalls that 'the scale of suffering and death in the Tet Offensive was staggering', enough to buckle the convictions of 'even the most traditionally patriotic, pro-military journalists'; their ideological defences had been overwhelmed and they could now see the war for what it really was, 'a lost cause, not worth American lives and treasure, ruinous to the Vietnamese'.[69]

Back in the United States, television coverage of the conflict became more graphic, as images of civilian casualties and urban devastation were broadcast an average of 3.9 times a week, four times the norm for the war as a whole. Daniel Hallin notes: 'Tet was the first sustained period during which it could be said that the war appeared on television as a really brutal affair.'[70] On 6 February 1968, a week after the offensive began, Ron Steinman telexed NBC headquarters in New York: 'Watch the newspapers and wires and us because the coming story is that of civilian casualties. By the look of things those are going to be painfully and tearfully high.'[71] Two days later, White House adviser Harry McPherson observed that the news coverage 'has had a stunning impact. TV and stills have been savage – they almost choke the viewer with horror.'[72] In the early months of 1968, it seems, the human cost of the military struggle became news in a way that it had not been before, and bodies seemed now as relevant to the story of Vietnam as geopolitics and strategic postures.

Just as the Tet offensive discredited the discourse of victory, placing a catalogue of grim statistics and images in the path of official rhetoric, so

---

[66] G. Hasford, *The Short-Timers* (London: Bantam, 1987), p. 80.

[67] *Ibid.*, p. 126.

[68] M. Herr, *Dispatches* (London: Picador, 1979), p. 60.

[69] Laurence, p. 84.

[70] Hallin, *The 'Uncensored War'*, p. 171.

[71] Steinman, pp. 239–40.

[72] McPherson to Christian, 8 February 1968, folder: 'ND19/CO312 3/10/68–3/18/68', Box 232, White House Central File, LBJL.

too did it provoke doubts about the extent of the control exercised over the national war effort by both civilian leaders in Washington and their military representatives in Saigon. The scope and vigour of the enemy's mobilization against US and ARVN positions now forcefully cast into question not only the ingenuousness of earlier official estimates of communist battlefield strength, but also the quality of American military intelligence and its data-gathering and processing structures. More than ever before, the audience for official press briefings was sensitized to the possibility that crucial information was being withheld or misinterpreted for reasons of incompetence as well as dark Machiavellian cunning. Either way, an increment of provisionality had been added to perceptions of official truth.[73] In addition – for all its eventual success in responding to the enemy offensive – the US command forfeited much of what remained of its reputation for an assured technocratic style of conflict management in the first days of the offensive, when the countrywide picture of what had been taken and what had been held was confused and military defeat – to a few observers, at least – seemed a genuine possibility.[74]

At home, meanwhile, the Johnson administration appeared unable to provide any firm public assurance that the war was under control and, indeed, spent several subsequent weeks in often heated private debates about whether the military situation in Vietnam merited the commitment of a further 200,000 troops. On the broader socio-political canvas, the assassinations of Robert Kennedy and Martin Luther King, riots in downtown Washington, DC, and the electoral insurgencies of Eugene McCarthy and George Wallace all indicated that the centre was not holding. At the Democratic National Convention in Chicago, mainstream reporters as well as anti-war protestors endured police beatings, and thus received a poignant lesson in just how brutal and indiscriminate the state-sanctioned use of force could be.[75] The events of 1968 suggested, not least to American journalists, that cracks were appearing in the calm neo-classical façade of national authority, that working assumptions of institutional professionalism had to be revised to admit the potential for chaos and transgression,

[73] William Hammond notes that, by the late 1960s, journalists were becoming less dependent than previously upon government sources. Perspectives gathered from official news conferences and press releases were increasingly supplemented with independently researched information and juxtaposed with comments from those critical of national policy. Hammond, *Public Affairs, . . . 1968–1973*, p. 102.

[74] Michael Herr asserts: 'We took a huge collective nervous breakdown, it was the compression and heat of heavy contact generated out until every American in Vietnam got a taste. Vietnam was a dark room full of deadly objects, the VC were everywhere all at once like spider cancer, and instead of losing the war in little pieces over years we lost it fast in under a week. After that, we were like the character in pop grunt mythology, dead but too dumb to lie down.' Herr, pp. 62–3.

[75] David Armstrong notes that the national mainstream media unequivocally condemned the police violence at the convention, though they were inclined at the time to consider it an aberration. Armstrong, *A Trumpet to Arms: Alternative Media in America* (Los Angeles: J.P. Tarcher, 1981), p. 126.

and that sometimes no one – in the government, in the military and especially in the news media itself – knew what they were doing or really what
was going on. In such a context, it seemed much more conceivable that a
massacre on the scale of My Lai could have occurred, yet not be registered
either by senior officials or the large corps of reporters dispersed throughout South Vietnam at the time.

In these three ways – by persuading many Americans to moderate their
expectations of what national policy might achieve in Indochina, thereby
limiting the scope for the discourse of victory to override ethical misgivings; by sensitizing a sluggish public sphere to the human costs of the
war; and by stimulating a new appreciation of just how much went on in
Vietnam outside the jurisdiction of benign and competent authority – the
events of Tet helped to create a space within the culture of war reporting
that would eventually permit the revelations about the My Lai massacre to
be believed, registered as significant and published as news.

This is not to assert, however, that the American news media and the
wider public sphere were now unflinching in their willingness to confront
the darker aspects of the Vietnam war. Following the disillusioning events
of 1968, a desire for retrenchment – for the closure of debates that questioned the national purpose – was also evident in much public discourse.
Indeed, the victory strategy of the new Nixon administration – requiring
as it did both the intensification of military pressure upon the enemy and
the deintensification of the anti-war protests that might lead Hanoi to
question how much longer that pressure could be applied – implicitly
depended on the preservation of media silence on the human misery that
US policies were still perpetuating in Vietnam.[76]

In addition, a number of the factors which had operated before the Tet
offensive to inhibit the reporting of civilian casualties continued to influence the content of news in its aftermath. Events that were not witnessed
personally by reporters were still unlikely to be communicated to the
public unless official channels formally or informally drew that event to
the attention of the press. Following Operation Speedy Express, conducted
in the upper Mekong Delta between December 1968 and May 1969, the
Army's Ninth Infantry Division claimed 10,883 enemy dead, but only 748
weapons captured. The disparity between these two figures indicated that
much of the body count consisted of non-combatants; until *Newsweek*
magazine began an investigation in November 1971, however, the murderous excesses of the operation largely escaped media scrutiny.[77] The civilian
victims of the raid carried out on Thanh Phong by Bob Kerrey's team
of Navy Seals were described in Kerrey's communiqué as enemy killed-
in-action. Although the district military advisory headquarters received
reports from village elders that atrocities had been committed, nobody

[76] Kimball, p. 90.
[77] Lewy, pp. 142–3; Knightley, pp. 438–40.

there seemed anxious to conduct a proper investigation, and so news of the killings never reached the press.[78]

In addition, although the media's characterization of American troops had changed in the wake of Tet, with representations of the committed professional warrior yielding to images of self-doubt and existential strain, its coverage continued to manifest a sympathetic identification between soldier and newsman which served to subdue editorial comment on the ethics of particular actions.[79] In September 1968, NBC broadcast a report on the burning of a Vietnamese village by American soldiers. Its correspondent Howard Tucker presented evidence that the village functioned as a base for the Vietcong. Noting, however, the assertion of the commander – a lieutenant – that his unit had received fire from its vicinity, Tucker declared that he had personally heard no shots. He concluded that the officer 'would have to live with his decision'. In the view of Daniel Hallin, Tucker – though sceptical – retained a respect for the lieutenant's judgement, indicating 'that the lieutenant, the reporter, and the audience all belong to the same moral community, sharing common values by which they judge one another's actions'.[80]

Efforts to chronicle the consequences of the fighting for the inhabitants of Vietnam – in particular by displaying images of the wounded and the dead – still sat as uneasily with the commercial interests of American media outlets as they had in the early years of the war. During the Tet offensive, a NBC camera crew travelled to My Tho in the Mekong Delta and filmed Vietnamese soldiers – wearing face masks to block out the smell – burying in mass graves hundreds of their compatriots who had died in the battle for the town. These pictures were spliced together with footage of crowded hospitals around the country in an attempt, Ron Steinman recalls, to communicate something of 'the wantonness of war'. Believing the report merited immediate broadcast, Steinman asked to use an expensive satellite feed, rather than air transportation, to send it to the United States. His producers in New York, however, rejected the idea: as the story did not involve American troops, its value as news was judged to be limited, and the costs of its transmission therefore had to be contained.[81]

Although the editors at *Life* paid a sizeable sum for the rights to Ronald Haeberle's images of the dead at My Lai (4), they elected not to display them on the magazine's front cover, fearing – Joe Eszterhas recalls – that 'newsstand buyers would be repulsed'. To illustrate a story about wildlife photography in Africa, an antelope appeared instead.[82]

[78] Vistica, *The Education of Lieutenant Kerrey*, pp. 93–7.
[79] Hallin, *The 'Uncensored War'*, p. 180.
[80] *Ibid.*, p. 150.
[81] Steinman, pp. 233–4.
[82] Eszterhas, p. 479; *Life* (5 December 1969).

The media's uncertainty about what constituted reprehensible behaviour in wartime also survived into the post-Tet period; indeed, as the conflict became cast as a dirty, regrettable business in virtually all respects, it seemed somewhat pedantic and severe to isolate specific examples of moral turpitude. In August 1969, when eight members of US Special Forces were charged with the murder of a suspected South Vietnamese double agent, *Time* reacted with agnostic bemusement. The rationale behind the decision to prosecute, it asserted, was known only to the US Army.[83] *New York Times* columnist Russell Baker was more offended by the manner of the killing – a bullet through the head followed by disposal of the body in a weighted sack at sea – than by the notion that American soldiers were engaging in summary executions. The affair, he commented, 'violates every rule in the style book . . . really now, if our Government has to be tough, can it not do better than emulate the odious style of the mafia?'[84] There were few complaints from the media when the charges were eventually dropped.

That same month, *Esquire* reported on an atrocity that had occurred nearly three years before, when a squad of US Marines had gang-raped one Vietnamese woman and murdered her husband and son and three members of her husband's family.[85] The editors led the issue with the article, and sent proofs to the major newspapers, but – anxious not to seem sensationalist – they otherwise underplayed it. No illustrations were used. Their ambivalence towards the story was reflected in the reaction of its readers. Some apparently believed the report was a hoax, consistent with the magazine's reputation for playful, satiric journalism. The newspapers showed little interest, and so the story died.[86] What the revelatory violence of Tet had initially revived in the way of moral seriousness, it had eventually also worn down, until irony and ennui had become the characteristic responses of both the newsman and his audience to the ongoing devastation of Vietnam. 'The television networks, the press, the government and the general public,' John Laurence observes, 'had become so accustomed to the weekly toll of dead and wounded that violence no longer surprised them.'[87]

In the autumn of 1969, those who wished to bring the massacre at My Lai (4) to the attention of the American public were obliged to negotiate this fluid, uncertain context. Eighteen months earlier, when the massacre had occurred, there had been no independent journalist on the scene, and therefore no non-military source to challenge the official account of the operation presented by the task-force command: that it had engaged

[83] *Time* (3 October 1969), p. 50.
[84] *New York Times* (21 August 1969), p. 40.
[85] N. Poirier, 'An American Atrocity', *Esquire* (August 1969), pp. 59–63, 132–41.
[86] Polsgrove, pp. 208–10; Knightley, pp. 433–4.
[87] Laurence, pp. 530–1.

enemy forces, killing 128, and capturing three weapons.[88] Nor, following the incorporation of that account into a press release at brigade head-quarters, did any correspondent critically examine the information provided and enquire precisely how it was that 125 of those certified as dead Vietcong appeared not to have been armed.[89] Allegations advanced in enemy radio propaganda broadcasts that 500 people had been massacred in the action and investigations conducted in late March and early April by local government officials after they had heard rumours of the killings were either ignored by American reporters or, more probably, simply never came to their attention.[90] These were not the sort of places that they looked for their news.

In the absence of immediate external scrutiny, the task force, brigade and divisional commands were left alone to write up the events that had occurred in Son My in whichever way they thought appropriate. They thought evasion appropriate. Warrant Officer Hugh Thompson, the pilot of a helicopter engaged in aerial surveillance for the task force, observed evidence during the operation that civilians were being deliberately killed and reported what he had seen to Major Frederic Watke, his commanding officer. Watke subsequently related Thompson's allegations to Lieutenant Colonel Barker, the task force commander, and Brigadier General George Young, the assistant commander of the Americal Division. Young in turn related them to the Division Commander, Major General Samuel Koster.[91] Both Barker and Koster, together with the commander of the 11th Brigade, Colonel Oran Henderson, had monitored the operation from the air and were already aware that non-combatants had been killed, even if they were uncertain of the number or of the manner in which they died.[92] According to MACV regulations, this knowledge should have been immediately communicated to higher headquarters, but it was not; similarly, as soon as commanders were told of Thompson's allegations, they should have been forwarded to a higher authority but, once again, they were not.[93] Instead, General Koster asked Henderson to look into the matter, which he did with a politic discretion and economy of energy. Henderson

[88] Goldstein *et al.*, p. 106. Major General Winant Sidle, later to become the Army's Chief of Information, notes that the siege at Khe Sanh dominated the attention of the American press corps in South Vietnam at the time of the massacre. Sidle, 'Massacre at My Lai', in J. Gottschalk (ed.), *Crisis Response: Inside Stories on Managing Image Under Siege* (Detroit: Visible Ink, 1993), p. 333.

[89] For discussion of the reported body- and weapons-count and subsequent press releases, see Goldstein *et al.*, p. 233; Hammer, *One Morning in the War*, pp. 6–9; and S. Hersh, *Cover-Up: The Army's Secret Investigation of the Massacre at My Lai 4* (New York: Random House, 1972), pp. 101, 120–1.

[90] Copies of an NLF propaganda script for radio broadcast and of the local government investigative reports can be found in Peers, pp. 276–86. See also Goldstein *et al.*, pp. 269–76; and Hersh, *Cover-Up*, pp. 180–95.

[91] Goldstein *et al.*, pp. 239–45.

[92] *Ibid.*, pp. 234–6.

[93] *Ibid.*, pp. 215–22.

spoke to Captain Medina who asserted that he had seen between 20 and 28 non-combatant casualties in My Lai (4) and who responded in the affirmative when Henderson asked him if they had been killed by artillery and gunship fire.[94] Henderson also assembled a group of soldiers from Charlie Company and enquired whether any of their number had killed civilians during the operation. This was not the method of a man who really wished for candid answers, and the response he received was accordingly negative. Henderson deemed these denials of sufficient weight to discount Thompson's charges and so he brought his investigation to a close. Koster was content to accept Henderson's conclusions, and to let the matter rest.[95]

The rumours and allegations of unwarranted killings drifting around enemy and local government channels by early April, however, prompted Koster and Henderson to return to the incident. Once more, Koster failed to communicate these allegations to higher headquarters, as MACV directives required; nor did he seek to appoint an independent investigating officer. He simply asked Henderson to submit a written report on his earlier enquiries.[96] The general seems to have been concerned that the circle of knowledge was widening and that he might need to demonstrate at some point in the future that an investigation had been undertaken and no firm evidence of malfeasance found. Henderson spoke to the commander of the local ARVN division and to the government's province chief, both of whom, he later said, seemed satisfied that the charges circulating were a confection of enemy propagandists and without real substance.[97] In his subsequent written report, submitted to Koster on 24 April, Henderson concluded that twenty non-combatants had been inadvertently killed during the operation 'when caught in the area of preparatory fires and in the cross fires of the US and VC forces'. He further concluded that 'no civilians were gathered together and shot by US soldiers'. The allegations that mass killings had occurred, Henderson said, were 'obviously a Viet Cong propaganda move to discredit the United States in the eyes of the Vietnamese people in general and the ARVN soldier in particular'.[98]

In Koster's view, however, Henderson's report did not carry conviction, because it was not only the enemy which was advancing accusations of massacre: the testimony of Thompson also had to be addressed. Koster asked Henderson to provide a more extensive analysis, a task which Henderson assigned to Colonel Barker, consistent with his concern to keep the matter contained within the immediate operational command.

94 Hersh, *Cover-Up*, pp. 154–5.
95 *Ibid.*, pp. 262–4.
96 *Ibid.*, p. 284.
97 *Ibid.*, pp. 281–3.
98 Henderson to Koster, 'Report of Investigation', 24 April 1968, folder: 'Master File [Copy 2]', Box 16, Records Created After the Completion of the Peers Inquiry (RCCPI), RPI, RAS, RG319, NACP.

Submitted in mid-May alongside fifteen to twenty signed witness state-ments, Barker's report reaffirmed Henderson's earlier conclusion about the extent and the cause of civilian casualties.[99] According to one officer who saw the report (which subsequently disappeared), all the accompany-ing statements were written in the same hand. This might have indicated nothing amiss (it was not unusual for an interrogating officer to transcribe responses himself) had any of the individuals most likely to have been interviewed by Barker in connection with the allegations subsequently recalled his investigation.[100] Henderson, however, did not enquire into the integrity of Barker's research, recommending that Koster accept the report; Koster was content to do so, it seems.[101] The rumours of what had really hap-pened in My Lai (4) were thereupon kicked with relief into the long grass.[102]

Within Charlie Company itself, meanwhile, a mixture of denial, moral confusion, guilt and fear of retribution functioned to sustain a brittle col-lective silence about the massacre. One soldier, Michael Bernhardt, who had not participated in the killings and who was known for his independ-ence of mind was warned by Captain Medina not to write to his congress-man; the consequences of such an action for Bernhardt's personal well-being were not stated, but they were understood. From that moment on, Bernhardt was kept out in the field, away from the rear areas where he might spread word of what the company had done; virtually every day he was ordered to walk point.[103] Accounts of the massacre did circulate around the 11th Brigade and the division headquarters at Chu Lai, but only one of those who heard them – Ronald Ridenhour – cared enough to find out more, and it took him some time. As the weeks and months passed, many of the personnel involved rotated out of service, or were moved to duties in other areas, and gradually, with no formal investiga-tion to sustain them, the mess hall whisperings died away.[104] US civilians who worked closely with the provincial government in Quang Ngai appar-ently heard nothing about the massacre, consistent with the view of its senior officials that nothing untoward indeed had occurred.[105] It is not

[99] Hersh, *Cover-Up*, pp. 208–10.

[100] *Ibid.*, p. 222; Goldstein *et al.*, p. 293.

[101] Hersh, *Cover-Up*, p. 210.

[102] The Peers Inquiry was unable to locate any copies of Barker's report and found no other witnesses beyond Koster and Henderson willing to attest to its existence (Barker himself had been killed in a helicopter collision in June 1968). The inquiry concluded that 'no such formal report of investigation ever existed' (Goldstein *et al.*, p. 293). After the inquiry had closed, however, two soldiers serving in the division headquarters recalled seeing a file that contained the report, and another – a clerk with the 11th Brigade – that he had typed it (Hersh, *Cover-Up*, pp. 222–5, 290).

[103] R. Ridenhour, 'Heroes at the Massacre', *Playboy* (March 1993), pp. 88–90, 144–9.

[104] Peers, p. 127.

[105] Goldstein *et al.*, p. 313. After the first significant news stories about My Lai appeared in November 1969, however, one Canadian doctor who had worked at a Quaker hospital in Quang Ngai City declared that he had heard of the massacre within days of its occurrence (Hersh, *Cover-Up*, pp. 237–8).

perhaps surprising, then, that members of the American press corps, based hundreds of miles to the south in Saigon, continued to be excluded from the circle of knowledge.

Even as the army embarked upon a more serious inquiry in the spring of 1969, following the receipt of Ridenhour's letter, the American public remained oblivious to the massacre.[106] In so far as it can be determined, military sources breathed nothing of the investigation to the media at this time. This was undoubtedly due in part to institutional self-interest, and in part also to a concern that premature disclosure would compromise any subsequent prosecutions.[107] It took a number of months, moreover, for the investigation to yield conclusive evidence that serious crimes had indeed been committed in My Lai (4). An initial survey of Americal Division records in Chu Lai, conducted by the Office of the Inspector General, yielded nothing that substantiated Ridenhour's claims and led the investigator to suggest that 'the complainant has grossly exaggerated the military action in question'.[108] Back in the United States, Colonel William Wilson was tracking down the men who had spoken to Ridenhour about the killings, and was seeking to contact others. By 5 May, he had interviewed four witnesses, as well as Ridenhour himself, and had come to the conclusion that the weight of the testimony was too great 'for the tale of mass murders to have been conjured up out of whole cloth'.[109] However, it was only in mid-July, when he interviewed Paul Meadlo, that Wilson obtained a confession of guilt from a soldier who had actually participated in the massacre. Meadlo was also a crucial witness because, having been seriously wounded and evacuated out of the unit the day after the operation in Son My, his testimony would not have been 'influenced by barracks-room discussions' with other members of Charlie Company. After speaking to Meadlo, Wilson considered the case closed and returned to Washington to report his findings.[110]

The outcome of Wilson's enquiries, however, was not in itself enough to propel the case into the public domain. His function was simply to determine whether the events in My Lai (4) merited a full criminal investigation. That having been determined, the Office of the Inspector General turned over the case in early August to the Office of the Provost Marshal General and to a team of detectives from its Criminal Investigation Division (CID), led by Chief Warrant Officer André Feher. At that time, the case retained its 'Sensitive' status to avoid the release of information that

[106] For a copy of Ridenhour's letter, see Goldstein *et al.*, pp. 34–7.

[107] W. Wilson, 'I had prayed to God that this thing was fiction . . .', *American Heritage* (February 1990), p. 46.

[108] Whitaker, 'Preliminary Inquiry Concerning Alleged Massacre of All Vietnamese Residents of My Lai (BS 728795) by US Soldiers', 17 April 1969, folder: My Lai 8/40, Papers of *Four Hours in My Lai*, LHCMA, KCL.

[109] Wilson, p. 49.

[110] *Ibid.*, pp. 52–3.

might prejudice future legal proceedings.[111] Moreover, though Wilson clearly took the view that Meadlo's testimony confirmed the essential veracity of Ridenhour's claims, others still needed to be convinced. Feher himself recalled that he did not obtain 'hard evidence that something real bad had happened' until he interviewed Ronald Haeberle on 25 August and was shown Haeberle's photographs of the massacre victims.[112]

Only when the decision was taken to prefer criminal charges against individuals would the army be compelled to release details of the case to the press, and throughout most of August the issue of charges remained unresolved. If any soldiers were to be charged in relation to the massacre, William Calley would have to be amongst them; most of the witnesses who had been interviewed by that stage, and especially Paul Meadlo, had placed Calley at the scene and in immediate command during the worst of the slaughter.[113] Calley, however, was due to leave the army on 6 September and thus sail out of the jurisdiction of the military justice system at a time when the most damning evidence against him was still being collected. In addition, the power to prefer charges against Calley lay not with the Office of the Inspector General nor with the Office of the Provost Marshal General, but with his local commanders and the staff judge advocates at Fort Benning, and they were initially unconvinced that the evidence presented to them by the Office of the Inspector General – which consisted solely of Meadlo's testimony – was sufficient to merit such an action.[114]

The staff judge advocates requested a more detailed briefing, which was provided by Colonel Wilson on 19 August. Thereafter, the commanding general at Fort Benning made the decision to retain Calley on active duty until the conclusion of the investigation, whilst the staff judge advocates conducted their own interview with Meadlo and travelled to the Office of the Judge Advocate General in Washington to discuss the drafting of charges. Wilson, however, had not provided any guidance concerning the final disposition of the allegations, and in late August or early September, the Office of the Judge Advocate General contacted the staff judge advocates at Fort Benning and told them: 'Do nothing until you hear from us.' It was only on 4 September that the authorities at Fort Benning were given the clearance to make their decision. The executive officer of the Student Brigade – the unit with immediate jurisdiction over Calley – discussed the evidence with his legal officer and the staff judge advocates and, considering it now sufficient, signed the charge sheet either that evening, or on the morning of 5 September.[115]

[111] Wallace to Whitaker, 4 August 1969, folder: 'My Lai Cases – General', Box 15, John Dean Subject Files, Staff Members and Office Files, White House Special Files, Nixon Presidential Materials (NPM), NACP.

[112] Feher to Bilton, 20 August 1990, folder: My Lai 8/35, Papers of *Four Hours in My Lai*, LHCMA, KCL; Haeberle, 'Witness Statement', 25 August 1969, folder: My Lai 8/38, Papers of *Four Hours in My Lai*, LHCMA, KCL.

[113] Wilson, p. 52.

[114] *United States* v. *Calley*, 46 CMR 1131 (ACMR 1973), in Goldstein *et al.*, p. 478.

[115] *Ibid.*, pp. 478–9.

The process of preferring the charges against Calley and thus, by extension, inviting the press to turn its attention to the massacre was made more complicated by the eddies of political and institutional interest that those involved in the process perceived to be flowing around them. Some time in August, a rumour that the case was receiving the attention of President Nixon reached both the senior staff judge advocate at Fort Benning and Captain William R. Hill, the Student Brigade's legal officer.[116] The White House had been informed about the move towards a full criminal investigation, with disciplinary or legal proceedings to follow, on 4 August.[117] Captain Hill discussed the possibility of Presidential intervention with three of the junior judge advocates at the base, who took the view that, if such an intervention occurred, it would most probably weigh against the preferral of charges.[118] This would have seemed consistent with the hold order issued by the Office of the Judge Advocate General. The lawyers at Fort Benning could certainly assume that new revelations about American atrocities in Vietnam would not be welcomed by an executive branch anxious to contain opposition to the war; they could also surmise that, given the sympathies extended at that time by press and public alike towards those accused of murder in the Special Forces case, the White House might discount the political liabilities that would be attached to a decision not to prosecute the perpetrators of the massacre at My Lai (4) if the decision was ever revealed. (A few weeks later, indeed, Nixon and his advisers conspired to have the charges against the Special Forces soldiers dropped, instructing the CIA to refuse to allow its agents to testify in the case.)[119] The group concluded that Captain Hill should sign the charge sheet even if the word was passed from higher authority not to do so; Hill might be disciplined, but the judge advocates would remain in post to carry the charges through to prosecution.[120]

The balance of evidence suggests, however, that the White House was not actively contemplating a precipitate intervention in the Calley case. In early September, the Department of the Army prepared briefing papers for the President on the subject of My Lai that seem to presuppose a readership basically uninformed about the facts of the massacre, the progress of the ongoing investigation, and the impact that a court martial might have upon administration policy in Vietnam. 'Publicity attendant upon such a trial', Nixon was told, 'could prove acutely embarrassing to the United States. It might well affect the Paris peace talks, and those nations opposed to our involvement in Vietnam will certainly capitalize

[116] *Ibid.*, p. 479.

[117] Wallace to Whitaker, 4 August 1969, folder: 'My Lai Cases – General', Box 15, John Dean Subject Files, Staff Members and Office Files, White House Special Files, NPM, NACP.

[118] *United States* v. *Calley*, 46 CMR 1131 (ACMR 1973), in Goldstein *et al.*, pp. 479–80; R. Hammer, *The Court-Martial of Lt Calley* (New York: Coward, McCann & Geoghegan, 1971), pp. 30–2.

[119] Haldeman, diary entries, 25 and 29 September 1969, in H. Haldeman, *The Haldeman Diaries: Inside the Nixon White House* (New York: Putnam, 1994), pp. 90–1.

[120] Hammer, *The Court-Martial of Lt Calley*, pp. 31–2.

upon the situation. Domestically, it will provide grist for the mills of antiwar activists'.[121] The papers indicate, moreover, that if any institution expressed strong convictions about the case, and claimed the principal power of decision over its prosecution, it was the Department of the Army, not the White House. Nor do the papers exhibit much regard for the right of Calley's local commanders to make an independent judgement about the disposition of the investigation. On 2 September, a memorandum from the Judge Advocate General still discussed the question of Calley's indictment in conditional terms: 'If the charges are preferred. . . .'[122] A day later, however – and at least twenty-four hours before the charge sheet was signed at Fort Benning – the Secretary of the Army, Stanley Resor, informed the Secretary of Defense, Melvin Laird: 'It is planned to prefer charges of murder against Lieutenant Calley on 4 or 5 September 1969'.[123] A memorandum was sent to the President on 4 September, similarly asserting that 'court martial charges will be preferred'. The 'known facts' about the massacre, the President was told, 'leave no doubt about the necessity of prosecution'.[124] That same day, the Army's Chief of Information dispatched public affairs guidance to the authorities at Fort Benning which also assumed that charges would be preferred.[125]

For most of August, then, a certain irresolution seems to have characterized the attitude of military authorities in Washington towards the prospect of massacre prosecutions; by early September, however, their attitude had changed dramatically. Such was their determination now to see Calley tried, indeed, that – had it been communicated to those officers at Fort Benning responsible for preferring charges against the lieutenant – it might well have constituted improper command influence.[126] This sudden acceleration towards a judicial accounting was most likely occasioned not by

[121] Packard to Nixon, 'The My Lai atrocity', 4 September 1969, folder: 'Possible My Lai Commission', Alexander Haig Special File, Box 1004, National Security Council Files, NPM, NACP. See also unsigned draft memorandum and attachment: 'The My Lai Atrocity', undated, folder 'Lt. Calley/My Lai Village', Box 15, John Dean Subject Files, Staff Members and Office Files, White House Special Files, NPM, NACP.

[122] Hodson to Westmoreland and Resor, 'Alleged Murder of Vietnamese Civilians', 2 September 1969, folder: 'My Lai Allegations', Box 16, RCCPI, RPI, RAS, RG319, NACP.

[123] Resor to Laird, 'The My Lai Atrocity', 3 September 1969, folder: 'My Lai Cases – General', Box 15, John Dean Subject Files, Staff Members and Office Files, White House Special Files, NPM, NACP.

[124] Packard to Nixon, 'The My Lai atrocity', 4 September 1969, folder: 'Possible My Lai Commission', Alexander Haig Special File, Box 1004, National Security Council Files, NPM, NACP.

[125] Coats to Connor, 'Public Affairs Guidance – 1LT Calley', 4 September 1969, folder: 'Master File [Copy 2]', Box 16, RCCPI, RPI, RAS, RG319, NACP.

[126] Calley's defence counsel did assert unlawful command influence when petitioning for a new trial in 1973, but lacked documentary evidence to give the allegations force. It is necessary to note, however, that all of the officers at Fort Benning involved in the processing of charges testified that they had received no instructions from the Department of Defense concerning the disposition of the case. The issue turns, perhaps, on the distinction between direct instructions and knowledge of command preferences and expectations. *United States* v. *Calley*, 46 CMR 1131 (ACMR 1973), in Goldstein *et al.*, pp. 475–84.

the conclusion of a probably phantom presidential review, but by the revelations that resulted from André Feher's interview with Ronald Haeberle on 25 August. Neither Haeberle's witness statement nor the photographs he had taken of the victims of the massacre provided much specific support for the case against Calley himself, but they did offer the most compelling evidence yet available to investigators that large groups of civilians – women and children included – had been shot in My Lai (4). Even more critically, perhaps, the interview indicated to Pentagon officials that news of the massacre could not be contained. Haeberle informed Feher that he had already shown his pictures to over 600 people whilst lecturing to civic groups in his home state of Ohio.[127] In its memorandum of 4 September, the Department of Defense drew the attention of the President to these lectures and concluded that, even if no courts martial were held, 'the incident will almost surely find its way into the public press by other means'.[128] There was an implicit corollary to this conclusion: that by the time the story – complete with its searing visual content – broke, the US military needed to have done as much as it could do to disassociate itself from the crimes committed in My Lai (4). That meant charging the soldiers responsible and not letting them go free.

The Pentagon, perhaps, assumed too much about the vigilance of the press. Still tethered to official sources, and culturally discomfited by atrocity stories, the mainstream news media in the autumn of 1969 spurned a number of opportunities to bring the events in Son My to the attention of the public. The images of massacre that Ronald Haeberle displayed to lecture audiences around Ohio appear to have entirely escaped the notice of reporters in that state. Doubtful that the military could be trusted to investigate itself, meanwhile, Ronald Ridenhour hired a literary agent to approach a handful of news magazines with an account of the killings, and was turned down by all. Editors apparently asked his agent: 'What are you associating yourself with something like this for?'[129]

In early September, when the American military made its first public acknowledgement of the case, in a news release which stated that Lieutenant Calley had been charged with murder, the national press again responded with inattention and incuriosity. Admittedly, military public affairs officials did what they could to keep the disclosure out of the headlines. Although it was composed by the army's Office of the Chief of Information (OCINFO), the news release was not issued in the Pentagon, where it would invite the scrutiny of experienced beat reporters, but at Fort Benning, where the accused was being held. It provided little indication

[127] Haeberle, 'Witness Statement', 25 August 1969, folder: My Lai 8/38, Papers of *Four Hours in My Lai*, LHCMA, KCL.

[128] Packard to Nixon, 'The My Lai atrocity', 4 September 1969, folder: 'Possible My Lai Commission', Alexander Haig Special File, Box 1004, National Security Council Files, NPM, NACP.

[129] *New York Times* (29 November 1969), p. 14.

of the scale of Calley's alleged crimes: whilst the charges specified that he had killed 109 Vietnamese civilians, the release made no mention of these numbers. Aside from Calley's service history, information officers at Fort Benning were instructed not to give the press any further details of the case without first consulting OCINFO. Nor were they to refer any enquirers directly to OCINFO, or mention the office's role in coordinating the news release.[130] That a lieutenant in the US Army stood accused of the murder of non-combatants in Vietnam was to be presented as a matter of purely local interest, with the hope that the story would thereby disappear into the stream of innocuous wire reports flowing daily from the provinces.

The military spoke *sotto voce* of atrocity and the media slept on. A short *Associated Press* report appeared on an inside page of the *New York Times*; the information officer at Fort Benning, it said, had given few details of the incident, other than to confirm that the charges against Calley related to the death of more than one civilian.[131] *Associated Press* itself neglected to pursue the story any further.[132] A brief item was broadcast on *NBC Nightly News*, noting that Calley was accused of the 'premeditated murder of a number of South Vietnamese civilians'.[133] The charges attracted a front-page headline in the *Ledger-Enquirer*, a journal which served the community of Columbus, Georgia, near Fort Benning.[134] Calley's home-town newspaper, the *Miami Herald*, also carried a report.[135] These limited manifestations of media interest aside, the information office at Fort Benning recorded, the news release 'went virtually unnoticed'.[136]

For another two months thereafter, the story lay dormant. CID detectives continued their inquiries into the massacre, whilst the authorities at Fort Benning began an investigation under Article 32 of the Uniform Code of Military Justice to ascertain whether the evidence against Lieutenant Calley merited court martial. A number of witnesses still on active duty in the army were invited to a hearing at Fort Benning from 20 to 23 October.[137] It was around this time, as the official investigations into the killings at My Lai (4) began to take the form of a judicial process, and tested the discretion of more and more military sources, that the seeds of the decisive press revelations of mid-November were sown. Seymour Hersh, a freelance reporter based in Washington, received a call from Geoff Cowen,

---

[130] Coats to Connor, 'Public Affairs Guidance – 1LT Calley', 4 September 1969, folder: 'Master File [Copy 2]', Box 16, RCCPI, RPI, RAS, RG319, NACP.

[131] *New York Times* (7 September 1969), p. 14.

[132] Hammer, *One Morning in the War*, p. 172.

[133] Hersh, *My Lai 4*, p. 130.

[134] *Columbus Ledger-Enquirer* (6 September 1969). Another report on the case appeared the following day: *Columbus Ledger-Enquirer* (7 September 1969).

[135] Hersh, *My Lai 4*, p. 129.

[136] Office of the Information Officer, Headquarters US Army Infantry Center, Fort Benning, 'Public Affairs Aspects of Calley Court-Martial', *c*. April 1971, folder: My Lai 8/31, Papers of *Four Hours in My Lai*, LHCMA, KCL.

[137] Belknap, pp. 114–15.

a writer on the *Village Voice*, who had learnt – he said – that the army was conducting a secret court martial at Fort Benning of a lieutenant charged with killing seventy-five Vietnamese civilians.[138] The process of military-media Chinese whispers had probably converted the Article 32 hearing into an actual trial. Hersh obtained some 'sketchy details' about the case from a friend on Capitol Hill, and then (on the afternoon of 23 October) he phoned the information office at Fort Benning to ask about a 'classified trial' being held there. He was told that no such trial was taking place, but when it became clear that his lead related to the Calley investigation, the information officer read him the report that had appeared in the *New York Times* in early September. Hersh spoke again to his friend in Congress, and sought to mine his contacts at the Pentagon for further details – largely without success, because most refused to talk.

The next morning, Hersh called the information office at Fort Benning again to ask for Calley's home address and the name of his defence attorney, George Latimer of Salt Lake City. A few days later, Hersh flew down to Salt Lake City to interview Latimer, who was willing to discuss the case. Subsequently, Hersh also travelled to Fort Benning where he spent an evening with Calley himself. Each time he spoke to the information office at the base, meanwhile, the contact was reported to OCINFO in Washington.[139]

Although gossip about the investigation into My Lai had probably reached the ears of journalists other than just Cowan and Hersh, the latter was almost alone in deciding to pursue the story. His independent status provides much of the explanation. Hersh was not subject to the institutional routines and daily deadlines which informed the preference of his accredited peers for conventional, clearly-defined stories prompted by the activities of officialdom, and led them to ignore enigmatic leads which would necessitate days and weeks of research and might still turn out to be no more than another wild Washington rumour.[140] Nor had he so strongly internalized the corporate concern with 'taste' which had deterred many salaried newsmen from pursuing atrocity stories in the past. Hersh had also never served as a reporter in Vietnam, and was firmly opposed to the American presence there. As a result, he suffered little from the jaundiced ethics and divided loyalties which kept more experienced war correspondents passive and discreet before the manifold cruelties that they witnessed. At the same time, however, Hersh represented the more reputable end of radical investigative journalism. Cowan had apparently passed on the

[138] D. Obst, *Too Good To Be Forgotten: Changing America in the '60s and '70s* (New York: John Wiley & Sons, 1998), p. 160; S. Hersh, 'How I broke the Mylai story', *Saturday Review* (11 July 1970), p. 46.

[139] Tucker, 'Calley Case', 27 October 1969, folder: My Lai 8/31, Papers of *Four Hours in My Lai*, LHCMA, KCL; Hersh, 'How I broke the Mylai story', pp. 46–9.

[140] Hersh noted later: 'catastrophe via telephone tip is a cheap commodity in Washington, DC', Hersh, 'How I broke the Mylai story', p. 46.

information about the case because he did not want the story buried in a local counter-cultural news outlet like the *Village Voice*. Hersh had worked for a number of years as the Pentagon correspondent for *Associated Press*; he had served as Eugene McCarthy's press secretary during the presidential primary campaigns of 1968; and his writing style conformed to the 'objective' register favoured by the mainstream media.[141] As a result, he had a better chance than Cowan of getting the story the public attention that it deserved.

Despite Hersh's professional credentials, the major national journals were still reluctant to publish his story, for reasons that were not fully articulated. As his research progressed, Hersh contacted *Life* magazine, only to be informed that publication was, 'Out of the question'. After some initial editorial interest, *Look* also turned the story down.[142] Doubts about the news value of American atrocities in what was already widely acknowledged to be an ugly war probably played a part in these responses: for some editors, that Hersh was the first reporter to investigate the allegations against Calley may have indicated not so much the story's status as an important exclusive as the likelihood that nobody else had found it interesting.[143] In these circumstances, publishing Hersh's article would invite the charge that their journal had a singular morbid obsession with the seamier side of national life. The prospect that the story would not be validated by the interest of their peers, however, may have concerned other editors less than the intensity of the reaction that it might provoke. In their hegemonic role as gate-keepers of the national consensus, the news magazines were perhaps even more uncomfortable than usual during these troubled times with stories that dwelt upon the pathologies evident in American society, and particularly with stories that emphasized the corruptions of purpose afflicting its leading institutions, such as the US military. Either way, this was hazardous news territory, and individual journals were reluctant to travel there alone.

Unable to steer his story past the editorial conservatism of the popular news magazines, Hersh placed it instead with the *New York Review of Books*, a liberal intellectual journal with a reputation for publishing articles strongly critical of the Vietnam war. Following an argument with the review's editor, however, the piece was left again without a home.[144] Hersh then turned to a small news agency, the *Dispatch News Service*, which was located at the interstices of the mainstream press and the alternative media of the New Left. It had been founded the previous year by David

[141] *Ibid.*, p. 49; Obst, p. 160.

[142] Hersh, 'How I broke the Mylai story', p. 47.

[143] David Obst – who eventually distributed Hersh's report through his *Dispatch News Service* – recalls his response when first told of the charges against Calley: 'I said big deal, it happens all the time, our guys can't tell the difference between the Vietcong and noncombatants' (Obst, p. 160).

[144] *Ibid.*, pp. 160–1.

Obst, a former student at the University of California, to provide a means of distributing stories about the war of the kind that had hitherto tended not to appear in American newspapers – stories of corruption, ineptitude and casual slaughter. The principal market for these accounts – mimeographed and sent out by mail – was college and radical counter-cultural publications, though on occasion customers did include mainstream journals.[145] Hersh's article on the investigation into My Lai, however, was written with the readers of established daily newspapers in mind. Improvising his sales technique on the spot, therefore, Obst began cold-calling news desks around the country, intimating – initially, not entirely candidly – that other papers had agreed to run the story. It was not the most conventional marketing method, but it promised the news service a reasonable financial return whilst – rather crucially – offering to editors the professional comfort of knowing that they would probably not be alone in ascribing news value to the atrocity. Around fifty newspapers asked Obst for a telexed copy of the article.[146]

When editors received the report, the dispassionate manner in which it was written may have further eased their concerns about its likely reception. In addition, the telex provided details of Hersh's credentials as a correspondent, noting his time with *Associated Press* and listing the major newspapers in which his previous work had been published, including the *New York Times* and the *Washington Post*.[147] Hersh had also taken the precaution – contrary to normal journalistic practice – of reading his story to George Latimer, Calley's defence counsel, before it was distributed. He realized that editors would wish to check the story prior to publication and, given the continuing silence of the Pentagon, Latimer was the only source who could vouch for its accuracy.[148]

On 13 November, Hersh's story appeared in thirty-five newspapers around the country.[149] That same day, the *New York Times* published a less detailed story on the Calley case by a staff reporter, which was distributed nationally by its own news service and reprinted in a number of other regional papers.[150] A correspondent for the *Washington Post* summarized the content of Hersh's article under his own byline.[151] Other papers carried a brief *Associated Press* dispatch on the case.[152] The previous day,

[145] *Ibid.*, pp. 124–5.
[146] *Ibid.*, pp. 164–6.
[147] *Dispatch News Service* telex, 12 November 1969, folder: 'Case Folder: 1LT – William L. Calley, Jr [Part 2 of 2]', Box 6, Records Pertaining to the My Lai Massacre, 1969–74, Records of the Vietnam War Crimes Working Group, Office of the Deputy Chief of Staff for Personnel, RAS, RG319, NACP.
[148] Hersh, 'How I broke the Mylai story', p. 49.
[149] See, for example, the *Boston Globe* (13 November 1969), p. 2; Bilton and Sim, pp. 253–4.
[150] *New York Times* (13 November 1969), pp. 1, 7. The *Cleveland Plain Dealer* was one of the other journals to carry the *NYT* report: *Cleveland Plain Dealer* (13 November 1969), pp. 1–A, 6–A.
[151] *Washington Post* (13 November 1969), p. 1.
[152] See, for example, the *Albuquerque Journal* (13 November 1969), p. 2.

a report about the investigation had appeared in the *Alabama Journal*, whilst the CBS network broadcast a short item on the affair during its evening bulletin.[153] Twenty months after it occurred, the My Lai massacre had finally become news.

That the massacre would evolve into one of the most momentous media stories of the Vietnam era, however, was far from immediately apparent, despite the publication of Hersh's report. In mid-November 1969, there were three stories with more urgent claims upon the front pages of the national press: American astronauts were preparing to land on the moon for the second time; in Washington, three hundred thousand people converged on the Mall for an anti-war rally and then besieged the Justice Department, prompting mass arrests by the local police; and Vice-President Spiro Agnew, speaking in Des Moines, Iowa, delivered a bilious attack upon what he considered to be the 'effete' liberal bias of news commentators. All these stories had a relevance to ongoing debates about the national character and purpose, all engaged with the question: Who speaks for America – the brave pioneers of space exploration, the peace-makers or the President, media elites or the 'silent majority'? In a public discourse dominated by such powerful symbols, a lowly army lieutenant in Georgia seemed to merit only passing attention.

In addition, the information about the massacre available to newspaper readers across the nation in mid-November 1969 varied from region to region, and from city to city. Some editors had decided not to publish Hersh's article, either relying on the less thorough accounts provided by other news services or else electing not to report the story at all. Those newspapers that did carry the article, were unlikely to have printed it in full.[154] Even where the most complete versions of the report appeared, the response of readers was hardly predetermined. Hersh certainly described some of the more compelling aspects of the case. He noted that, across the six specifications of murder, Calley was alleged to have killed a total of 109 civilians. 'In terms of numbers slain', Hersh asserted, '"Pinkville" is by far the worst known US atrocity case of the Vietnam war'.[155]

---

[153] Bilton and Sim, p. 254; *CBS Evening News*, 12 November 1969, VTNA. The newsman responsible for the *Journal*'s piece, Wayne Greenhaw, was – like Hersh – later to write his own book-length account of the My Lai massacre and its aftermath: see Greenhaw, *The Making of a Hero: A Behind-the-Scenes View of the Lt William Calley Affair* (Louisville: Touchstone, 1971).

[154] The *Boston Globe* excised about 600 words from the original, including statements supportive of Calley from fellow officers at Fort Benning, a brief comment from the lieutenant himself and details of his service record, *Boston Globe* (13 November 1969), p. 2.

[155] 'Pinkville' was the informal name by which American soldiers referred to the sub-hamlet of My Lai (1). Some commanders believed that the headquarters of the Vietcong's 48th Battalion were located in My Lai (1), and it was coloured pink on US military maps. Other commanders identified the sub-hamlet of My Lai (4), west of My Lai (1), as the battalion headquarters, and that was actually where most of the killing occurred during the operation of 16 March 1968. Hammer, *One Morning in the War*, p. 6; Goldstein *et al.*, p. 90.

He recorded the belief of 'many military officers and some well-informed congressmen' that the affair would become 'far more controversial' than that of the Special Forces. In one of the most expressive sections of the report, Hersh quoted an officer at the Pentagon who, tapping his knee, said of Calley: 'Some of those kids he shot were this high. I don't think they were Viet Cong. Do you?' The article, however, contained statements from other officers who maintained that what had occurred in the village was nothing out of the ordinary. 'It could happen to any of us', said one. 'He's killed and seen a lot of killing . . . Killing becomes nothing in Vietnam. He knew that there were civilians there, but he also knew that there were VC among them'.[156] The same judicious and objective tone, moreover, which had facilitated the dissemination of the article also possibly served to mute its impact upon those who read it. To the attentive reader, the extraordinary nature of the charges against Calley was probably evident, but to many others – dependent upon the normal significations of a story's importance, such as the front-page splash and urgent official comment – Hersh's account of the case may have appeared to be just one more contribution to the daily flow of regrettable news from the war.

For the next week, indeed, the national media seemed unable to resolve its doubts about the news status of the massacre. The official sources upon whom correspondents usually relied for confirmation of a story's significance largely remained silent. On 6 November, the Article 32 investigation into the charges against Calley produced a recommendation for court martial, whilst inquiries into the conduct of other members of Charlie Company continued.[157] Given the increasing likelihood of a judicial resolution, military spokesmen remained anxious not to say anything about the case that might be deemed prejudical either to the prosecution or the rights of the accused. They refused to confirm, for example, the accuracy of Hersh's assertion that Calley had been charged with the murder of a total of 109 civilians. On 14 November, reporters were given brief details of an Article 32 investigation into Staff Sergeant David Mitchell, who had served in Calley's platoon.[158] The following day, the information office at Fort Benning – in liaison with Calley's defence counsel – gave the news media an opportunity to take pictures of the lieutenant.[159] This was consistent with the continuing desire of OCINFO to keep the locus of press enquiries at the base and away from the Pentagon; it repeated its instruction

[156] *Dispatch News Service* telex, 12 November 1969, folder: 'Case Folder: 1LT – William L. Calley, Jr [Part 2 of 2]', Box 6, Records Pertaining to the My Lai Massacre, 1969–74, Records of the Vietnam War Crimes Working Group, Office of the Deputy Chief of Staff for Personnel, RAS, RG319, NACP.

[157] *United States* v. *Calley*, 46 CMR 1131 (ACMR 1973), in Goldstein *et al.*, p. 480.

[158] Sidle to Woolnough *et al.*, 'Public Affairs Guidance – My Lai Case', 14 November 1969, folder: 'Master File [Copy 2]', Box 16, RCCPI, RPI, RAS, RG319, NACP.

[159] Office of the Information Officer, Headquarters US Army Infantry Center, Fort Benning, 'Public Affairs Aspects of Calley Court-Martial', *c*. April 1971, folder: My Lai 8/31, Papers of *Four Hours in My Lai*, LHCMA, KCL.

to local information officers that the ongoing coordination with Washington was not to be mentioned to reporters.[160]

Although a number of papers assigned correspondents to pursue the story, their coverage in general indicated its secondary rank on the news agendas of the moment. In the six days following its initial article on 13 November, the *New York Times* published only one further front page report on the massacre, with no report appearing in the newspaper at all on 18 November.[161] The case also provoked no editorial comment at this time. On 13 and 14 November, none of the three network evening news programmes carried items on the story. By the beginning of the next week, they had located Ronald Ridenhour in California and interviewed him about the massacre and the letter he had sent calling for an investigation.[162] Their correspondents in Vietnam, meanwhile, found their way to refugee camps close to My Lai (4) where they spoke to survivors.[163] None of these reports, however, led the evening broadcasts, and on 19 November, with a moon walk in progress, the massacre was once again entirely ignored. When the networks did discuss the story, their tone remained cautious. ABC's Jack Davenport noted that Ridenhour wanted the United States to withdraw from Vietnam and that he had not personally witnessed the killings.[164] All three networks reported the assertion of Colonel Khien, the South Vietnamese province chief, that any civilian casualties had been accidental.[165] NBC anchor David Brinkley informed his viewers: 'The full truth is not yet obtainable'.[166]

What appeared on the television screen and on the front page may have been tentative and slight; in the newsrooms and out in the field, however, the story was gathering mass and momentum and beginning to slip beyond the military's control. The appetite of the press for information was such that it swiftly chewed up the six-month lead that army detectives had established in their investigation of the case. Only a day or so after Andre Feher had travelled to Son My for the first time to inspect the massacre site and interview survivors, news reporters arrived in the area seeking to do the same.[167] Back in Ohio, Ronald Haeberle read accounts of the killings and the charges against Calley and, on 17 November, decided to take his

[160] Sidle to Woolnough *et al.*, 'Public Affairs Guidance – My Lai Case', 14 November 1969, folder: 'Master File [Copy 2]', Box 16, RCCPI, RPI, RAS, RG319, NACP.

[161] *New York Times* (17 November 1969), pp. 1–3.

[162] *ABC News*, 17 November 1969, Vanderbilt Television News Archive (VTNA); *CBS Evening News*, 17 November 1969, VTNA; *NBC Nightly News*, 17 November 1969, VTNA.

[163] *ABC News*, 18 November 1969, VTNA; *CBS Evening News*, 18 November 1969, VTNA; *NBC Nightly News*, 18 November 1969, VTNA.

[164] *ABC News*, 17 November 1969, VTNA.

[165] *ABC News*, 17 November 1969, VTNA; *CBS Evening News*, 17 November 1969, VTNA; *NBC Nightly News*, 18 November 1969, VTNA.

[166] *NBC Nightly News*, 18 November 1969, VTNA.

[167] Gustafson to Westmoreland, 'My Lai Investigation', 20 November 1969, folder: 'Master File [Copy 1]', Box 15, RCCPI, RPI, RAS, RG319, NACP; Feher, 'Witness Statement', 16 November 1969, folder: My Lai 8/35, Papers of *Four Hours in My Lai*, LHCMA, KCL.

pictures of the operation, including images of the dead and the just-about-to-die, to his local newspaper, the *Cleveland Plain Dealer*. Joe Eszterhas, a reporter on the paper, contacted the Public Information Department at OCINFO to confirm Haeberle's service record and his presence in My Lai (4) during the massacre. When the department stalled, asserting that confirmation would take a number of weeks, Eszterhas phoned Aubrey Daniel, a judge advocate at Fort Benning assigned to the Calley case, and told him that the *Dealer* was planning to publish Haeberle's photographs. Daniel's dismayed reaction was enough to verify the evidentiary status of the pictures.

The moonwalk coverage scheduled to lead the paper's 20 November edition was quickly shunted aside: 'Fuck the moonwalk,' said the night managing editor when he viewed the massacre images. 'It's just a routine moonwalk'.[168] On the afternoon of 19 November, before the pictures even appeared in the *Dealer*, Eszterhas travelled to New York to offer the colour reproduction rights to *Life* magazine.[169] As the investigative activities and interests of the press began to reach beyond Fort Benning and the charges against William Calley to explore the actions of other members of Charlie Company in My Lai (4), OCINFO was obliged to abandon the fiction of localized news management and to assume explicit responsibility for coordinating relations with the media on the subject of the massacre. By 18 November, noting 'continued pressure for all details of [the] case', OCINFO was preparing to release upon request the service records of four more soldiers: Ernest Medina, Paul Meadlo, Ronald Ridenhour – and Ronald Haeberle.[170]

On 20 November, the dam finally broke, as narratives of the massacre and images of its victims flooded the national media. That day, the *Dispatch News Service* circulated a second report by Seymour Hersh, providing an account of interviews with three GIs who had been present at the time of the killings. One of the soldiers, Michael Bernhardt, commented: 'The whole thing was so deliberate. It was point-blank murder and I was standing there watching it'.[171] Details of a telephone interview with Bernhardt also appeared on the front page of the *New York Times*, whilst his testimony at a press conference was broadcast on both the CBS and NBC network news programmes. Asked by a reporter whether the inhabitants of My Lai (4) were Vietcong, Bernhardt was shown responding: 'Some of the people in the village weren't old enough to walk yet. I don't see how they could be Vietcong'.[172] As if to confirm Bernhardt's

[168] Eszterhas, p. 457.
[169] *Ibid.*, p. 462.
[170] Sidle to Woolnough *et al.*, 'Public Affairs Guidance – My Lai Case', 18 November 1969, folder: 'Master File [Copy 2]', Box 16, RCCPI, RPI, RAS, RG319, NACP.
[171] *Cleveland Plain Dealer* (20 November 1969), p. 5–B.
[172] *New York Times* (20 November 1969), pp. 1, 14; *CBS Evening News*, 20 November 1969, VTNA; *NBC Nightly News*, 20 November 1969, VTNA.

assertion, the *Cleveland Plain Dealer* published Haeberle's photographs of the massacre; posted on the front page was an image of twenty dead villagers lying in a road, young children clearly visible among them.[173] That night, the same image – the camera closing in on the body of a baby – appeared on national television, as *CBS Evening News* exhibited the photographs, one after another, in complete silence.[174] The pictures were also reprinted by a number of other newspapers in the following days, whilst *Life* paid $20,000 for the right to reproduce them in colour.[175]

What had left CBS at a loss for words finally required the Pentagon to speak. As US senators and representatives began to call for a congressional inquiry, and correspondents reported expressions of horror from abroad, the army sent out its General Counsel, Robert Jordan, to talk to the press. Jordan himself was not particularly forthcoming. He refused to confirm details of the allegations against Calley and Mitchell because to do so, he declared, might prejudice their legal rights. He could provide at best some limited information about the scope of the ongoing criminal investigation.[176] What Jordan said, however, was probably less important than the fact that he spoke at all. For Bill Downs of *ABC News*, his statement amounted to the first public expression of concern by a 'high defense official' that American troops in Vietnam 'might have committed genocide'.[177] Official comment, guarded though it remained, had at last validated press interest in the story. On 22 November, the *New York Times* published its first editorial on the subject, asserting that reports of the atrocity were 'so shocking, so contrary to principles for which this country has always stood, as to be beyond belief. Yet the evidence mounts daily that something horrible did take place'. The paper called for 'a thorough, public investigation of this sordid affair'.[178] Two days later, the commanding general at Fort Benning, Major General Orwin Talbott, made a formal determination that Calley should face a court martial; upon that decision, the specifications of the charges against the lieutenant were released to the press, finally providing official confirmation that he was alleged to have killed a total of 109 Vietnamese civilians.[179] That same day, *CBS Evening News* broadcast an extended interview with Paul Meadlo, another member of Charlie Company, in which Meadlo – slow, passive, defeated – admitted killing 'just too many' civilians in My Lai (4), women

---

[173] *Cleveland Plain Dealer* (20 November 1969), pp. 1, 4–B, 5–B.

[174] *CBS Evening News*, 20 November 1969, VTNA.

[175] The other newspapers which printed Haeberle's photographs included the *New York Post* (21 November 1969), pp. 1, 4 and the *New York Times* (22 November 1969), p. 3. *Life* published the colour images in its 5 December issue, available at news-stands from 1 December.

[176] *New York Times* (21 November 1969), pp. 1, 18; *New York Times* (22 November 1969), pp. 2–3, 36; Bilton and Sim, pp. 256–8.

[177] *ABC News*, 21 November 1969, VTNA.

[178] *New York Times* (22 November 1969), p. 36.

[179] *United States* v. *Calley*, 46 CMR 1131 (ACMR 1973), in Goldstein *et al.*, p. 480; *New York Times* (25 November 1969), p. 1.

and children amongst them. 'And babies?' asked the interviewer, Mike Wallace. 'And babies', Meadlo replied.[180]

By this time, reports on the massacre had become an established feature of network television news shows and the front pages of America's mainstream news journals. On 26 November, ABC, CBS and NBC all led their evening news broadcasts with items on My Lai.[181] There seemed to be enough in the story to sustain press interest for a number of months. The media now awaited Calley's court martial, whilst inquiries into the conduct of other members of Charlie Company – and the broader CID investigation of the massacre – continued. On 24 November, the army directed Lieutenant General William Peers to lead an investigation into the response of brigade and division commands to the atrocity allegations that had emerged in the immediate aftermath of the Son My operation.[182] The House Armed Services Committee also announced that it would examine the affair.[183]

What occurred during the course of November 1969 was what the US military had feared for eight months, ever since Ronald Ridenhour's account of the killings at My Lai (4) had arrived at the Pentagon: the loosening of its control not just over the distribution of knowledge about the atrocity, but also over the process of investigation and prosecution, and over the future of its own public reputation and the reputation of the war it was fighting in Vietnam. Soon after CBS had aired its interview with Paul Meadlo, the military judge in the Calley case, Colonel Reid Kennedy, received a joint motion from the defence and prosecution counsel asking him to prohibit all further pre-trial publication and broadcast of witness statements and images relating to the massacre. Kennedy acknowledged the danger that the media's coverage could compromise the army's capacity to find an impartial jury and to conduct a fair trial, but believed that an order granting the motion might well contravene the First Amendment.[184] The massacre was now out of the box, and there was nothing much that anyone could do to get it back inside. Indeed, the sheer scale of national and international press interest in the My Lai story – and, perhaps, also the perception that reporters were now accumulating information about the case at a pace which rivalled that of CID's own detectives – prompted the army to establish a special task force, with markedly enhanced resources, to

---

[180] *CBS Evening News*, 24 November 1969, VTNA. A transcript of the interview was printed in the *New York Times* (25 November 1969), p. 16. The interview had been arranged by the *Dispatch News Service*. Hersh had tracked down Meadlo, and Obst subsequently offered his testimony to CBS in return for $10,000. Hersh said later: 'I do not claim this as the greatest day in my professional life' (Obst, pp. 169–70); Belknap, pp. 120–1.

[181] *ABC News*, 26 November 1969, VTNA; *CBS Evening News*, 26 November 1969, VTNA; *NBC Nightly News*, 26 November 1969, VTNA.

[182] *New York Times* (25 November 1969), p. 16; Resor and Westmoreland to Peers, 'Directive for Investigation', 26 November 1969, in Goldstein *et al.*, p. 33.

[183] *New York Times* (25 November 1969), p. 16. See also M. Carson, 'F. Edward Hébert and the congressional investigation of the My Lai massacre', *Louisiana History*, 37 (1996), 61–79.

[184] *New York Times* (2 December 1969), pp. 1, 12; Belknap, pp. 149–51.

allow the investigation to proceed more expeditiously.[185] In the White House, Bob Haldeman – Nixon's chief of staff – noted in his diary entry of 25 November that the President was 'now realizing [the] harm' that the massacre could cause in terms of public support for the Vietnam war.[186] A week later, he recorded that Nixon had asked him 'to set up a My Lai planning group to figure how best to control the whole problem – which is, as of now, pretty well out of hand'.[187]

The story of My Lai had finally entered the field of public knowledge because the intricate relations of power that had functioned, very often unconsciously and as a matter of unreflective routine, to hold it outside had been displaced, at least temporarily. Within the American military, as within the broader public sphere, there was in the post-Tet period a greater readiness to accept that events like My Lai could occur, that even the most controlled and conventional operational environments contained the potential for aberration and chaos. Moreover, as the aims of national policy in Vietnam changed, the armed forces were unable to trust their public image to the eventual achievement of victory; in the absence of such victory, military leaders were more likely to be called to account for the conduct of their organization and required to demonstrate in particular that criminality was not tolerated within its ranks. Of course, the likelihood that news of the massacre would seep out into wider circulation through the chatter of GIs and Haeberle's illustrated lectures was probably not entirely irrelevant to the decision to press charges against William Calley. The institutional instinct towards self-preservation and secrecy also remained, manifested in the decision to release details of the Calley charges at Fort Benning and not in Washington, and in the reluctance of army spokesmen to comment on the case following the publication of Hersh's first article. Nevertheless, that the investigation into the massacre was proceeding indicates the extent to which the military was now conscious of the need to address, and to be seen to address, its own moral lapses and limitations.

The fact that the authorities in the Pentagon were prepared to subject the conduct of American soldiers at My Lai (4) to a criminal investigation

[185] Asserting the need for a 'substantial task force', Colonel Henry Tufts of CID noted: 'The Army position is questioned by three US Senators, all the news media, the public in general, and foreign governments. This matter assumes an immediate criticality'. Tufts, 'Exploitation of My Lai', 28 November 1969, folder: 'Master File [copy 2]', Box 16, RCCPI, RPI, RAS, RG319, NACP. See also 'The CID Investigation of the Son My Incidents', 31 December 1970, folder: My Lai 8/36, Papers of *Four Hours in My Lai*, LHCMA, KCL.

[186] Haldeman diary entry, 25 November 1969, folder: 'H.R. Haldeman Journal Volume III, September 23, 1969 – January 12, 1970', Box 1, Handwritten Journals and Diaries of Harry Robbins Haldeman, Box 32, Staff Members and Office Files: Haldeman, White House Special Files, NPM, NACP.

[187] Haldeman diary entry, 1 December 1969, folder: 'H.R. Haldeman Journal Volume III, September 23, 1969 – January 12, 1970', Box 1, Handwritten Journals and Diaries of Harry Robbins Haldeman, Box 32, Staff Members and Office Files: Haldeman, White House Special Files, NPM, NACP.

did not in itself guarantee that the fate of the settlement would come to be exposed in the national press. The failure of reporters accredited to mainstream journals to investigate the charges against Calley following the initial, furtive September news release, and to respond as Hersh did to subsequent rumours about the massacre, together with the reluctance of the same journals to commit to publication when approached by, first, Ridenhour and then Hersh, indicates the degree to which the media remained hesitant about stories of American atrocities in the absence of an unambiguous official lead.

Nevertheless, the specific dynamics of the My Lai case, combined with broader changes occurring in the national media culture by the autumn of 1969, ensured that this particular atrocity story was eventually able to attain the status of news. First of all, the very fact that the inquiry was taking place more than a year after the event, when many of those involved had rotated out of the war-zone and in some cases out of military service altogether, meant that the principal locus of reporting on the affair was the United States, not Vietnam. That is, the personal loyalties and logistical dependencies that had sometimes encouraged correspondents in the field to overlook or euphemize atrocities committed by American troops, and the corrosive effects of prolonged combat experience upon their moral response to the killing of civilians, informed the way in which the massacre was reported in the mainstream media much less than they might have done if the news had broken several months before. Key components of the story did not have to process through the peer group metabolism of war reporters in Vietnam before arriving in the public sphere. Moreover, as a number of those who had been present in My Lai (4) had now returned to civilian life within the United States, there existed a plenitude of sources outside the reach of military discipline and unit-level retribution to verify the story and, through the compelling details of their testimony, to magnetize the attention of the public, even as official channels maintained their silence.

It was not enough, however, that witnesses to the massacre were accessible to reporters subject neither to jaundiced ethics or fraternal affinities for those fighting the war. The conservative practices and attitudes of the established press – if left to themselves – might still have continued to circumscribe media responses to the case of William Calley as it passed through the court-martial system, discouraging the pursuit of the story through all available sources and ultimately restricting its capacity to arouse national concern. The news of My Lai reached the American public in the autumn of 1969 precisely because the established press was not left to itself, but exposed to journalistic influences and initiatives from beyond its own rarefied professional culture. Largely separate and mutually suspicious in the 1950s, the radical and mainstream presses experienced a tentative and uneven rapprochement towards the end of the next decade, allowing a small cohort of individuals and institutions to operate at their interstices and combine politically engaged reportage with professional respectability.[188] The rumours of atrocity, for example, found their way to Seymour Hersh because his credentials as a reporter were sufficiently orthodox to offer them the possibility of mainstream publication. He was, however, also sufficiently independent and enterprising not to be deterred when formal government information channels kept quiet. Hersh's political allegiances, meanwhile, encouraged him to pursue the case, where accredited reporters might have been inhibited by corporate distaste for atrocity stories, yet he had also been socialized into a style of writing that made his reports compatible with the 'objective' idiom of conventional news outlets. Moreover, he was assisted by the recent establishment of a news agency radical enough to be untroubled by the content of his article, but sufficiently commercial to disseminate it widely, thus overcoming the reluctance of individual editors to publish the story alone.

Finally, the elevation of the massacre to the status of front-page news occurred because, as witness and participant accounts began to confirm the scale of the killings in My Lai (4), members of the media became more confident that this was no ordinary atrocity, if such a thing existed. The continuing accretion of detailed evidence, attesting both to the absence of enemy forces in the settlement at the time of the operation and the specific outrages committed by Charlie Company, addressed the concern of editors that – in prioritizing such a story – they might be basing their news judgement on standards of behaviour which were unrealistic in war. The emerging testimony also provided armour against the otherwise predictable charge that the reporting of this atrocity once again demonstrated the unwarranted obsession of the press with the most regrettable aspects of the military effort in Vietnam. My Lai seemed to transcend all that. Similarly, the discourse of 'taste' which had previously limited pictorial representations of civilian casualties sounded morally anorexic when confronted with images of a whole community being put to the sword; thus, where visual evidence of other atrocities had often in the past been left in the editorial drawer, Ronald Haeberle's graphic photographs of dead women and children were splashed across the front page. By the end of November, the massacre had become one of the rare stories to which the day-to-day professional compromises of mainstream journalism appeared no longer to apply, engaging instead with some of the highest aspirations of the news trade: enterprising investigative reportage, unflinching pictorial coverage and thoughtful, critical editorial analysis.

[188] For discussions of the radical press in the 1960s, see Armstrong, *A Trumpet to Arms* and J. Aronson, *Deadline for the Media: Today's Challenges to Press, TV and Radio* (New York: Bobbs-Merrill Co., 1972).

2

Containing culpability

At the end of November 1969, a fortnight after the initial media revelations concerning My Lai (4), reporters from the *Wall Street Journal* interviewed more than 200 people in a dozen cities around the United States and discovered 'a great number' unwilling to credit the allegation that American soldiers had perpetrated a massacre in the settlement. 'I don't believe it actually happened,' said one Los Angeles salesman. 'The story was planted by Vietcong sympathizers and people inside the country who are trying to get us out of Vietnam sooner.'[1] In December, researchers from the Wright Institute in California conducted a survey of Oakland residents and also encountered significant resistance to the idea that American troops had been to blame. One of those interviewed asserted: 'Our boys wouldn't do this. Something else is behind it.'[2] In Columbus, Georgia – close to Fort Benning where William Calley was being held – the mother of a soldier who had been killed in Vietnam told a reporter for *CBS Evening News*: 'Our men are calm soldiers. Our men are brave soldiers – that's the way they're trained. We don't have bad soldiers.'[3] Around the same time, 43 per cent of Minnesota residents polled recalled that their first reaction to the massacre stories had been to consider them untrue.[4]

The origins of such responses may lie, as one Wright Institute psychologist suggested, in the self-centred refusal of individuals to assume moral responsibility for actions undertaken in their collective name, and in a concomitant reluctance to commit themselves to a campaign for a political accounting. Simple ignorance, however, may also have played an important role.[5] In view of what, hitherto, had and had not been reported in the American press about the ethical content and human consequences of the

[1] *Wall Street Journal* (1 December 1969), p. 1.

[2] E. Opton, 'It never happened and besides they deserved it', in N. Sanford *et al.*, *Sanctions for Evil* (San Francisco: Jossey-Bass, Inc., 1971), p. 62.

[3] *CBS Evening News*, 16 December 1969, VTNA.

[4] *Minneapolis Tribune* (21 December 1969), p. 4B.

[5] Opton, in Sanford *et al.*, p. 61.

nation's war-fighting methods in Vietnam, it was perhaps not surprising that when the grim details of the atrocities in My Lai (4) were finally revealed, many in the United States initially experienced a kind of cognitive dissonance and sought refuge in denial. During the previous five years of conflict, editors and correspondents had consistently withheld from their readers and viewers the sort of information that would have made the news of the massacre appear a little less implausible when it eventually broke. Press coverage of the story thereafter was in most respects serious and responsible, but much of the damage had already been done. The radical disjunctures between the attitudes held by media professionals and the perspectives of large sections of their audience which occasionally became evident during the news life of the massacre were products in part of the divergent knowledges of the Vietnam conflict possessed by these parties at the moment that the first accounts of the killings appeared.

Although many remained sceptical, for others the incredible was rapidly becoming credible. By the end of November, the sombre tones of television anchormen, the monochrome images carried in the newspapers, the confessions contained in their reports and the solemn columns of editorial comment, were all giving discursive weight to the bloody deeds that had taken place in Son My twenty months earlier. Within the less obstinate sectors of the public consciousness, a set of recognizable symbols – maps of central Vietnam (sometimes shown splashed with blood), aerial views of My Lai (4), bodies on a road, Calley in his uniform, the words of Paul Meadlo – was cohering to represent the materiality of the event and, thus reified, the search for its causes could begin.

At that moment, it appeared possible that the country would embark upon a fearless accounting of what had happened in the village, and certainly, over the course of the next year and a half, what seemed to many Americans to be a painful and comprehensive national debate did take place. A vast array of different cultural actors – politicians from left and right, radical and traditional veterans' groups, intellectuals and ordinary Americans – joined with the military and the news media to discuss the causes of the massacre and where responsibility lay. Consensus, however, remained elusive. The deliberations and judgments of the military courts were too provincial, too contradictory and too easily attributed to institutional self-interest to have a decisive effect upon public perception. The hegemonic coalition between the state and the mainstream media, meanwhile, was struggling to contain its own internal disputes and had forfeited much of the power that it once possessed to channel and discipline popular responses to the events of the war. At a time, moreover, when relationships between the individual and the collective were being busily contested and renegotiated across the national culture, unsettling traditional assumptions about the viability of moral autonomy and the locus of moral authority, it was unlikely that any single explanation of the constellation of responsibility for the massacre would attract unanimous public approval.[6]

On the critical issues of causation and culpability, three distinct interpretations emerged. For many of those contributing to the debate, the origins of the massacre lay in the broader culture of American warmaking in Vietnam. If the soldiers of Charlie Company had slaughtered civilians at will, it was only because they had considered their conduct consistent with the attitudes and practices of their GI peers, with the policies of the military command, and with the conscience of the political nation at home. Others drew the circle of responsibility more broadly still, as broadly, perhaps, as it could be drawn: atrocity, like war, was an eternal recurrence in human affairs, an expression of the unchanging primal essence of man. Some Americans, however, judged such ruminations nebulous, and argued robustly that the only meaningful explanation for the killings lay in the specific criminality of Charlie Company, with the actions of Ernest Medina, William Calley and the men they led into My Lai (4) that day. A range of professional practices and institutional investments, together with the dynamics of the story when it first became news, served to establish and sustain this particular interpretation.

The proposition that the events at My Lai (4) were explicable in terms of the depravity of a small group of soldiers was implicit in the content of the story as it broke upon the public consciousness during the course of that November. The massacre, after all, had been drawn to the attention of the media, and then the nation, as a result of legal proceedings which sought to establish the culpability of individuals. The charges against Calley had been the principal concern of Seymour Hersh's first article. On 24 November, the army announced that the lieutenant would be court-martialled.[7] Meanwhile, inquiries continued into the conduct of other members of Charlie Company, Medina included, as did the Article 32 investigation which followed the preferral of charges against David Mitchell. The military justice system thus ensured that the personal guilt of the soldiers actually present at the time of the killings would remain a significant theme of both press coverage of the story and the debate about responsibility in the wider public sphere, at least until the verdict against Calley was reached in March 1971.

That the legal process emphasized the agency of a small number of individuals no doubt reinforced the inclination of the media to adopt what was in any case a common news practice when engaging with events as complex and enigmatic as those which had occurred at My Lai (4): to gain narrative and analytical traction by reducing the frame of reportage,

---

[6] A small group of moral philosophers commissioned to consider the allocation of responsibility for the massacre diverged widely in both their theoretical assumptions and in their eventual conclusions. See P. French (ed.), *Individual and Collective Responsibility* (Rochester, VT: Schenkman Books, 1998). This volume was first published in 1972.

[7] *New York Times* (25 November 1969), p. 1.

focusing upon the fate of one or two actors. This was most evident with regard to William Calley. As the first soldier to be publicly connected with the story, he immediately became the focus of attention from journalists seeking to discover more about the massacre. Before writing his initial article, Seymour Hersh travelled to Fort Benning to speak to Calley himself. They ate dinner together, with Calley confirming for Hersh the number of people he had been accused of killing.[8] The day Hersh's story appeared, Calley had lunch with a reporter from the *New York Times*, which published an account of the meeting on 14 November.[9] Neither conversation yielded much further information about what had happened at My Lai (4), for Calley's military counsel refused to let his client discuss in any detail the charges against him. Nevertheless, the articles which resulted from these meetings represented the first stage in the media's conversion of William Calley into a curious kind of celebrity. Hersh's report began with a description of his subject: 'a mild-mannered, boyish-looking Vietnam combat veteran with the nickname of "Rusty"'.[10] The *New York Times* noted that Calley's blond hair was 'thinning at the temples' and that he ate his food 'without enthusiasm'; it also provided details of his height and weight, together with a brief account of his education and life before joining the army.

By this time, a number of national news outlets had sent reporters to Fort Benning, and were pressing for an opportunity to photograph the lieutenant which, with Calley's consent, the information office at the base duly arranged.[11] On 17 November, *CBS Evening News* broadcast images of Calley in uniform, walking across a road at Fort Benning with one of his military lawyers.[12] Four days later, a drawing of Calley's head appeared on the backdrop of the *NBC Nightly News* anchor desk, as anchorman Chet Huntley introduced an item about the case.[13] On 24 November, ABC reported the decision to court-martial the lieutenant; the backdrop consisted of a photograph of the accused from his shoulders up, next to a large splash of blood.[14] Photographs of Calley were printed by *Newsweek* in its issue of 24 November, by the *New York Times* on 25 November, and by *Time* magazine in its 28 November issue.[15] On 26 November,

[8] Hersh, 'How I broke the Mylai story', p. 49.

[9] *New York Times* (14 November 1969), p. 16.

[10] *Dispatch News Service* telex, 12 November 1969, folder: 'Case folder: 1LT – William L. Calley, Jr [Part 2 of 2]', Box 6, Records Pertaining to the My Lai Massacre, 1969–74, Records of the Vietnam War Crimes Working Group, Office of the Deputy Chief of Staff for Personnel, RAS, RG319, NACP.

[11] Sidle to Woolnough *et al.*, 'Public Affairs Guidance – My Lai Case', 14 November 1969, Box 16, RCCPI, RPI, RAS, RG319, NACP; Office of the Information Officer, Headquarters US Army Infantry Center, Fort Benning, 'Public Affairs Aspects of Calley Court-Martial', *c*. April 1971, folder: My Lai 8/31, Papers of *Four Hours in My Lai*, LHCMA, KCL.

[12] *CBS Evening News*, 17 November 1969, VTNA.

[13] *NBC Nightly News*, 21 November 1969, VTNA.

[14] *ABC News*, 24 November 1969, VTNA.

[15] *Newsweek* (24 November 1969), p. 40; *New York Times* (25 November 1969), p. 16; *Time* (28 November 1969), p. 18.

NBC broadcast interviews with Calley's fifteen-year-old sister Dawn, his best friend Chuck Queen, and the former Dean of Boys at his old high school in Miami.[16] The following week, Calley's face appeared on the front covers of both *Time* and *Newsweek*.[17] Inside, *Time* carried an account of his life, illustrated with a picture taken from his high school yearbook.[18]

Over the course of the next eighteen months until the end of his court martial, images of Calley – alongside Ronald Haeberle's photographs of the dead in My Lai (4) – became the dominant visual content of the story: reports on the case were typically accompanied by pictures of the lieutenant entering or leaving the courthouse at Fort Benning or relaxing in his apartment after the trial had adjourned, or by sketch-artist impressions of his appearance on the witness stand.[19] On the eve of his court martial in November 1970, a 'search for William Calley' was broadcast by *ABC News*, the narrative of his life accompanied by images of his childhood home in Miami, the schools he attended, a railroad train (to indicate his work as a switchman), railroad tracks reaching into the distance (to signify his travels before enlisting in the army), a military parade ground, and, finally, the Fort Benning courthouse where, the reporter declared, the search for William Calley came to an end.[20] *Esquire* magazine distilled material from a long series of interviews with Calley and published it in the form of a three-part pseudo-memoir, entitled his 'confessions'.[21] The cover of the issue which contained the first extract from these 'confessions' featured a portrait of Calley in uniform sitting with four sombre-faced Asian children, one – little more than a baby – resting in the crook of the smiling lieutenant's arm. On the day of the court-martial verdict, Calley's image once again appeared behind the anchor desk of *ABC News*, emblazoned this time with the words 'My Lai' and 'Guilty'.

By 1 April, two days later, 96 per cent of Americans polled were professing that they had either 'heard, seen or read about the conviction of Lt William L. Calley in connection with the My Lai massacre'.[22] Calley and the proceedings against him became the subject of a series of swiftly published books, some of which were thorough, insightful analyses, others no

[16] *NBC Nightly News*, 26 November 1969, VTNA.

[17] *Time* (5 December 1969), p. 1; *Newsweek* (8 December 1969), p. 1.

[18] *Time* (5 December 1969), p. 25.

[19] For an example of all three of these representative tropes, see *Life* (5 March 1971), pp. 22–9.

[20] *ABC News*, 9 November 1970, VTNA.

[21] 'The Confessions of Lieutenant Calley', *Esquire* (November 1970), pp. 113–19, 227–8; 'The Continuing Confessions of Lieutenant Calley', *Esquire* (February 1971), pp. 55–9, 114; 'The Concluding Confessions of Lieutenant Calley', *Esquire* (September 1971), pp. 85–9, 224–8.

[22] Opinion Research Corporation poll, 1 April 1971. Data provided by Roper Center for Public Opinion Research, www.ropercenter.uconn.edu (accessed November 2003).

more than opportunistic sleeve notes to an atrocity.[23] Thus, though he was of little initial use as a source of information, the media's need to convey the story of My Lai in familiar, human terms had ultimately resulted in the transformation of Calley into the massacre's most pervasive living symbol.

To be so closely associated with the crimes committed at My Lai (4) was effectively to be incriminated: that was the assertion not just of Calley's own defence counsel but also of a number of other authorities both before and after the trial, including the American Civil Liberties Union and Judge Robert Elliott of the United States District Court for the Middle District of Georgia. 'It is our conclusion', wrote the executive and legal directors of the ACLU's New York chapter in a letter to the Secretary of Defense in December 1969, 'that it is now impossible for Lt Calley to receive a fair trial.'[24] Responding to a petition for writ of habeas corpus filed by Calley's lawyers in February 1974 after they had exhausted all other avenues for appealing his conviction, Judge Elliott determined that the media's coverage of the massacre allegations had indeed been corrosive of the presumption of Calley's innocence. 'Never in the history of the military justice system, and perhaps in the history of American courts,' he said, 'has any accused ever encountered such intense and continuous prejudicial publicity as the Petitioner herein.'[25]

These arguments were not entirely persuasive. The US Court of Appeals for the Fifth Circuit rejected Elliott's reasoning, noting, first, that the coverage he considered so prejudicial had hardly neutralized public sympathy for the lieutenant, and second, that no evidence existed to suggest that it had actually influenced the verdict reached by the jurors.[26] Furthermore, the media's reporting of the story was not uniformly uncharitable towards Calley: Hersh's initial article, for example, included a series of supportive comments from officer peers at Fort Benning, whilst the reporter himself later wrote in quite fraternal terms of the evening he had spent in Calley's company: 'Hell, he was nice . . . It could have been a night with any old friend.'[27]

---

[23] A. Everett, K. Johnson and H. Rosenthal, *Calley* (New York: Dell Publishing Co., 1971); Greenhaw, *The Making of a Hero*; Hammer, *The Court-Martial of Lt Calley*; J. Sack, *Lieutenant Calley: His Own Story* (New York: Viking Press, 1971); T. Tiede, *Calley: Soldier or Killer? (Your Decision)* (New York: Pinnacle Books, 1971). Tiede's volume was the least thoughtful of these works on Calley, though it was far from the worst 'instant' book to be written on the subject of the massacre. For the most rancid example of the genre, see M. Gershen, *Destroy or Die: The True Story of My Lai* (New Rochelle: Arlington House, 1971).

[24] Pemberton and Wule to Laird, 10 December 1969, folder: My Lai 8/11, Papers of *Four Hours in My Lai*, LHCMA, KCL.

[25] *Calley* v. *Callaway*, 382 F. Supp. 650 (1974), in Goldstein *et al.*, pp. 535–40.

[26] *Calley* v. *Callaway*, US Court of Appeals for Fifth Circuit, 10 September 1975, in *ibid.*, pp. 556–64.

[27] *Dispatch News* Service telex, 12 November 1969, folder: 'Case folder: 1LT – William L. Calley, Jr [Part 2 of 2]', Box 6, Records Pertaining to the My Lai Massacre, 1969–74, Records of the Vietnam War Crimes Working Group, Office of the Deputy Chief of Staff for Personnel, RAS, RG319, NACP; Hersh, 'How I broke the Mylai story', p. 49.

Moreover, although Americans were continually being invited by the news media to gaze upon William Calley as if an explanation of the massacre might lie somewhere therein, his image in itself would have rarely directed a final resolution of their thoughts on the subject. Calley's image, like his personality, was pliable and under-determined, offering little resistance to whatever preconceptions its viewers brought to their text. Soon after the initial massacre revelations, the Art Workers Coalition (AWC) – a radical group of artists and critics opposed to corporate control of major art institutions and to the Vietnam war – manufactured thousands of masks bearing a photograph of Calley's face. These were to be worn at an anti-war march to affirm the responsibility that all Americans carried for the atrocities committed at My Lai (4). As AWC member Lucy Lippard later recalled, however, some observers took the masks to be an expression of support for the accused lieutenant, which was not quite the same thing: 'A lesson was learned about the transferral of esthetic ambiguity into the streets.'[28] That his image could be appropriated both by those who sympathized with his predicament and by those who considered him guilty of mass murder was recognized by Calley himself. After he had appeared on the front cover of *Time*, 200 people sent Calley copies of the picture, asking for his signature. 'God! I haven't the vaguest idea of why they would want this,' he commented. 'To hang it next to Hitler? Or to hang it next to Santa Claus?'[29]

What the media actually wrote and said about William Calley, and the liberal use that they made of his image, ultimately had no decisive perjorative effect upon the outcome of his case; but it did have an impact upon the broader public debate about the killings. The pre-eminent status of the lieutenant within popular massacre discourse encouraged Americans to engage with and assess one particular conception of causation before all others: that the locus of guilt was narrow, and centred on Charlie Company, 1st Platoon and the men who led them into My Lai (4). Calley operated as a kind of lightning rod, attracting the rhetorical energies of most of those who held strong views about the massacre, whether they insisted upon his personal culpability or contested it, demanding either that the search for guilty parties be suspended or that it be directed elsewhere. Indeed, in the attitudes of many who considered it unjust, Calley's prosecution produced an equal and opposite reaction, imitative in its excesses of the same judgments that it condemned: the war criminal became a martyr, the anti-hero a hero.

[28] L. Lippard, *A Different War: Vietnam in Art* (Seattle: The Real Comet Press, 1990), p. 24. Lippard asserts that the protest in question was the Moratorium march in Washington on 15 November, 1969, but images of Calley could not have been in public circulation by that point. The November event was actually known as the Mobilization; the Moratorium demonstration had occurred in October.
[29] 'The Confessions of Lieutenant Calley', *Esquire* (November 1970), p. 116.

Responses to the massacre, which affirmed the essential culpability of the soldiers present in My Lai (4) at the time may also have been informed by the media's early and intensive deployment of witness and participant testimony in its reports. The passage of atrocity stories to acceptance as legitimate news was never an easy one, as editors who had scrutinized and censored such stories in the past knew very well. During this period of asserted administration attacks upon the negativity of the media, it became all the more important that, having decided that the story of the massacre merited broadcast or publication, editors should ensure that the reports carried on their programmes or in their journals contained compelling and convincing evidence of the scale of the killings, the defence-less nature of the victims and the casual, intimate callousness of those engaged in the slaughter.[30] The accumulation of persuasive first-hand testimony was also necessary to sustain the credibility of the story in the face of a declaration by the South Vietnamese Ministry of Defence that no massacre had occurred, as well as initial indications of public scepticism about the allegations.[31]

Hence the swelling of editorial confidence evident in the massacre coverage from 20 November on, when Michael Bernhardt and Michael Terry, who had served with Charlie Company during the operation in Son My, and Ronald Haeberle, who had been present as an army photographer, made themselves available to the news media. That day, the *New York Times* published an account of a telephone interview with Bernhardt, one of the few members of the company not to have participated in the killings, whilst his press conference was featured on both the CBS and NBC evening news broadcasts.[32] In his interview with the *New York Times*, Bernhardt estimated that he had personally witnessed about 100 people being killed or lying dead, but noted that, within the company itself, a total body-count of 300 had been mentioned. He had seen no military-age Vietnamese males present in the village and recalled of the massacre: 'They would get the people together and gather them in groups. Then they would shoot them with rifles and machine guns.'

On *NBC Nightly News*, Michael Terry recalled one such incident of mass killing: 'they had rounded up about twenty, maybe thirty people and most of them were women and children. There might have been a few old men in the group – but they'd rounded them up just right over a ditch bank and shot 'em all with machine guns and left 'em in the

---

[30] Vice-President Agnew had followed his criticism of network news commentators on 13 November with an assault a week later on the liberal print press, and the *New York Times* in particular. For texts of these speeches, see T. Goldstein (ed.), *Killing the Messenger: 100 Years of Media Criticism* (New York: Columbia University Press, 1991).

[31] For the South Vietnamese declaration, see Bunker to Rogers, 'Quang Ngai Incident', 25 November 1969, folder: 'Department of State', Box 2, Administrative and Background Materials Files – Open Inventory, 1967–1970, RPI, RAS, RG319, NACP.

[32] *New York Times* (20 November 1969), pp. 1, 14; *CBS Evening News*, 20 November 1969, VTNA; *NBC Nightly News*, 20 November 1969, VTNA.

ditch.'[33] Two days later, the *New York Times* described an interview with William Doherty – later charged with premeditated murder, though the case was eventually dismissed – who gave his own account of the massacre, estimating that over 100 civilians had been killed.[34] On 25 November, after Paul Meadlo had appeared on *CBS Evening News* and confessed to shooting babies, the entire transcript of the interview was printed in the *New York Times*.[35] On 27 November, the *New York Times* reported the admission of Varnado Simpson of the company's 2nd platoon that he had personally been responsible for the deaths of ten people in the village.[36]

The use of first-hand accounts to legitimize press interest in the story of My Lai, therefore, had the effect of emphasizing the primary responsibility of those who had actually carried out the killings. Furthermore, the prominence given to such testimony often seems to have produced a explicitly prosecutorial tone in both the reporting of the story and subsequent editorial comment. When Ronald Haeberle's photographs of the massacre were printed in the *Cleveland Plain Dealer* on 20 November, the paper consciously positioned the images, together with Haeberle's personal account of what had occurred, as powerful and credible evidence of aberrant criminality on the part of the American troops involved. Haeberle himself was cast as a dynamic yet responsible witness, motivated by nothing more complicated than a desire to see wrongdoing exposed. The story, crafted by *Dealer* reporter and later Hollywood screenwriter Joe Eszterhas, quoted Haeberle's assertion that he was 'just an average American with an upper-middle-class background who was drafted'; it noted also that he was not against the war in Vietnam and that he had received an honourable discharge after his army service.[37] The report implicitly aligned Haeberle with the ongoing criminal inquiry into the massacre, declaring that three months previously he had 'provided' army investigators with his photographs, along with a six-page statement.

Two images of Haeberle telling his story to Eszterhas accompanied the article, both of which presented him as an animated, passionate witness, his face expressive, hands raised up in mid-motion. Haeberle's personal condemnation of the killings was prominently featured, with the first sentence of the article quoting his description of civilians 'indiscriminately and wantonly mowed down' by US troops. The article also accentuated the criminality of the massacre by citing Haeberle's view that such atrocities deviated from the norms of American conduct in Vietnam: 'I felt nauseated to see people treated this way. American GIs were supposed to be protecting people and rehabilitating them and I had seen that. But this was incredible.'

[33] *NBC Nightly News*, 20 November 1969, VTNA.
[34] *New York Times* (22 November 1969), p. 2.
[35] *New York Times* (25 November 1969), p. 16.
[36] *New York Times* (27 November 1969), p. 18.
[37] *Cleveland Plain Dealer* (20 November 1969), pp. 1, 6–A.

Haeberle's photographs were thus presented to the readership of the *Cleveland Plain Dealer* in the context of an account which located the cause of the massacre in the homicidal viciousness of a small group of soldiers, whose reckless savagery was irreconcilable with the normal practices of the US military in Vietnam and with the conscience of ordinary Americans. The constructed nature of this moral positioning – and the absence of any essential relationship between knowledge of what happened at My Lai (4) and the kind of vigilant ethical concern affected by Haeberle – becomes evident when one considers what the story omitted. Haeberle was not quite the dynamic, uncomplicated force for the exposure of wrongdoing that the *Dealer*'s article seemed to suggest. The article, for example, did not address Haeberle's own behaviour in the village – that his response to the killings that he witnessed was not to intervene, but to continue taking pictures. Nor did it address his failure to report the massacre to higher authority when he returned to base camp, despite the evidence carried in his camera.[38] Although Haeberle had indeed 'provided' army investigators with copies of his photographs, and a statement, he had done so only when they contacted him, seventeen months after the event: at that time, moreover, he was not entirely certain whether he would be willing to serve as a witness for the prosecution if the case went to court.[39]

Indeed, as Eszterhas later recorded, Haeberle had been largely untroubled by thoughts of the massacre since his return from Vietnam: 'He was doing all right, gaining weight, making a little money, and the memory of that day at Mylai did not bother him at all.'[40] When he delivered illustrated lectures to civic groups around Ohio, the images of those who had died at the hands of Charlie Company were interwoven with pictures he had taken of other aspects of the conflict – GIs handing out chocolate bars to Vietnamese children, army medics at work. Haeberle made no attempt to mobilize the conscience of his audiences, to enlist them behind a call for justice: there the massacre was, a moment of grisly spectacle in the wider panorama of war, and that was all. He told his story to Eszterhas in the same matter-of-fact manner. He only became expressive, Eszterhas recalled, for the benefit of the paper's photographer, who told him 'to make some hard-hitting faces so we'd have our art to illustrate his art. Ron twisted his face, pushed his eyebrows up, made sweeping gestures.'[41]

---

[38] The report of the Peers Commission later judged Haeberle's conduct to have been deficient on five counts, including the failure to make any effort to prevent the killings, the failure to inform appropriate authorities of what he had witnessed and the suppression of evidence (Goldstein *et al.*, p. 344). At Calley's court martial, Haeberle testified that he had never heard of the MACV directive requiring military personnel to report war crimes to their commanding officer (Hammer, *The Court-Martial of Lt Calley*, p. 91).

[39] Asked by André Feher if he would testify in court, Haeberle replied: 'At this time I do not want to commit myself either way. However it is more on the favorable side.' Haeberle, 'Witness Statement', 25 August 1969, folder: My Lai 8/38, Papers of *Four Hours in My Lai*, LHCMA, KCL.

[40] Eszterhas, p. 456.

[41] *Ibid.*, pp. 459, 461.

In addition, Haeberle's motivation for bringing his story to the attention of the press did not consist entirely of the outraged humanity exhibited in the *Dealer*'s article. When he had been interviewed by Army CID agents in August, showing them his slides of the massacre, one of the detectives had speculated that the images could be worth a million dollars. In mid-November, reading news of the charges against William Calley, Haeberle remembered the conversation and contacted Eszterhas, whom he had known at Ohio University.[42] Together they decided to use the *Dealer* as a showcase for the photographs, selling the reproduction rights elsewhere.[43] The day before the pictures appeared, with the initial asking price set at $100,000, Eszterhas flew to New York to offer the rights to *Life* magazine.[44] The tiny annotation '© 1969, Ronald L. Haeberle', printed under each of the pictures, was the only indication in the original *Dealer* report that the photographer was planning to profit financially from their publication. The *Dealer*, indeed, seems to have discarded all elements of Haeberle's story which would have disrupted the impression of an authentic, unequivocal moral response to the massacre and thus denaturalized the prosecutorial tone of its coverage.

In the case of the *Cleveland Plain Dealer*, therefore, the deployment of witness testimony, together with direct visual evidence, pulled coverage of the story in a prosecutorial direction, though the actions of the witness himself suggested that there was no inevitable progression from personal experience of the atrocity to the pursuit of a full judicial accounting. The relationship between the publication of first-hand accounts and the moral condemnation of those involved in the killings became even more explicit in the next issue of the newspaper. The previous day, the *Dealer* had primarily relied upon Haeberle's testimony, carefully massaged, to draw the attention of readers to the evidence of criminality at My Lai (4). Editorial comment was limited to a statement from William Ware, the *Dealer*'s executive editor, which explained why the photographs were published despite the assertion of the US Army that this might prove prejudicial to the rights of individuals charged in connection with the case. Briefly acknowledging the possibility that the pictures were not genuine images of the massacre, Ware argued that the readers of the paper were 'entitled to see them for what they purported to be by the man who gave them to The Plain Dealer for publication: Photographs taken at a village in Vietnam.'[45]

By the next morning, however, editorial opinion had been brought into line with the tone of the news coverage, emboldened perhaps by the interest shown in the exclusive by other media outlets in the United States and

[42] *Ibid.*, p. 457.
[43] *Ibid.*, p. 458.
[44] *Ibid.*, p. 462.
[45] *Cleveland Plain Dealer* (20 November 1969), p. 6–A.

overseas.[46] Having invested their paper's prestige in the story, the *Dealer*'s editors might also have been concerned to confront the ambivalence that its reporters discovered when they canvassed readers for a response to the pictures: many either offered no opinion or professed scepticism about the allegations of massacre.[47] Thus, under the forceful heading, 'They Butchered a Village', the paper's leader column on 21 November announced: 'In March, 1968, the soldiers of C Company, 1st Battalion, 200th Infantry Regiment, 11th Light Infantry Brigade mass-murdered the men, women, children and babies who were virtually the entire population of My Lai No. 4, a little village in the Son My area.' Any military rationalizations, it declared, were 'pitifully refuted' by 'the bodies of poor, naked babies'. The column concluded: 'Whatever justice can be done must be done.'[48]

When the colour reproductions of Haeberle's photographs were first published by *Life* magazine in its issue of 5 December, alongside detailed witness and participant accounts, the actions of American troops at My Lai (4) were summarized in similarly censorious terms.[49] The introduction to the article, to which Eszterhas contributed, as part of the reproduction agreement negotiated in New York, rejected the assertion of the South Vietnamese government that the allegations of mass killings were simply enemy propaganda: 'This is not true. The pictures shown here by Ronald Haeberle, an Army photographer who covered the massacre, and the interviews on the following pages confirm a story of indisputable horror – the deliberate slaughter of old men, women, children and babies.' Eyewitness testimony, *Life* stated, indicated 'that the American troops encountered little if any hostile fire, found virtually no enemy soldiers in the village and suffered only one casualty, apparently a self-inflicted wound. The people of Mylai were simply gunned down.'[50] In the case of one witness, Varnado Simpson, the article juxtaposed his account of shooting a woman and child with a photograph of the victims lying dead in the courtyard of a hut. Simpson was also pictured just below the image of those he had killed, looking straight at the camera, adjacent to the following text in large black type: 'Someone will always be pointing a finger at me and saying, "He was one of them."'[51]

[46] Newspapers and broadcasters from around the world had contacted the paper requesting permission to print the photographs. *Cleveland Plain Dealer* (21 November 1969), p. 12–A. The previous evening, the images had also been shown on *CBS Evening News. CBS Evening News*, 20 November 1969, VTNA.

[47] *Cleveland Plain Dealer* (21 November 1969), pp. 1–A, 12–A.

[48] *Cleveland Plain Dealer* (21 November 1969), p. 10–A.

[49] For an illuminating analysis of the *Life* article, see R. Slotkin, *Gunfighter Nation: The Myth of the Frontier in Twentieth-Century America* (New York: Atheneum, 1992), pp. 581–91.

[50] *Life* (5 December 1969), p. 36.

[51] *Life* (5 December 1969), p. 42. Simpson's account was not entirely reliable. He asserted that the woman and child (Truong Thi Huyen and Nguyen Tan) had been accompanied by a man, who managed to get away. In fact, as another photograph makes clear, there were three bodies lying together in the courtyard, including that of Nguyen Gap, a male aged around 50. See the key to Haeberle's pictures produced by CID investigators: folder: My Lai 8/34, Papers of *Four Hours in My Lai*, LHCMA, KCL.

There was nothing in the photographs that Ronald Haeberle had taken at My Lai (4) which, inevitably, required the journals that first published them to adopt an interpretation of causality which stressed the elemental guilt of those involved in the killings. None of the images actually depicted members of Charlie Company shooting civilians in the village, and, in any case, the principal alternative interpretations of culpability – which attested to the correlations between atrocity and broader national policy in Vietnam, or between atrocity and the general proclivities of humankind towards violence – were not grounded in a denial that they had done so. (Nor was there any reason why the deployment of first-hand testimony should in itself preclude earnest reflection upon the more diffuse forces that might have contributed to the events at My Lai (4).) Nevertheless, there was something about Haeberle's photographs of dead children which seemed to quicken the prosecutorial pulse, making it a little bit harder to believe that the killings were somehow necessary and that the killers had no choice. A survey conducted at Ohio State University indicated that students who were shown the massacre images were more likely to regard what happened at My Lai (4) as 'an example of brutal and cold-blooded murder' than students who viewed only written descriptions.[52] A number of the attorneys who contested the massacre courts martial appear to have predicted this effect. Although the photographs revealed nothing directly about William Calley's conduct in My Lai (4), the army prosecutor Aubrey Daniel nevertheless introduced them as exhibits, enlarged and in colour. The size of the exhibits provoked a member of the lieutenant's defence team to complain that Daniel was attempting to improperly influence the jury.[53] In the trial of Ernest Medina, the evidence contained within the photographs was much more material to the prosecution's case – because they demonstrated that Medina had indeed moved around the settlement and seen the bodies of those killed by his men. Nevertheless, the defence counsel managed to have the images declared inadmissible.[54]

When coverage in the media drew most extensively on witness accounts and the images provided by Haeberle, then – as in the weeks immediately following the initial massacre revelations – a conscious editorial emphasis upon the guilt of individuals does seem to have been produced, as the treatment of Varnado Simpson in *Life* clearly demonstrates. This manner of media address, however, reflected not just whatever logic of personal culpability was suggested by the visual evidence of the crimes and the disclosures of the men present at the time they were committed, but also – once again – the legal dynamics of the story when it first broke. Press

[52] K. Thompson, A. Clarke and S. Dinitz, 'Reactions to My-Lai: a visual–verbal comparison', *Sociology and Social Research*, 58 (January 1974), 122–9.

[53] Hammer, *The Court-Martial of Lt Calley*, pp. 86–9; Bilton and Sim, p. 335. In the trial of Private Michael Schwarz for the atrocities committed at Son Thang, the defence counsel similarly argued that the sole purpose of the prosecution in introducing colour photographs of the victims' bodies as evidence was 'to inflame the minds of the jury' (Solis, pp. 138–9).

[54] Bilton and Sim, pp. 283, 348.

interest in the circumstances of the massacre had been stimulated by judicial developments which directed attention to the question of the criminality of the soldiers who had actually entered My Lai (4) – primarily the members of Charlie Company. Crucially, however, that interest was engaged before the legal defences of those implicated had been able to cohere into an alternative set of explanations.

On the advice of his military counsel, William Calley himself did not speak to the media about the details of the Task Force Barker operation, the orders he had been given and his own conduct in the village.[55] For his part, George Latimer, Calley's civilian counsel, had refused to listen to the lieutenant's version of what had happened before he agreed to take on the case, and he displayed little interest in hearing it any time thereafter.[56] Had his research been more rigorous, Latimer might have refrained from some early public assertions – such as his statement to Seymour Hersh that whatever deaths had occurred resulted from a firefight – which quickly proved to be unsustainable.[57] In addition, lucid analyses of the broader context in which the atrocities had been committed were rarely forthcoming either from participants who were unlikely to be charged because they had already left military service or from witnesses who had stood aside from the slaughter.[58]

With those most closely involved in the massacre offering no convincing rationalizations of their conduct, interpretations which stressed the role of broader structural or cultural forces emerged somewhat hesitantly. In the first few weeks of the story's life, therefore, a prosecutorial tone was often adopted by the press because, at this time, the basic fund of news content which set the parameters for editorial positioning consisted almost exclusively of the perspectives of those with the most intimate personal experience of the killings – the men who had actually fired their weapons at the people of My Lai (4) and the men who had watched them do it.

The American media's initial preoccupation with the immediate guilt of Charlie Company emerged, then, as a consequence of both its reliance on first-hand accounts to give credibility to a controversial story and

[55] *New York Times* (14 November 1969), p. 16.

[56] Hammer, *The Court-Martial of Lt Calley*, p. 61.

[57] *Dispatch News Service* telex, 12 November 1969, folder: 'Case folder: 1LT – William L. Calley, Jr [Part 2 of 2]', Box 6, Records Pertaining to the My Lai Massacre, 1969–74, Records of the Vietnam War Crimes Working Group, Office of the Deputy Chief of Staff for Personnel, RAS, RG319, NACP.

[58] In his CBS interview, Paul Meadlo was asked: 'It's hard for a good many Americans to understand that young, capable, American boys could line up old men, women and children and babies and shoot them down in cold blood. How do you explain that?' He replied: 'I wouldn't know.' *New York Times* (25 November 1969), p. 16. In the *Life* article, both Simpson and Sergeant Charles West emphasized the order to destroy the settlement which had been issued by Captain Medina. Neither, however, seemed entirely convinced that this absolved them of blame, with West acknowledging that Medina 'didn't give an order to go in and kill women or children', *Life* (5 December 1969), pp. 39, 42.

the desultory manner in which the legal process, at this early stage, fed alternative perspectives into the national debate. Other forces – more profound and pervasive, though difficult to define – may also have been at work. Whilst the events of the late 1960s certainly disrupted the ideological affinities between press and state, which had inhibited critical reporting of the military's conduct in the first few years of the Vietnam war, they did not prompt media institutions to entirely abandon their hegemonic role. Throughout this troubled period, many mainstream news outlets continued to articulate a vision of a righteous, moderate and cohesive national community. It was not always clear – especially when confronted with the polarizing strategies of the Nixon administration or those size-able sections of popular opinion lighting out for the political extremes – whether this vision represented reality or aspiration. Nevertheless, as the discursive status of the massacre shifted from allegation to certified crime, a number of media commentaries sought to preserve the protective cast around the national self-image, asserting the aberrant nature of the events at My Lai (4) and, by implication, the elemental and exclusive guilt of Medina, Calley and their men.

Thus, a regular feature of early media reactions was the assertion that American atrocities of this kind were isolated and infrequent; if any side in the conflict had adopted a calculated policy of violence against non-combatants, it was the enemy, not the United States. In his commentary for *ABC News* on 24 November, anchorman Howard K. Smith rejected the view, expressed by Senator Stephen Young of Ohio, that the massacre was comparable to atrocities committed by the Nazis: 'Well, it's not. Nazi atrocities, like the daily ones of the Vietcong, are acts of national policy. This, if it happened, is a violation of national policy.'[59]

Two days later, Smith repeated the lesson, holding up to the camera what he called a 'scholarly' book on the Vietcong, written by Douglas Pike, which contained statements from the movement's leaders asserting that torture and murder were essential to the prosecution of their struggle: 'So we should be careful about equating us with the Vietcong. There is no equation.'[60] A report on the terror tactics of the enemy was included in *Time*'s coverage of the story, beginning with the assertion: 'For shocked Americans, what happened at My Lai seems an awful aberration. For the Communists in Viet Nam, the murder of civilians is routine, purposeful policy.' The report was illustrated with a photograph of the burnt bodies of Montagnard tribespeople, including babies, killed by the enemy in 1967.[61]

It was at this moment that the media revived the memory of the battle for Hué, taking their cue from a captured enemy document released by the American military mission in Saigon. With remarkable serendipity, the

[59] *ABC News*, 24 November 1969, VTNA.
[60] *ABC News*, 26 November 1969, VTNA.
[61] *Time* (5 December 1969), p. 29.

document had apparently been discovered in the mission's files only a few days before. According to reports, it described how, during the course of the siege, communist forces had deliberately killed nearly 3,000 of the city's inhabitants.[62] Both CBS and ABC reported the discovery in their news broadcasts; behind the ABC anchor desk, a large splash of blood, which had earlier appeared on a map of Vietnam to mark the location of Son My, was now used to identify Hué.[63] On 28 November, NBC anchor Chet Huntley introduced a report from the city with the observation: 'The massacre at My Lai – if there was one – was not the only one committed during the Vietnam war. And probably the worst was the work of the enemy.' Citing the civilian death-toll mentioned in the captured document, correspondent Robert Hager commented: 'The immense proportions of the crime against humanity committed at Hué is hard for the mind to comprehend.' The victims, he said, had been marched in groups to the edge of holes, shot and pushed in. Their bodies still lay buried under fields flooded by the monsoon rains.[64]

These comparisons between the normative ethics of the two sides functioned to intercept the attribution of guilt for the massacre before it could reach the American nation as a whole: if My Lai indeed represented simply a single, extraordinary lapse within a national culture of war-fighting which remained in large measure disciplined and moral, despite the utmost provocation from a deliberately vicious foe, then neither the US military command nor the people at home were obliged to feel any meaningful responsibility for what had transpired. The implications of such comparisons for the guilt of those who participated personally in the massacre, however, were rather more complex. References to the conduct of the communist forces could establish a context in which the atrocities committed at My Lai (4) might appear more consistent with the behavioural norms of a cruel war, or indeed as an understandable, though regrettably indiscriminate, convulsion of vindictive rage against an elusive and demonic enemy.[65]

Alternatively, after years of exposure to press reports on the conflict in which the North Vietnamese and the Vietcong were routinely dehumanized, described as 'savage' or 'half-crazed', many Americans who witnessed

[62] *New York Times* (25 November 1969), p. 6.

[63] *ABC News*, 24 November 1969, VTNA; *CBS Evening News*, 24 November 1969, VTNA.

[64] *NBC Nightly News*, 28 November 1969, VTNA. For a sceptical discussion of the massacre at Hué, and particularly the allegation that the enemy was responsible for the murder of thousands of civilians, see Herman and Chomsky, pp. 323–5.

[65] In its first major report on the massacre, *Newsweek* explicitly sought to place the actions of Charlie Company in such a context. Publishing a photograph of a line of skulls and other bones belonging to those killed by the communists during the siege of Hué, and commenting also that the Vietcong forces in the area surrounding My Lai (4) were 'uncommonly ferocious', the journal concluded that the atrocity served 'as a stark reminder of the brutalizing effect that war – and particularly the war in Vietnam – has had upon all too many of those unfortunate enough to become involved in it', *Newsweek* (1 December 1969), pp. 36–7.

media commentaries categorizing the actions of Charlie Company along-side those of enemy forces may have registered the very possibility of such an analogy as a sign of the company's peculiar degradation, embedding the impression of its criminality still further.[66]

The inclination of some sections of the media to reassure their audience that the causes of the massacre lay outside the national sociology was particularly apparent in a report carried in *Life* magazine on 12 December, the week after it had published Ronald Haeberle's colour images of the victims at My Lai (4). The article described the fate of a young Vietnamese girl called Nguyen Thi Tron who, two years previously, had 'lost' half her right leg in an 'inadvertent' US helicopter attack near her village. *Life* had first reported on her recovery from the injury in November 1968; now returning to the story, it noted that the initial article had prompted 'an outpouring of money and gifts to Tron and her family' from readers in the United States. Tron was pictured smiling happily, holding up – the caption recorded – 'dolls and stuffed animals from California, the latest in a year-long flood of gifts'. In three other images, she was shown – again smiling – with a new artificial leg and shoes bought for her by the magazine's photographer, Larry Burrows.[67]

The story of Tron was almost perfectly positioned to ease concerns about the disintegration of national virtue, precipitated by the recent revelations about the acts committed by American soldiers in Son My. The US military had injured a child, but only by accident. Though they bore no direct responsibility for her fate, the response of Americans – rendered instinctive by the naturalizing language of an 'outpouring' and 'flood' – was to offer assistance, as a result of which the 'lost' limb could be restored, happiness be regained and a young life proceed along its allotted path. If this was the real America, however, the delinquency of those involved in the killings at My Lai (4) became all the more apparent.

In much of the media's initial reaction to the massacre revelations, then, the attribution of primary responsibility to Calley, Medina and their men functioned as a kind of default editorial setting. It was a position adopted in the absence of overt prompting from national institutional forces – which were largely silent in the early weeks of the story, apparently due to concerns about prejudicing the case – and informed instead by news content which drew attention to the immediate circle of perpetrators, by the sluggishness with which those accused mobilized to defend themselves, and by the investment of the mainstream press in a culturally self-confident community of readers and viewers. In view of their reticence on the subject of the massacre, the state authorities were perhaps fortunate that media coverage did not discomfort them more. Though both the US Army and the Nixon administration obviously would have preferred the

[66] On press representations of the enemy, see Hallin, *The 'Uncensored War'*, p. 158.
[67] *Life* (12 December 1969), pp. 85–6.

massacre to attract no press attention at all, the emphasis upon a narrow locus of guilt, which characterized much of the early reporting and editorial comment, was less inconvenient to their interests at this time than coverage that placed the question of culpability in broader cultural and institutional frames.

In so far as the army's leaders were consistent about anything in the wake of the media revelations concerning My Lai, they were consistent in their efforts to inoculate their institution against some of the massacre's more damaging potential consequences. For a number of reasons, the army command was anxious to maintain the distinction between the norms of military conduct and the actions of Calley and his men. As a result of studies conducted during the course of 1969, it appeared increasingly likely that the Nixon administration would soon decide to end the draft system of military recruitment and establish all volunteer armed services.[68] In the near future, the army would be unable to rely upon conscription to bridge any gap between the number of enlisted soldiers and its actual personnel requirements. To avoid such shortfalls, and attract the necessary volume of sound and capable young men into its recruiting offices, it was essential that the service both improve the financial incentives towards a military career and reverse the impact of recent vicissitudes upon the level of esteem in which it was held by the American public.

The massacre disclosures came as a terrible malediction for an institution whose long-term survival depended upon the consonance of its own reputation with the aspirations and values of the nation's young male citizens and – at least as pertinently – those of their parents. Twenty years on, CID detective André Feher recalled that, though he endeavoured to be fair and impartial throughout his investigation of the events at My Lai (4), his principal concern was that the atrocities 'would make the Army's conduct of the Vietnam war look very bad in the eyes of the public and that many mothers would feel that this was *not* the place for their sons to be'.[69] Myrtle Meadlo, mother of Paul, famously complained to a CBS correspondent: 'I had raised him up to be a good boy and did everything I could, and he *was* a good boy. They come along and they took him to the service, and I said he fought for his country and then, I said, look what they've done to him, I said. They've made a murderer out of him, to start with.'[70]

The conviction of army leaders in Washington that the massacre could not go unprosecuted, even if the power of decision lay formally with base commanders elsewhere, reflected their awareness of the need to make

[68] For an account of decision-making on the all volunteer force, see G. Lee and G. Parker, *Ending the Draft – The Story of the All Volunteer Force* (Alexandria: Human Resources Research Organization, 1977). See also G. Flynn, *The Draft, 1940–1973* (Lawrence: University Press of Kansas, 1993), pp. 224–71.

[69] Feher to Bilton, 20 August 1990, folder: My Lai 8/35, Papers of *Four Hours in My Lai*, LHCMA, KCL (emphasis in original).

[70] *CBS Evening News*, 25 November 1969, VTNA (emphasis in original).

manifest in action the institutional line that ethics and discipline continued to be embedded in army culture, that atrocity was not tolerated. The court-martial process, by isolating individuals and contesting their allegiance to military values and military law, could provide a dramatic signification of the position publicly adopted by the army command in response to My Lai: that the behaviour of Charlie Company was aberrant, in conflict with service norms. For the same reason, the command rejected a proposal that all the massacre cases be prosecuted together in a single court proceeding, a little like Nuremberg, because this might create the impression that the institution itself was on trial.[71] To the mothers of America, the message of the army was this: 'Trust us. Charlie Company is the exception. We will not make murderers out of your sons.'

In Vietnam at this time, the army was also experiencing an attrition of battlefield discipline and troop morale: developments which lent additional urgency to its efforts to buttress the distinction between the good and bad soldier. If the licence implied by the failure to punish many earlier atrocities had contributed to the conditions in which My Lai had occurred and, thereafter, been deleted from the operational record, then what horrors might be committed by GIs who had witnessed their most senior commanders allowing an acknowledged mass murderer to escape justice? Within the ranks of the junior officer corps, the prosecution of William Calley was undoubtedly regarded with a measure of ambivalence. At Fort Benning, a number of Calley's peers expressed anger at the decision to prefer charges.[72] In Vietnam, meanwhile, junior troop commanders were anxious that political pressures acting upon the army leadership were coarsening the application of military justice: might they too be court-martialled if civilian deaths, however accidental, occurred on their operational watch?[73] In the view of many in the professional officer corps, however, Calley was a horribly poor specimen of their kind; there would be very little left to recommend continued army service, they believed, if the institution itself did not undertake to demonstrate that babykillers were an aberration within its ranks.[74] During Calley's court martial, the journalist Richard Hammer was stopped by one West Point graduate who asserted that the regular army wanted the lieutenant not just convicted, but hanged:

Goddammit, I didn't go around massacring civilians when I was in Viet-Nam like that little son of a bitch. But now, whenever I wear the uniform off the base, it's damn obvious that people think I did, that they think everyone over

[71] Hammer, *The Court-Martial of Lt Calley*, pp. 37–8.

[72] Hersh, 'How I broke the Mylai story', p. 48.

[73] Responses to a questionnaire distributed among the soldiers and officers of the Americal Division by the investigative subcommittee of the House Armed Services Committee in early 1970, folder: My Lai 8/12, Papers of *Four Hours in My Lai*, LHCMA, KCL; Milloy to Zais, 30 April 1970, folder: My Lai 8/64, Papers of *Four Hours in My Lai*, LHCMA, KCL.

[74] General Charles W. Dyke, interview with author, Washington, DC, 5 September 2003.

there is butchering babies. I don't know whether it's ever going to be possible now to persuade people that I didn't fight a war like that and neither did a lot of other guys, but if they don't convict Calley and hang him or throw away the keys, nobody's ever going to believe we didn't.[75]

As details of the killings, and particularly their scale, began to percolate out into the public consciousness, so too did suspicions that the divisional command must have known what had happened, yet failed to investigate. On 20 November, General Westmoreland – now Army Chief of Staff – received a summary of preliminary findings from the CID investigation which indicated that Colonel Henderson, General Young and General Koster had all been informed of Thompson's allegations of massacre and that the outcome of their subsequent enquiries was as yet unclear.[76] On 24 November, apparently over the opposition of officials in both the White House and the Department of Defense, Westmoreland directed General Peers to explore the nature and scope of these inquiries and to determine their adequacy.[77] According to Peers, Westmoreland privately stressed to him 'the importance of my assignment and the effect it would have on the image of the Army in the eyes of the American public.'[78] At a time when the army was preparing to prosecute junior officers and ordinary soldiers for violations of the laws of war, it needed to demonstrate that the enforcement of those laws was not simply subject to the discretion of the military command. The inquiry team that Peers assembled, however, was more independent of mind than many in the higher echelons of the army might have liked. 'It was *not* our job,' Peers later commented, 'to be concerned about what effects the Inquiry might have on the Army's "image" or about the press or public's reaction to our proceedings'.[79] His commission's conclusions, when they came to be submitted, proved profoundly discomfiting to an army leadership which was otherwise endeavouring to present the massacre at My Lai (4) as an event almost entirely inexplicable in terms of its own institutional culture.[80]

[75] Hammer, *The Court-Martial of Lt Calley*, pp. 376–7.

[76] Gustafson to Westmoreland, 'My Lai Investigation', 20 November 1969, folder: 'Master File [Copy 1]', Box 15, RCCPI, RPI, RAS, RG319, NACP.

[77] Conversations between Lieutenant General William R. Peers and Lieutenant Colonel Jim Breen and Lieutenant Colonel Charlie Moore, Senior Officers Debriefing Program, 14 April 1977, William R. Peers Papers, USAMHI; William C. Westmoreland Project 1982–F Oral History Interview 1982, conducted by Lieutenant Colonel Martin L. Ganderson, folder: 'Volume 1 – Unbound', Box 3, William C. Westmoreland Papers, USAMHI; Westmoreland and Resor to Peers, 'Directive for Investigation', 26 November 1969, in Goldstein *et al.*, p. 33.

[78] Peers, pp. 8–9.

[79] *Ibid.*, p. 10 (italics in original).

[80] Congressman F. Edward Hébert, who headed the subcommittee of the House Armed Services Committee which was also investigating the massacre, recalled that the army had exerted constant pressure upon him to reach a favourable verdict on its handling of the affair, calling him on Capitol Hill, at home, and at his daughter's house: 'Hell, they even called me back in a Boston hospital [when I was] recuperating from an [eye] operation' (Carson, p. 70).

The desire to distinguish between the killings at My Lai (4) and the conduct and conscience of the US Army as a whole was also evident in the testimony of Army Secretary Stanley Resor before the Senate Armed Services Committee on 26 November. As the first senior Pentagon official to comment substantively upon the allegations, Resor asserted that – if the massacre had indeed occurred – then it was 'wholly unrepresentative of the manner in which our forces conduct military operations in Vietnam'. The 'over-all record' of the American troops who had served in southeast Asia during the last few years had been 'one of decency, consideration and restraint towards the unfortunate civilians who find themselves in a zone of military operations'. The senators present, Resor declared, might feel a great sense of dismay and outrage that 'such a thing could occur in our armed forces', but 'it could be no greater than mine, nor than that experienced by the thousands of loyal and brave officers and men who have labored so long and sacrificed so magnificently in search of the just peace we all seek in Vietnam'.[81] Within the army leadership itself, Resor's words were welcomed, but judged to have been 'couched in lawyer's language and not sufficiently hard hitting'. It was suggested that, if the public reputation of the army was to be maintained and its soldiers reassured that their time in uniform would be regarded with honour, General Westmoreland should make a prime-time television statement emphasizing the aberrant nature of crimes committed at My Lai (4) and his personal determination to ensure that justice was done.[82] Such a statement, however, would have required the consent of the President; nothing seems to have come of the proposal.

The army command and the Nixon administration had a common investment in establishing a distinction between the actions of Charlie Company and the broader ethos of American war-fighting in Vietnam, even if, as in the case of the Peers investigation, they sometimes contested the best means of so doing. Like the General Staff, the executive branch could hardly feel sanguine about the prospect of a further decline in army discipline and morale, or about a scenario in which the political liability of the draft gave away only to the disaster of a force unable to attract recruits. A shared strategic calculus, meanwhile, may have also recommended to both institutions the course of prosecuting the immediate perpetrators of the massacre. In so far as the court-martial process would direct the public's attention towards the conduct of individuals and away from the ethical content of the Vietnam war as a whole, it would serve the interests of the executive and its military servants. This was a period, after all, in which the United States was actually intensifying, rather than

[81] *New York Times* (27 November 1969), p. 18.

[82] See Schopper, 'CofSA Talking Paper for SA and SECDEF', 4 December 1969 and attached 'Talking Paper: Internal and External Reaction to the My Lai Incident and Other Recent Army Bad Publicity', folder: 'My Lai Allegations', Box 16, RCCPI, RPI, RAS, RG319, NACP.

de-escalating, many aspects of the war, most obviously pacification programmes and bombing operations. Nixon and his advisers – partial as
they were to grand geopolitical conceptualizations of international affairs
– placed a premium on credibility: they judged confidence in the United
States to be fundamental to the maintenance of stability and cohesion in
the non-communist world. As a consequence, throughout 1969 and most
of 1970, their essential policy ambition remained military victory, whereby
the communist regime in North Vietnam and its Vietcong allies would
be brought by force of American arms to accept the permanent non-
communist status of the regime in the South.[83] If this objective was to be
achieved, however, the overall levels of firepower applied to the military
effort would have to increase – to persuade the North that the costs of
continuing the conflict were too great and, whilst they were being so
persuaded, to compensate for the numbers of US troops sent home to
propitiate domestic opinion.[84]

The consequences of these policies for those at the raw end of the
pacification process or resident at the ground zeroes of the expanded
bombing campaigns seem rarely to have been considered by Nixon and
his advisers, except in so far as their suffering might provoke a new
controversy at home, quickening the pulse of public opposition to the
war, confirming to Hanoi the brittleness of the American commitment to
Vietnam and thus extinguishing any hopes that the administration could
force a settlement from a position of strength. The revelations about
My Lai, therefore, presented a significant threat to the aims of the Nixon
administration: if the national debate about the causes of the massacre
was allowed to evolve into a more general interrogation of military policy
in south-east Asia, the strategy which the executive had devised to bring
the war to a favourable conclusion might unravel entirely. In addition, if
the massacre was cast as anything other than the aberrant act of a rogue
company, it would neutralize one of the principal justifications advanced
by the President for staying the course in Vietnam, a justification forcefully reiterated in his recent 'silent majority' address: that a communist
victory would result in a bloodbath.[85] To weave My Lai into a much broader
pattern of indiscriminate killing by American forces was to dissolve the
moral distinctions between the United States and the other side, and
thereby also public confidence that there remained any meaningful
humanitarian purpose to the defence of South Vietnam.

[83] Kimball, pp. 67, 90, 233.

[84] For discussions of military policies in south-east Asia during the early years of the
Nixon administration, see R. Hunt, *Pacification: the American Struggle for Vietnam's Hearts
and Minds* (Boulder: Westview Press, 1995); Kimball, pp. 91–176; and L. Sorley, *A Better
War: The Uncensored Victories and Final Tragedy of America's Last Years in Vietnam*
(New York: Harcourt Brace & Company, 1999).

[85] S. Hersh, *The Price of Power: Kissinger in the Nixon White House* (New York: Summit
Books, 1983), p. 131.

Richard Nixon's policies in Vietnam, therefore, were vulnerable to any development which further advertised the malignancy of the United States presence there. For as long as media interest in the massacre revelations remained somewhat hesitant, the White House maintained its silence. A presidential statement on the affair at this time would not just risk the integrity of the judicial process; it would also breathe additional life into what might otherwise turn out to be only a momentary public embarrassment. On 21 November, national security adviser Henry Kissinger suggested to Bob Haldeman, Nixon's chief of staff, that a 'good deal of the current heat on this case is due to a concern by the press that there might be a cover-up. Once it is announced that there will be a court martial, some of this pressure should dissipate.' As a consequence, Kissinger recommended 'that we keep the President and the White House out of this matter entirely'.[86] The desire of the executive branch to do nothing that might either prolong or intensify media scrutiny of the massacre also may have informed its apparent opposition to the establishment of the Peers Inquiry.

As the days passed, however, as the *New York Times* called for a full investigation of the massacre, and as Paul Meadlo told the nation how he had fired his gun into a ditch full of women and children, the White House came to realize that something more than silence was required. 'I would doubt the war effort can ever now be the same', Daniel Patrick Moynihan informed the President on 25 November.[87]

If Nixon's advisers had once hoped that the massacre could be held outside the horizon of public concern, that hope had finally faded. The ongoing revelations, and their implications for the President's policy of persistence in Vietnam, would have to be actively managed, and the reaction of the public steered away from those interpretations of the massacre which were most irreconcilable with the administration's objectives. In particular, it was essential that popular perceptions of My Lai be kept as separate as possible from popular perceptions of the war. According to Bob Haldeman, writing in his diary on 25 November, Nixon felt 'that we have to make the point that this was totally contrary to national policy'.[88] The next day, Nixon's press secretary Ronald Ziegler told a news conference that an incident of the kind alleged to have occurred at My Lai (4) 'is in direct violation not only of United States military policy, but is also

[86] Kissinger to Haldeman, 'Lieutenant Calley Case', 21 November 1969, folder: 'Lt Calley/My Lai Village', Box 15, John Dean Subject Files, Staff Members and Office Files, White House Special Files, NPM, NACP.

[87] Moynihan to Nixon, 25 November 1969, folder: 'My Lai Incident [1 of 2]', Alexander Haig Special File, Box 1004, National Security Council Files, NPM, NACP.

[88] Haldeman diary entry, 25 November 1969, folder: 'H.R. Haldeman Journal Volume III, September 23, 1969–January 12, 1970', Box 1, Handwritten Journals and Diaries of Harry Robbins Haldeman, Box 32, Staff Members and Office Files: Haldeman, White House Special Files, NPM, NACP.

abhorrent to the conscience of all the American people.'[89] The President, meanwhile, expressed his approval of a cartoon published in the *Birmingham News* entitled 'For Us ... One Time Is Too Much.' The cartoon depicted an American GI staring at his left hand, which was dripping with blood. An enemy soldier stood nearby, his whole left arm bathed in blood, his large ape-like body bearing the legend 'communist atrocities as standard operating procedure'. Nixon told Herbert Klein, White House Director of Communications, to 'try to get this syndicated'.[90]

On 1 December, the issue of *Life* magazine containing Ronald Haeberle's colour images of the massacre arrived on the nation's newsstands. That afternoon, the President held a meeting with Secretary of State William Rogers, Secretary of Defense Melvin Laird, Attorney-General John Mitchell, and Henry Kissinger. My Lai dominated the discussion. The same day, Nixon asked Haldeman to establish a planning group which would be responsible for bringing the problem back under control.[91] Accounts of other atrocities committed by American soldiers in Vietnam had begun to appear in the press, and the President told Kissinger to find out from the Pentagon whether it expected any more revelations of this kind.[92] To Haldeman, he reiterated the need 'to get out the other side of the story'.[93] On 4 December, Kissinger gave the President a list of 'humanitarian actions' undertaken by American forces in Vietnam which, he suggested, might be used to reinforce the administration's argument that the massacre at My Lai (4) 'was an isolated incident, was contrary to the orders under which our forces are operating and wholly unrepresentative of the manner in which these orders are carried out'. He also provided brief details of the 'terror tactics' used by communist forces in South Vietnam, including the assertion that 'an estimated 3,500 citizens were shot, strangled or clubbed and buried alive' during the enemy's three-week occupation of Hué in 1968.[94]

The efforts of the Nixon administration to classify the massacre as something apart, and to keep it segregated from discussions of wider national policy in Vietnam, were not assisted by the proposal, advanced from a variety of quarters, that the President establish some kind of independent

[89] *New York Times* (27 November 1969), p. 1.

[90] Annotated copy of *Birmingham News*, 26 November 1969, folder: My Lai 8/83, Papers of *Four Hours in My Lai*, LHCMA, KCL.

[91] Haldeman diary entry, 1 December 1969, folder: 'H.R. Haldeman Journal Volume III, September 23, 1969–January 12, 1970', Box 1, Handwritten Journals and Diaries of Harry Robbins Haldeman, Box 32, Staff Members and Office Files: Haldeman, White House Special Files, NPM, NACP.

[92] Brown to Kissinger, 2 December 1969, folder: 'Possible My Lai Commission', Alexander Haig Special File, Box 1004, National Security Council Files, NPM, NACP.

[93] Haldeman diary entry, 3 December 1969, folder: 'H.R. Haldeman Journal Volume III, September 23, 1969–January 12, 1970', Box 1, Handwritten Journals and Diaries of Harry Robbins Haldeman, Box 32, Staff Members and Office Files: Haldeman, White House Special Files, NPM, NACP.

[94] Kissinger to Nixon, 'My Lai Incident', 4 December 1969, folder: 'My Lai Incident [2 of 2]', Alexander Haig Special File, Box 1004, National Security Council Files, NPM, NACP.

public inquest into how it was that such an appalling catalogue of atrocities came to be committed by a company of American soldiers. Urging the President to 'undertake some larger effort at understanding than can be had from a court martial,' Moynihan proposed that he 'empanel a group of serious and distinguished men to look into this whole area of experience in Vietnam'.[95] Writing in the *New York Times*, James Reston asserted the necessity of a presidential commission. 'If this was an isolated case in which a few soldiers acted against orders,' he said, 'we need to know what has happened to the discipline of our armed forces. If it was an example of the bewildering pressures of war itself, or the dehumanizing and brutalizing influences of the struggle, we need to know that too.'[96]

Two senior US Senators, John Stennis and Margaret Chase Smith, recommended the appointment of 'a blue ribbon panel', independent of the Pentagon, 'to assemble all relevant facts and to submit an objective report to the President'.[97] On 5 December, thirty-four eminent lawyers and law professors signed an open letter to the President proposing that he mandate a commission 'of unquestionable impartiality' to determine whether US military operations in Vietnam were being conducted in a manner consistent with the laws of war.[98]

The proposition that the White House might authorize a commission, independent of its own control, to elaborate whatever dynamics of culture and practice connected the behaviour of American soldiers at My Lai (4) with the broader national military effort in Vietnam produced allergic reactions amongst many of the President's advisers. Deputy Secretary of Defense David Packard and General Alexander Haig, Kissinger's second-in-command, both expressed strong reservations.[99] Any such commission, Haig warned, would 'heighten public attention to the incident' and impact adversely upon a military 'which was still attempting to conduct a war for better or worse under already stringent restrictions'. Haig also informed Kissinger that he could 'think of nothing worse than assembling a group of high-level civilians to look into the ethics of conducting military operations'. It would constitute, he suggested, another effort to 'civilianize' the armed services; in the past, initiatives of this kind had served only to 'shatter military discipline to a degree that the effectiveness of our military was seriously hampered'.[100]

[95] Moynihan to Nixon, 25 November 1969, folder: 'My Lai Incident [1 of 2]', Alexander Haig Special File, Box 1004, National Security Council Files, NPM, NACP.

[96] *New York Times* (30 November 1969), p. 12.

[97] Harlow to Nixon, 'My Lai Atrocities', 3 December 1969, folder: 'My Lai Incident [2 of 2]', Alexander Haig Special File, Box 1004, National Security Council Files, NPM, NACP.

[98] Goldberg *et al.* to Nixon, 5 December 1969, folder: '[cf.] ND18–4 War Crimes – Trials [1969–70]', Box 43, Confidential Files, White House Special Files, NPM, NACP.

[99] Harlow to Nixon, 'My Lai Atrocities', 3 December 1969, folder: 'My Lai Incident [2 of 2]', Alexander Haig Special File, Box 1004, National Security Council Files, NPM, NACP.

[100] Haig to Kissinger, 'My Lai Atrocities', 4 December 1969, folder: 'My Lai Incident [2 of 2]', Alexander Haig Special File, Box 1004, National Security Council Files, NPM, NACP.

On 8 December, after discussing the matter with Haldeman and others, Kissinger recommended against the creation of a commission unless there emerged a need to pre-empt congressional inquiries into the massacre or unless additional atrocities surfaced 'which would fundamentally change the character of the phenomenon'.[101]

Those who attended the President's news conference that evening witnessed a recitation of what had now emerged as the administration's standard script whenever it was obliged to speak publicly about the massacre. Nixon expressed his conviction that the massacre was 'an isolated incident' and asserted that, in contrast with an enemy 'which has atrocity against civilians as one of its policies', the overall record of American soldiers in their interactions with the Vietnamese had been one 'of generosity, of decency'. In 1969 alone, he said, US Marines had 'built over 250,000 churches, pagodas, and temples for the people of Vietnam' – a figure later abbreviated by the White House Press Office to 251 schools and 117 churches, pagodas and temples. Asked whether he would establish a civilian commission of inquiry into the massacre, the President emphasized the need to first allow the judicial process to take its course, in view of the effect that such a commission might have upon the rights of the accused in the case. However, if the judicial process 'does not prove to be adequate in bringing this incident completely before the public, as it should be brought before the public', then, he said, he was prepared to establish a commission, 'but not at this time'.[102]

As his actions at the end of Calley's court martial in March 1971 reveal, Nixon's tender expression of concern for the integrity and independence of the military justice system primarily reflected political convenience, not procedural principle. Following Calley's conviction, Nixon ordered him to be released from the stockade for the duration of the appeal process and announced that, whatever the final legal outcome, the fate of the lieutenant would be a matter for presidential review, taking into account all factors in the case, non-judicial as well as judicial. In spring 1971, of course, the political environment was very different to that which had prevailed sixteen months before, when the interests of the executive had been served by the legal investigation, by a judicial circus which directed the attention of its audience to the actions of a small number of individuals, and away from the institutional context in which those actions had occurred.

In the weeks immediately following the initial disclosures about the massacre at My Lai (4), a range of different factors – the early content of the story, the conventions of news reportage, the inability of those implicated

101 Haig to Cole, 'Attached Letter from Arthur J. Goldberg', 8 December 1969, folder: '[cf.] ND18–4 War Crimes – Trials [1969–70]', Box 43, Confidential Files, White House Special Files, NPM, NACP.
102 'The President's news conference of *December* 8, 1969', *Public Papers of the Presidents of the United States: Richard Nixon, 1969* (Washington, DC: US Government Printing Office, 1971), pp. 1003–5.

to offer a coherent response to the allegations, and the desire of the mainstream media to uphold the image of a benign national community – intertwined to produce a discursive emphasis within the public sphere upon the guilt of a handful of men, an emphasis which so matched the political and strategic interests of the state that it chose to offer no alternative perspective.

The public sphere, however, is not quite the same thing as public opinion. As early as mid-December 1969, it was evident that the patronage of the press, the army brass and the White House had not secured for their preferred interpretation of the massacre a full popular endorsement. Certainly, Richard Nixon would have been relieved to discover that, despite the wide dissemination of accounts of the killings and Haeberle's images of the victims, overall levels of public support for the Vietnam war remained essentially unchanged. Reflecting on the *vox populi* interviews that its reporters had conducted around the country, the *Wall Street Journal* noted that the massacre revelations seemed to have prompted very few Americans to reassess their attitudes towards the nation's military involvement in Vietnam: those who had previously been opposed to that involvement were still opposed; those who had given it their support continued to do so.[103] One polling organization which questioned its respondents on the wisdom of the original decision to send troops to Vietnam found that the percentage of those who considered the decision to have been a mistake increased by only a single point from September 1969 to January 1970.[104] Contrary to the administration's initial expectations, the British ambassador in Washington reported, the massacre 'has not led to many new questions' about the President's policies in Indochina.[105] Though the story remained subject to 'enormous television emphasis,' wrote Bob Haldeman in his diary on December 16, '[the] public seems to have taken it pretty well in [its] stride and then become bored'.[106]

Yet the resilience of popular support for Nixon's pursuit of a favourable settlement in Vietnam cannot be ascribed to the persuasiveness of his argument that the atrocities committed at My Lai (4) revealed nothing about the manner in which the war as a whole was being fought, and that the most convincing explanations of the massacre were likely to be yielded by the process of court martial, and the fathoming of individual moral failure that would take place therein. If reports of civilians corralled into a ditch to await a decimating stream of American bullets did not disturb the pattern of popular attitudes towards the war, it was at least partly

---

[103] *Wall Street Journal* (1 December 1969), p. 1.

[104] Mueller, pp. 54–5.

[105] Freeman to Greenhill, 15 December 1969, PREM 13/3552, National Archives, Kew.

[106] Haldeman diary entry, 16 December 1969, folder: 'H.R. Haldeman Journal Volume III, September 23, 1969–January 12, 1970', Box 1, Handwritten Journals and Diaries of Harry Robbins Haldeman, Box 32, Staff Members and Office Files: Haldeman, White House Special Files, NPM, NACP.

because many Americans took the view that this was what war did. And if this was what war did, then the men who pointed their guns at the ditch and pressed their fingers against the trigger could not be held personally responsible for the deaths that occurred a moment thereafter. In mid-December, only 12 per cent of Minnesota residents registered the opinion that blame for the killings lay 'mostly' with the soldiers of Charlie Company, with 55 per cent preferring to attribute them instead to 'the fact that war tends to make people brutal'.[107]

Shortly afterwards, a poll conducted for *Time* magazine found only 22 per cent of respondents ready to express clear moral repugnance at the massacre, with 65 per cent favouring the assertion that 'incidents such as this are bound to happen in a war'. Fifty-five per cent agreed that Lieutenant Calley was 'being made a scapegoat by the Government'. Surveying the distance in ethical reasoning that lay between these reactions and their own apprehension of My Lai as murderous aberrance, *Time*'s editors reflected gloomily that Americans seemed prepared 'to tolerate the intolerable, which is not always a virtue'.[108]

Through all the initial massacre revelations, then, majority opinion in the United States continued to express support for the national endeavour in Vietnam and for the American troops, support which extended even to those soldiers accused of war crimes. The odious acts committed by Calley haunted these citizens less than the ambivalent spectacle of his trial for murder by the same institution which had ordered him overseas to kill for his country. It seemed likely, moreover, that as the judicial investigation entered its court-martial stage, the individuals charged and their defence counsels would seek to mitigate the impression of aberrant criminality by locating the killings at My Lai (4) in the context of a war fought with extortionate brutality on all sides. Furthermore, as the story matured, news outlets themselves would explore alternative frames of analysis, in part to refresh their own coverage of the case and retain the attention of readers and viewers. In many later contributions to the national debate about the causes of My Lai, therefore, the peculiar pathologies of Charlie Company would be ascribed little explanatory value.

The prosecutorial perspective, however, continued to characterize much of the media's reporting of the massacre story, even in the wake of Calley's conviction – when the wider public mood was one of hostility to the verdict and the President himself intervened to stress its provisionality. The editorial positions adopted in response to the initial revelations may have exerted the pull of precedent upon subsequent coverage, but other factors also operated to sustain the correlations between the narratives that appeared in the press and the efforts of the state, through the judicial process, to contain the attribution of responsibility. Until Richard Nixon

[107] *Minneapolis Tribune* (21 December 1969), p. 4B.
[108] *Time* (12 January 1970), pp. 8, 10–11.

renewed his interest in the case in late March 1971, indeed, the overall balance of official comment and information on the subject of My Lai remained consistent with renditions of the massacre as exception, to be explained primarily by reference to the individual transgressions of the soldiers on the scene.

That consistency, however, was not always easily and openly achieved, as the army's management of the report of the Peers Inquiry indicates. In February 1970, the scope of the inquiry had been extended beyond simply an examination of the original investigation into the allegations of civilian deaths in the settlement of My Lai (4); it was now commissioned to explore what had actually happened in that settlement, and also the actions of Task Force Barker soldiers in the rest of Son My village.[109] Submitted in mid-March, the final report delivered a powerful indictment of the suppressions and evasions that had marked the brigade and division responses to the massacre and also provided a discussion of the factors that had contributed to the massacre itself, including: the frustrations of counterinsurgency warfare, the inadequacies of troop instruction concerning the rules of engagement, permissive command attitudes towards the killing of non-combatants, the prevalence of anti-Vietnamese prejudice amongst task force personnel, and the failure of the orders issued by Barker and his subordinates to provide for the safe conduct of civilians encountered in the area of operation.[110] Peers and his team identified twenty-eight officers and two enlisted men that it suspected of omissions and commissions in connection with the massacre cover-up and – because the two-year statute of limitations on military offences was soon to expire – assisted the Office of the Judge Advocate General in the preparation of criminal charges to be preferred against eleven, including General Koster and Colonel Henderson. Two military members of the inquiry prepared charges against four other officers, General Young amongst them.[111] In addition, the Peers report revealed that, during the same Task Force Barker operation, as many as 90 non-combatants had been killed by the soldiers of 1st Platoon, Bravo Company, in the coastal sub-hamlet of My Hoi, identified by the Americans as My Khe (4).[112] The inquiry had already brought this incident to the attention of the army's legal authorities, with the result that, on 10 February, war crimes charges were preferred against the lieutenant who had led 1st Platoon, Thomas Willingham.[113]

To read the account provided in the Peers report of the activities of Charlie Company in My Lai (4) is to be left in little doubt that its soldiers

---

[109] Westmoreland and Resor to Peers, 'Son My Investigation', 2 February 1970, in Goldstein *et al.*, p. 43.
[110] Goldstein *et al.*, pp. 192–206, 299–313.
[111] *Ibid.*, pp. 317–19; Peers, pp. 214–16.
[112] Goldstein *et al.*, pp. 167–81.
[113] Peers, p. 197.

had freely engaged in the mass killing of non-combatants.[114] Peers himself later commented that, given the crimes he had committed, William Calley was 'real fortunate to come out with his neck'.[115] The most original contributions that the commission might have yielded to the national debate about My Lai, however, resided in the sections of its report that complicated the story of the massacre as the outcome of factors entirely local to Medina, Calley and their men. In its forceful denunciation of senior officers for their negligent and self-serving responses to a serious war crime, in its assertion that dynamics of training, command, culture and environment – dynamics that may well have been familiar to American soldiers elsewhere in Vietnam – were critical to an understanding of why the killings had occurred, and in its revelation that a couple of kilometres down the road, another company of US infantry troops had also fired indiscriminately upon civilians, the report offered to its readers clear evidence that the relationship between the army and atrocity was not fully disclosed in either its formal regulations or its subsequent processes of prosecution and punishment.

In short, the Peers report was trouble. In the White House, Kissinger expressed concern about the use that those opposed to the Vietnam conflict might make of its conclusions.[116] No doubt partly because its disclosure might prejudice current criminal investigations and future court proceedings, but also partly because much of what it contained reflected adversely upon both the army and the war, all but fifty fairly innocuous pages of the four-volume report remained classified.[117] Only in November 1974, after Calley's sentence had been upheld by the Court of Military Appeals, did the army release Volume I of the report, comprising the inquiry's findings and conclusions.[118]

Though the army could justify imposing a quarantine upon the report itself, it could not avoid making some public comment on what the inquiry had actually revealed. Following the submission of the report, Peers was informed that a news conference would be held on 17 March. He prepared a statement to read out to the press. Having reviewed the statement, however, the army's Chief of Information, General Winant Sidle, asked him not to use the term 'massacre' to describe what had happened in My Lai (4). Peers and his team objected, threatening not to participate unless

[114] Goldstein *et al.*, pp. 127–45.

[115] Conversations between Lieutenant General William R. Peers and Lieutenant Colonel Jim Breen and Lieutenant Colonel Charlie Moore, Senior Officers Debriefing Program, 14 April 1977, William R. Peers Papers, USAMHI.

[116] Record of phone conversation between Westmoreland and Palmer, 16 March 1970, folder: 'Fonecoms Jan–Mar 70', Box 26, William C. Westmoreland Papers, USAMHI.

[117] 'Statement of Secretary of the Army Howard H. Callaway to accompany release of the Peers Report, November 13, 1974', in Goldstein *et al.*, pp. 20–3; Hersh, *Cover-Up*, p. 247.

[118] Volume III was also released in November 1974. Volumes II and IV, which contained witness testimony and CID statements, were released the following year, although the names of individuals were deleted and a code provided to allow the identification of only those personnel who had previously been publicly connected with the affair (Peers, p. 244).

they could speak candidly about their findings. The issue was not resolved until the morning of the conference, when Peers – conscious that Sidle's intervention reflected the wishes of the Secretary of the Army – finally agreed to refer instead to 'a tragedy of major proportions'. He later recalled, however, that the pressure to which he had been subjected had led him to enter the conference 'in an irritated and apprehensive mood', and that as a result, the answers he had given to reporters were not 'as clear and responsive as I would have liked'.[119] Although he announced details of the charges preferred against senior officers, Peers avoided any mention of the massacre at My Khe (4). He was asked whether any evidence existed to indicate 'that the type of behavior that the charges are based on was more widespread than what happened at My Lai on March 16? In other words, other days or other places?' Peers replied: 'If there is, I have no knowledge of it.' In response to an query concerning the charges preferred against Thomas Willingham, whose company had been operating elsewhere in Son My, not in My Lai (4), Peers chose to address only the confusion in local nomenclature, and his answer was not followed up. He subsequently commented to a colleague that, despite his 'three hours of hell' just prior to the conference, 'there were no tough questions asked'.[120]

In spring 1971, Seymour Hersh resumed his enquiries into the massacre at My Lai (4), having gained access to the still-classified Peers report. In articles for the *New Yorker* and a book entitled *Cover-Up*, and with all the fanfare normally accorded to a sensational new disclosure, Hersh combined the information provided in the report with his own witness and participant interviews to construct an account of Bravo Company's assault upon My Khe (4). As Hersh acknowledged, however, the story of the My Khe massacre had not entirely escaped the attention of other news reporters. In late November 1969, *Associated Press* had described an interview with Terry Reid, a former private in Bravo Company, which had been published by a local newspaper in Oshkosh, Wisconsin. Reid asserted that he had personally witnessed an incident in which US troops had entered a village and killed sixty old men, women and children. It was this report, indeed, which prompted Richard Nixon to ask whether the Pentagon expected any other accounts of American atrocities to emerge.[121] In January 1970, two months later, the journalist Richard Hammer was researching the events at My Lai (4) when he came across evidence of the killings in My Khe (4). He shared his information with a senior member of the Peers commission and included testimony from some of My Khe (4)'s surviving inhabitants in his book *One Morning in the War*, published

[119] *Ibid.*, pp. 216–17.

[120] Hersh, *Cover-Up*, pp. 248–51.

[121] Brown to Kissinger, 2 December 1969, folder: 'Possible My Lai Commission', Alexander Haig Special File, Box 1004, National Security Council Files, NPM, NACP; Kissinger to Laird, 'Vietnam Atrocity Stories', 8 December 1969, folder: 'Possible My Lai Commission', Alexander Haig Special File, Box 1004, National Security Council Files, NPM, NACP.

later that year.[122] In mid-February, meanwhile, *NBC Nightly News* broadcast a lengthy report on the allegations of massacre at My Khe (4). Its correspondent Kenley Jones visited the sub-hamlet and interviewed witnesses, whilst in the studio, Robert Goralski described how the episode had been uncovered during the course of the Peers Inquiry. Were My Lai (4) and My Khe (4), he asked, 'isolated incidents in the Vietnamese war? It appears that only the army can answer these questions.'[123]

In the end, however, news reporters did not force the army to do so. Until Hersh's later disclosures, these stories represented pretty much the only significant examples of media interest in the massacre at My Khe (4). If correspondents had secured a more confident knowledge of what Willingham and his platoon had effected in that settlement, then their attributions of guilt with respect to My Lai might well have been revised, exposing to a harsher interrogative light the culture of command existing within Task Force Barker itself and the wider army beyond. As it was, the Peers Inquiry – rather ironically, given the contents of its report – seems actually to have enhanced the public reputation of the army command. Following the press conference on 17 March and the announcement of the charges against Koster, Young and other senior officers, *ABC News* anchorman Frank Reynolds observed that the army

> is probably the last place where those who have lost faith in the establishment – or say they have – would expect to find this kind of soul-searching, this 'eyes-wide-open' type of self-examination. So let them think about that. It might be somewhat reassuring for all of us to consider that while the Pentagon is the headquarters of the military, today's action demonstrates it is not the headquarters of militarism. There is a big difference.[124]

The Peers investigation, therefore, had offered a serious challenge to some of the more simplistic articulations of the prosecutorial perspective, but that challenge had been successfully contained. The inclination of the national media to explicate the My Lai massacre principally in terms of individual acts and individual guilt was subsequently reinforced by the education that a number of its representatives received in the essential details of the killings from their presence in the courthouse when the Calley case eventually came to trial. The news life of most front-page stories is short, and the correspondent responsible may often have no expertise of his or her own to invest in the report, relying instead upon statements from others, such as government officials or academic specialists, to provide authoritative interpretations of the events described. My Lai was different; as the charges against Calley and others slowly made their way through the military justice system into the courts, reporters assigned to the case were themselves often able to build up a detailed fund of knowledge about the deeds perpetrated by the men of Charlie

---

[122] Hammer, *One Morning in the War*, pp. xii, 145–7.
[123] *NBC Nightly News*, 18 February 1970, VTNA.
[124] *ABC News*, 17 March 1970, VTNA.

Company. Once again, the information emerging from these legal proceedings was more likely to emphasize the specific actions of individuals rather than the context in which they occurred and more likely, therefore, to reinforce impressions of guilt over those of extenuating circumstance. For many members of the media, the court martial of William Calley represented an indispensable corollary to the massacre narratives that they had been constructing ever since November 1969, when the story had first broken. For one reporter covering the trial, the opening statement by the prosecuting counsel, Captain Aubrey Daniel, confirmed all that he had read and heard about My Lai: 'All my life I've almost automatically sided with the defense whenever I've covered a court case; it's just kind of natural. Not this time. This is the first time I can remember when I'm all for the prosecution.'[125]

The trial proceedings, of course, gave Calley and his legal representatives an opportunity to disrupt these confident attributions of blame by framing accounts of his behaviour within a range of mitigating contexts. After all, they might have argued, this was a war in which guerrilla intent was often dressed in civilian guise. If it was obvious in retrospect that the people of My Lai (4) presented no menace to the soldiers of Charlie Company, this could not have been safely assumed at the time, especially in the light of intelligence reports that the 48th Vietcong battalion was present in the settlement. Innocents had died because Calley and his men had been edgy and insecure – understandably so – and whilst this was certainly a source of regret, it was not, in a just world, a cause for criminal conviction.

The defence might also have asserted that, even had the non-combatant status of the villagers been totally self-evident to the lieutenant, their killing was hardly his responsibility alone. The company's second platoon, commanded by Lieutenant Stephen Brooks, had also participated in the carnage, whilst two kilometres away, as part of the same operation, Bravo Company's 1st Platoon was moving through the sub-hamlet of My Khe (4) shooting everyone in sight.[126] The orders Calley received from the task force command had evinced no concern for the fate of the inhabitants of My Lai (4): their homes were to be destroyed, yet no provision was made for their safe conduct from the scene.[127] Senior officers monitoring the assault on the hamlet from helicopters circling two thousand feet above,

[125] Hammer, *The Court-Martial of Lt Calley*, p. 79.

[126] The Peers commission estimated that between 50 and 100 inhabitants of My Lai (4), 'comprised almost exclusively of old men, women, children, and babies', had been killed by Brooks' platoon. Goldstein *et al.*, p. 134.

[127] William Peers concluded that Lieutenant Colonel Barker had been aware that civilians would be present in Son My, but gave no instructions to his subordinates about how they were to be handled. This omission 'created the potential for grave misunderstandings as to his intentions and for interpretation of his orders as authority to fire, without restriction, on all persons found in the target area' (*Ibid.*, pp. 94–5). Mary McCarthy commented: 'The men were to murder a hamlet; on that point, the instructions were clear. A veil was drawn as to what was to become of the population. They were to be disregarded, just as though they did not exist. The next step, to conduct them from virtual to real non-existence, then became easy', McCarthy, *Medina* (London: Wildwood House, 1973), p. 32.

together with Captain Medina on the ground, must have known something of what was being perpetrated there, yet they apparently elected not to intervene until it was too late.[128]

In addition, his lawyers might have argued, Calley's permissive reinterpretation of the rules of war represented simply an over-enthusiastic improvisation around the ethical latitudes which the army itself was regularly observing in Vietnam, as it wrenched thousands of civilians from their homes and the means of life, decanted upon them an exotic brew of chemicals and munitions if the injunction to leave was ignored or misunderstood, and responded with inertia and indulgence to instances of rape, mutilation and murder committed by American troops. It was sad but not surprising – the defence might have concluded – that their client should have calibrated his conception of justifiable force against these informal institutional norms rather than the brief, token instruction in the laws of war which he received during his time at Officer Candidate School.

These were not arguments which would have immunized Calley against conviction, nor would they have convinced all in the courtroom that he was totally without sin but, if they had been advanced purposefully and consistently, they might have made the prosecution's task of delineating the exact parameters of his personal guilt much more arduous and difficult than, in the event, it turned out to be. As it was, the lieutenant's legal representatives, led by George Latimer, seemed to have little idea what they were trying to prove. Having been afforded nearly a year to prepare for the trial, they still turned in a quite wretched performance. Latimer remained unwilling to listen to Calley's version of events, and he displayed no interest in the interviews which his assistant, Captain Brooks Doyle, had conducted with potential witnesses.[129] As a result, each successive line of defence offered by Latimer during the course of the court martial was quickly overpowered by conflicting testimony, until the only resource he had left was the story he had not heard – Calley's own account: an unconvincing narrative, irreconcilable with the weight of the evidence and punctuated with the sort of conspicuous evasions that a half-competent attorney would have told him to either abandon or properly resolve. The incoherence of the case for the defence was at one point so transparent that Colonel Kennedy, the trial judge, summoned Latimer and his colleagues to his chambers and warned them of the harm that they themselves were inflicting upon their client's prospects of acquittal.[130]

At first, then, Latimer tried to suggest that those who had died at My Lai (4) had been the victims of helicopter gunships and the long-range artillery bombardment intended to clear a landing zone near the settlement before Charlie Company arrived.[131] Later, he asserted that many of

[128] Goldstein *et al.*, p. 142.
[129] Belknap, pp. 148, 170.
[130] *Ibid.*, p. 169.
[131] Hammer, *The Court-Martial of Lt Calley*, p. 87.

the dead had been Vietcong guerrillas.[132] Successfully proving neither of
these propositions, Latimer raised the issue of combat stress, backing
himself into a sanity defence, and effectively acknowledging both that
Calley had been involved in the killings and that his actions had no military justification. According to this new line of argument, the people of
My Lai (4) met their deaths not as collateral casualties, nor as the wages
of enemy allegiance, but because the lieutenant was mentally incapable.[133]
However, when all three 'expert' witnesses summoned to attest to Calley's
disordered state of mind were swiftly discredited under cross-examination,
this attempt to locate the causes of the massacre in the clinical realm was
also abandoned. Subsequently, during the lieutenant's own testimony,
Latimer seemed content for his client to confute the admission of agency,
which had implicitly accompanied the sanity defence. Calley asserted that
he had not personally participated in any mass killings, shooting only six
to eight times into the ditch, and recalled that the principal intent behind
the orders that he issued to his men – Meadlo in particular – had been the
removal of the villagers from the scene.[134] His own interpretation of the
orders he had received from Medina, however, did allow that they could
be 'wasted' if removal became difficult.[135]

The view which the defence projected of the events which had occurred
in My Lai (4) – and of Calley's role in them – therefore lacked consistency
and coherence. In addition, Latimer and his team were unable to blur the
parameters of their client's responsibility for the massacre by establishing
a direct causative line between his actions – whatever they may have been
– and the commands issued by his superior officers, or between his actions
and the behavioural cues of the broader American military effort in
Vietnam. According to the defence, Calley was merely a neutral instrument
of Captain Medina's will; if the settlement had been destroyed, it was
because Medina had ordered it so.[136] A number of defence witnesses
had indeed affirmed that Medina's briefing to the company had contained
an instruction to 'kill everything that breathed', but their accounts were
rebutted by others.[137] In his testimony, moreover, Medina denied giving
any such direction; the killing, he said, had gone on at Calley's initiative.[138]

One man's account effectively stood against another's, and for many
spectators, as Richard Hammer notes, it was Medina's story which carried

[132] *Ibid.*, p. 179.

[133] *Ibid.*, pp. 214–26.

[134] *Ibid.*, pp. 253–4, 269. In the course of psychiatric evaluations, never released to the
court, Calley acknowledged killing many more civilians than he admitted during his trial
(*Ibid.*, pp. 255–6).

[135] *Ibid.*, pp. 253–4, 269.

[136] *Ibid.*, pp. 184–5.

[137] Belknap, pp. 171, 179.

[138] Hammer, *The Court-Martial of Lt Calley*, pp. 311, 316. The Peers Inquiry concluded
that Medina's orders 'left little or no doubt in the minds of a significant number of men in his
company that all persons remaining in the My Lai (4) area at the time of combat assault were
enemy, and that C Company's mission was to destroy the enemy' (Goldstein *et al.*, p. 98).

'the truer ring'.[139] In any case, even had the defence provided unimpeach-able evidence that Medina had indeed ordered a massacre, its effect upon the court's appreciation of Calley's guilt would have been palliative at best. As both Captain Daniel and Judge Kennedy emphasized in their closing statements to the jury, it was Calley's lawful duty both as an officer and as 'a man of ordinary sense and understanding' to do whatever he reasonably could to stand between what would have been a trans-parently illegal directive and its execution.[140] Instead, he had picked up his rifle and briskly gone to work.

Furthermore, in seeking to prove that the essential responsibility lay with Calley's immediate superior, Latimer permitted the structure of com-mand, which stretched upwards from Medina, to escape the courtroom scrutiny which it was surely due. The culture of negligence and licence which seemed to characterize Task Force Barker and the Americal Division went largely unexplored. Latimer asserted that Calley was a scapegoat, but he did not demonstrate for whom. Of Calley's defence team, only Major Kenneth Raby, a military lawyer, consistently sought to weave the events at My Lai (4) into a wider canvas. Raby suggested that American troops in Vietnam commonly killed unarmed civilians. His efforts to sub-stantiate this proposition, however, were never very successful. On one occasion, he was persuaded by the trial judge not to question a witness about an incident near Duc Pho in which a squad of soldiers had been directed to kill all the inhabitants of a village. As the judge pointed out, the officer concerned had subsequently been talked, by his men, into rescinding the command – testimony that would hardly be helpful to a defence which was otherwise insisting that orders were orders, that subordinates like Calley had no scope for discretion.[141]

The defence was compelling only in its incompetence. Most damagingly, Latimer and his colleagues were unable to disrupt the impression left upon the court by a parade of prosecution witnesses who testified that it had been Calley, not Medina, who had directed the killing on the ground, ordering his men to fire upon the inhabitants of My Lai (4), emptying his rifle on many of them himself.[142] Daniel asked Paul Meadlo: 'Did Lieutenant Calley or did Captain Medina order you to kill?' Meadlo replied: 'I took my orders from Lieutenant Calley.'[143]

Thomas Turner described how he had watched for over an hour as Calley ordered successive groups of villagers into the ditch, collapsing each in turn with bursts from his gun.[144] Indeed, the trial so effectively demonstrated Calley's personal enthusiasm for the grim task of slaughter

[139] Hammer, *The Court-Martial of Lt Calley*, p. 322.
[140] *Ibid.*, pp. 344–53.
[141] *Ibid.*, pp. 196–8.
[142] *Ibid.*, p. 116.
[143] *Ibid.*, p. 163.
[144] Belknap, pp. 162–3.

that the subsequent legal proceedings against Ernest Medina, in which the captain was charged with premeditated murder, came to have little prospect of success. Medina could not be indicted for ordering the massacre, for his denial that he had done so had contributed to Calley's conviction.[145] If the army were to establish Medina's guilt, therefore, it had to prove that he had been aware of the killings as they went on and yet had not acted to stop them, an issue on which the evidence was conflicting and conjectural.[146] The judgment against Calley did not simply affirm his own individual culpability; it actually queered the pitch for the judicial attribution of blame to others, embedding still further the impression that guilt was concentrated, and that the principal cause of the massacre was the murderous aberrance of a single lieutenant. Daniel's response to the closing statement of the defence expressed the point precisely. 'They tell you that the accused was not the only man responsible,' he said. 'Well, I ask you, did anyone else do any more that day than he did?'[147]

In convicting Calley of the premeditated murder of an unknown number of Vietnamese civilians (certainly no fewer than twenty-two), and in sentencing him to life imprisonment with hard labour, the jury in the court martial delivered its assessment of the scale of his crimes in My Lai (4) and the price that he should pay in terms of his own comfort and freedom for what he had done. In terms of the evidence with which it was presented, the court's judgment seems fair, perhaps even generous. Public opinion, however, operated according to a different rationale, consisting in part of the assumption that if guilt was to be ascribed, it had to be shared. Of the 79 per cent of poll respondents who expressed their disapproval of the court's verdict, only 20 per cent did so because they believed that what had happened at My Lai (4) had not been a crime. Seventy-one per cent of the remainder – that is, 56 per cent of the total number polled – disapproved because they took the view that Calley was not the only soldier responsible.[148] By the time of Calley's conviction, David Mitchell and Charles Hutto had both been court-martialled and found not guilty, the charges against Thomas Willingham had been dismissed, Generals Koster and Young had escaped with letters of censure and the effective end of their military careers, whilst Captain Medina and Colonel Henderson had yet to be tried (though they too were eventually acquitted).

To many Americans, therefore, all the burden of guilt and punishment for the massacre at My Lai (4) – a crime in which others were undoubtedly complicit – had fallen upon the shoulders of one man, a fate he seemed to bear with an appealing dignity, as if it was just one more duty to fulfil in a

[145] Major William Eckhardt, Daniel's supervisor, had instructed him not to call Medina as a prosecution witness, because by doing so the government would be seen to have vouched for his credibility. However, the jury in Calley's court martial wanted to hear Medina's account, and so the damage was done (Belknap, pp. 180–3); McCarthy, pp. 60–1.

[146] McCarthy, pp. 60–4.

[147] Belknap, p. 185.

[148] *New York Times* (4 April 1971), p. 56.

long record of loyal military service. Informed of his sentence by the president of the court, Calley saluted and replied: 'I'll do my best, sir'.[149] Very swiftly, therefore, he became the symbol not of atrocity, but of stoicism in the face of conspicuous injustice; the prosecutorial process, through a peculiar inversion, had led to the making of a hero.

Audie Murphy, the most decorated American soldier of the Second World War, told reporters that, in similar circumstances, he might have done the same thing.[150] Interviewed at a rally he had organized in Columbus, Georgia – the closest town to Fort Benning – the Revd Michael Lord, amid scenes of near hysteria, compared the fate of Calley to that of the crucified Christ.[151] In his own moment, this inadequate young lieutenant seemed to magnetize all the frustrations and resentments which had been generated by the war in Vietnam, even more so than Richard Nixon. 'Calley for President?' queried the *National Review*, indeed, as it reflected upon his passage to the centre of public concern.[152]

Over the long months of Calley's trial, the courthouse at Fort Benning and its immediate environs became home not just to the judge and his clerks, to the jury and to Latimer, Daniel and their respective colleagues, but also to a corps of reporters from the national press. Whilst some correspondents visited the trial briefly and went away again, others remained for the duration, witnessing – just as the jury did – the progressive accumulation of evidence against the accused and the poverty of his defence. Their experience may have been critical in determining the reaction of the mainstream media to the verdict against Calley and to the spasm of popular indignation which followed in its wake. The collective education which these reporters received in the damning details of the lieutenant's actions in My Lai (4) provided their institutions with a fund of knowledge and moral conviction, which sustained editorial support for the judgment of the court even in the face of widespread public dissent, even as the White House itself trimmed its response to match the prevailing national mood. In the view of Richard Hammer, most of those who attended the trial throughout, who listened to all the evidence, believed that the jury 'could have arrived at no other decision than the one they did'.[153] Howard K. Smith, commenting for *ABC News*, agreed: 'In this case – from the evidence – it's hard to see that any other verdict but 'guilty' of a clearly forewarned crime was possible.'[154] According to *Life*, 'acquittal

[149] Hammer, *The Court-Martial of Lt Calley*, p. 368.

[150] *New York Times* (2 April 1971), p. 16.

[151] *CBS Evening News*, 31 March 1971, VTNA.

[152] *National Review* (20 April 1971), pp. 408–12.

[153] Hammer, *The Court-Martial of Lt Calley*, p. 6.

[154] *ABC News*, 29 March 1971, VTNA. The following day, in what was, for television news commentators, a rare dissent from the prosecutorial perspective, Smith's colleague, Harry Reasoner, told ABC viewers: 'it is too hard for it to come down to one simple and unprepared man out of the morass of all the confused and casual killing. I could not have voted guilty in this trial', *ABC News*, 30 April 1971, VTNA.

would have been a disaster: here was a responsible officer, not even in the position of being fired upon, who callously mowed down women and children'.[155] The *New York Times* declared that the sentence imposed – life imprisonment with hard labour – afforded 'ample recognition of the seriousness of crimes which no civilized society could condone and of Lieutenant Calley's personal responsibility as an active participant in the slaughter of unarmed civilians and as officer in charge of the troops most directly involved'.[156]

Both *Life* and the *Times*, together with the *Washington Post*, criticized Richard Nixon's decision to release Calley from the stockade pending an appeal and to review the case at the end of the legal process. The President's intervention, *Life* asserted, was 'reckless and dismaying'.[157] The inclination of many Americans to accord the lieutenant the status of martyred hero, meanwhile, was described by *Time* as 'an astounding, indeed sickening distortion of moral sensibility'.[158] Returning to the subject of the court martial, Howard Smith chastised the Revd Francis Sayer, dean of Washington Cathedral, for his declaration that 'Calley is all of us. He is every single citizen in our graceless land.' Smith commented:

> Rev. Sayer may be Calley, but I'm not. Among the many others who are not Calley are the almost 1,000 other platoon leaders in Vietnam who could have, but never did, wilfully shoot children and unarmed women point blank. If it is said that Calley acted on orders, well he was told that such orders were illegal and not to be obeyed. The fact that he ordered one of his men to shoot one of the My Lai victims and that soldier refused shows it can be done.[159]

Even in the American south, the heartland of support for the convicted man, newspapers were prepared to issue correctives to popular assumptions about the case. The *Atlanta Constitution* editorialized: 'War does not excuse the murder of unarmed men, women and children in a non-combat situation no matter how many people say so or how many similar incidents may be cited. And My Lai, by the weight of evidence, was such a situation.'[160] In the Midwest, the fiercely conservative *Chicago Tribune* informed its readers that 'if the jury's finding holds up, the country should resign itself to the fact that a punishable crime did take place and that it can't be brushed under the rug as "part of war" or blamed on Washington'.[161]

The most prominent national news outlets, together with many in the regions, adhered to the prosecutorial perspective, then, even as the majority of Americans registered their disagreement with the judgment of the court,

[155] *Life* (16 April 1971), p. 40.
[156] *New York Times* (1 April 1971), p. 40.
[157] *New York Times* (4 April 1971), 'The Week in Review', p. 12; *Washington Post* (4 April 1971), p. D6; *Life* (16 April 1971), p. 40.
[158] *Time* (12 April 1971), p. 14.
[159] *ABC News*, 5 April 1971, VTNA.
[160] *Atlanta Constitution* (2 April 1971), p. 4–A.
[161] *Chicago Tribune* (1 April 1971), p. 26.

with the notion that Calley should be held legally responsible for his conduct in My Lai (4). For the news magazines in particular, this was a somewhat discomfiting experience, not just because the public response revealed the existence of sizeable cavities within the nation's moral imagination, but also because their staff were unused to this degree of editorial estrangement from the main currents of popular opinion.[162] In mid-April, *Time* reflected anxiously upon what it all meant, comparing the agitation against the verdict to the reopening of a 'wound in American life', a wound caused by the war in Vietnam, a wound 'that will not heal'; the court's judgment had provoked 'an angry, troubling and sometimes ugly hemorrhaging of national passions'.[163] For the editors of *Life*, the controversy surrounding the case revealed a 'kind of masochism', an 'increasing feeling of shame and revulsion at the war'.[164] At this time, these explanations of the public temper were lacking in conviction, for neither journal really understood what was going on; it was as if all rational men had departed for the moon.

As the days and weeks passed, however, the confidence of media institutions in the probity of their editorial support for the verdict seems to have increased, reflecting a decline in the intensity of popular protest and the movement of the Nixon administration, after its initial interventions, towards a more circumspect and judicious public posture on the case. A number of senior officials and advisers, including Secretary of Defense Laird, and John Dean, Nixon's legal counsel, had cautioned against intervention prior to the President making his decisions.[165] Dean informed Haldeman and John Ehrlichman that the trial had revealed evidence of 'particularly aggravated conduct on the part of the accused, even taking into account the combat environment'. Although political considerations determined the President's actions in the short term, the balance of opinion within the executive branch thereafter shifted in favour of those who wanted to elevate the White House above the continuing massacre controversy and out of the military justice system. Legal specialists within the administration had been confronted with a difficult enough challenge constructing post-facto procedural justifications for the decisions already made, and they advised against any further intervention or public comment lest this provoke charges of command influence upon the appellate

[162] For one contemporary analysis of the divergence between media and public reactions to the court-martial verdict, see J. Kraft, 'Lt Calley no media hero', *Washington Post* (4 April 1971), p. D7.

[163] *Time* (12 April 1971), p. 13.

[164] *Life* (16 April 1971), p. 40.

[165] See 'statement on the Calley trial recommended by Secretary Laird', 31 March 1971, folder: 'Calley case 160', Box 18, Ronald Ziegler Numerical Subject File, Staff Members and Office Files, White House Special Files, NPM, NACP; Dean to Ehrlichman and Haldeman, 'Presidential Response – Calley Court-Martial Case', 1 April 1971, folder: 'Chronicle – April 1971', J. Fred Buzhardt Chronological Files, Box 1, Staff Members and Office Files, White House Special Files, NPM, NACP.

process or imply a prejudgment of the case prior to the final presidential review.[166]

Melvin Laird, meanwhile, sent the White House a strongly-worded memorandum expressing the conviction of both the Department of Defense and the Department of the Army that the court-martial verdict had been necessary and just and that 'responsible officials' should do nothing that might encourage the American people to form a different impression. The document stated that 'Calley is not a scapegoat, nor a poor lieutenant singled out to bear the entire burden of a difficult war. His act stands alone in infamy among known atrocities by US Forces in the war.' To pardon him or to drastically reduce his sentence would 'lend substance to the charge that his actions were the product of the war policy', and suggest to American soldiers that 'anything goes'. The implications of such a lesson, for the army and for the nation, were 'incalculable but clearly intolerable.'[167]

By the second week in April, with opinion polls indicating that the American public had overwhelmingly endorsed his decisions with regard to confinement and review, Nixon's advisers seem to have judged that additional interventions in the case would yield only diminishing returns.[168] John Davies of Gallup informed the White House that, having successfully responded to demands for compassionate action, the President would risk an accusation of meddling if he became any more deeply involved.[169] Nixon himself noted with approval the view advanced by Patrick Buchanan that the administration should now move to reaffirm its defence of the Army, 'the process of law in this country, [and] our belief that excesses in combat will not be tolerated'. The President stated: 'This is our position.'[170]

The most notable challenge to the efforts of the administration to affect a Solomonic posture – to suggest that it had maintained a judicious balance between the claims of democratic opinion and the requirements of due process – came from Captain Aubrey Daniel, the prosecutor in Calley's court-martial. On April 3, he wrote a letter to the President in

[166] Fygi to Dean, 'Presidential Actions in the General Court-Martial Case of United States v. Calley', 6 April 1971, folder: 'Calley: April–May 1971', Box 14, John Dean Subject Files, Staff Members and Office Files, White House Special Files, NPM, NACP; Dean to Ehrlichman, Haig and Krogh, 'Discussion Memorandum Re War Crimes Cases', 14 May 1971, folder: 'War Crimes Study', Box 15, John Dean Subject Files, Staff Members and Office Files, White House Special Files, NPM, NACP.

[167] Attachment: Haig to Ehrlichman, 'My Lai', 7 April 1971, folder: 'Calley – April-May 1971', Box 14, John Dean Subject Files, Staff Members and Office Files, White House Special Files, NPM, NACP.

[168] *New York Times* (4 April 1971), p. 56; Opinion Research Corporation poll, 5–6 April 1971. Data provided by Roper Center for Public Opinion Research: www.ropercenter. uconn.edu (accessed November 2003).

[169] Chapin to Haldeman, 9 April 1971, folder: '[cf] ND 8 Military Personnel [1971–74]', Box 41, Confidential Files, White House Special Files, NPM, NACP.

[170] Huntsman to Buchanan, 'Your memorandum dated April 5th entitled "The Calley Situation"', 15 April 1971, folder: 'Staff Memoranda Received, 1971–1972', Box 3, Patrick Buchanan Name File: Action Memos 1971, Staff Members and Office Files, White House Special Files, NPM, NACP.

which he forcefully defended the fairness of the trial and the justice of the jury's verdict and asserted that he would have expected the White House to have done the same. Instead, he said, 'political expediency' had motivated the President to intervene in the case in a manner that 'damaged the military judicial system and lessened any respect it may have gained as a result of these proceedings '.[171]

Identified as 'a hot one' upon its arrival at the White House, Daniel's letter was released to the press on 7 April.[172] Privately, it provoked streams of invective from the President, who labelled Daniel a 'little jerk captain' and ordered Haldeman to call Laird and demand the resignation of Stanley Resor, the Secretary of the Army, whom he suspected of sponsoring the prosecutor's initiative.[173] Nixon also wanted Ehrlichman to 'answer this head on' in a briefing to the press, but Ehrlichman advised against any reflexive public response, judging that it would perpetuate what was probably only 'a one-day story'.[174] Thereafter, in its response to Daniel's allegations, the White House sought to maintain a magisterial façade. During a news conference on 16 April, Nixon expressed his respect for Daniel and the court-martial jury, whilst reiterating that his interventions had been consistent with both the national interest and the integrity of military justice.[175] Having attempted in vain to persuade Secretary Resor to answer Daniel's letter on the President's behalf, the White House settled for a brief reply, signed by one of John Dean's assistants, asserting that the continuing appellate review made it inappropriate for the President 'to respond to the points you have raised' in any greater detail than he had already done and conveying to the prosecutor the President's appreciation that he had been given 'the benefit of your personal views on this subject'.[176]

[171] Daniel to Nixon, 3 April 1971, folder: 'Calley', Box 16, John Ehrlichman: Alphabetical Subject File, Staff Members and Office Files, White House Special Files, NPM, NACP.

[172] Campbell to Cole, 6 April 1971, folder: 'Calley', Box 16, John Ehrlichman: Alphabetical Subject File, Staff Members and Office Files, White House Special Files, NPM, NACP.

[173] Conversation with Haldeman, 7 April 1971, Conversation No. 246-5, White House Reference Cassette No. 419, NPM, NACP. Resor had served as Secretary of the Army under President Johnson and had been retained in the post by the new administration. Although Nixon's advisers were keen to install Republican appointees into all significant posts, Melvin Laird had determined that Resor should be kept on, precisely so that he could act as reviewing officer when the Calley court-martial came to an end. The Secretary of Defense, it seems, wanted any controversial post-trial decisions to be made by a Democrat. Flanigan to Haldeman, 21 July 1970, folder: My Lai 8/83, Papers of *Four Hours in My Lai*, LCHMA, KCL; Flanigan to Haldeman, 'Secretary of the Army', 14 December 1970, folder: My Lai 8/83, Papers of *Four Hours in My Lai*, LCHMA, KCL.

[174] Haldeman diary entry, 7 April 1971, Audio Cassette No. 6, Part 2, Diaries of Harry R. Haldeman, NPM, NACP.

[175] 'Panel interview at the Annual Convention of the American Society of Newspaper Editors', 16 April 1971, *Public Papers of the Presidents: Richard Nixon, 1971* (Washington, DC: US Government Printing Office, 1972), pp. 537–9.

[176] Fielding to Daniel, 21 April 1971, folder: 'Chronicle – 1971', Box 1, J. Fred Buzhardt: Chronological Files, Staff Members and Office Files, White House Special Files, NPM, NACP; Belknap, pp. 203–6.

In the immediate aftermath of the Calley court martial, news reporters found it difficult to identify individuals outside of the media itself who were ready to publicly defend its outcome, with the exception of one of the jurors, Major Harvey Brown, who was interviewed by both CBS and NBC on 1 April.[177] However, as the Nixon administration became less willing to associate itself with those who dissented from the verdict, so press coverage of the national reaction to the trial gradually changed: the early tone of uncertainty and alarm gave way to more assertive attempts to narrate and validate the other side of the story. On 5 April, the television networks reported the views of Senators Jacob Javits and Adlai Stevenson, both of whom denied that any miscarriage of justice had occurred, as well as the conclusion of legal expert Telford Taylor that 'an acquittal here would be disastrous'.[178] Two days later, NBC's Robert Goralski noted that many people in the Pentagon, following his letter to the President, considered Aubrey Daniel to be a kind of hero.[179]

Over time, a certain ease and confidence was also restored to the massacre reporting of the news magazines, and the irrational and amoral tendencies previously detected in popular responses to the Calley trial receded from the centre of editorial concern. In its issue of 23 April, *Life* asserted that the 'wide outrage' which had greeted the verdict 'is less strident now, and a new wave of public opinion is washing over the lieutenant. These second thoughts – displaying less certainty about the harshness of the treatment Calley received – distinguish between the legitimate exigencies of war and murderous excess.'[180] There was a degree of assurance about *Life*'s coverage which had been missing from that of *Time* a week or so earlier. The captions accompanying *Life*'s images of Calley's supporters were neutral in tone – wry, detached vignettes of groups and individuals passing from political significance.[181] In one full-page picture, Anne Moore, the lieutenant's girlfriend, was shown leaving his apartment; taken from a distance, with no indication that Moore knew she was being observed, the image has the cool stigmatizing quality of a surveillance photograph – of the kind, indeed, that investigative writers were to take of Calley himself years later, as they revisited the story of My Lai and he sought obscurity in the routines of an ordinary life.[182]

In the same issue, *Life* reported approvingly on Captain Daniel's letter to the President.[183] Daniel was pictured in military uniform, looking straight

[177] *CBS Evening News*, 1 April 1971, VTNA; *NBC Nightly News*, 1 April 1971, VTNA.

[178] *ABC News*, 5 April 1971, VTNA; *CBS Evening News*, 5 April 1971, VTNA; *NBC Nightly News*, 5 April 1971, VTNA.

[179] *NBC Nightly News*, 7 April 1971, VTNA.

[180] *Life* (23 April 1971), p. 23.

[181] *Ibid.*, pp. 24–5.

[182] See, for example, an image of Calley in 1991 leaving his father-in-law's jewellery store in Columbus, Georgia: Bilton and Sim, p. 241.

[183] The nation's 'second thoughts' about the legitimacy of Charlie Company's actions in My Lai, *Life* asserted, 'were best put into focus not by a politician or a general but by the young Army lawyer who had prosecuted Calley', *Life* (23 April 1971), p. 23.

at the camera. The issue also contained a profile of Major Brown. *Life* noted that Brown was an army veteran of 15 years: he had served two tours in Vietnam and held the Bronze Star for valour. In the initial aftermath of the verdict, the article recorded, the jurors had attracted a 'flood of hate-mail', but now the letters Brown received came 'not from extremists but from people in the center of the spectrum'. These correspondents, Brown said, 'seem to understand what we were faced with and what we tried to do'. On the subject of the killings, Brown commented: 'You don't just round up the enemy and summarily execute them. It's not morally right to do it. Common sense would dictate that'.[184] In reporting thus, *Life* refrained once more from dilating the locus of culpability for the massacre at My Lai (4). William Calley was not presented here as a symbol of America and the condition of its conscience. That status was instead reserved for those who had worked for his conviction and those who had judged him guilty.

By early June, opinion polls conducted for a sociological research programme were indicating that public dissent from the prosecutorial perspective had moderated in intensity since its peak immediately after the end of Calley's court martial, though there remained a stark disparity between the attitudes of the American majority and the editorial positions adopted by the mainstream news media.[185] Fifty-eight per cent of respondents asserted that they disapproved of the lieutenant having been brought to trial. The researchers concluded that those registering this opinion were most likely to come from demographic backgrounds consistent with the expectation that the rules of social behaviour would be set by others, that those rules had to be followed and that as long as an individual did so, he or she would not be held personally responsible for any adverse consequences. According to contemporary sociological theory, this expectation – which was reflected in a strong identification with Calley's defence that he was only following orders – represented the 'normative level' of integration into the national system.

Those who approved of the trial, meanwhile, tended to be grouped in higher socio-economic and educational categories, and were most likely to be integrated into the national system at what the researchers called the 'ideological' or 'role-participant' levels. Ideological integrants in particular were the system's most reliable source of long-term support, because they identified its values with their own, but they were also more capable of discerning when individual system policies departed from those values and, in such instances, of engaging in disobedience or dissent. Thus, respondents approving of the trial were inclined to conceive of Calley's actions in My

[184] *Ibid.*, pp. 26–7.

[185] H. Kelman and L. Lawrence, 'Assignment of responsibility in the case of Lt Calley: preliminary report on a national survey', *Journal of Social Issues*, 28 (1972), 177–212; H. Kelman and L. Lawrence, 'American response to the trial of Lt William L. Calley', *Psychology Today*, 6 (June 1972), 41–5, 78–81.

Lai (4) as a violation of national values rather than as an outcome of system rules, and to believe that, whatever the pressures exerted upon him by senior commanders, it should have been possible for him to have exercised personal responsibility and put down his gun.

The model of ideological integration, interestingly, is compatible with Daniel Hallin's application of the Gramscian theory of hegemony to the mainstream American news media.[186] In Hallin's view, those who work in the media certainly tend to exhibit a reverence for political authority and to subscribe to the ideologies dominant within the nation's political establishment. However, they also maintain a commitment to the ethics of their profession, to the image of the journalist as responsible critic, and to a philosophy of liberal individualism, which can leave them alert to contradictions between the actions of elites and national values and suspicious of the assertion that a respect for authority necessitates the abrogation of personal conscience and responsibility. In similar, though not quite identical ways, both the professional soldier and the professional journalist looked at Calley and saw someone more impoverished than themselves: he was guilty of a kind of capitulation as well as of atrocity.

In contrast to the silences which had earlier prevailed on the subject of My Lai, the period from Seymour Hersh's reports of massacre allegations to the controversy surrounding Calley's judicial fate (from November 1969 to April 1971), was filled with an urgent babble of voices. Only traces of this discursive vortex are recoverable now, in particular the articulations reified by the media in newsprint, cartoons, photographs and recorded television newscasts. By no means all responses to the affair that can be retrieved exhibit satisfaction with the trajectory of its central narratives – the passage from press exposé to court case, from army officer to convict, from acclaimed operational success to certified war crime. Nevertheless, the supposition that the causes of the massacre were essentially local, rooted in the aberrant criminality of a small group of men – whose guilt had a density which could be meaningfully measured through a judicial process – remained a significant trope of the debates about My Lai which took place in the public sphere.

The continued prominence of the prosecutorial perspective was not simply a function of its convenience to power. In late 1969, it was certainly in the interests of the US military and the administration of Richard Nixon to quarantine the massacre within the national consciousness, to limit the extent to which My Lai would produce a new public interrogation of the broader culture of American war-fighting in Vietnam. Such an interrogation might expose current combat tactics in all their diverse dirtiness, exhaust the popular support upon which Nixon's long-term pursuit of a favourable resolution to the conflict relied, and fatally degrade the prestige

---

[186] Hallin, *We Keep America on Top of the World*, esp. pp. 1–55; Hallin, *The 'Uncensored War'*, pp. 5–8.

of the armed services just as they were moving towards a voluntary man-power model. That the executive branch would have been prepared to exploit its institutional prerogatives to prevent the massacre from sabot-aging its policy objectives was apparent from Nixon's later interventions in the case. In the immediate aftermath of the revelations, however, such interventions were not necessary, because the patterns of public and media response did not conflict overtly with administration interests. The machinations of the state, therefore, cannot explain the currency of the view that the primary responsibility for the slaughter at My Lai (4) lay not with the negligent many but instead with the murderous few.

Nor can it be entirely explained by conceptions of the mass media as a hegemonic force, functioning to preserve plebeian confidence in the existing politico-economic order and its core values. A degree of cultural defensiveness was undoubtedly evident in some media responses to My Lai, as editors and commentators sought to establish both the uniqueness of the massacre and the aberrance of its perpetrators within what essen-tially remained a righteous and benign national community. Ultimately, however, the emphasis placed by the press upon the guilt of individuals reflected a set of more mundane factors – the professional imperatives, practices and ethics of mainstream journalism. From the time of the first public revelations in November 1969 onwards, the most immediate news content of the massacre story generally consisted of the changing dynamics of the legal process; it was not the progressive delineation of the institu-tional and cultural context in which the killings at My Lai (4) occurred that constituted the day-to-day development of the story, but rather the movement of the case into its court-martial stages. The prosecutorial perspective was reinforced by the media's need to authenticate and legiti-mize an obscure and controversial news item through the deployment of first-hand testimony, which could never describe the broader constella-tion of responsibility for the massacre as compellingly as it could the flow of fire from one person's gun to another's body, and the fall of that body to the ground.

The obscurity which initially surrounded the events at My Lai (4) also encouraged reporters to explicate the story in simple, human terms, to concentrate their attention on the role of a handful of actors – Calley in particular – who came to embody almost by default all the complex causative forces which converged to effect a massacre in the settlement. In addition, the attitudes of many correspondents most familiar with the case may well have been informed by the failure of the accused them-selves – both in response to the initial revelations and later as their charges came before the courts – to offer a coherent defence of their actions, or at least to mitigate impressions of their personal culpability by illuminating the sanguinity with which the US military as a whole drew down death upon civilians during the war. Finally, it was difficult for representatives of the press – subscribing as they did to a set of professional values which stigmatized meek submission to power – to maintain an empathetic identification with men who claimed to have killed upon demand. Indeed, the affinities between journalistic culture and the prosecutorial perspective were so intimate that they help to explain not just why the media responded in the way that it did to the judicial outcomes of the massacre, but also why most Americans did not.

3

Dispersing culpability

Before the revelations about the massacre at My Lai (4), the indifference with which US armed forces regarded the ambiguities of civilian political allegiance in South Vietnam, and the carelessness and callousness with which they often determined the fate of civilians in the line of American fire, had constituted a form of forbidden knowledge. It was held close both by those who fought the war and by those who reported it, lest disclosure embarrass official narratives of military competence and virtue. Even after the massacre story had broken, and accounts of atrocities committed elsewhere in Vietnam pursued it into the public sphere, most members of the mainstream press did not believe, or want to believe, that there was something systemic about the manner in which American bombs, shells and bullets were felling Vietnamese non-combatants. After all, they could assert, there were locations in the battle zone where the war seemed under control, where officers were conscientious and soldiers well-policed, where firepower was applied with scrupulous accuracy, where the human wreckage was contained. Admittedly, the war in Quang Ngai was not under control, and those responsible for fighting it – the leaders of the Americal Division – offered little moral direction to their men, yet there was no reason to assume, even in that 'horrible, malignant place', that massacre was inevitable.[1] Personal ethics, if robustly professed and expressed in action, should still have exercised a suppressive effect upon whatever pathologies had been excited by battlefield circumstance and licenced by the local command. Most correspondents, like most professional soldiers, would have registered the point – forcefully made years later by novelist Tim O'Brien, who had served as an infantryman in Quang Ngai during 1969 – that context was not everything: 'What about those of us who went through exactly what Charlie Company went through? I went through

---

[1] For an illuminating account of the military situation in Quang Ngai, see H. Norman Schwarzkopf, *It Doesn't Take a Hero: The Autobiography* (London: Bantam Press, 1992), pp. 150–73. On the Americal Division, see Hersh, *Cover-Up*, pp. 26–42.

exactly what they went through in the same place, and we weren't killing babies.'[2]

The elliptical and evasive quality of the media's earlier coverage of the war, however, contributed to the instability and confusion that marked the public response to news of the My Lai massacre. Unbelieving at first, many Americans swiftly thereafter became receptive to the argument that what had happened in the village was, at most, only a modest departure from the behavioral norms of the US military in the conflict at large. To a number of observers, this seemed an illogical reversal of attitudes, but it was broadly consistent with the abrupt change in the volume and tone of available information about the human costs of the war which occurred in late 1969, from incidental whispers of civilian casualties to a clamour of gruesome revelations that cumulatively evoked images of a landscape littered with Vietnamese corpses. Moreover, the passage from scepticism about the reports of an American massacre to an avowal of that massacre's exemplary status required no immediate dissolution of patriotic identifications with the national cause in Vietnam, or of empathetic identifications with the men fighting there. As one member of Calley's local American Legion post in Columbus, Georgia, told *CBS Evening News*: 'First of all I don't believe it happened and I won't believe it happened until somebody proves it to me. And I said in the second place, assuming that it happened, we as veterans can understand how it might happen.'[3]

Public attitudes towards the massacre at My Lai (4), its causes and its correlations with wider American combat practices in Vietnam, were complex and subject to dramatic mutations. The variations in knowledge that informed them and the internal inconsistencies that they often contained render any conclusions about their origins and inspirations tentative at best. In the wake of the massacre disclosures, for example, the critiques of the US military establishment advanced by the anti-war movement were unusually (though not entirely) consonant with the perspectives of the national majority. Most Americans, whether actively opposed to the conflict or not, were prepared to describe the events in the settlement as a crime, and favoured forcing those they considered responsible to account for their actions before a court of law. Most were also inclined to allocate the balance of blame to those situated higher in the military system than the men of Charlie Company, judging either that the killing of civilians had reflected the orders actually given to the soldiers or that it had resulted from other invidious forms of pressure or culpable negligence on the part of the command. What gave unity to this fragile coalition was the conviction that something more than individual malfeasance had effected a massacre and that something more than the imprisonment of William Calley was required before the matter could be laid to rest.

[2] T. O'Brien, 'The mystery of My Lai', in Anderson, p. 174. For an account of his experiences in Quang Ngai, see O'Brien, *If I Die in a Combat Zone* (London: Granada, 1980).
[3] *CBS Evening News*, 16 December 1969, VTNA.

Yet the precise apportionment of responsibility throughout the gradations of military and political authority remained a subject of contention.
Different contributors to the debate often measured very differently the
structuring stimuli given to the massacre by the omissions and commissions that had occurred at various levels of the war command, within the
army leadership in Quang Ngai and Saigon, within the Pentagon and the
Johnson White House, within the wider political and economic establishment, and within the stratum of ethical oversight attended by the demos
itself – the citizens of the United States.

As attributions of blame proliferated, so too did prescriptions for
reform, from the exemplary punishment of culpable senior personnel, to
the revision of military doctrine, to a citizens' inquiry into the scale and
the causes of American war crimes in Vietnam, to withdrawal from the
war, to social revolution, to national acts of atonement and subsequent
spiritual rebirth. The only corrective measures actually enacted, however,
were those that coincided with the self-interest of specific institutions:
for example, the army's introduction of new regulations for training on
the laws of war, which – in return for a modest investment of time and
resources – provided corroboration for the service's claim that it could
learn lessons from experience and implement change, whilst also probably promising some genuine dividends in the form of improved troop
discipline. Otherwise, reform proposals were too controversial or the
reform impetus too evanescent, like a collective sigh for a better America.
On the most contentious issue of all – whether to stay the course in
Vietnam – the massacre left the balance of public attitudes unchanged.
The coalescence of majoritarian and protest sentiment did not stretch as
far forward as ultimate purposes, or as far back as ultimate motivations.
If most Americans were impatient for a conclusion to the conflict,
they maintained a respect for national institutions and for the integrity of
national power, and did not want the United States to be seen to have 'cut
and run' from its commitments; nor were they as exercised as members of
the anti-war movement by the ration of suffering which their country's
arms were daily inflicting upon the population of South Vietnam.[4] Accordingly, they were less troubled than the movement by news of what had
been perpetrated at My Lai (4) and less compelled to support the project
of reparation and reform. Indeed, many of those who, if asked directly,
would have deferred to the position that the massacre was a crime, who
might have allowed in addition that responsibility was corporate and thus
merited some kind of legal or civic inquisition beyond that provided by
the trial of Lieutenant Calley, would have also been amongst the majority
recorded by a Harris poll in January 1970 who affirmed that 'incidents
such as this are bound to happen in a war' – a response which intimated

⁴ H. Schuman, 'Two sources of antiwar sentiment in America', *American Journal of
Sociology*, 78 (1972), 513–36.

the currency of apathy and indulgence more than it did that of conscience and critique.[5]

Though commendable and necessary, the effort to consign elsewhere whatever surplus of guilt had been left unclaimed by the members of Charlie Company was not without hazards. As, under scrutiny, responsibility was dispersed, it became dissipated too, ultimately dwindling the momentum towards reform; a finite supply of outrage chased an almost unlimited number of malefactors (some observers, after all, indicted the entire nation), until virtually everybody apart from Calley eluded a proper accounting. Once liberated from the essential content of the atrocity – the decision made by each soldier to shoot defenceless civilians – guilt expanded to occupy the horizon and so began to look like the condition of life itself. As the philosopher H.D. Lewis commented:

> If blame is in order at all, we tend to shift it from those directly involved to their superiors, and from them to the politicians, and from them to the present state of the community, to 'us all', or indeed to the state of the world at the present time and the course of history. The buck is no longer being passed; it does not come to rest, even on the desk of the President, and it has just disappeared into a morass of hypostatized abstractions.[6]

In a culture where the guilt of massacre is permitted to dissolve into mist, slaughter in war will seem incorrigible; it will resist the jurisdiction of human authority and any measures of redress. In such a culture, it will be those who presume to judge who become the object of contempt. Thus, for many Americans in 1971, what was criminal about the My Lai affair was not what Calley and his men had done in the settlement but the arbitrary justice which had selected him for trial. The communalization of guilt did not lead inevitably to its abstraction, but neither was it obvious where the communalization process should end. As a consequence, though the final attribution of the massacre to some essential component in the constitution of man is the subject not of this chapter, but of the next, the pessimism and anarchy that it invited stalked much of the discourse to be presently surveyed.

The reaction of the American public to the revelations of massacre at My Lai (4), and to the subsequent trial of Lieutenant Calley, exhibited a noticeable intensity, whilst structuring itself in complex and surprising ways; some of the more common judgements made about the massacre, meanwhile, challenged national myths in ways that their exponents seem not to have examined. By April 1971, public attitudes had become volatile and abrasive, less deferential to the opinion and authority of traditionally hegemonic institutions, such as the mainstream news media, the military and even the Presidency: the letters, telegrams and cards sent to the

---

[5] *Time* (12 January 1970), pp. 8, 10–11.
[6] H. Lewis, 'The non-moral notion of collective responsibility', in French, p. 183.

White House by ordinary Americans in the wake of the Calley verdict were, one official noted, 'exceptionally intemperate in nature'.[7] The credibility of these institutions – and their power to discipline public sentiment – seemed to be declining all over, and not just because they often failed, at this time, to speak with a common voice. The status of the media as an objective witness of contemporary events, of the kind that could be trusted to deliver disinterested judgements on matters as controversial as the morality of national policy in Vietnam, was being contested both from within and without.[8] The leaders of the military, meanwhile, had already forfeited much of their hold upon popular esteem by throwing more and more young American bodies at a war which they appeared not to know how to win, and they were in any case implicated in the massacre itself and its subsequent cover-up.

Richard Nixon may have constructed a 'silent majority', but he had done so at the expense of national consensus, stigmatizing opposition and attenuating respect for the Presidency beyond the perimeter of his own electoral base. In addition, whilst the President was quick to collect the immediate political dividends which accrued from his public intimations of sympathy for Calley, he was unwilling to explicitly connect his action to any particular view of where responsibility for the massacre actually lay – ostensibly because that would amount to command influence upon the process of military justice, but also perhaps because the logic of his intervention pointed to the culpability of others more elevated than the convicted lieutenant – those who had directed the war and those who had supported it, Richard Nixon amongst them.

What American political culture lacked in this period, therefore, were clear, cooperative centres of moral authority, willing and able to direct the national debate about the causes of the My Lai massacre into constructive channels, to chasten its excesses, to effect judicial and extrajudicial accountings where merited, and to implement necessary measures of reform. Much of public discourse on the massacre seemed tainted in some way, by political or institutional interest, by the desire to escape criticism or punishment, by ignorance, or by the pursuit of money. For Seymour Hersh, a freelance reporter with no certain source of income, and David Obst, operating his news service on a shoestring, the massacre demanded attention, but it was also a commodity. Obst's telemarketing of the initial story, Hersh commented, was akin to the selling of Campbell's soup. They accepted $10,000 for delivering Paul Meadlo to CBS, 'We needed our expenses covered,' Obst later recalled.[9]

[7] Melencamp to Price, 'Acknowledgment of Communications about the Calley Case', 7 April 1971, folder: 'Calley correspondence', Box 14, John Dean Subject Files, Staff Members and Office Files, White House Special Files, NPM, NACP.

[8] J. Boylan, 'Declarations of Independence', *Columbia Journalism Review*, (November/December 1986), pp. 29–45.

[9] *Time* (5 December 1969), p. 75; Obst, pp. 169–70.

More entrepreneurial still were Ronald Haeberle and Joe Estzerhas, who offered exclusive rights to Haeberle's images of the atrocity to *Life* magazine in return for $120,000. In the event, *Life* bought the US rights for $20,000, with another $15,000 coming from papers overseas.[10] *Esquire* paid $30,000 for the 'confessions' of William Calley, $20,000 of which the lieutenant took himself, the rest going to John Sack, who wrote up his account for publication.[11] Of those who contributed to the massacre story, Ronald Ridenhour and Hugh Thompson were most clearly beyond reproach: they had registered the atrocity for what it was and done what they could to bring it to account, seeking no benefit for themselves. Ridenhour's immediate reward for his endeavours, however, was to be trailed by an investigator working for the White House, at the direct request of President Nixon, who wanted to know 'who is backing him'.[12] Thompson, meanwhile, attracted hate mail, as well as hostile questioning when he appeared before Congress.[13] At moments in the controversy, the culture seemed to judge itself short of the few good men required to render an authoritative verdict on the affair. Almost by a process of will, it failed also to acknowledge those who, by their conduct, had complicated the easy attribution of massacre to culture or nature and made evident just how far from virtue the soldiers of Charlie Company had fallen.[14]

In the view of the men implicated in the killings, they had not actually fallen very far. The first duty of a soldier, they declared, was to follow orders, and with respect to My Lai the orders were, Calley recalled of Captain Medina's briefing on the evening before the assault, 'to go in rapidly and to neutralize everything. To kill everything.'[15] Although this defence ultimately did not convince the jury at the lieutenant's court mar-tial, it received some corroboration from witnesses who had no reason to lie. At his press conference on 20 November, a week after the massacre story had first appeared, Michael Bernhardt – who had not fired a shot in My Lai (4) – was asked whether he was suggesting that Calley, in orches-trating the slaughter in the village, had been carrying out the orders of his commanding officer. He replied: 'I'm not suggesting. I'm saying that's exactly what he did.'[16] Outside the court, the assertion that orders were

[10] Eszterhas, p. 466; Bilton and Sim, pp. 263–4.

[11] Polsgrove, p. 221.

[12] Brown to Butterfield, 10 December 1969, folder: '[cf.] ND 18–4 War Crimes – Trials [1969–70]', Box 43, Confidential Files, White House Special Files, NPM, NACP; Butterfield to Nixon, 'Ronald Lee Ridenhour (And Other Information re My Lai)', 17 December 1969, folder: My Lai 8/83, Papers of *Four Hours in My Lai*, LHCMA, KCL.

[13] T. Angers, *The Forgotten Hero of My Lai: The Hugh Thompson Story* (Lafayette: Acadian House, 1999), pp. 164–70, 178.

[14] Researchers from the Wright Institute found that only a handful of respondents recalled that some of the soldiers in My Lai had refused to shoot civilians. Opton, in Sanford *et al.*, p. 64.

[15] 'The Concluding Confessions of Lieutenant Calley', *Esquire* (September 1971), p. 85.

[16] *CBS Evening News*, 20 November 1969, VTNA.

orders reflected common understandings of military culture; the caveat that the principle of obedience was itself constrained by the laws of war was no better comprehended by most civilians than it seemed to have been by the men under Medina's command. Assessing Paul Meadlo's role in the massacre, Robert Hale – the manager of a pool hall in Meadlo's home town of New Goshen, Indiana – commented: 'He was under orders. He had to do what his officer told him.' Hale's associate, Dee Henry – a veteran of the Second World War and Korea – agreed: 'Anybody who's had any affiliation with the service knows you do what you're ordered to do – no questions asked.'[17]

To believe, as many Americans apparently did, that the behaviour of Charlie Company in My Lai (4) directly reflected the orders it had been given was to shift much of the burden of guilt from the soldiers on to their officers, particularly – if Calley's contention was correct – to the company's commander, Captain Medina, but also conceivably beyond. Medina, of course, rejected the claim that he had instructed his men to kill everyone in the village, and he was not alone in doing so, but even those attentive readers and viewers who registered this dissent might still have elected to assign to him and his superiors the larger share of the blame. Having informed their soldiers (on the basis of erroneous intelligence) that they would confront a hardened enemy force in My Lai (4), no one in the operational command, from Medina upwards, provided any guidance on the treatment of non-combatants encountered in the course of the expected battle. As Charles West recalled in *Life* magazine: 'Nobody told us about handling civilians, because at the time I don't think any of us were aware of the fact that we'd run into civilians. I think what we heard put fear into a lot of our hearts. We thought we'd run into heavy resistance.'[18] Moreover, as the assault proceeded, and as the inhabitants of My Lai (4) were shot on sight or else gathered in groups and mown down en masse, the key figures in the command – Medina, Barker, Henderson, Koster – either paid no attention to what was going on, or chose not to intervene. The precise details of what the command knew and how it had acted did not emerge particularly clearly from media reports on the massacre, but it was nonetheless possible to conclude from the coverage that there had been something seriously amiss with the operation as a whole and to subsequently decide, in Ronald Ridenhour's words, that 'there are a lot of bigger fish in this kettle and they aren't being caught'.[19] In April 1971, 76 per cent of respondents to a Harris poll asserted that 'soldiers at My Lai were only following orders from their higher ups'.[20] Sixty-nine per cent

[17] *New York Times* (26 November 1969), p. 10.
[18] *Life* (5 December 1969), p. 39.
[19] *New York Times* (16 November 1969), p. 58.
[20] Harris to Higby, 5 April 1971, folder: 'Calley', Box 16, John Ehrlichman: Alphabetical Subject File, Staff Members and Office Files, White House Special Files, NPM, NACP.

of those questioned by Gallup, meanwhile, agreed that Calley 'is being made the scapegoat for the actions of others above him'.[21]

That the task force command might have neglected to provide for the safe conduct of civilians in its area of operations, or even that it had knowingly allowed them to be killed, or – worse still – that it had actually ordered their deaths, was a conclusion made more tenable by other atrocity revelations which appeared in the American media in the wake of the My Lai story. What these revelations seemed to suggest was that, all over Vietnam, US soldiers were merrily disregarding the laws of war, and that their officers very often were permitting them – perhaps indeed encouraging them – to do so. On 29 November, the *Chicago Sun-Times* published two photographs on its front page, apparently of an enemy prisoner being thrown from an American helicopter. It printed the commentary of the soldier who took the pictures: 'And here he takes a sky dive without the aid of a parachute. Instant Paratrooper!'[22] Recalling his experience as a correspondent in Vietnam, Frank McCulloch of *Time* stated: 'I have seen men pushed out of airplanes, shot with their hands tied behind their backs, drowned because they refused to answer questions.'[23] On 2 December, *CBS Evening News* broadcast a report from a hamlet in the Mekong Delta, where American troops – nervous after the explosion of a mine – had allegedly poured machine-gun fire into nearby houses, killing a number of those who lived there.[24]

The media's coverage of the massacre and the subsequent trial of William Calley prompted many military veterans to disclose that they too had witnessed or participated in crimes of war whilst serving in Vietnam, either because they judged that there was now a greater likelihood that their claims would be taken seriously and properly investigated, or else to suggest the absurdity of prosecuting individual soldiers for actions that had analogues across the whole of the combat zone. The quantum of atrocity allegations submitted to US Army CID, most of them by active or former service personnel, increased markedly in the final quarter of 1969 and the first half of 1970.[25] Responding to the pictures of the massacre published in the *Cleveland Plain Dealer* on 20 November, one veteran commented: 'I saw things just like that only on a smaller scale, and it never hit the papers.'[26] In March 1971, an NBC reporter interviewed a veteran living in Columbus, Georgia – close to Fort Benning where Calley was being court-martialled. He was asked: 'Why don't they try me? I did

[21] G. Gallup, *The Gallup Poll: Public Opinion 1935–1971: Volume Three 1959–1971* (New York: Random House, 1972), p. 2296.

[22] *Chicago Sun-Times* (29 November 1969), p. 1.

[23] *Time* (5 December 1969), p. 30.

[24] *CBS Evening News*, 2 December 1969, VTNA.

[25] Schopper, 'War Crimes Allegations Other than Son My', 17 January 1971, folder: 'Messages 1971', Box 23, William C. Westmoreland Papers, USAMHI.

[26] *Cleveland Plain Dealer* (21 November 1969), p. 12–A.

the same thing he done.'[27] After the lieutenant's conviction, ten Vietnam veterans in Albuquerque, New Mexico, tried to have themselves arrested, asserting that they were also guilty of war crimes by the definition of the court's verdict. One of the veterans, Chris Vineyard, told Bob Knight of NBC that he had been ordered to bomb and napalm a Vietnamese village: 'I have no idea how many people I killed, but I didn't see anyone come out.'[28]

As atrocity allegations proliferated, and as a number of those who had fought in the war sought to relate their own experiences to what they knew of the massacre in My Lai (4), many Americans found it difficult to discriminate clearly between the actions of Charlie Company and the ethical content of the wider conflict. In April 1971, 50 per cent of those questioned by Gallup took the view that 'the incident for which Lt Calley was tried' was a 'common' occurrence in the war.[29] Eighty-one per cent of respondents to a Harris survey were certain, at the very least, that 'there were other incidents like My Lai involving US troops that have been hidden.' Louis Harris himself commented: 'Most Americans clearly are convinced that Calley was caught up in a web of military orders and practices, common in the Vietnam conflict, and now has been singled out as an object lesson for a crime most believe thousands of other American soldiers probably also committed.'[30] The particular desolation that Calley, Medina and their men had effected in My Lai thus seemed to recede into a conflict-wide tableau of excessive American violence and Vietnamese suffering. The typology of the crime became indistinct, to the point that it could be found everywhere, and to the point that the search for its authors had to be directed to a higher plane, to those whose authority encompassed the war as a whole.

For many veterans who had returned from Vietnam disillusioned with the progress of the conflict and appalled by the human waste that it caused, the revelations about My Lai seemed to offer an opportunity to awaken the American public to the horrors being committed in their name, to generate new momentum towards withdrawal, and to indict senior civilian officials and army commanders for their role in initiating and perpetuating an illegitimate war. Two organizations, their relationship oscillating between competition and alliance, were instrumental in promoting these perspectives: the National Committee for a Citizens' Commission of Inquiry on US War Crimes in Vietnam (CCI) and the Vietnam Veterans Against the War (VVAW). Veterans played little role in coordinating the activities of the CCI, which had been inspired by the work of the International War Crimes Tribunal founded by Bertrand Russell in 1967, but throughout 1970, they were invited by the committee to attend a series of public

[27] *NBC Nightly News*, 22 March 1971, VTNA.
[28] *NBC Nightly News*, 1 April 1971, VTNA; *New York Times* (4 April 1971), p. 56.
[29] Gallup, p. 2296.
[30] Harris to Higby, 5 April 1971, folder: 'Calley', Box 16, John Ehrlichman: Alphabetical Subject File, Staff Members and Office Files, White House Special Files, NPM, NACP.

hearings and press conferences around the country and to speak about their experiences in the war.[31] These events culminated in the National Veterans' Inquiry into US War Crimes held in Washington, DC, in December 1970, at which witnesses recalled the regular use of torture to elicit intelligence from suspected enemy soldiers and supporters, as well as instances when prisoners and civilians were deliberately killed.[32]

Largely dormant since the presidential election of 1968, meanwhile, the VVAW had been revived in the final months of 1969, inspired partly by the nationwide anti-war protests that occurred in October and November, but also because, after the My Lai disclosures, its leaders believed that a more receptive audience might now exist for its views: the movement had been contacted by a number of reporters seeking to follow up on the massacre story.[33] During much of 1970, the VVAW assisted the CCI in its efforts to use the testimony of veterans as a weapon against the war, but in time – having become uncomfortable with the committee's wider ideological agenda – it moved to organize hearings of its own.[34] In late January and early February 1971, the movement hosted the 'Winter Soldier Investigation' at a Howard Johnson's motel in Detroit, during which over a hundred veterans provided accounts of their service in Vietnam, including war crimes that they had witnessed or indeed committed themselves.[35] In April, determined to force the political nation to pay attention to both their stories and their dissent, the VVAW sponsored 'Operation Dewey Canyon III', co-opting the codename for US and South Vietnamese military raids into Laos for its own 'limited incursion into the country of Congress'.[36] Camping at night on the Washington Mall, veterans lobbied members of the legislature and engaged in 'guerrilla theater' (undertaking, for example, mock search-and-destroy missions against government buildings); in a dramatic finale, many threw away their service medals, casting them over a fence at the west steps of the Capitol.[37]

The veterans' argument that the war needed to be stopped because it was causing atrocities reflected a sensitivity not just to the well-being of the population of Vietnam, but also to their own best interests as a distinctive social group. To assert that the crimes of war and other acts of atrocity committed by US servicemen in Vietnam were primarily a product

[31] R. Stacewicz, *Winter Soldiers: An Oral History of the Vietnam Veterans Against the War* (New York: Twayne Publishers, 1997), p. 235.

[32] J. Higgins, 'Horror takes the Stand', *Nation* (4 January 1970), pp. 6–8.

[33] Stacewicz, pp. 205, 233, 235.

[34] W. Scott, *The Politics of Readjustment: Vietnam Veterans Since the War* (New York: Aldine De Gruyter, 1993), p. 18; A. Hunt, *The Turning: A History of Vietnam Veterans Against the War* (New York: New York University Press, 1999), pp. 45, 61–5.

[35] Scott, pp. 18–19; Hunt, pp. 68–72. For extracts from the hearings, see *The Winter Soldier Investigation: An Inquiry into American War Crimes by the Vietnam Veterans Against the War* (Boston: Beacon Press, 1972).

[36] Stacewicz, pp. 240–1.

[37] Scott, pp. 20–3; Stacewicz, pp. 241–9; Hunt, pp. 94–119.

of the conflict itself was to suggest that responsibility for those crimes should not be borne by individual soldiers, but either by those who had exercised executive power over national war policy or by the American people as a whole, for their refusal to take notice of what was really going on. '[U]nless we exposed how the service trained us and how society used us,' recalled one of the 'Winter Soldiers' later, blame for wartime atrocities 'wouldn't be redirected toward the government – it would be directed down toward the GIs, servicemen, and lower-ranking officers.'[38] For this reason, perhaps, a number of witnesses who testified at the National Veterans' Inquiry and at the VVAW hearings in Detroit were unwilling to cooperate with criminal investigations into their claims: until the army was prepared to indict the men that the veterans judged most responsible, every ordinary soldier prosecuted for war crimes would be a scapegoat.[39] It was for this reason, most certainly, that anti-war veterans were active in the dissent against the trial and conviction of William Calley. At a VVAW demonstration in New York, John Kerry – then a prominent member of the veterans movement, more recently a candidate for the White House – declared: 'We are all of us in this country guilty for having allowed the war to go on. We only want this country to realize that it cannot try a Calley for something which generals and Presidents and our way of life encouraged him to do. And if you try him, then at the same time you must try all those generals and Presidents and soldiers who have part of the responsibility. You must in fact try this country.'[40]

Also informing the activities of the anti-war veterans movement were a nascent set of socio-psychological ideas about the relationship which needed to be negotiated between civilian society and the soldiers who had returned or would eventually return home from Vietnam. These ideas originated in the observation that many former servicemen were struggling to readapt to civilian life. Early investigations suggested that veterans' difficulties were often exacerbated by feelings of guilt and/or trauma, attributable in some way to their experiences in the war. Two kinds of experience were most commonly held to stimulate such feelings: the death of comrades and participation in acts of atrocity.[41] Sometimes unable or

---

[38] Stacewicz, pp. 239–40.

[39] Schopper, 'War Crimes Allegations Other than Son My', 17 January 1971, folder: 'Messages 1971', Box 23, William C. Westmoreland Papers, USAMHI; memo extract: '"Winter Soldier Investigation" Testimony" (WSI)', 7 January 1972, folder: 'Action File – "Winter Soldier Investigation" Hearings, 1971 [Part 1 of 2]', Box 4, Vietnam War Crimes Working Group Central File, Records of the Vietnam War Crimes Working Group, Office of the Deputy Chief of Staff for Personnel, RAS, RG319, NACP. The refusal of witnesses to cooperate with investigators, combined with instances when their accounts either could not be substantiated or were contradicted by other evidence, provoked the historian Guenter Lewy to criticize the sponsors of both the CCI and VVAW hearings for favouring sensation over veracity. See Lewy, pp. 313–19.

[40] *Time* (12 April 1971), p. 15.

[41] R. Lifton, *Home From the War: Vietnam Veterans: Neither Victims nor Executioners* (London: Wildwood House, 1974), pp. 100–1.

unwilling to tell their stories to their immediate families and friends, small, disparate groups of veterans around the country began to meet together to discuss what they had witnessed and what they had done in Vietnam, and what they now thought about their time in the service and the ongoing war.[42] In their own rough, independent fashion, these veterans were pursuing a talking cure for their troubles.

They were encouraged in this therapeutic endeavour by the attentions of Robert Jay Lifton, a psychiatrist known for his work with survivors of Hiroshima. In November 1969, Lifton had read an account of the My Lai massacre in the *New York Times* and resolved thereafter to apply his professional expertise in ways that might also serve the project of ending the conflict in Vietnam: in particular, he advanced the hypothesis that the conditions of warfare prevailing in that country made atrocities inevitable.[43] To this end, Lifton conducted an intensive series of interviews with Michael Bernhardt and in late 1970, having met with members of the VVAW in New York, he agreed to participate in and lend a clinical perspective to the weekly veterans 'rap groups' which the local chapter hosted in its office.[44] As a result of his association with the veterans, Lifton became convinced that the Vietnam war was indeed 'an atrocity-producing situation'. In his view, the frustrations of fighting against an enemy, which was often indistinguishable from the civilian population, combined with the undifferentiated insistence upon aggression to which military recruits were exposed during training, with the command emphasis upon high body counts and the routine dehumanization of the Vietnamese, created a combat environment in which 'men of very divergent backgrounds – indeed just about *anyone* – can enter into the "psychology of slaughter"'. The behavioural traits fostered by this environment had been revealed in their essence during the massacre at My Lai (4), which Lifton considered 'exceptional only in its dimensions'.[45]

Atrocity was responsible for the veterans' distress, the war was responsible for atrocity, and the American nation as a whole, Lifton asserted, was basically responsible for the war. That the American people were ultimately implicated in the crimes committed against the Vietnamese was a truth about which they remained largely in denial, and whilst that was still the case, the veterans could not achieve a full recovery from their experience. They could find some solace and some resource for transformation in talking to other veterans, but until their words began to be carried beyond the confines of their local rap groups, even those with access to psychiatric expertise, the cure would be fragile, incomplete, prone to regression. In Lifton's view – and it was a view that came to influence many subsequent socio-psychological reflections upon the veterans'

---

[42] *Ibid.*, pp. 295–8; Scott, pp. 6–7, 14–15.
[43] Lifton, pp. 16–17.
[44] *Ibid.*, pp. 17–18; Scott, pp. 14–15; Hunt, pp. 86–8.
[45] Lifton, p. 42.

condition – what they required (and what American society itself required before it too could 'heal' from the Vietnam war) was the communalization of their guilt and their trauma.[46]

'[T]o do what the veterans ask,' Lifton declared, 'would mean confronting the responsibility of the society as a whole, and of its leaders in particular, for the killing and dying. It would require the most intense exploration of shared forms of guilt as well as revitalizing images beyond that guilt.'[47] When the anti-war veterans discarded the traditional symbols of martial prowess, when they invited the media to broadcast their confessions of atrocity, and when they insisted that blame could not be ascribed just to themselves, they were engaged in a quest for the relief of their pain as well as in a dissent against national policy in Vietnam: 'For such people not only is protest necessary to psychological help – it *is* psychological help.'[48]

The veterans associated with the CCI and the VVAW were animated by their own particular peer-group interests as they sought to advertise the wider constellation of agency and power that they considered responsible for American atrocities in Vietnam. However, though their motivations (and many of their methods) may have been unique, their critiques coalesced with arguments advanced in other prominent commentaries upon the war and, more specifically, upon the massacre at My Lai (4). One such contribution to the national debate about the massacre was made by Telford Taylor, who had served as a senior American prosecutor in the trials of the Nazi elite at Nuremberg, and was now teaching law at Columbia University. In late 1970, Taylor published *Nuremberg and Vietnam*, a volume that assessed the applicability of the legal principles developed during those trials and during the prosecution of Japanese leaders to the war that the United States was currently waging in Indochina. Most strikingly, he concluded that the same judgment handed down in the trial of General Tomayuki Yamashita by the US military commission in Manila – that he had failed to exercise effective control over his soldiers, thus fostering a permissive environment in which they committed a whole catalogue of atrocities – could be used to indict the highest levels of the American military command in Vietnam. The massacre at My Lai (4), Taylor noted, was in its dimensions probably 'out of the ordinary', but there were 'numerous indications that our troops have killed many other civilians under parallel circumstances, and equally in violation of the laws of war'.[49]

---

[46] See, for example, A. Egendorf, *Healing from the War: Trauma and Transformation after Vietnam* (Boston: Shambhala, 1986), and J. Shay, *Achilles in Vietnam: Combat Trauma and the Undoing of Character* (New York: Atheneum, 1994).

[47] Lifton, p. 132.

[48] *Ibid.*, p. 69 (italic in original). *Life* described the Winter Soldier Investigation as 'a sort of mass therapy session with political overtones.' *Life* (9 July 1971), p. 25.

[49] T. Taylor, *Nuremberg and Vietnam: An American Tragedy* (Chicago: Quadrangle Books, 1970), p. 139.

Whilst the army's written directives on the rules of engagement and the treatment of non-combatants were – as the published fragments of the Peers report indicated – 'virtually impeccable', the quality of initial training in their provisions had been poor, with minimal command reinforcement taking place in the field.[50] In the combat environment of Vietnam, where US military forces would routinely encounter civilians in the course of their operations, 'it should have been a matter of the highest priority to insure, by indoctrination and subsequent policing, that the troops should treat the Vietnamese as human beings with lives worth preserving'. Instead, Taylor asserted, 'it is all too clear that the Army's attitude and performance in this area have been woefully inadequate'.[51] To the army's further dismay, Taylor appeared on the Dick Cavett television show in January 1971, along with a representative from the CCI, and declared that if the standards of Nuremberg were indeed applied to the conduct of the conflict in Vietnam, General Westmoreland might well be convicted of war crimes.[52]

In the view of other observers, the massacre at My Lai – like many acts of destruction committed elsewhere in the war-zone – was as much the product of deliberate policy as of command negligence. Reporting for the *New Yorker* in 1967, Jonathan Schell had described how those managing and implementing the American programme of pacification, which sought to divorce enemy guerrillas from their sources of food, shelter and support amongst the rural population, had come to the conclusion that, in the most contested areas, this could only be achieved through the complete destruction of Vietnamese villages and the wholesale relocation of their inhabitants to refugee camps under government control. These camps, however, were poorly provisioned and quickly became overcrowded, with the result that – as the US military proceeded with its side of the pacification effort – it began to receive requests from officials in charge of resettlement operations that no further refugees be generated.[53]

In late November 1969, Schell, writing once more in the *New Yorker* (and also in a letter, co-signed by his brother Orville, to the editor of the *New York Times*), stressed the continuities that had existed between pacification as actually practised and the recently reported massacre. Instructed not to evacuate any more people from the villages they destroyed, American military units had simply decided to destroy the people too, bombing them from the air, often without warning. In the sense that it was committed by troops on the ground, the slaughter in My Lai (4) may have been unusual, Schell declared, but 'there can be no doubt that such an atrocity was possible only because a number of other methods of

[50] *Ibid.*, pp. 167–8.

[51] *Ibid.*, p. 174.

[52] Schopper, 'War Crimes Allegations Other than Son My', 17 January 1971, folder: 'Messages 1971', Box 23, William C. Westmoreland Papers, USAMHI.

[53] Schell, *The Real War*, p. 257.

killing civilians and destroying their villages had come to be the rule, and not the exception, in our conduct of the war'. He concluded, therefore, that 'the issue of the massacre at My Lai is inextricably bound up with the issue of our entire presence in Vietnam. And although any men who are accused of participation in the massacre cannot be exonerated on this account, when we ask ourselves who is responsible we cannot rest the blame on them alone, nor can we exonerate ourselves by imposing heavy penalties on them.'[54]

That the behaviour of William Calley and the rest of Charlie Company could not be explained (or judged) without reference to the wider attrition of ethics, pity and care that now seemed evident in almost every aspect of the American war effort was a view often reprised in the liberal news media in late 1969, for it was consistent with the posture of opposition to the conflict that virtually all of these outlets had adopted by this time. In its first editorial on the massacre, the *New York Times* observed: 'The face-to-face shooting of civilians in a village street is not far removed morally, if at all, from the indiscriminate shelling or bombing of civilians from a distance, as happens regularly in the "free fire zones." '[55] What had happened in My Lai (4), commented the *Washington Post*, 'cannot be written off as some isolated aberration. For all its horror, in a certain sense it is part and parcel of the war, removed only in degree from what is known to be commonplace: the indiscriminate killing of South Vietnamese civilians by American saturation bombing, by American artillery fire, by isolated infantry skirmishing.'[56]

Between the initial massacre disclosures and the end of Calley's court martial, with no imminent withdrawal in sight, with the conflict having been widened into both Cambodia and Laos, the inclination of these newspapers to devolve My Lai into what they considered the larger crime of the war itself seems to have deepened, even as they continued to hold the individual soldiers who had killed civilians in the village personally responsible for their actions. 'We kill civilians because the enemy is among them,' wrote Frank Mankiewicz and Tom Braden in a commentary published in the *Post*. 'We kill their livestock because it may feed the enemy. We use chemicals forbidden in the United States because – although they may cause deformed births – they defoliate so that the enemy can be found. By these standards, can [Captain] Medina be far from the mark in suggesting that there was no "atrocity" in My Lai?'[57]

Discussing the question of war crimes in the *New York Times Book Review*, Neil Sheehan declared that Calley and his men 'were doing with their rifles what was done every day for reasons of strategy with bombs

[54] *New York Times* (26 November 1969), p. 44; J. Schell, 'Notes and comments: talk of the town', *New Yorker* (20 December 1969), pp. 27–9.
[55] *New York Times* (22 November 1969), p. 36.
[56] *Washington Post* (26 November 1969), p. 12.
[57] *Washington Post* (4 April 1971), p. A21.

and artillery shells'.[58] Whatever was eventually learnt about the disposition of responsibility for the massacre, the *Times* itself editorialized, the most immediate priority 'should be to end a conflict that has become a continuing atrocity, "wasting" the moral and physical resources of everyone involved'.[59]

The mass killing of Vietnamese civilians in My Lai (4), asserted other commentators, correlated with the practices of the American military elsewhere in Vietnam, not just because non-combatant casualties had become, across the whole of the conflict, an acceptable residual of the application of force; rather, it expressed precisely the underlying logic of US national policy in the war, which was genocide. The introduction of that arresting word – genocide – into sober discussions of Vietnam predated the massacre by a number of months. In his address to the Russell tribunal in 1967, the French philosopher Jean-Paul Sartre had argued that the leaders of the United States, considering the war to be a test of their military and political credibility, had insisted that the people of Vietnam make a choice between submission to American power and their own destruction.[60] Submission, the Vietnamese understood, would constitute just another kind of collective death, so they resisted; what resulted, thereafter, was genocide, 'total war waged to the end by one side and with not one particle of reciprocity'.[61]

Two years later, Townsend Hoopes – who had served in the administration of Lyndon Johnson as Under-Secretary of the Air Force – came close to conceding the charge, albeit with a graceful twist of reasoning which converted genocide into a deliberate decision of the Vietnamese themselves; confronted with 'unanswerable military power', yet retaining a 'capacity for endurance in suffering' characteristic of the Asian poor, they had elected to persist in their struggle, thus 'inviting' their fate.[62] Writing after the close of the My Lai courts martial, the journalist Frances Fitzgerald observed that, though William Calley and his men could not be absolved entirely of blame for the massacre, 'there was a certain sense in which it could be said that the responsibility belonged to American policy in Vietnam'.[63] Atrocity mimicked strategy in both its causes and effects. For those directing the war just as much as for ordinary GIs, the distinction between communist guerrillas and civilians was more difficult to define than the divide that prevailed between Americans and Vietnamese. Whilst resistance continued, punishment would have to be collective, for there was no other way of ensuring that the enemy indeed would be punished. 'No one in the American government consciously planned a

[58] Sheehan, 'Should we have war crimes trials?', p. 31.

[59] *New York Times* (1 April 1971), p. 40.

[60] J.-P. Sartre, 'On Genocide', in Limqueco and Weiss, pp. 350–65.

[61] *Ibid.*, p. 364.

[62] T. Hoopes, *The Limits of Intervention* (New York: David McKay Company, Inc., 1969), pp. 128–9.

[63] F. Fitzgerald, *Fire in the Lake: The Vietnamese and the Americans in Vietnam* (Boston: Little, Brown and Co., 1972), p. 372.

policy of genocide,' Fitzgerald asserted. 'The American military commanders would have been shocked or angered by such a charge, but
in fact their policy had no other military logic, and their course of action
was indistinguishable from it.'[64]

'This stuff would stop if we'd hang a couple of senior commanders.
If it's no longer condoned, then it will cease.' Such was the conclusion of
Lieutenant Colonel Anthony Herbert, the highest ranking officer to participate in the Winter Soldier investigation.[65] It did not seem an entirely
frivolous endeavour, in the eighteen or so months after the revelations of
massacre at My Lai (4), to assert that those who had directed the conflict
in Washington and Saigon should be held to judicial account for whatever
contribution they had made to a combat situation in which US soldiers
were regularly committing acts of atrocity against Vietnamese civilians:
for failures of indoctrination in and enforcement of the rules of engagement; for establishing a culture of strategic violence so liberal that indiscriminate killing looked like official policy to many of their men; and, in
the view of some legal commentators, for initiating and prosecuting a
conflict that conformed to the Nuremberg definition of an 'aggressive war'.
It did not seem an entirely frivolous endeavour, in particular, to General
Westmoreland, who viewed the allegations with such concern that he
commissioned army lawyers to write a lengthy report defending his conduct of the conflict.[66]

Yet even the most forthright critics of the moral character of the war
seemed to hesitate before the proposition that its most senior military and
civilian commanders should all be arrested and put on trial. They may
have sensed that the American public had no stomach for such a show,
retaining doubts about the reach of criminal liability to individuals who,
though probably negligent, had directed no atrocities themselves. In the
late spring of 1971, a majority of poll respondents agreed that officers
senior to Lieutenant Calley bore much of the blame for his deeds; only
22 per cent, however, believed it reasonable to convict American generals for crimes they had not personally ordered.[67]

Amidst ambivalence of this kind, any campaign to reprise the proceedings of Nuremberg with respect to Vietnam was likely to fail. In the view
of Telford Taylor, Westmoreland was comparable to Yamashita, but it was
less essential that this analogy be tested in court than that the nation
embark upon 'a dispassionate, thorough inquiry into our conduct of the
war'.[68] In his celebrated essay on the subject, Neil Sheehan came to the

[64] *Ibid.*, p. 375.

[65] *Life* (9 July 1971), p. 24.

[66] 'Final Report of the Research Project: Conduct of the War in Vietnam, May 1971',
Box 25, William C. Westmoreland Papers, USAMHI. See also S. Zaffiri, *Westmoreland: A
Biography of General William C. Westmoreland* (New York: William Morrow & Co., 1994),
pp. 342–3.

[67] Kelman and Lawrence, 'Assignment of responsibility', pp. 188, 199.

[68] Taylor, *Nuremberg and Vietnam*, p. 182; *Life* (9 April 1971), p. 23.

same cautious conclusion: 'the cleansing of the nation's conscience and the future conduct of the most powerful country in the world towards the weaker peoples of the globe, demand a national inquiry into the war crimes question. What is needed is not prison sentences and executions, but social judgments soberly arrived at, so that if these acts are crimes, future American leaders will not dare to repeat them.'[69]

Whatever crimes recent American leaders had committed (and whatever crimes current leaders continued to commit) occurred primarily because their policies were compatible with the tolerance levels of the national majority, or because that majority was indifferent to its own obligation of oversight. In the view of those implicated in the My Lai massacre, civilians had been killed in the settlement because – of the outcomes available in that particular situation – it seemed the one most closely akin to a military victory, and victory, after all, was the will of the American people. 'At times now, I lie awake,' Calley stated after his conviction. 'I think of Mylai and say, *My god. Whatever inspired me to do it?* But truthfully: there was no other way. America's motto there in Vietnam is "Win in Vietnam," and in Mylai there was no other way to do it. America had to kill everyone there.'[70] To the extent that guilt existed, therefore, it was collective, a condition from which even – perhaps especially – the arbiters of justice themselves could not escape. Speaking on the day after the jury had returned its decision in the Calley court martial, Ernest Medina declared: 'I think we all as American citizens must share in the guilt of Lt Calley. I think that every member in the United States Army and each member of the jury, as members of the United States Army, will also share in that verdict of guilty.'[71]

Of course, it was in the interests of both Medina and Calley to insist that culpability was dispersed, but the claim that the American nation as a whole was implicated in their crimes was not made by them alone. Surveying the massacre for its wider meanings, many commentators arrived at similar conclusions, some no doubt simply because there was an agreeable ring of moral profundity to the assertion that 'we all share the guilt'. For others, however, the massacre had identifiable origins in the failures of national politics and the content of national culture. The inhabitants of My Lai (4), they asserted, might not have died had the American people more swiftly registered the extent of the support that existed in South Vietnam for the insurgency against the regime in Saigon. Such an recognition would have raised an awareness that the human costs of US military intervention would be extortionate, with no certainty of mission success. The outcome of Calley's trial, declared the *Nashville Tennessean*, 'reflects back on the country that sent him to Vietnam to save democracy in the

[69] Sheehan, 'Should we have war crimes trials?', p. 33.

[70] 'The Concluding Confessions of Lieutenant Calley', *Esquire* (September 1971), p. 86 (italics in original).

[71] *CBS Evening News*, 30 March 1971, VTNA.

form of the Thieu government, to fight a different war than he had ever known in a way that was to shock Americans, at last, by the brutality of it'.[72] As civilian casualties indeed began to accumulate, additional commentaries suggested, they had received little attention within an obtuse and incurious American public sphere. 'The press is guilty,' wrote Mankiewicz and Braden, 'not for doing what Agnew said it was, but for not doing it enough.' They went on: 'The American people are guilty, too – we didn't want to hear it the way it was.'[73] 'Few of us,' observed Wright Institute psychologist Edward Opton, 'have done much that was person-ally inconvenient to discover or to fight against either the root sources or the proximal causes of My Lai.'[74]

A memory of collective indifference to the consequences of war, there-fore, contributed to assertions that the American nation itself bore re-sponsibility for the massacre; so too did the perception that what Charlie Company had perpetrated in My Lai (4) had been informed by values, attitudes and practices which were actually conspicuous across much of mainstream American society and culture: ideological anti-communism, racial prejudice, warrior models of masculinity, a willing submission to authority. As one combat veteran, Master Sergeant Don Duncan, declared of those who had confessed to atrocities during the Winter Soldier hear-ings in Detroit: 'Whatever it was that was in these men, that allowed them to do the things they did, is in all of us. We start taking it in, if by no other process, at least by osmosis, from the day we are born in this country.'[75] The apparent ordinariness of the soldiers involved, the absence of any radical disparities between their cultural and psychological formation and that undergone by most other young American males, was often a theme of commentaries upon the massacre.

'The deed was not performed by patently demented men,' *Time* pointed out. 'Instead, according to the ample testimony of their friends and rel-atives, the men of C Company who swept through My Lai were for the most part depressingly normal. They were Everyman, decent in their daily lives, who at home in Ohio or Vermont would regard it as unthinkable to maliciously strike a child, much less kill one.'[76] In November 1970, the first extracts from William Calley's 'confessions' appeared in *Esquire*, complete with a photograph on the cover of the lieutenant – smiling – in the company of four small Asian children. John Sack, the writer who had prepared the article for publication, hoped that Americans would look at the image and say: 'He isn't a murderer. *And ask*, Well who is the murderer then? *And the answer*, It's us.'[77]

[72] *Nashville Tennessean* (31 March 1971), p. 10.
[73] *Washington Post* (4 April 1971), p. A21.
[74] Opton, in Sanford *et al.*, p. 58.
[75] *The Winter Soldier Investigation*, p. 167.
[76] *Time* (5 December 1969), p. 23.
[77] Polsgrove, p. 229 (italics in original).

1 Inhabitants of Xom Lang/My Lai (4) lie dead on a trail. Amongst the victims were Truong Thi Thu (4) and Truong Thi Bi (13).

2 Women and children in Xom Lang/My Lai (4), moments before they were killed. US Army CID identified the victims as: Do Thi Be (far left), Do Thi Phu, Ba Moi and Ba So (front), Do Thi Can and her son Do Hat (right), and Do Thi Nhut (far right).

3 General William Peers (with cigar) visits the site of the massacre, January 1970.

4 A view of Xom Lang at the time of Peers's visit, during the rainy season.

5 William Calley with his attorney, George Latimer, outside the courthouse at Fort Benning, February 1970.

6 A statue expresses pity and defiance at the Son My memorial, February 2004.

7 The ditch at which many inhabitants of Xom Lang were killed, February 2004.

8 The reception building and garden at the Son My memorial, February 2004.

9 The museum at the Son My memorial, February 2004.

10 The hospital in Son My, built by an American charity, February 2004.

In the view of *The Progressive*, reflecting on the popular response to the outcome of the Calley trial, Americans judged themselves complicit in the crimes committed at My Lai (4): 'If he is guilty, they say, so are we. He is, and we are.'[78] This was not purely an editorial conceit. Many ordinary US citizens, though they often lived and worked at a considerable geographical and functional remove both from the execution of the massacre and from the direction of the war, did indeed feel some measure of personal responsibility for the fate of the settlement, some sense of national shame. When questioned by *Wall Street Journal* reporters about her reaction to the initial news of the killings, Mrs James Greene of Los Angeles replied: 'I was appalled. I didn't know we were like the Germans in World War II.'[79] In a second survey conducted by the Wright Institute in spring 1970, several respondents expressed their conviction that 'Americans, including themselves, were ultimately responsible for My Lai'.[80] When, after the end of Calley's court martial, the ten veterans from Albuquerque declared themselves also to be war criminals and asked to be arrested, they were accompanied by four women who professed, according to NBC reporter Bob Knight, that they too were guilty 'because they paid taxes that supported incidents such as the one at My Lai'.[81] On 2 April, Barbara Sherman of Goldendale, Washington, composed a poem about the trial, entitled 'Wars of Men', a copy of which she later mailed to the lieutenant. The final verse asked:

Is it prison, or should we stand
    by his side?
Now it [is] the time for all America to
    decide.
But remember, did he want guns or
    to give commands,
Was he given a choice of war, or
    of his own home land,
Is it only he, that should be
    sentenced and crucified
Was he the only man to cause others
    to die?[82]

It is evident, in addition, that many Americans looked at the men of Charlie Company, and William Calley in particular, and did indeed recognize themselves, although it was far from inevitable that these identifications, when they occurred, would admit any mutuality of remorse. Those who

[78] 'Calley: Thee and We', *The Progressive* (May 1971), pp. 5–6.
[79] *Wall Street Journal* (1 December 1969), p. 1.
[80] Opton, in Sanford *et al.*, p. 64.
[81] *NBC Nightly News*, 1 April 1971, VTNA.
[82] Sherman to Calley, *c.* December 1971, folder: 'Incoming Public Letters – Calley Case, 1972 (Unanswered)', Box 25, Records of the Calley General Court-Martial, 1969–1974, Office of the Clerk of the Court, Records of the Judge Advocate General (Army), RG153, NACP.

imagined a walk in Calley's shoes, from civilian life to the army, from the massacre to the courthouse, might well have been projecting a perception of their own submission to the work of arbitrary powers, rather than a conviction that it was they as much as Calley who had been represented in his crimes. Whichever it was – guilt that was shared or not claimed at all – the ethical distance between the public and the immediate perpetrators of the massacre appeared to diminish, and in some instances, perhaps, it entirely collapsed.

The assertion that the nation itself was responsible for what happened at My Lai (4), that Calley was merely an ordinary young American doing what he reasonably believed to be his job, was a prominent feature of the defence offered by George Latimer during the lieutenant's trial, inside the courthouse and, probably more effectively, also outside, in his statements to the press. Latimer adopted a sorrowful, paternal tone when speaking of his client, invoking his service in the army, contemplating his fate at the hands of the court. On the day of the verdict, Latimer's lament at the outcome was carried on *CBS Evening News*: 'Persons can go and not be drafted: they'll get six months or a year. Boy goes over there, is loyal enough to go over and fight. He fights, kills somebody in fighting and he gets the gallows.'[83] The next afternoon, before the jury retired to decide upon a sentence, the attorney informed them that 'some small considera- tion should be given to a boy who did not necessarily want to go to Vietnam but was sent there, a boy who did not want to kill anybody but who thought he had to'.[84]

The point may have been reinforced, not always intentionally, by the media's coverage of the massacre story. To reduce the frame of reportage, to look for clues to an event in the lives of one or two of the individuals involved, was a strategy often used by the press when the wider contours of that event remained rather indistinct; it was a means of achieving a degree of news definition. In the case of stories like My Lai, this manner of address might produce a confusion of the clue with the cause, em- bedding the impression of a limited circumference of guilt. Yet, when the men of Charlie Company were represented in the media, it was frequently as members of a recognizable national community, in army uniform or at home, in the company of family and friends, surrounded by the routine goods and chattels of an ordinary American life. In his first report on the case, Seymour Hersh described William Calley as 'boyish-looking' (as did an early story in the *New York Times*), mentioned his nickname, 'Rusty', and detailed the normative aspects of his military service: 'Until the incident at Pinkville, he had received nothing but high ratings from his superior officers, and also was scheduled to be awarded, he said, the Bronze and

[83] *CBS Evening News*, 29 March 1971, VTNA.
[84] Hammer, *The Court-Martial of Lt Calley*, pp. 366–7.

Silver stars for his combat efforts.'[85] As other newsmen moved in to investigate the allegations, their reports were regularly accompanied by images of the lieutenant, neatly attired in military dress.[86]

Reading newspapers and magazines, surveying the coverage on television, Americans were also given the opportunity to imagine the men of Charlie Company in a civilian landscape, as people they grew up with, as people they knew well. After Paul Meadlo had appeared on *CBS Evening News*, the *New York Times* reported from his home town of New Goshen, Indiana. In this place of 'chunky church spires and white clapboard houses,' Meadlo – or 'Paul David', as the article called him – was apparently 'a familiar figure shouldering up to the bar at Hutch's Hut or warming his hands over the pot-bellied stove at Olivero's Grocery'. He was also popular: 'Townspeople questioned today responded with one voice: "A very nice boy", "the nicest guy you'd ever want to meet", "easy-going, got along with everybody", "never had any trouble out of him. Wish I could say the same about some other youngsters around here."' The article ended with Meadlo's mother offering an arresting counter-image to her son's testimony on television: 'Showing a visitor a picture of Paul, his wife, Mary, and his two babies, Paul Jr, 2½, and Tresa Lynn, 15 months, Mrs Meadlo said through her tears: "When he's around his babies he'll pick 'em up and love 'em. Just love 'em."'[87]

It was the character of William Calley, of course, which most interested the press. In late November, NBC interviewed the former Dean of Boys at Calley's old high school in Miami, who stated (somewhat contrary to an official record of mediocre academic performance) that 'if you would have met him, you would have been impressed . . . He was well-liked. He was just an average American boy.'[88] *Time* took that final phrase, with a query appended, as the title of its own account of the lieutenant's life. Illustrated with a photograph of Calley borrowed from his high-school yearbook, the article declared that there was 'little' in his past that might have foretold an involvement 'in so horrible a nightmare as the My Lai massacre'.[89] On the eve of his trial, embarking upon its 'search for William Calley', *ABC News* displayed an image of his childhood home: 'It's a pleasant house, in a pleasant neighborhood of Miami. It could be any middle

---

[85] *Dispatch News Service* telex, 12 November 1969, folder: 'Case folder: 1LT – William L. Calley, Jr [Part 2 of 2]', Box 6, Records Pertaining to the My Lai Massacre, 1969–1974, Records of the Vietnam War Crimes Working Group, Office of the Deputy Chief of Staff for Personnel, RAS, RG319, NACP; *New York Times* (14 November 1969), p. 16.

[86] *New York Times* (25 November 1969), p. 16; 'The Week in Review', *New York Times* (30 November 1969), p. 1; *New York Times* (6 December 1969), p. 1; *Time* (28 November 1969), p. 18; *CBS Evening News*, 17 November 1969, VTNA; *NBC Nightly News*, 18 November 1969, VTNA.

[87] *New York Times* (26 November 1969), p. 10.

[88] *NBC Nightly News*, 26 November 1969, VTNA. Calley was ranked 666th in his high school graduation class of 731. Belknap, pp. 28–9.

[89] *Time* (5 December 1969), p. 25.

class house anywhere in America, just as it seems William Calley could be any American boy.' Until he had entered My Lai, the report concluded, 'he was completely typical of his people and his time. Rusty Calley could have been any one of us. There is no clue, no sign that he was any different.'[90]

Until the latter stages of his court martial, Calley himself kept his distance from the press, with the initial exception of Hersh and, subsequently, John Sack, who was preparing his 'confessions' for *Esquire*. Calley apparently distrusted reporters, believing they wanted him hanged, whilst Sack was anxious to protect his exclusive. The editors at *Esquire*, however, fretted at the disparities evident between the portrayal of the lieutenant offered in its account and the representations appearing in the rest of the press, and they urged Sack to allow other newsmen access to his charge, in the hope that they might develop a more sympathetic view.[91] Calley began thereafter to invite journalists back to his apartment, including *Time* correspondent Peter Range, who – according to Richard Hammer – became a close friend.[92] After the court had reached its verdict, in an article entitled 'Rusty Calley: Unlikely Villain', Range recorded his impressions: 'He is not a monster, not a callous warrior, not the tattooed caricature of the professional killer who does target practice on weekends and keeps a rifle mounted in the rear window of a pickup truck. In the evening, casually attired in blue jeans or bell-bottoms, he could be any young American.' Calley liked to mix drinks and cook food for his friends, Range said: 'he is a partygoer, a host'.[93] Later that April, *Life* printed a picture of Calley, wearing a track-suit top, standing at the bar in his apartment, a can of Coca-Cola, an iced drink and a pack of cigarettes all within reach.[94]

These were the environments from where the killers had come, and to which they had now returned. Like the killers themselves, they looked not much different from the rest of America, perhaps precipitating the thought: if these men, from these places, could unload their weapons upon Vietnamese women and children, how many Americans could say for certain that, in the same situation, they would not have acted the same way? If Calley had been black, as one commentator pointed out, the response to his trial might have been different: 'Would Athens, Georgia, have rallied to his defense?'[95] If he had done his killing at home, amongst his own kind, who then would have claimed him? The inhabitants of My Lai (4) were no less innocent and no less cruelly hastened to their deaths than those murdered at the Los Angeles home of Sharon Tate in August 1969; yet the chief perpetrators of these two crimes, coming to public attention at around

[90] *ABC News*, 9 November 1970, VTNA.
[91] Polsgrove, p. 230; Hammer, *The Court-Martial of Lt Calley*, pp. 171–4.
[92] Hammer, *The Court-Martial of Lt Calley*, pp. 356–9.
[93] *Time* (12 April 1971), p. 17.
[94] *Life* (23 April 1971), p. 22.
[95] M. Novak, 'The Battle Hymn of Lt Calley . . . and the Republic', *Commonweal* (30 April 1971), p. 184.

the same time, were represented in the media in very different ways. On 5 December, a photograph of Calley appeared on the front cover of *Time*, together with a diagonal banner asking 'Where Does the Guilt Lie?' *Time* rendered the image more diffuse by placing several layers of coloured plastic on top of the original and shooting it again. According to the journal's publisher, Henry Luce III, the result was intended 'to suggest the mist of horror surrounding the massacre and any who participated in it'.[96] Two weeks later, however, when Charles Manson was displayed on the front cover of *Life*, the horror with which he was associated had no quality of mist: he was shown staring wild-eyed, beneath a heading that read 'The Love and Terror Cult'.[97] As both the Manson 'family' and Calley trials came to a close in the spring of 1971, an editorial in the *Washington Post* confirmed the former's exclusion from the national community: 'the perpetrators appear to be stripped of humanity and thus scarcely to be fit objects of human compassion'.[98] Considering his response to the judgment against Calley, President Nixon told Bob Haldeman: 'It gets to the question of whether this man is a criminal who should be treated like Manson, and the answer is no.'[99]

There were makers of atrocity, therefore, in whom Americans were prepared to recognize themselves, and others in whom they most assuredly were not. The violent murder of a young Hollywood actress and her company of friends was, it seems, a crime too abhorrent to admit any redistribution of blame, aside from one or two ruminations on 'the dark edge of hippie life'; by contrast, the killings in My Lai (4) were something to be shared.[100] One of the motifs appearing most regularly in discussions of the massacre was that of the reflected image. Historically, the mirror has been used in cultural discourse to evoke the promise of valuable revelation, as well as the dangers of inversion, deception and narcissism.[101] In public modes of representation, it provides a means of expressing collective self-perception, particularly at moments when a culture is uncertain and requires either affirmation of its own viability or confirmation that its anxiety is justified, that decay has begun and must be addressed. In the wake of My Lai, the image of the mirror articulated the need for American society to confront the true reality of itself, as a prelude either to reform or to the fashioning of a new, more complex national self-knowledge.

[96] *Time* (5 December 1969), p. 14.

[97] *Life* (19 December 1969).

[98] *Washington Post* (2 April 1971), p. A26.

[99] Haldeman, diary entry, 1 April 1971, Audio Cassette No. 6, Part 2, Diaries of Harry R. Haldeman, NPM, NACP.

[100] The phrase 'the dark edge of hippie life' comes from the cover of *Life* (19 December 1969). For a further discussion of the relationship between hippies and violence, see *Time* (12 December 1969), p. 23.

[101] S. Melchior-Bonnet, *The Mirror: A History* (New York: Routledge, 2001).

It was a motif, perhaps, with a particular power at this time, given its appearance in the coverage of the first two moon landings, as newspapers and magazines published the famous photographs in which the image of the astronaut taking the picture, from whose perspective the reader is also gazing, is reflected in the visor of his colleague: these pictures invited the reader, albeit by some difficult suspension of their immediate world, to project himself or herself into a moment of national triumph.[102] In the case of My Lai, however, the mirror was invoked in order to challenge collective self-perceptions of this kind, to emphasize the dissonance that existed between conventional apprehensions of the national character and the more chastening reality. In a cartoon published both in the *Washington Post* and *Time*, Herblock depicted the finger of a clean white American hand pointing at a round mirror, with a finger dripping with blood and inscribed with the word 'ATROCITIES' pointing back as the reflected image.[103] The caption reads: 'The Other Side'. Herblock seemed to be asserting that the United States could no longer 'point the finger' at the enemy ('the other side') and claim ethical superiority for its own conduct in the war. The phrase 'The Other Side' also connotes the passage into darkness.

Shortly after the cartoon appeared, *ABC News* anchorman Frank Reynolds spoke to his viewers about the massacre, and suggested a similar lesson: 'We are now facing the kind of confusion and horror that comes from looking into a mirror and discovering that what we dread most is staring back at us. We must refrain from passing judgment on the accused men, but we must not avoid looking into that mirror, for there is no reason, no reason, to claim that the men of Company 'C' are anything but representative of us.'[104] After his court martial, William Calley remembered reading a letter which had been sent to the President protesting his prosecution. 'You, Sir, I and our nation must share the guilt of Vietnam,' the letter asserted. 'Calley is being tried by all conscience-stricken citizens, who see him as a reflection of themselves.'[105]

If many Americans, as it seems, were looking at William Calley and seeing their own image, they may have also been looking at the pictures of the massacre and seeing their own crimes. The actual reaction of ordinary citizens to the photographs taken by Ronald Haeberle has been the subject of only limited formal enquiry. In the survey conducted amongst students at Ohio State University, slides depicting the killings were significantly more likely than written descriptions to elicit condemnatory responses; they were also marginally more likely to provoke dissent from the statement: 'If one feels a need to place the blame for [the My] Lai

---

[102] See, for example, the cover of *Life* (10 August 1969); *New York Times* (28 November 1969), p. 34.
[103] *Washington Post* (26 November 1969), p. 12; *Time* (5 December 1969), p. 27.
[104] *ABC News*, 28 November 1969, VTNA.
[105] Sack, p. 20.

incident, all he need do is look in the mirror.'[106] It is evident, however, that there was little in the content of Haeberle's images that would necessarily disrupt the moral appropriation of the crime by those who viewed them. As Susan Sontag has pointed out, photographers rarely occupy a totally innocent space with respect to their subjects, and in the case of Haeberle, this was particularly true. Electing not to intervene whilst the slaughter proceeded around him, he had – in Sontag's formulation – chosen the photograph over the life.[107] His, then, was an ethically compromised view, and it was from this position, eventually, that the rest of America looked on. Haeberle's pictures, indeed, were the fruit of a licence that could have been patterned on the sanction that Americans had accorded to the war as a whole: this may continue, as long as we can watch.

What the photographs offered to the viewer, moreover, was a peculiarly faithful record of what the perpetrators themselves would have seen as they went about their business. It is now a commonplace observation that a camera frames its subject through optical sights much like a rifle, until the photographer locates the image that he wants to possess, and depresses his finger. There, usually, the simile ends. In My Lai (4), however, death had a habit of following Haeberle around, often arriving from the same direction from which his camera scanned the scene, sometimes around the same moment that he composed himself to 'shoot'. Years later, he recalled: 'I noticed this one small boy had been shot in the foot. Part of the foot was torn off, he was walking toward the group of bodies looking for his mother. I put my camera to my eye, I was going to take a photograph, I didn't notice a GI kneeling down beside me with his M-16 rifle pointed at the child. Then I suddenly heard the crack and through the viewfinder I saw this child flip over on top of the pile of bodies.'[108]

In one of the photographs that appeared in *Life*, two small children lie in the middle distance, by the side of a road. One of them is looking back towards the direction of the camera. Haeberle explained what happened: 'When these two boys were shot at, the older one fell on the little one, as if to protect him. Then the guys finished them off.'[109]

Almost to the limit of their power to do so, therefore, the pictures of the massacre replicate the gaze of the killers. Rarely, moreover, did the view of the victims provided in the pictures disclose the agency of those most immediately to blame for their fate. In one of the images published in *Life*, a soldier throws baskets onto a fire; in the picture of the boys fallen in the road, the hat and arm of an American GI are just visible on the right; but that was about it. There was no photograph of William Calley at the ditch. Haeberle had watched as – outside the village, about fifty yards from where he stood – a machine-gunner started firing into a group of

[106] Thompson *et al.*, pp. 125, 127.
[107] S. Sontag, *On Photography* (New York: Dell Publishing, 1978), pp. 11–12.
[108] Bilton and Sim, p. 133.
[109] *Life* (5 December 1969), p. 38.

women and children. He told army investigators, however: 'I did not take a picture of this.'[110]

Nor subsequently was he able to identify the perpetrators, in part because he had joined the company to cover only that particular operation and did not know its members by name, and in part because, as once again he informed investigators, 'There were too many people shooting.' The prosecuting authorities were able to identify some of the soldiers responsible for the deaths of those shown in the pictures (the scene of devastation at the trail was scrutinized closely by the jury at Calley's court martial as it sought to determine how many people he had killed); but few attributions of this kind appeared in the press.[111] The captions and commentaries which accompanied the images were often confined to the baldest statements of content, such as that provided by the *Cleveland Plain Dealer*: 'A clump of bodies on a road in South Vietnam', or borrowed, like those in *Life*, from Haeberle's own name-free narration.[112] Sometimes, as when the pictures were displayed on *CBS Evening News*, there were no captions or commentaries provided at all.[113] Moral ownership of the atrocity was still open to be claimed.

That the photographs themselves (and the reticent manner of their display) yielded few clues about who had actually conducted the killings was unlikely to dissolve in the viewer all awareness that accountable individuals would have been involved, or to disarm their desire – if that was their desire – to see the guilty parties brought before a court. The images were certainly not irrelevant to the prosecution of the case. Yet they were also not incompatible with efforts to characterize the massacre as a collective crime, as one particular example of their use confirmed. It was the conviction of the artists and critics affiliated with the AWC that responsibility for the atrocities committed at My Lai (4) was shared by every American, a conviction they sought to illustrate by manufacturing masks of Calley's face to be worn by those marching against the war.[114] Their most notable production, however, was a colour poster of the photograph Haeberle had taken by the trail, superimposed onto which was an extract from Paul Meadlo's interview with Mike Wallace of CBS: '*Q. And babies? A. And babies.*'

In December 1969, fifty thousand copies of the poster, approximately 2 ft by 3 ft in size, were printed and distributed for free to anti-war activists all around the country. The image was pasted throughout the New York City subway system, and coalition members also staged a demonstration at the Museum of Modern Art, parading the poster in front of Pablo Picasso's

---

[110] Haeberle, 'Witness Statement', 25 August 1969, folder: My Lai 8/38, Papers of *Four Hours in My Lai*, LHCMA, KCL.

[111] Hammer, *The Court-Martial of Lt Calley*, p. 361.

[112] *Cleveland Plain Dealer* (20 November 1969), p. 1; *Life* (5 December 1969), pp. 36–45.

[113] *CBS Evening News*, 20 November 1969, VTNA.

[114] Lippard, p. 24.

Guernica and thus comparing the dead of My Lai (4) to the victims of fascism.[115] Supplies were exhausted within two weeks, prompting calls for a new edition.[116]

What the photographs of massacre offered to their viewers, then, was the option of shame, a chance to map any continuities that existed between what they had done (at home, in work, in politics) and what they now saw (Vietnamese bodies on a trail). Perhaps they offered even more. In her classic study *On Photography*, Susan Sontag argued that, in modern industrial societies, there had occurred a steady attrition of the distinction between participation in events and the examination of those events in the form of the photographic image: when present at an event, we take photographs to establish (for ourselves as much as for others) incontrovertible proof that we were really there; when we were not present, photography provides a means by which we can nevertheless take possession of the experience.[117] '[R]eality,' she wrote, 'has come to seem more and more like what we are shown by cameras.'[118]

Similar thoughts, of course, have excited theorists of postmodernity who have proposed that we now live in the society of the spectacle, suffused by images to the point that the real (or at least our confidence in it) has entirely disappeared. Turning to the war in Vietnam – which, depending on whom one reads, was either the midwife or the progeny of the postmodern condition – these theorists search out evidence that the Americans who fought in the conflict and those who watched it at home perceived their experience in terms of a movie, acting out roles, passively observing the parade of images, the association with entertainment arresting their moral response.[119] In a more recent intervention, however, Sontag has criticized the postmodern perspective as 'a breathtaking provincialism', asserting that it was 'absurd to generalize' about the ability of people to respond to images of atrocity and the suffering of others.[120] It may have been the case, during Vietnam, that the boundary between observation and authorship became somewhat indistinct, but the mystery could as readily resolve itself through the assumption of agency as it could in denial. As Michael Herr recalled: 'It took the war to teach it, that you were

[115] For accounts of the production and distribution of the poster, see *ibid.*, pp. 27–8; J. Aulich, 'Vietnam, fine art and the culture industry', in J. Walsh and J. Aulich (eds), *Vietnam Images: War and Representation* (Basingstoke: Macmillan, 1989), p. 82; and F. Frascina, 'Meyer Schapiro's Choice: My Lai, Guernica, MOMA and the art left, 1969–70 [Parts 1 and 2]', *Journal of Contemporary History*, 30 (1995), pp. 481–511, 705–28.

[116] Schwartz to Hightower, 18 May 1970, file no. 8: 'Art Workers Coalition Materials and Information', Box 5, Series III, John B. Hightower Papers, Museum of Modern Art Archives.

[117] Sontag, *On Photography*, pp. 24, 155–61.

[118] *Ibid.*, p. 161.

[119] M. Bibby, 'The post-modern condition', in Bibby (ed.), *The Vietnam War and Postmodernity* (Amherst: University of Massachusetts Press, 1999), pp. 143–71; M. Clark, 'The work of war after the age of mechanical reproduction', in Bibby, pp. 17–47.

[120] S. Sontag, *Regarding the Pain of Others* (New York: Farrar, Straus and Giroux, 2003), pp. 108–11.

as responsible for everything you saw as you were for everything you did.'[121] At the moment of the My Lai revelations, Americans were being encouraged to look upon another event which had unfolded far from their homes and to claim collective ownership thereof. If they turned in the same acquisitive spirit from pictures of the second moon landing to those of the massacre, they would have been effectively gazing, as Jonathan Schell suggested, 'through the eyes of the perpetrators'.[122]

Yet, as Schell himself warned, to identify with the perpetrators was not necessarily to assume any moral responsibility for their crimes. After Calley's court martial, respondents to two opinion polls were asked what they would have done if, as a soldier in Vietnam, they had been ordered by a superior officer to shoot all the inhabitants of a village suspected of aiding the enemy, including old men, women and children. Respectively, 51 per cent and 43 per cent of those questioned affirmed that they would have obeyed such an order. In one of the surveys, 29 per cent of respondents registered their conviction that Calley had done 'what any good soldier would do under the circumstances'.[123] In March 1971, an elderly lady from Columbus, Georgia, interviewed by *NBC Nightly News*, volunteered the conclusion: 'They went in there, were told to shoot so they shot. I would too, wouldn't you?'[124]

Many Americans, it seems, were prepared to project themselves into the scenario of massacre, and to see themselves in the soldiers of Charlie Company, but it was usually through the prism of social function – class loyalty, almost – that they made that identification, not through the mist of collective guilt. The majority of those who responded in this way (like the majority of those who disapproved of Calley's trial) came from the socio-economic and educational backgrounds most likely to condition them to the notion that orders had to be obeyed. They had abdicated control over their own working lives in return for the assurance that, whatever the consequences of their actions, they would not personally be held to account.[125] According to this logic, largely untroubled as it was by value judgements about outcome, the images of the dead in My Lai (4) were actually evidence of a job well done. It was the images of Calley leaving the courthouse under guard that quickened these Americans to anger, for the scene seemed to revoke the entire contract with authority around which they had structured their lives, a contract that – at a time of rising unemployment and inflation – was already draining empty of its wider integrity and promise.

[121] Herr, p. 24.

[122] Schell, 'Notes and comments: Talk of the town', *New Yorker* (20 December 1969), p. 27.

[123] Harris to Higby, 5 April 1971, folder: 'Calley', Box 16, John Ehrlichman: Alphabetical Subject File, Staff Members and Office Files, White House Special Files, NPM, NACP; Kelman and Lawrence, 'Assignment of responsibility', p. 193.

[124] *NBC Nightly News*, 22 March 1971, VTNA.

[125] Kelman and Lawrence, 'Assignment of responsibility', pp. 203–10.

Many Americans were undoubtedly persuaded that the massacre at My Lai (4) was a crime in which the whole nation was implicated; others were not, with some taking the view that it was not a crime at all. The assertion of collective responsibility, and the reflections that it stimulated about national moral character, were probably features more evident in media and liberal-left discourses on the killings than they were in the thoughts of ordinary citizens. 'My Lai – those women and children are in our consciousness now,' said Frank Reynolds of *ABC News*, 'and they are also *on* our conscience. The national soul *is* wounded and because those men came *from* us and acted *for* us, the wound is self-inflicted.' He went on: 'because of what it is said happened there our spirit as a people *is* scarred.'[126] Eric Sevareid also invoked the image of a national wound in his commentary for CBS. The news of the massacre, he declared, 'plunges the reputation of America to a new low among foreign peoples, many of them all too ready to think ill of us. A moral abscess, like one in the body, can only be lanced and drained – it cannot be bandaged over.'[127]

Just how bad things had become, indeed, was indicated by the comparisons made by some contributors to the debate between the atrocities in My Lai (4) and the actions of Nazi Germany. 'If these stories are true,' stated an editorial in the *Nation*, 'the Americans involved behaved with an on-the-spot savagery that exceeded even that of the Germans at Lidice in World War II. The Nazis wiped out the village, shot all the men, and dragged the women and children off to concentration camps.'[128] More disturbing still, perhaps, than the analogous content of the crimes was the conclusion reached by the researchers from the Wright Institute: that, with respect to both My Lai and the Vietnam war as a whole, many American citizens – like the citizens of Germany as the Holocaust gathered speed – had simply decided that the killing of innocents did not merit their concern.[129]

What the massacre represented for those who claimed it as the outcome of a national dereliction, and who drew attention to its analogues in the crimes of other states, was a challenge to the long and widely-held belief that America was different. As Deborah Madsen notes, the concept of exceptionalism has been at the centre of debates about American identity since even before the nation itself was founded.[130] According to Perry Miller, the seeds of exceptionalist doctrine were sown by the Puritan migrants of the seventeenth century, who sought to establish in New England a working model for the full religious reformation that had still to be achieved at home. In Miller's view, this notion of a special spiritual

---

[126] *ABC News*, 28 November 1969, VTNA (italics reflect emphasis in original).

[127] *CBS Evening News*, 28 November 1969, VTNA.

[128] 'The American conscience', *Nation* (8 December 1969), p. 619.

[129] Opton, in Sanford *et al.*, pp. 49–70.

[130] D. Madsen, *American Exceptionalism* (Edinburgh: Edinburgh University Press, 1998), pp. 1–2.

destiny for the Puritan community became somewhat secularized as the prospect of a return to Europe receded, as Enlightenment science contracted the spheres in which the workings of God's grace were accorded primary explanatory power, and as the increasing material prosperity of New England indicated to its people that they basked in the approval of the Lord and that there was no longer quite the same need for them to abase themselves before the knowledge of their own sin, despite the jeremiads of preachers who continued to insist that they should.[131]

Sacvan Bercovitch, however, asserts that Miller proposed a false opposition between the spiritual lamentations of the Puritan churches and the secular processes through which wider society became American, for the jeremiad – and its avowal of the gap between the collective moral ideal and contemporary moral practice – flourished as a rhetorical model well beyond the colonial period. For Bercovitch, the historic distinctiveness of the American nation was expressed in and affirmed by the jeremiad; in contrast to the European form which invoked the distance between the injunctions of God and the conduct of man as evidence of the latter's essential depravity, the American jeremiad was intended to induce reform within its audience and to propel the nation on towards the fulfilment of its special destiny. At the same time as it diagnosed delinquency, therefore, the jeremiad professed optimism and faith. For Americans, the act of gazing upon themselves and registering their sinfulness was a necessary stage in their communal passage towards reformation and redemption, when the profane countenance of man would dissolve, giving way to the divine.[132]

As both Loren Baritz and Trevor McCrisken have demonstrated, the conviction that the United States represents a virtuous alternative to an old world resigned to its own amorality has been a consistent feature of American thinking on foreign affairs since the birth of the republic, even as the national policy posture shifted markedly from one of aloofness in the early 1800s to one of global intervention by the high-tide of the twentieth century. Meanwhile, the conversion of national economic power into international predominance also refracted back to further confirm the validity of assumptions about the uniquely righteous character of American civilization: that the United States had come to stand at the commanding heights of the international system was evidence of the blessings bestowed upon a worthy people by an approving God.

[131] P. Miller, *The New England Mind: From Colony to Province* (Cambridge: Harvard University Press, 1953); Miller, *The New England Mind: The Seventeenth Century* (Cambridge: Harvard University Press, 1954), especially pp. 463–91; Miller, 'Errand into the wilderness', in Miller, *Errand into the Wilderness* (Cambridge: The Belknap Press of Harvard University Press, 1964), pp. 1–15.

[132] S. Bercovitch, *The American Jeremiad* (Madison: University of Wisconsin Press, 1978), pp. 3–30; Bercovitch, *The Puritan Origins of the American Self* (London: Yale University Press, 1975), pp. 14–15.

As a consequence of the war in Vietnam, however, these two components of exceptionalist doctrine were exposed to unprecedented critical
scrutiny.[133] The experience of military defeat by an ostensibly weaker foe
disrupted the narrative of accumulating national power. Atrocities such as
the massacre at My Lai (4), meanwhile, cast into doubt the ability of
Americans to live up to the ethical standards that they had ascribed to
themselves.

For a number of commentators and many ordinary citizens, the effort
to do so was futile: the American people were condemned to exist in
the same moral space as everybody else and were subject to the same
elemental dispositions towards selfishness and violence. From this state
of nature, there was no hope of escape. Yet for others, the promise of the
American jeremiad still held: that through collective self-reflection and
a commitment to reform, the United States could and should transcend
the pathologies that had revealed themselves at My Lai (4) and return
once again to the path of righteousness and the condition of national
exception. 'The massacre calls for self-examination and for action,' wrote
Jonathan Schell. 'If we deny the call and try to go on as before, as though
nothing had happened, our knowledge, which can never leave us once we
have acquired it, will bring about an unnoticed but crucial alteration in us,
numbing our most precious faculties and withering our souls. For if we
learn to accept this, there is nothing we will not accept.'[134]

In the view of some observers, the peculiar commitment of the American people to a exemplary standard of national conduct, and the peculiar
intensity of their distress when that standard was debauched, had already
been made evident in their initial reaction to the massacre. *Newsweek*
declared that 'it is America's strong image of itself as a country attached
to traditions of human decency and fair play that helps explain the guilt,
shame and horror that have swept the US in the wake of revelations about
Song My'.[135] Others, of course, were also monitoring the public response to
the news and finding those sensations of 'guilt, shame and horror' hardly
evident at all. Whatever conclusions were reached on that particular point,
something more was probably needed. Daniel Patrick Moynihan, noting
that the nation was 'being judged', suggested to President Nixon that he
declare 'a day of prayer for the dead of Mylai. A day of atonement. A day
in truth of prayer for the United States of America.'[136] Six months later,
during the Cambodian incursion, Dr Irving Greenberg from New York

[133] L. Baritz, *Backfire: A History of How American Culture Led Us into Vietnam and
Made Us Fight the Way We Did* (New York: William Morrow & Co., 1985); T. McCrisken,
American Exceptionalism and the Legacy of Vietnam: US Foreign Policy Since 1974
(Basingstoke: Palgrave Macmillan, 2003).
[134] Schell, 'Notes and comments: Talk of the town', *New Yorker* (20 December 1969), p. 29.
[135] *Newsweek* (8 December 1969), pp. 34–5.
[136] Moynihan to Nixon, 25 November 1969, folder: 'My Lai Incident [1 of 2]', Alexander
Haig Special File, Box 1004, National Security Council Files, NPM, NACP.

submitted a similar proposal to the Senate Foreign Relations Committee, which was conducting hearings on the 'moral and military aspects' of the war in Vietnam. A 'final moral disaster', Rabbi Greenberg told the committee, was soon likely to befall the American nation in south-east Asia unless it learned from an ancient model of collective atonement provided in the Bible: 'the community, led by its leaders, become one by confessing its errors and sins before God and to those whom it had harmed. Then it turned together to new ways of life affirmation to overcome the evils of the past.'[137] Another possible source of national redemption, according to its numerous advocates, was a commission of inquiry into US war crimes in Vietnam. If the conscience of the American people was to be cleared, asserted the thirty-four eminent jurists who recommended such a venture to President Nixon in the wake of the massacre disclosures, they had to show themselves 'manifestly unafraid to examine all the evidence, to review the context within which the alleged acts occurred, and if required, to make reparations and institute the changes in policy and procedure necessary to restore our good standing as a moral leader among nations'.[138]

These propositions, however, were unlikely to progress very far. The constituencies that actively sought to engage the American people in communal rites of atonement were modest in size and persuasive power. This was as true on the liberal left as it was everywhere else. Within the central currents of American culture, the challenge presented by the massacre to the doctrine of exceptionalism may not have been registered very much at all. For many of those more invested in dissent and critique, it was providentialism itself that consisted of a dubious prospectus; efforts to recuperate the myth of essential national goodness through acts of penance and absolution would serve only as a distraction from the most critical questions of ideology and power. The 'pseudo-moral discussion' that had followed the revelations about My Lai, argued the *Nation*, 'was as ephemeral as the frontier evangelism from which it is derived and which went hand in hand with the slaughter of Indians'.[139]

Similarly, just as Richard Nixon resisted proposals for an official war crimes commission, fearing it might reveal rather too much about the way in which the conflict was being fought, so reservations were also likely to be expressed by the left. No commission composed, as the jurists suggested, of '[r]etired judges of superior federal and state courts, leaders of the bar, distinguished professors of law and retired general officers of our armed forces' could be expected to produce the sort of systemic

[137] 'Statement of Dr. Irving Greenberg', 7 May 1970, in US Congress, Senate, Committee on Foreign Relations, *Moral and Military Aspects of the War in Southeast Asia: Hearings Before the Committee on Foreign Relations*, 91st Congress, Second Session, 1970 (Washington, DC: US Government Printing Office, 1970), p. 13.

[138] Goldberg *et al.* to Nixon, 5 December 1969, folder: '[cf.] ND18-4 War Crimes – Trials [1969–70]', Box 43, Confidential Files, White House Special Files, NPM, NACP.

[139] 'The war system', *Nation* (15 December 1969), p. 650.

indictments and recommendations for wholesale reform favoured by radical activists, for whom these sorts of people were part of the problem.[140]
The establishment could not be trusted to return an honest verdict on
itself. Indeed, if the carnage that national policy had effected in Vietnam
was to receive a proper accounting, it was the establishment that would
have to be changed – and that, as Noam Chomsky noted, 'would require
social revolution, leading to a redistribution of power throughout the
industrial as well as the political system'.[141]

This was the difficulty. As the circle of responsibility for the atrocities
in My Lai (4) became increasingly enlarged, extending beyond individual
soldiers and specific institutions, the more likely it was that the implicated
parties would evade the operations of justice and ignore any demands for
radical transformation of their conduct. William Calley might be convicted,
but he could not be kept in jail. The army could expand its requirements
for troop instruction in the Hague and Geneva conventions, revise its
directives with regard to the reporting of crimes of war, and generally
amplify the emphasis given to ethics throughout its service schools.[142] Yet
internal studies which diagnosed a crisis of values and integrity within
the service as a whole, from the general staff down, were held in limited
circulation and their prescriptions for reform left largely unaddressed.[143]
The broader the indictment, the more interests there are motivated to
resist, and the reformist impulse begins to wither in the face of the scale
of the task, to the point that the problem itself comes to seem simply like
a fact of human existence: American soldiers kill civilians; American generals ignore bad news; the configuration of national power is impervious
to change.

It was, therefore, the fate of some of the more expansive reflections upon
the causes of the massacre to congeal at length into intellectual pessimism. This was true, perhaps most notably, of enquiries into the apparent
readiness of American soldiers at My Lai (4) to suspend their own powers
of ethical judgement and, upon the instruction of authority, kill defenceless

[140] Goldberg *et al.* to Nixon, 5 December 1969, folder: '[cf.] ND18-4 War Crimes – Trials
[1969–70]', Box 43, Confidential Files, White House Special Files, NPM, NACP.

[141] N. Chomsky, 'Foreword', in Limqueco and Weiss, p. 26.

[142] Army Regulation No. 350–216: 'Training: The Geneva Conventions of 1949 and Hague
Convention No. IV of 1907', 28 May 1970, folder: 'Laws of War Reference File, 1975 – Folder
#1', Box 14, RCCPI, RPI, RAS, RG319, NACP; MACV Directive 20–4: 'Inspections and
Investigations: War Crimes', 10 July 1970, folder: 'Reporting and Investigating War Crimes
Allegations – Procedures and Regulations', Box 4, Vietnam War Crimes Working Group
Central File, Records of the Vietnam War Crimes Working Group, Office of the Deputy Chief
of Staff for Personnel, RAS, RG319, NACP; Cincinnatus, *Self-Destruction: The Disintegration and Decay of the United States Army During the Vietnam Era* (New York: Norton,
1981), pp. 174–7.

[143] There were two such studies, the first in 1970 and the second the following year, both
conducted by the Army War College. For accounts of their reception, see Cincinnatus,
pp. 130–1, 166–7; Zaffiri, pp. 344–5; J. Kitfield, *Prodigal Soldiers: How the Generation of
Officers Born of Vietnam Revolutionized the American Style of War* (New York: Simon
& Schuster, 1995), pp. 107–13.

civilians. For many commentators, the surrender made in this instance expressed not so much the peculiar meekness of the men actually involved, but rather a wider crisis of individual moral autonomy in the US military and throughout contemporary society beyond. It was a relatively minor test of memory, after all, to think back to 1963 and the publication of Hannah Arendt's *Eichmann in Jerusalem*, in which she provocatively asserted that it did not take a monster to commit the crimes for which Eichmann had been tried and convicted.[144] He had simply been acting in accordance with what the Nazi system required of a man in his position, requirements which included the suppression of personal moral scruple: 'this new type of criminal, who is in actual fact *hostis generis humani*, commits his crimes under circumstances that make it well-nigh impossible for him to know or to feel that he is doing wrong.'[145]

Around the same time, at Yale University, the psychologist Stanley Milgram was discovering that individuals willing to yield their inner convictions to authority were not just confined to totalitarian states. In a series of studies, which received considerable attention as the decade drew on, Milgram enlisted ordinary Americans to participate in what they were told was an experiment exploring 'the effects of punishment on learning'. In the most simple version of the experiment, they were asked to act as 'teachers', putting questions to 'learners' and administering electric shocks whenever an incorrect answer was given. The electric shocks would increase in voltage with each incorrect response. (In fact, the generator was fake, with the 'learner' – an actor – only simulating distress when the shock was applied.) Whenever 'teachers' became hesitant about administering the shock, they were enjoined to continue by an 'experimenter' who was apparently overseeing the test. Milgram was dismayed by what he found: 'Many subjects will obey the experimenter no matter how vehement the pleading of the person being shocked, no matter how painful the shocks seem to be, and no matter how much the victim pleads to be let out.'[146]

In the view of a number of theorists, what could be concluded from such experiments, and what had been confirmed by My Lai, was that it was not the Nazi system alone that created the conditions for 'guilt-free massacre'.[147] Most members of modern industrial society had become habituated to the subordination of their individual will to the larger organization and to higher authority, enervating the link between the profession and the realization of their values. If what seemed to be a

---

[144] H. Arendt, *Eichmann in Jerusalem: A Report on the Banality of Evil* (Harmondsworth: Penguin, 1977). *Time* referred to Arendt's volume in its early analysis of the My Lai massacre: *Time* (5 December 1969), p. 26.

[145] *Ibid.*, p. 276.

[146] S. Milgram, *Obedience to Authority: An Experimental View* (New York: Harper & Row, 1975), p. 5.

[147] T. Duster, 'Conditions for Guilt-Free Massacre', in Sanford *et al.*, pp. 25–36.

legitimate authority (such as a researcher at Yale) ordered them to undertake a task which conflicted with their ethical beliefs, it was the ethical beliefs that were likely to yield. Technological rationalism had evolved to the point, argued the political scientist Charles Drekmeier, that men and women now viewed themselves as instruments and judged others in that way, as either objects of practical value or else of no value at all. Their ability to place their actions in a broader moral perspective had become depleted, and because virtually everyone was abdicating their sense of autonomy to the system, the idea of moral responsibility itself was threatening to dissolve.[148] If this was true anywhere, suggested another political scientist, Carey McWilliams, it was true in the army, which had evolved into the exemplary bureaucracy of the liberal state, governed by role demands and system rules rather than by autonomous individuals: 'The very tendency of bureaucracy – and an aim of liberal theory – is to produce men with a desire to *avoid* responsibility and authority, who will fly to the safety of laws, rules and technique rather than imposing judgments of their own.'[149]

To find an example of such a man – someone who had willingly reduced himself to the instrument of others – one had to look no further than William Calley. According to one army psychologist who examined him, he had followed the line of least resistance all the way through his life. As a young man, Calley had not particularly enjoyed watching television or movies 'but watched them because others were doing so, and because it demanded less effort than reading'. His verbal responses to ethical questions 'can be considered normal', but in practice he was uncomfortable with the burden of judgement, ethical or otherwise. Calley, the psychologist concluded, 'appears to be rather rigid in his thinking, and following orders to the letter allows him to function in a robot-like fashion and relieves him of having to make decisions'.[150] The lieutenant's own attorneys, indeed, cited Milgram's research during the appellate process as evidence that most individuals of 'ordinary sense and understanding' – the standard of mental capacity that, if possessed by a soldier, allowed him to be judged – would not have realized in Calley's position that obedience to orders was wrong.[151] In an account of his experiments written in the early 1970s, Milgram himself asserted that the problem of obedience, in which

[148] C. Drekmeier, 'Knowledge as Virtue, Knowledge as Power', in Sanford *et al.*, pp. 192–243.

[149] W. Carey McWilliams, *Military Honor After Mylai* (New York: Council on Religion and International Affairs, 1972), pp. 28–9 (italics in original).

[150] Bond, 'Prisoner's Admission Summary Data', 22 November 1972, folder: My Lai 8/30, Papers of *Four Hours in My Lai*, LHCMA, KCL.

[151] Latimer and Gordon, 'Petition for Reconsideration: US Court of Military Appeals: *United States v. William L. Calley, Jr*', 4 January 1974, folder: 'Presidential/SA Review of Calley Appeal, Apr.–May 1974', Box 1, Records of the Calley General Court-Martial, 1969–74, Office of the Clerk of Court, Records of the Judge Advocate General (Army), RG153, NACP.

the operation of conscience was transformed by authority, had been 'revealed with special clarity' by the massacre at My Lai (4).[152]

If it were accepted, therefore, that the massacre emerged from a process of culture-wide socialization into instrumentalist habits of thought, which in turn had their origins in the dominant ideology of liberal rationalism, how might it be ensured that no such massacre occur again? After all, the response to Calley's conviction itself reflected the scale of the problem: there were many Americans who believed that they too would have killed women and children in Son My had they been ordered to do so. For Carey McWilliams, it was actually the army that constituted the most promising agent of reform, if it could dissolve its allegiance to instrumental and bureaucratic values and return to the traditional concept of 'military honor' as the basis for the conduct of both individual soldiers and service practice as a whole.[153] In doing so, perhaps, the army could offer an example to the rest of society.

It was a nice enough sentiment, but at a time when army recruiters were trying to convince young Americans that the service 'wants to join you', and when relations between the Pentagon and private corporations seemed about as intimate as they could get, there was little real likelihood that the US military would recluse itself from civilian culture and initiate the process of dismantling liberal rationalist doctrine.[154] Whilst believing 'our position is not hopeless', McWilliams nevertheless acknowledged that he had proposed 'a difficult, perhaps impossible, task'.[155] To read Stanley Milgram, meanwhile, was to confront the possibility that the easy capitulation of individual ethics to institutional authority was an anthropological phenomenon, invulnerable even to the most radical transformation of the prevailing social structure: 'This is a fatal flaw nature has designed into us, and which in the long run gives our species only a modest chance of survival.'[156] It was a melancholy thought: not just that every man might be a Calley, but that so might his sons, and his grandsons and so on, until eventually one or more of them, succumbing to the impulse to obey, would – most likely, via the nuclear trigger – compliantly bring the fate of the inhabitants of My Lai (4) down upon all the inhabitants of the earth.

Across a majority of national opinion, it was recognized that blame for the massacre at My Lai (4) could not just be confined to the soldiers of Charlie Company. There was more to the story than a few bad men slaughtering women and children in a village. In so far as the contexts in which

---

[152] Milgram, p. 183.

[153] McWilliams, pp. 29–32. A similar argument was made in R. Gabriel and P. Savage, *Crisis in Command: Mismanagement in the Army* (New York: Hill and Wang, 1978).

[154] See the US Army recruitment advertisement in *Life* (9 April 1971), pp. 52–3. On the military-industrial complex, see S. Melman, *Pentagon Capitalism: The Political Economy of War* (New York: McGraw-Hill, 1970) and Melman (ed.), *The War Economy of the United States* (New York: St Martin's Press, 1971).

[155] McWilliams, p. 32.

[156] Milgram, p. 188.

the killings occurred seemed to be subject to somebody's control, there was scope for the allocation of guilt beyond those actually present on the scene and also a potential for preventative reform. Of those contexts, the most conspicuous was the Vietnam war itself: it was logical that those who had exercised authority over the conflict – the military command, the civilian leaders in the Pentagon and the White House, and indeed the American people as a whole – should be ascribed some measure of the blame. The visual content of the massacre story, moreover, offered a medium through which the communalization of guilt might proceed, for it allowed Americans to identify with William Calley and with what he had done. It was logical also that the massacre would be used to buttress the case against the war, with some commentators arguing that the most immediately effective way to prevent such atrocities from happening again was to bring a swift end to the fighting.

Yet there were competing logics (and politics) at play. Even as they sought to redirect the balance of Calley's guilt up the chain of command, most Americans accepted that criminal responsibility had to end where the massacre orders had begun. According to that rationale, those who had never explicitly directed the killing of civilians, but who had, nonetheless, cultivated the conditions for the massacre (by failing to indoctrinate soldiers properly in the laws of war, by licensing the excesses of pacification, by deciding to contest an insurgency in a country where the insurgents had extensive public support), would not be required to join Calley before the courts. In Vietnam-era America, unlike post-war Germany and Japan, high-level war crimes prosecutions (and war crimes commissions) could only occur with the cooperation of national authority, and in the absence of revolution that was likely either to be denied or else lead to a whitewash. These were times in which authority could be challenged, but there seemed little real prospect that it could be pressured to surrender, or even to adopt radical changes of practice. Once that had been acknowledged, the conscientious mind had nothing left with which to respond to the massacre but vaporous rhetorics of atonement or gloomy reflections about the capacity of authority to summon men to its will, a capacity judged so resilient that, paradoxically perhaps, it was seen to lie beyond the reach of its own powers of reform.

The identifications that ordinary Americans made with William Calley did not, for the most part, proceed through the assumption of shared guilt, but instead through a perception that he – just like them – had no influence over the conditions or the content of his work. The anti-war veterans who had so publicly associated themselves with atrocities in an effort to force their countrymen to conscience were thus rather left out on a limb. Moreover, although they joined in the dissent against Calley's conviction, their motivations for doing so conflicted dramatically with those who responded to the verdict with the most energetic displays of dissent: traditional veterans' organizations and pro-war conservatives. It was not the suffering of the Vietnamese people that concerned these particular currents of opinion. On the contrary, what they resented was the refusal of the government – its attitude exemplified by the trial – to accept that the war should be prosecuted with all available means. Calley, they judged, had at least been doing his job, and those who were not, who had let the conflict slide into ignominious stalemate, had no right to judge. Against the lessons of military history, American leaders had tried to discipline the enemy through delicate calibrations of strategic force, a presumption of a piece with their insistence that a similar discretion be exercised by troops on the ground. Just as they had resisted the wisdom that wars had to be fought through the full mobilization of national power, so in convicting William Calley – his supporters asserted – those leaders were maintaining the delusion that war's violence could be controlled. 'Now what in the hell *else* is war than killing people?' Calley himself complained.[157] That it was nothing else was apparently a popular view, which ultimately aspired to dissolve into abstraction the causes of atrocities like My Lai, and to ease them out of history altogether.

---

[157] Sack, p. 23 (italics in original).

4

Abstracting culpability

To look upon the massacre at My Lai (4), as many Americans did, and to judge as overly harsh the attribution of essential guilt to the soldiers of Charlie Company, and yet to resist the reallocation of the balance of that guilt to any other party or parties (to those, for example, who had managed the Vietnam war, or even to the nation as a whole for having permitted the war to go on), was in effect to allow responsibility to drift. Settling nowhere, it seemed to become elemental, as indefinite as the weather in its origins and resolutions. There was nothing more to be said about My Lai and what had caused it to occur than there was about a thunderstorm; the massacre and, perhaps, also the war were the outcome of systems and conditions beyond human control and the hope of reform. A model for such despair could be found in American social science, its habitual enthusiasm for the promise of public policy exhausted, as it characterized the massacre and many other instances of violence as symptoms of problems – a culture of instrumentalism and obedience to authority – that appeared intractable and virtually timeless, stretching back at least to the first division of labour and, in the view of Stanley Milgram, perhaps as far as the story of Isaac and Abraham.[1]

Most Americans, of course, were not attending to their social science textbooks at this time. Those who arrived at a similar conclusion – that the massacre at My Lai (4) reflected a condition more profound and pervasive than the individual delinquencies of William Calley and his men, or the peculiar circumstances of the Vietnam war – were usually negotiating a variety of different knowledges and intuitions. By the turn of the decade, the war was becoming oddly detached from its own history, as the purposes for which it had been initiated (at least on the American side) came to seem either anachronistic or remote from any prospect of fulfilment. With its most immediate extrinsic meanings draining rapidly away, the national enterprise in Indochina was increasingly driven – to the extent that it had

---

[1] Milgram, pp. xi, 11.

any direction at all – by its own self-reflexive logics of violence and will. The soldiers fighting the war lacked compass and purpose, whilst their countrymen back home became impatient with detail: they were for the most part uninterested in the content of the Pentagon Papers, or in the modulations of current policy short of the polarities of withdrawal or major combat operations, or in the provisions of the Uniform Code of Military Justice.[2] News organizations started to wind down their coverage of the conflict, whilst the reporters that remained in Vietnam tended to tell the same story of military stalemate over and over again, collectively evoking – in Daniel Hallin's words – 'an image of war as eternal recurrence, progressing nowhere'.[3] Unable either to sustain mass mobilization or to convert a sporadic series of rallies and marches into influence over administration policy, many of those involved in the anti-war movement became disillusioned, convinced that the fighting would continue whatever they tried to do.[4] There was a general flattening of sensibility across the culture, to the point that the massacre at My Lai (4) began to look not just like the rest of this particular war, but like war itself as a historical constant in human affairs.

This perception was reinforced by the meanings imposed upon the massacre from without, in the form of emerging liberal and leftist critiques of America's past which traced a long narrative of national violence back from Vietnam through the suppression of insurgents in the Philippines, the Indian wars of the nineteenth century and beyond; the declarations made by a number of veterans of earlier military campaigns that, during the course of their service, they had committed acts similar to those for which William Calley and others were now being prosecuted; the insistence within hawkish circles, traditional veterans organizations prominent amongst them, that it was through the use of firepower of the kind that Calley had applied to the situation in Son My that the United States had won its earlier campaigns (it was fastidiousness about civilian casualties, therefore, which was preventing victory in Vietnam); and, less overtly, a discourse of conflict and violence particular to the American south, which was reactivated by the trials playing out in its midst, and which could aim to close the debate about who was to blame for the massacre by invoking the apologia offered by the Union general who had lain waste to the

[2] According to Charles Colson, polls conducted for the Nixon administration indicated that the controversy over the Pentagon Papers 'has not had the enormous impact on the public that one would expect from the intensive press coverage'. He went on: 'The heartland isn't really aroused over this issue. There is nothing like the Calley case here.' Colson to Haldeman, '*New York Times* Article', 25 June 1971, folder: 'Pentagon Papers', Box 9, Nixon Presidential Materials Project (1), America Since Hoover Collection, 1929–80, Gerald R. Ford Library.

[3] Hammond, *Public Affairs: The Military and the Media, 1968–1973*, p. 102–3; Hallin, *The 'Uncensored War'*, p. 176.

[4] C. DeBenedetti with C. Chatfield, *An American Ordeal: The Antiwar Movement of the Vietnam Era* (Syracuse: Syracuse University Press, 1990), p. 297.

region in 1864, William Tecumseh Sherman, in his later reflections upon his military career: 'war is hell'.[5]

Whatever measure of the public controversy about the massacre was tranquillized by the assertion that wars were always atrocious had the potential, however, to be revived by the anxieties this formulation might subsequently provoke concerning American national identity. According to the doctrine of exceptionalism, after all, the United States had been walking a higher path, at a conscientious remove from the litanies of slaughter that had punctuated the military histories of other major powers. The doctrine could accommodate a single American atrocity, or even a short atrocious war, because it had the jeremiad available to summon the people back to virtue. To declare, however, that all conflicts ever fought, by the United States as well as by everybody else, had involved the massacre of innocents was to suggest that the people (or, at least, the men they sent to war) had stopped listening to the jeremiad many decades before, and were now so distant from any unambiguous model or memory of righteous conduct that there was no prospect of return. If consolation were available, it lay instead in the discourse of authenticity, which reflected ambient cultural and countercultural ideas about the coexistence of good and evil within the human soul, and the primitive impulses which persisted beneath the civilized façade of modern man, and pop-psychological propositions which cast the experience of war and atrocity for individuals and nations alike as an existential rite of passage into the condition of self-knowledge and maturity. In committing massacre, therefore, Americans were communing with deeper forces. The revelations about My Lai and the national capacity for violence were actually mnemonic prompts to an older knowledge, as old as original sin or nature itself, in which the only essential parameters of experience were survival and death.

Although they encountered no enemy fire, though their victims were all non-combatants, many members of Charlie Company seem to have perceived their assault upon My Lai (4) in terms consistent with the script of a conventional infantry battle, of the kind that occurred relatively rarely in Vietnam. According to Michael Bernhardt, the soldiers kneeled and crouched whilst firing their weapons at the people in the settlement, as if they were in actual combat.[6] At the time, even Bernhardt himself was not entirely confident that a distinction existed between normal military practice and what was being perpetrated around him. 'Maybe this was the way wars really were', he recalled thinking. 'Maybe what we saw in the movies and on TV wasn't so, that war was running around and shooting civilians

---

[5] Prior to setting Atlanta aflame, Sherman told the city's mayor, 'War is cruelty and you cannot refine it', J. McPherson, *Battle Cry of Freedom: The Civil War Era* (Oxford: Oxford University Press, 1988), p. 809. The phrase 'war is hell' comes from the general's address to Michigan Military Academy in 1879: J. Keegan, *A History of Warfare* (London: Hutchinson, 1993), p. 6.

[6] Lifton, p. 50.

and doing this kind of thing. Maybe all along everyone else knew. I felt like I was left out, like maybe they forgot to tell me something, that this was the way we fought wars and everybody knew but me.'[7]

To other observers on the scene – most obviously, Hugh Thompson and his gunship crew – it was much more evident that Calley and his men were engaged in murder, not war, whilst after the massacre some of the participants became sufficiently sensitive to the aberrance of their own behaviour that they sought either to enforce silence across the company or, in contrast, to discuss their experience with somebody outside – enter Ronald Ridenhour.[8] Yet, others still exhibited a degree of pride in what they had done, as if there had indeed been a battle in the village, as if the scale of the slaughter was an index of operational success.[9] (In early 1970, one member of the company – its personnel having changed entirely since the time of the massacre – noted that the press revelations a month or so before had actually improved its morale, with the unit now referred to as the 'My Lai Boys'.)[10]

That the casualties of the operation had met their deaths in the course of combat (and that the work of their killers was therefore consistent with the obligations of military service) was a proposition advanced by Calley's legal representatives as soon as the charges against him became public knowledge. In Seymour Hersh's initial report on the case, George Latimer was quoted: 'Whatever killing there was was in a firefight in connection with an operation.'[11] A few days later, Latimer was asked by a reporter from *CBS Evening News* whether he believed the alleged incident was 'just a matter of war?' The attorney replied: 'Absolutely. The boys are over there, sent over there for war.'[12] He reiterated the point when interviewed by NBC: 'If Calley killed anybody, he killed them in the line of duty and to accomplish his mission.'[13] For the lieutenant himself, war was an objective, intractable condition, from which inevitably issued civilian casualties like those that had occurred in My Lai (4), rather than a mutable complex of contingencies and practices, pliant to the competence and conscience of the individual soldiers involved. 'I had been told what war is like,' he said, 'but I never knew until I got there. I was never taught the tragedy of war. After seeing war, you just sit down and cry.' He

[7] Hersh, *My Lai 4*, p. 186.

[8] Ridenhour, 'Heroes at the Massacre'.

[9] Lifton, pp. 53–6.

[10] Response of SSG John Moore to a questionnaire distributed amongst the soldiers and officers of the Americal Division by the investigative subcommittee of the House Armed Services Committee: folder: My Lai 8/12, Papers of *Four Hours in My Lai*, LHCMA, KCL.

[11] *Dispatch News Service* telex, 12 November 1969, folder: 'Case Folder: 1LT – William L. Calley, Jr [Part 2 of 2]', Box 6, Records Pertaining to the My Lai Massacre, 1969–74, Records of the Vietnam War Crimes Working Group, Office of the Deputy Chief of Staff for Personnel, RAS, RG319, NACP.

[12] *CBS Evening News*, 17 November 1969, VTNA.

[13] *NBC Nightly News*, 18 November 1969, VTNA.

went on: 'I'll be very proud to have been in the US Army and fought at My Lai if it shows the world just what war is.'[14]

In court, of course, the weight of witness testimony – largely provided by the men of Charlie Company themselves – quickly extinguished the contention that Calley had 'fought at My Lai', for nobody could offer any convincing evidence that enemy soldiers were present in the settlement, and their accounts of the lieutenant corralling successive groups of defenceless civilians into a ditch, thereafter opening fire, hardly conformed to conventional narratives of battle. Outside the court, however, the impact of this testimony was much more limited. Many Americans did not know precisely what had happened in My Lai (4), and thus their reactions to the eventual verdict seem to have been informed instead by impressionistic conceptions of the fog of war and killing through inadvertence. White House staff reported that a sizeable fraction of the letters, telegrams and cards received from the public in the wake of the Calley trial were 'based on false or misunderstood premises', with John Dean estimating that the error factor in the mail that he had answered 'at times ran between 10–15 per cent'.[15] Those who telephoned the Pentagon to protest against the verdict were often operating on the assumption that the civilians, whom the lieutenant had been convicted of murdering, had met their deaths when caught in a cross-fire.[16]

If many American citizens were prepared to subscribe to the defence offered by William Calley that his misadventures in My Lai (4) could best be explained by reference to the routine confusion and tragedy of war, it was probably because they shared a perception of the Vietnam conflict itself as ever more confused and ever more tragic: tragic, that is, not just in its effects, but also in the challenge that it presented to notions of human understanding and control. Almost everywhere one looked, the cultural and strategic coordinates that had given shape and meaning to the military endeavour in Vietnam were becoming increasingly unreliable, or else were simply disappearing from view. Talent had failed, and so apparently had technology and knowledge: the 'best and the brightest' had proved unable to bend the enemy to their will, even with all the data they had gathered about the progress of the war, all the computers they had used to crunch out the results, all the munitions they had expended to extort a favourable peace.[17] By the turn of the decade, moreover, the whole enterprise seemed futile, not just because victory remained elusive,

[14] *Time* (12 April 1971), p. 17.

[15] Melencamp to Price, 'Acknowledgment of Communications about the Calley Case', 7 April 1971, folder: 'Calley Correspondence', Box 14, John Dean Subject Files, Staff Members and Office Files, White House Special Files, NPM, NACP; Dean to Ehrlichman, 'Cost of Acknowledgment of Calley Mail', 17 May 1971, folder: 'JWD Chron File, May 1971', Box 2, John Dean Correspondence Files, Staff Members and Office Files, White House Special Files, NPM, NACP.

[16] Everett *et al.*, p. 291.

[17] D. Halberstam, *The Best and the Brightest* (New York: Ballantine, 1993).

but because changes in the regional geopolitical order – the right-wing counter-coup against Sukarno in Indonesia, the deepening of the Sino–Soviet dispute, and, ultimately, the move of both Moscow and Beijing towards détente with the United States – had evaporated most of the original strategic rationales for initiating and continuing the war. What once could have been defended, rightly or wrongly, as a test of America's reputation as a guarantor against the expansionist ambitions of an international communist confederation had withered, by the time of Calley's trial, into a struggle over the modalities of a ceasefire which was likely to be limited in its long-term effects even within Vietnam itself: US policymakers believed that they could secure nothing better from the settlement than a 'decent interval' before the regime in the south succumbed to pressure from the north.[18] Yet it continued to be a massively destructive war, an exercise in mutual punishment that, on the American side at least, seemed driven more by will than by purpose, in which the reasons for the violence were being rapidly obscured by the bodies and the rubble, to the point that it was perhaps only in the violence that any certain meaning inhered.

Within the American military, the impoverishment of the national objectives in Vietnam was reflected in increasing levels of desertion and drug abuse, and more frequent instances of inter-racial strife, corruption, indiscipline and displays of political dissent.[19] It was also evident in the retreat of the officer class towards careerist values, away from an ethos of proficient leadership, public service and personal integrity, as revealed in studies conducted by the Army War College. Time and time again, these studies observed, professional soldiers would return in interviews to the theme of the 'ambitious, transitory commander – marginally skilled in the complexities of his duties – engulfed in producing statistical results, fearful of personal failure, too busy to talk with or listen to his subordinates, and determined to submit acceptably optimistic reports which reflect faultless completion of a variety of tasks at the expense of the sweat and frustration of his subordinates'.[20] For many ordinary servicemen, Vietnam – already a strange and difficult place to fight a war – had become a kind of vacuum, indifferent to the pull of American power, in which history and time seemed to have been suspended, knowledge was unreliable and morality irrelevant; it was a vacuum, moreover, from which purpose had been expelled and all responsible leaders had fled. The veteran Tim O'Brien captured the condition of these soldiers in his novel *Going After Cacciato*, set in Quang Ngai in 1968:

[18] Kimball, p. 240.

[19] For contemporary analyses of the state of the army, see E. Sherman, 'A bureaucracy adrift', *Nation* (1 March 1971), pp. 265–75; R. Heinl, 'The collapse of the armed forces', *Armed Forces Journal* (7 June 1971), pp. 30–8.

[20] US Army War College, *Leadership for the 1970's: USAWC Study of Leadership for the Professional Soldier*, 20 October 1971.

They did not know even the simple things: a sense of victory, or satisfaction, or necessary sacrifice. They did not know the feeling of taking a place and keeping it, securing a village and then raising the flag and calling it a victory . . . They did not have targets. They did not have a cause. They did not know if it was a war of ideology or economics or hegemony or spite. On a given day, they did not know where they were in Quang Ngai, or how being there might influence larger outcomes. They did not know the names of most villages. They did not know which villages were crucial. They did not know strategies. They did not know the terms of the war, its architecture, the rules of fair play . . . They did not know how to feel when they saw villages burning. Revenge? Loss? Peace of mind or anguish? . . . They did not know good from evil.[21]

None of this, of course, made massacre inevitable; none of it justified what Calley and his men perpetrated in My Lai (4). Yet a crisis of purpose, knowledge and meaning, similar to that which pervaded the wider prosecution of the war, was evident in accounts of the killing in the village, and indeed was invoked by a number of commentators as they sought to illuminate the reasons why that killing had occurred. Of the briefing he received before the operation, Calley observed: 'Medina told us, "Kill everything." It made sense: it made as much sense as any of Charlie Company's missions the last quarter year, and I didn't question it.'[22]

Although the company had been told to expect a battle with the 48th Vietcong battalion in My Lai (4), the intelligence on which this assessment was based was at best ambiguous; some senior officers in the task force command, including Colonel Barker himself, believed that the battalion's headquarters were actually located a mile or so east in the sub-hamlet of My Khe, identified on American maps as My Lai (1) and known informally as 'Pinkville'. At province headquarters, meanwhile, intelligence officers judged that, following the Tet offensive, the battalion had retreated to the mountains west of Quang Ngai City, and were thus twenty or more kilometres away from the village of Son My.[23] After the operation, one soldier recalled, 'We all wondered where the enemy went.'[24] The massacre proceeded alongside elements of grim carnivalesque: one man was seen 'running down a trail, chasing a duck with a knife', another was cheerfully 'stabbing a calf over and over again'. The other cows in the village were also killed, as Jay Roberts, an army reporter who covered the operation with Haeberle, remembered: 'They had them in small pens. They'd shoot them – *paff, paff*, and the cow'd just go *moo*. Then *paff, paff, moo.*'[25] A group of soldiers continued firing at the head of a woman long after she was dead. 'You could see the bones flying in the air chip by chip,' Haeberle

[21] T. O'Brien, *Going After Cacciato* (London: Flamingo, 1988), pp. 255–6.
[22] 'The Concluding Confessions of Lieutenant Calley', *Esquire* (September 1971), p. 86.
[23] Goldstein *et al.*, p. 90; Hammer, *One Morning in the War*, p. 32; Hersh, *Cover-Up*, pp. 71, 96–7.
[24] *Life* (5 December 1969), p. 44.
[25] *Ibid.*, p. 43.

said later. 'Jay and I, we just shook our heads.'[26] In My Lai, Michael Bernhardt reflected, 'something was missing. Something you thought was real that would accompany this. It wasn't there . . . There was something missing in the whole business that made it seem like it really wasn't happening.' According to Robert Lifton, Bernhardt's account revealed an 'all-encompassing' condition of 'absurdity and moral inversion. The absurdity has to do with a sense of being alien and profoundly lost, yet at the same time locked into a situation as meaningless and unreal as it is deadly. The moral inversion, eventuating in a sense of evil, has to do not only with the absolute reversal of ethical standards but with its occurrence in absurdity, without inner justification, so that the killing is rendered naked.'[27]

In the *New York Times*, James Reston expressed the point more plainly: 'It is an appalling story of confusion and brutality, of gunning down children and women, of American soldiers who could not do it, and others who felt it was their duty to carry out orders, and some who were so brutalized or so confused or ignorant that they didn't know what they were doing or were being asked to do.'[28]

In the combat environment in which the members of Charlie Company operated in March 1968, atrocities may have occurred in part because some portion of their capacity for allocating weight and meaning to their actions, of calibrating means to ends, no longer worked. They may have occurred alternatively because in the commission of atrocity resided the promise of control: when everything else in the war seemed ambiguous and uncertain, this at least was something a soldier could do which had a definite, predictable result. Either way, the massacre expressed an experience of disorientation and frustration – ultimately resolved in excess – with which many Americans back home were able to identify as the conflict continued to resist the competence of national authority and their own understanding. In the wake of the Tet offensive, a significant minority of opinion poll respondents were prepared to support a dramatic escalation of the American commitment to Vietnam in order to win the war, apparently without much thought for the human consequences. In the same month as the massacre, 27 per cent of those polled agreed that the United States should use atomic weapons to achieve a military victory.[29] A year later, 32 per cent of respondents favoured the option: 'escalate war, go all out'.[30] At the time of the first massacre revelations, roughly the same percentage identified themselves as hawks, in line with the statement: 'People are called "hawks" if they want to step up our military effort in Vietnam.'[31]

[26] *Ibid.*, p. 41.
[27] Lifton, pp. 36–7.
[28] *New York Times* (26 November 1969), p. 44.
[29] Mueller, p. 129.
[30] Gallup, p. 2189.
[31] Mueller, p. 107.

In the White House, meanwhile, Richard Nixon and Henry Kissinger were conscious that, as congressional impatience with the continuation of the war increased and as US ground troops withdrew, their bargaining position with respect to the eventual settlement with Hanoi would progressively deteriorate. They endeavoured to compensate for that loss by ratcheting up the levels of aerial firepower applied against the enemy, first in South Vietnam, then (secretly) in Cambodia, and, with the support of 47 per cent of opinion-poll respondents, eventually also in the north.[32] According to Jeffrey Kimball, they even contemplated the use of nuclear weapons.[33]

To be drawn, as many Americans were, to the satisfactions of excessive force was not necessarily to forgive incidents like My Lai, but it undoubtedly restricted the grounds for moral critique. There may have been a moral distinction, as Mary McCarthy argued, between the acts of pounding a village with munitions from the air, in the knowledge that civilians would die as a result, and walking around the same village shooting its inhabitants with a rifle, but it was not necessarily clear to all those who paid attention to the case.[34] In a way, it all just looked like war. South Vietnam, CBS reporter Bert Quint stated in early December 1969, was 'full of hamlets and villages' in which people were suffering as a result of the conflict: 'To them, it's academic whether their children or their neighbours died because bombs fell or machine-gun bullets were fired, whether it was a communist or an American who looked through the sights. They do not die for democracy or for communism; they die because they are here.'[35]

Around the same time, one Indiana man interviewed by reporters from the *Wall Street Journal* declared: 'You drop bombs on a village and innocent bystanders get killed. Is that an atrocity? This is just the nature of war.'[36] After the verdict in Calley's court martial had been reached, *ABC News* anchorman Harry Reasoner observed: 'There are men wearing medals for what they did in Vietnam who killed more innocent civilians than Lt Calley even saw in My Lai. They did it from aeroplanes ... Is it murder if you can see them, and the nature of war if you cannot?' He was not sure it was: 'it is too hard for it to come down to one simple and unprepared man out of the morass of all the confused and casual killing. I could not have voted guilty in this trial.'[37]

The disappointments endured by the American people during the conflict in Vietnam had dismantled many of their traditional conceptions of war: as a site where violence could be morally redemptive and individuals could fashion their own fate, and as a field of imagination across which

[32] Kimball, pp. 136–7, 183–4, 316; Hammond, *Public Affairs ... 1968–1973*, p. 556.
[33] Kimball, pp. 145, 163, 313.
[34] McCarthy, pp. 41–2.
[35] *CBS Evening News*, 2 December 1969, VTNA.
[36] *Wall Street Journal* (1 December 1969), p. 1.
[37] *ABC News*, 30 March 1971, VTNA.

the creative intellect could play. By the late 1960s, war seemed a rather tedious enterprise, indifferent to human agency, unresponsive to thought.[38] Men killed and were killed, and there wasn't much more to be said about it than that. How death happened and where responsibility lay were matters only for the morbidly curious or for those who liked to make trouble. This was certainly the opinion of Mr and Mrs Robert F. Henry of Cincinnati, forcefully expressed in a letter to the army's Court of Military Review following the Calley verdict: 'One cannot convict a military man of premeditated murder, when his sole intent for being militarized, is to kill! One cannot disallow a military kill on one particular day; in one particular town; on some particular civilians.'[39] Asked for his view of the verdict by a reporter for NBC, Sergeant Richard Jupiter of the Americal Division, recently redesignated the 23rd Infantry Division, replied: 'I think it stinks, sir. I don't think he should have been convicted. War is war.'[40]

The enemy's atrocities, of course, were not as readily ascribed to the exigencies of combat, or even to its chaos, but it was no longer as contentious as it once had been to assert that a measure of moral equivalence obtained across all the parties in the war, to locate them within the same community of destruction. A village in the Mekong Delta, taken over first by the Vietcong, and then reclaimed with rockets and artillery by US forces and the South Vietnamese, was described by Bert Quint as a victim 'not just of Americans or of Communists, but a victim of man'. He concluded: 'One may ask "Whose fault is it?", and the only certain answer is that, in this war, there are few saints and many martyrs.'[41] Yet, as Americans became more aware of their national capacity for violence, more aware that malignancy of conduct was not confined to the other side, they did not necessarily connect this knowledge to the specific failures of military policy in Vietnam, taking it as a challenge to their conscience and as an inspiration for reform. Instead, to the dismay of those who had striven to confront the culture with the evidence of how the conflict was really being fought, in the hope that some such policy change would result, many citizens took the view that it was pointless and foolish to expect anything different from a war. As John Kerry of the Vietnam Veterans Against the War declared in testimony before the Senate Foreign Relations Committee in April 1971: 'We are faced with a very sickening situation in

[38] Tom Englehardt records that, over the course of the Vietnam war, the manufacturers of the action figure 'GI Joe' gradually withdrew the toy's more militaristic accessories from sale, in an effort to redefine him as a classic adventure hero. T. Englehardt, *The End of Victory Culture: Cold War America and the Disillusioning of a Generation* (New York: Basic Books, 1995), pp. 175–8.

[39] Mr and Mrs Robert F. Henry to 'US Army Court of Military Review Judges', 5 April 1971, folder: 'Incoming Public Letters – Calley Case, 1972 (Unanswered)', Box 25, Records of the Calley General Court-Martial, 1969–74, Office of the Clerk of the Court, Records of the Judge Advocate General (Army), RG153, NACP.

[40] *NBC Nightly News*, 30 March 1971, VTNA.

[41] *CBS Evening News*, 2 December 1969, VTNA.

this country, because there is no moral indignation and, if there is, it comes from people who are almost exhausted by their past indignations.'[42]

By the time of the massacre revelations, the war in Vietnam was already vulnerable to recontextualization. Credibility had drained from its original rationales; the power of human authority to influence its course (and, by extension, to control its excesses) seemed markedly diminished; popular frustration with the poverty of military progress, meanwhile, was reflected in demands for the dramatic escalation of violence as much as it was in calls for immediate withdrawal and peace. Into the flux of this period fell the news of My Lai, which exercised a discursive pull sufficient for the cohering of an alternative conception of war and its relation to ethics: that the pathologies exposed as Calley and his men proceeded through the settlement were not limited to them alone, or to the combat culture of US forces in Vietnam, but rather expressed moral ambivalences intrinsic to the whole broader profession of arms.

What the disclosures prompted, particularly amongst liberals and those on the left, was a re-evaluation of the military history of the United States and the pattern of its interactions with people of other races. This re-evaluation – which established that the atrocities at My Lai (4) had a plenitude of precedents stretching back throughout the nation's past – travelled some way beyond the usual parochial orbits of academic revisionism. The *New York Times* reminded its readers of two earlier massacres committed by American armed forces – of the Miniconjou Sioux at Wounded Knee in 1890, and of 600 Moros near Jolo in the Philippines in 1906.[43] Other journals carried detailed accounts of the war in the Philippines, noting the resemblance between the charges of misconduct advanced against the US Army in that particular campaign – that its soldiers routinely engaged in torture, in the wholesale destruction of villages and in the killing of prisoners and civilians – and those advanced against it in the present with respect to Vietnam.[44] 'Indeed,' said the writer of one such account, 'to follow the Philippine Insurrection in old newspapers and magazines is like sitting through a shabby drama for the second time.'[45] Hollywood, meanwhile, turned its attention to the Indian wars of the late nineteenth century: in the films *Little Big Man* and *Soldier Blue*, both produced in 1970, the army was depicted assaulting native American encampments, butchering women and children by the score.[46] In his

[42] 'Statement of John Kerry, Vietnam Veterans Against the War', 22 April 1971, in US Congress, Senate, Committee on Foreign Relations, *Legislative Proposals Relating to the War in Southeast Asia: Hearings Before the Committee on Foreign Relations*, 92nd Congress, First Session, 1971 (Washington, DC: US Government Printing Office, 1971), p. 184.

[43] *New York Times* (28 November 1969), p. 18.

[44] D. Schirmer, 'Mylai was not the first time', *New Republic* (24 April 1971), pp. 18–21; S. Miller, 'Our Mylai of 1900: Americans in the Philippine insurrection', *Trans-Action* (September 1970), pp. 19–28.

[45] Miller, p. 19.

[46] *Little Big Man*, dir. Arthur Penn (1970); *Soldier Blue*, dir. Ralph Nelson (1970).

reflections on the massacre at My Lai (4), Noam Chomsky asked: 'Is it an exaggeration to suggest that our history of extermination and racism is reaching its climax in Vietnam today?'[47]

It was not just liberal and left critiques, however, which asserted that the record of the US military was more familiar with atrocity than collective memory liked to allow. Taking the view that Calley's conviction represented a wilful denial of the harsh realities of combat, a succession of Second World War veterans publicly declared that they too had been guilty of war crimes according to the definition of the court. Raymond Hufft, a retired major general, told reporters that he had once ordered his men to take no prisoners: 'We shot everything that moved . . . If the Germans had won, I would have been on trial at Nuremberg instead of them.' In Coventry, Rhode Island, Carl Savard announced that he had killed a mother with a baby in her arms, as well as a 10-year-old boy who had shot his radio man, and requested to be placed in jail. 'If he [Calley] can be tried for those crimes,' he said, 'I would like to be tried for crimes I committed in World War II.'[48] *CBS Evening News* reported from a rally in Waterloo, Illinois, organized to protest the verdict against the lieutenant, and filmed a member of the American Legion informing the crowd: 'He only did what he was told to do, what he was asked to do, what he was trained to do, and what millions of the rest of us did in World War One, Two and the Korean War.'[49]

Indeed, it was the traditional veterans' community which was probably the source of many of the initial public expressions of sympathy for William Calley and, as his trial came to an end, it was the institutions of that community which provided a clearing-house for public dissent from the verdict and an organizational framework for subsequent demonstrations and petitions. In its attempt to account for the ease with which the nation had accommodated the revelations about the massacre, *Time* noted: 'There are, after all, millions of adult Americans who have fought from the Argonnes to Inchon and carry their own private knowledge of the necessities – and the better-forgotten brutalities – of personal combat.'[50] Although those who disapproved of Calley's prosecution were no more likely to have served in the military than those who approved, if they had seen such service, it was more likely to have occurred during a war, and more likely also to have included experience of combat.[51]

The national veterans organizations, such as the American Legion and the Veterans of Foreign Wars, took no official stand on the massacre case in the weeks after it was revealed, but local members were not

[47] N. Chomsky, 'After Pinkville', in Limqueco and Weiss, pp. 45–6.
[48] *New York Times* (1 April 1971), p. 18.
[49] *CBS Evening News*, 2 April 1971, VTNA.
[50] *Time* (12 January 1970), p. 8.
[51] Kelman and Lawrence, 'Assignment of Responsibility', p. 203.

discouraged from engaging in activities of their own. In Columbus, Georgia, six miles from Fort Benning, the American Legion post sponsored a campaign to raise money for Calley's legal defence.[52] After the court returned its verdict, the post became a cell of local resistance, as it announced a petition of protest and a fund-raising drive to pay for the lieutenant's appeal; many reporters headed to its hall to capture snappy examples of veterans dissent.[53] 'I thought he would be found not guilty,' declared one member of the legion to a film crew from NBC, 'because you send a man into combat, you train him to be a killer and then he does, why, then you prosecute him!'[54]

As soon as the verdict was reached, however, the veterans' protest went national. The American Legion informed White House staff that it was receiving telephone calls, night and day, from every state in the union, 'from people who are in turn responding to hundreds of calls in their localities'.[55] Herbert Rainwater, Commander-in-Chief of the Veterans of Foreign Wars, wrote to more than 12,000 officers in his organization, exhorting them to send a letter or telegram immediately to the President and their congressional representatives, urging that the verdict be overturned. He had travelled to Washington from the VFW's national headquarters in Kansas City in order 'to personally work on this matter'.[56] On 31 March, Rainwater met with the heads of other major veterans' organizations; they decided collectively 'to demand to see the President to express their unanimous feeling that if this is the way we treat our Military personnel, we should stop fighting immediately'.[57] Rainwater told the press: 'There have been My Lais in every war. Now for the first time in our history we have tried a soldier for performing his duty.'[58]

In their communications with the White House, the veterans leaders reported 'that the feeling in the South is near revolt'.[59] Most indices of public sentiment – opinion polls, editorials in local newspapers, letters and telegrams sent to the President and to Congress – confirm the impression that if the people of any particular region were especially exercised

[52] *CBS Evening News*, 16 December 1969, VTNA.

[53] *CBS Evening News*, 30 March 1971, VTNA.

[54] *NBC Nightly News*, 29 March 1971, VTNA.

[55] Bell to Colson, 'Reactions to Calley Verdict', 1 April 1971, folder: 'Calley verdict', Box 42, Charles Colson Subject Files, Staff Members and Office Files, White House Special Files, NPM, NACP.

[56] Rainwater to Commanders, 1 April 1971, folder: 'Veterans of Foreign Wars [2 of 3]', Box 120, Charles Colson Subject Files, Staff Members and Office Files, White House Special Files, NPM, NACP.

[57] Colson to Haldeman, 1 April 1971, folder: 'Chuck Colson April 1971 [2 of 2]', Box 77, Harry R. Haldeman: Alpha Name Files, Staff Members and Office Files, White House Special Files, NPM, NACP.

[58] Tiede, p. 130.

[59] Colson to Haldeman, 1 April 1971, folder: 'Chuck Colson April 1971 [2 of 2]', Box 77, Harry R. Haldeman: Alpha Name Files, Staff Members and Office Files, White House Special Files, NPM, NACP.

by the conviction of William Calley, it was the people of the south.[60] Vietnam itself, as Joseph Fry has pointed out, was a war disproportionately waged by southerners: initiated by Johnson of Texas and Rusk of Georgia and for the most part cheered on by southern politicians, with the eleven states of the former Confederacy supplying nearly a third of the total number of US combat personnel. In national opinion surveys, southerners were always more confident than Americans elsewhere about the efficacy of military force in Vietnam; they were always more ready to support the unrestrained pursuit of military victory, and always more irritated when those restraints failed to come off.[61] When southerners looked at the men charged with atrocities in My Lai (4), they saw their own sons and brothers, arraigned before a court for actions that seemed – at least, to the superficial glance – roughly consistent with the policy that they believed should have been adopted all along. A good many members of Charlie Company, after all, had sprung from the south: at the trial of Ernest Medina, Mary McCarthy observed, the company delivered its testimony 'in all the black and white varieties of southern speech'.[62]

In February 1971, 50 per cent of those polled in the south considered Calley's shooting of civilians to have been justified (compared with 36 per cent in the West and Midwest, and 25 per cent in the East), and 56 per cent judged that it was 'more right' to follow orders to shoot old men, women and children in a village where the civilians were suspected of aiding the enemy than it was to refuse (compared with 34 per cent in the West, 37 per cent in the Midwest, and 41 per cent in the East).[63]

Medina's court martial took place at Fort McPherson in Atlanta – the site, as McCarthy noted, of 'an earlier war crime', when General Sherman had torched the city and laid waste to much of the rest of Georgia on his march to the sea.[64] Fort Benning, where Calley was tried, was less than a hundred miles away. What southerners thought about Vietnam, and what they thought about My Lai, may well have been informed by sectional memories of the Civil War, of a conflict that had been waged through the total mobilization of a society's resources and eventually resolved by means of their total destruction. 'I know that you've got to destroy the enemy's

[60] Twenty-eight per cent of respondents who expressed disapproval of the trial in early summer 1971 came from the south, compared with 22 per cent of the total survey sample. The respective figures for other regions were as follows: East – 39 per cent and 43 per cent; Midwest – 21 per cent and 18 per cent; West – 12 per cent and 16 per cent. Kelman and Lawrence, 'Assignment of Responsibility', p. 202. See also: W. Garber, 'Editorial reaction of selected daily newspapers to the Calley conviction' (MA thesis, University of Florida, 1972), pp. 66–7; Higby to Haldeman, 1 April 1971, folder: 'Calley', Box 16, John Ehrlichman: Alphabetical Subject File, Staff Members and Office Files, White House Special Files, NPM, NACP; *New York Times* (3 April 1971), p. 14.

[61] J. Fry, *Dixie Looks Abroad: the South and US Foreign Relations 1789–1973* (Baton Rouge: Louisiana State University Press, 2002), pp. 261–73.

[62] McCarthy, p. 66.

[63] Harris poll data, folder: My Lai 8/83, Papers of *Four Hours in My Lai*, LHCMA, KCL.

[64] McCarthy, p. 67.

resources,' Jay Roberts said as he recalled Charlie Company's actions in My Lai (4). 'It's an old tactic and a good one. Sherman's march to the sea. You've just got to. We saw soldiers drag a body from a hut and throw it in a well to destroy the water supply.'[65] Close to Fort Benning, the owner of a gas station responded to the court's judgment against Calley by quoting Sherman's most famous words on his forecourt sign: 'War is hell. Free Lt Calley.'[66] Releasing Calley from confinement in September 1974, Judge J. Robert Elliott of the United States District Court for the Middle District of Georgia, Columbus Division, justified his decision through lengthy reference to the conduct and philosophy of Sherman's campaign in the south: 'The point is that Sherman was absolutely right; not about what he did, but about the nature of war; war *is* hell.'[67]

The trial of William Calley exacerbated, therefore, a long-gathering crisis in southern attitudes towards the Vietnam conflict, for now it seemed apparent that not only was the national leadership not in the war to win, but that it was also intent on the persecution of any American soldiers who were. If that was the case, then the South wanted out. Around the region, and also elsewhere, local draft boards refused to conscript any more young men until the decision was reversed.[68] In Athens, Georgia, the entire draft board resigned, its chairman telling a reporter for *NBC Nightly News* that he was not prepared to procure soldiers for the military when obedience to orders might mean a share in Calley's fate.[69] George Wallace, governor of Alabama, directed his officials to investigate whether he could suspend the draft in the state as a means of forcing a pardon.[70] Other prominent southern politicians, such as the governor of Mississippi, declared that, if the President did not intervene in the case, they would insist upon immediate American withdrawal from the war.[71]

For a White House that was endeavouring to cultivate a new Republican south, and also to preserve the coalition of sentiment in favour of staying the course in Vietnam (of which the traditional veterans organizations were another important part), these demands for intervention were difficult to ignore. As the President told Henry Kissinger on 1 April, 'We're dealing really with the bigger cause, which is the question of how can we hold enough support for a year and a half to maintain our conduct of the war.' If he failed to act, Nixon believed, that support 'will evaporate or become discouraged'. To uphold the judicial process offered, in contrast, very few political rewards: 'There is not enough in it for us to fight for

[65] *Life* (5 December 1969), p. 43.

[66] Everett *et al.*, p. 283.

[67] *Calley* v. *Callaway*, 382 F. Supp. 650 (1974), in Goldstein *et al.*, pp. 554–5 (italics in original).

[68] B. Asbell, 'The day America could have used a psychiatrist', *Today's Health* (August 1971), p. 29.

[69] *NBC Nightly News*, 30 March 1971, VTNA.

[70] Asbell, p. 29.

[71] *ABC News*, 31 March 1971, VTNA.

the military.' In the event that he moved to commute Calley's sentence, the President proposed to make a statement addressing 'the obsolete idea that war is a game with rules', asserting that, though the lieutenant's actions could not be condoned, 'when men serve their country you cannot during this crisis of war follow this line [of prosecution] unless there's a direct clear breach of orders'. He wanted to 'make the point that war is bad so we've got to avoid more bad wars'.[72] As it happened, he did not actually go quite this far. When he released Calley from the stockade pending his appeal and announced that he would personally review the case at the end of the appellate process, Nixon justified those decisions primarily in terms of his duty as President to ease public disquiet.[73] Nevertheless, his intervention was informed by a perception that his principal constituencies of support were far more concerned about the fate of William Calley than about what Calley himself had done to the inhabitants of My Lai (4). As Nixon explained to Kissinger, 'most of the people don't give a shit whether he killed them or not'.[74]

Although the President's actions in the wake of the court martial were warmly received by the vast majority of Americans, they did not entirely soothe the resentment and despair that Calley's conviction had provoked, especially within hawkish circles.[75] Perhaps influenced in addition by the failure of the recent South Vietnamese incursion into Laos, approval ratings for Nixon's policies in Vietnam fell precipitiously, from 41 per cent in early March to 32 per cent at the start of April.[76] It was a response that caused some consternation in the White House, with the President himself regarding the results as 'absurd', and indeed it was only a temporary decline, with the index of support returning to its previous levels over the next few weeks.[77]

More enduring were the effects of the case upon underlying attitudes towards the war as a whole. In January, 47 per cent of poll respondents had judged that it was morally wrong for the United States to be fighting in Vietnam. By April, the figure had risen to 58 per cent, with the trend sustained through October, when 65 per cent of those polled registered an

[72] Haldeman, diary entry, 1 April 1971, Audio Cassette No. 6, Part 2, Diaries of Harry R. Haldeman, NPM, NACP.

[73] 'Panel interview at the Annual Convention of the American Society of Newspaper Editors', 16 April 1971, *Public Papers of the Presidents: Richard Nixon, 1971*, pp. 537–8.

[74] Conversation with Kissinger, 8 April 1971, Conversation No. 475–16, White House Reference Cassette No. 453, NPM, NACP.

[75] *New York Times* (4 April 1971), p. 56; Opinion Research Corporation poll, 5–6 April 1971. Data provided by Roper Center for Public Opinion Research: www.ropercenter. uconn.edu (accessed November 2003).

[76] Opinion Research Corporation polls, 6–7 March, 1 April 1971. Data provided by Roper Center for Public Opinion Research: www.ropercenter.uconn.edu (accessed November 2003).

[77] Conversation with Haldemen, 7 April 1971, Conversation No. 246–7, White House Reference Cassette No. 422, NPM, NACP; Opinion Research Corporation polls, 5–6 April, 22 April 1971. Data provided by Roper Center for Public Opinion Research: www.ropercenter. uconn.edu (accessed November 2003).

ethical dissent from the war. Perhaps the most dramatic shift of sentiment on this question occurred in the south, as the proportion of southerners declaring the war to be morally wrong increased from 38 per cent to 58 per cent between January and April, stabilizing somewhat thereafter.[78] The stimulus for these misgivings was unlikely to have been the massacre itself, the essential dimensions of which had been disclosed a long time before, or the incursion into Laos, for that was just the sort of initiative that the south tended to support. Rather, it was the sight of an American soldier on trial for his life, abandoned by the army, harried by its lawyers, eventually condemned to its stockade, that seemed to be their source. That is, when they were asked about the ethical content of the conflict, many poll respondents did not think about its impact upon the Vietnamese at all, but about the duty of the US military to honour the service of its own men: to prosecute the war in good faith, not the soldiers who fought it. It was in the dereliction of that duty that the moral failing lay.

The argument advanced by hawks and doves alike that the killings in My Lai (4) had ethical analogues in earlier national campaigns represented a more serious challenge to the doctrine of exceptionalism than the massacre had just on its own. It was not only the reputation of the US military in the present day that was now cast into ambiguity, but all claims of a higher virtue made in relation to the country's martial past. To assert that 'war is hell' was to cloud many of the distinctions previously held to obtain between the manner in which, historically, the United States had fought its battles and the combat practices of other national armed forces, even those of regimes that commonly had been considered beyond the ethical pale. It was self-deceiving to pretend, declared the *New York Times*, 'that wanton violence is new, to this nation or any other. It is as old as the maddened passions of war and hate'.[79] *Time* was unsure whether the massacre could be classified as a historical aberration. In previous wars, it acknowledged, acts of brutality had also been committed by US troops, though it considered these distinct from the atrocities in which other countries had engaged, for they were rarely the result of 'a deliberate national policy of terror'. The journal offered the following circumspect conclusion: 'The tragedy shows that the American soldier carries no immunity against the cruelty and inhumanity of prolonged combat.'[80] Two weeks later, *Time* examined foreign newspaper coverage of the story and, in much the same tone, informed its readers: 'In the end, if any reaction to the massacre of My Lai was shared by honest men, it was that the world expects the worst from warriors – even American warriors.'[81]

---

[78] Harris poll data, folder: My Lai 8/83, Papers of *Four Hours in My Lai*, LHCMA, KCL.
[79] *New York Times* (30 November 1969), p. 12.
[80] *Time* (28 November 1969), p. 19.
[81] *Time* (12 December 1969), p. 17.

That the tale of a single sub-hamlet put to the sword contained universal lessons about the true nature of war was a proposition that found echoes in the broader public response to the affair. 'Oh fiddle! Every war has that. War is war,' said Mrs Mary Halsem of Los Angeles, when asked for her reaction by reporters for the *Wall Street Journal*. The sentiments expressed by Patrick Kupper, an elevator starter from Boston, were even more robust: 'It was good. What do they give soldiers bullets for – to put in their pockets? That's the way war is.'[82] Both local and national opinion polls found majorities ready to assert that events like My Lai were inevitable in war, given the tendency of combat to 'make people brutal'.[83] After Calley had been convicted, *Time* observed that, for many Americans, the notion that laws existed in conditions of conflict was simply 'absurd'.[84] It was not necessarily the case, however, that those who judged it axiomatic that wars produced atrocity were thereby entirely reconciled to the human implications of that view, or to the conclusion that, in conflict, anything goes. 'I don't approve of women and children being killed,' one survey respondent declared, 'but unfortunately in war these things happen.'[85] At Ohio State University, roughly 80 per cent of students polled agreed that 'Incidents such as My Lai are bound to happen in war.' Yet much the same proportion also registered their dissent from the statement: 'War is war – nothing wrong with what happened at My Lai.'[86]

Not everyone who attributed the massacre to the sociology of armed conflict did so in the belief that the actions of Charlie Company were consistent with normal military ethics and practice. An alternative, slightly more nuanced perspective was available: that, in any large battle zone, in any conflict of duration, some soldiers, somewhere, could be expected to succumb to the strains (and opportunities) of war, making victims, most likely, of defenceless civilians. Absent the condition of war, these men would not behave in such a way; ergo, it was war that was to blame.[87]

Atrocities in war were caused by war: in its most routine articulations, this explanation of the massacre withered the moral autonomy of the individual soldier at least as much as did the alternative defence that 'orders were orders', to the point, indeed, that it was only the chance contingencies of combat (and not his attributes of character, the quality of instruction and leadership to which he was exposed, or the ethical lessons that he

---

[82] *Wall Street Journal* (1 December 1969), p. 1.
[83] *Minneapolis Tribune* (21 December 1969), p. 4B; *Time* (12 January 1970), p. 8.
[84] *Time* (12 April 1971).
[85] Kelman and Lawrence, 'American response to the trial of Lt William L. Calley', p. 78.
[86] Thompson *et al.*, p. 127.
[87] Daniel Patrick Moynihan offered a similar evaluation to President Nixon in November 1969: 'It is not the American character that came out at Mylai. It is what war can do to that or any character. I joined the Navy in 1944 at age 17, and am proud of it. I later served as a gunnery officer on a ship at sea. I have seen what the mere proximity to violence does to certain personalities.' Moynihan to Nixon, 25 November 1969, folder: 'My Lai Incident [1 of 2]', Box 1004, Alexander Haig Special File, National Security Council Files, NPM, NACP.

drew from the practices of the military command) which were held to determine whether or not he participated in slaughter. Other reflections on the massacre, however, offered an even more abstracted reading of its causes: it was not their experience of war which made soldiers engage in atrocity, but the fact that they were human, thus harbouring in their hearts some base attraction to sin and a capacity for violence.

Anthony Lewis, London correspondent for the *New York Times*, reported that, in Europe, My Lai was 'seen as a reminder that there is a dark side to all human beings, to all societies'.[88] *Time* magazine observed that good and evil were 'intertwined and inseparable' components of human exist- ence; whilst acknowledging that wrongdoing was 'not to be shrugged off with easy references to human nature', it concluded that 'to ignore the persistent dark element in man can be as misleading, and intolerant, as to see only the dark'.[89] These meditations often took a genealogical turn, alluding to the survival of the savage beneath the rational, urbane façade of modern man. Until the causes of war were finally eliminated, asserted a *New York Times* editorial, 'it remains the burden of democratic govern- ment and of the national conscience to chain the bestial instincts which war unleashes and which, unchecked, threaten a people's heart and soul'.[90] Writing in the same paper, Tom Wicker proposed that the massacre proved 'nothing specific about Vietnam; it only shows once again what man is capable of once he lets loose the beast within himself'.[91] The argument concerning the true nature of 'the human animal', Eric Sevareid told viewers of *CBS Evening News*, 'has been going on for several thou- sand years. It's far from settled.'[92] Later, after the end of Calley's trial, Sevareid assessed the mood in Washington, and reported that many people there were 'thinking some long thoughts about the fragile construction of civilization and what endless war gradually does to the mirror image of a people who always thought that they had at the least a general goodness'.[93]

These challenges to the polarities of good and evil, civilization and savagery, reflected a range of long-established cultural assumptions, as well as more contemporary intellectual developments. Much of Christian theology – not least in its concept of original sin – asserted the coexist- ence of good and evil within man.[94] The political principles of conservat- ism (undergoing a revival in these years) were underpinned by a Hobbesian conception of human relations in their natural state as anarchic, com- petitive and brutal. Presented with the opportunity to condemn the My Lai

---

[88] *New York Times* (29 November 1969), p. 32.
[89] *Time* (5 December 1969), p. 27.
[90] *New York Times* (30 November 1969), p. 12.
[91] *New York Times* (2 December 1969), p. 54.
[92] *CBS Evening News*, 28 November 1969, VTNA.
[93] *CBS Evening News*, 9 April 1971, VTNA.
[94] In its ruminations upon the massacre, indeed, *Time* cited Martin Luther: 'man is *simul justus ac peccator* – saint and sinner at once', *Time* (5 December 1969), p. 27.

massacre, most conservative religious leaders elected to pass.[95] In the references to the persistence of primal energies, there were traces of Frederick Jackson Turner's iconic American frontiersman, operating at 'the meeting point between savagery and civilization' – a figure, as John Hellmann has noted, which had been recently revived for the era of modern warfare in the form of John F. Kennedy's Green Berets.[96] Perhaps most influential, however, were the neo- and post-Freudian manifestoes of the 1960s' counter-culture which asserted the need to acknowledge and emancipate the natural instinct-life of the human species, long suppressed by the role demands of modern technocratic capitalism.[97] Not all did so without critical reservations, because the survival of ethics in an uninhibited society could not be entirely guaranteed: the passage of the Manson family from free love to gleeful killing offered good reason to be cautious. As Theodore Roszak observed: 'No sooner does one speak of liberating the non-intellective powers of the personality than, for many, a prospect of the starkest character arises: a vision of rampant, antinomian mania, which in the name of permissiveness threatens to plunge us into a dark and savage age.'[98] Nevertheless, the pathologies that resulted from repression were considered more destructive than those that might accompany the condition of liberation. Consciousness of one's own irrational urges was healthier than denial. Thus, argued the sociologist Robert Bellah, the young cultural dissenters of the day possessed a better understanding of the darkness that lay within and 'a deeper sense of what it means to be human' than many of their elders, for whom evil had always been projected outwards onto others.[99]

To identify atrocity as an authentic expression of what it is to be human was to engage with the proposition that something of value can accrue

[95] In the wake of Calley's court martial, the liberal Catholic journal, *Commonweal,* urged the National Conference of Catholic Bishops to speak out about the massacre: 'If they hope to have any influence at all as moral leaders in the future, they must now vigorously and courageously summon the nation back from the precipice of barbarism.' The bishops seem not to have heeded the call. See J. Benestad and F. Butler (eds), *Quest for Justice: A Compendium of Statements of the United States Catholic Bishops of the Political and Social Order 1966–1980* (Washington, DC: National Conference of Catholic Bishops, United States Catholic Conference, 1981). President Nixon asked Daniel Moynihan to elicit the views of Revd Billy Graham on the Calley case. Graham's response, whatever it was, clearly did not deter the President's intervention. Haldeman, handwritten note, 1 April 1971, folder: 'H Notes April–June 1971 Part 1', Box 43, Harry R. Haldeman: Notes, Staff Members and Office Files, White House Special Files, NPM, NACP.

[96] F. Turner, 'The significance of the frontier in American history', in Turner, *The Frontier in American History* (New York: Henry Holt, 1931), p. 3; J. Hellmann, *American Myth and the Legacy of Vietnam* (New York: Columbia University Press, 1986), pp. 41–53.

[97] See, for example, H. Marcuse, *Eros and Civilization* (London: Sphere Books, 1969); Marcuse, *One-Dimensional Man: Studies in the Ideology of Advanced Industrial Society* (London: Routledge, 1991); C. Reich, *The Greening of America* (New York: Bantam Books, 1971); T. Roszak, *The Making of a Counter-Culture: Reflections on the Technocratic Society and Its Youthful Opposition* (London: Faber & Faber, 1970).

[98] Roszak, p. 73.

[99] R. Bellah, 'Evil and the American Ethos', in Sanford *et al.,* p. 190.

from the act – in particular, a form of existential knowledge. That the experience of release from ethical restraint might provide access to essential truths about the nature of man was a postulate of many contributions to American cultural discourse in the late 1960s and early 1970s. In 1972, in a collection of lectures, Lionel Trilling contended that works of literature which evinced the quality of 'sincerity' were now considered anachronistic and quaint; over the course of the twentieth century, 'authenticity' had become the identifying mark of literary merit. To Trilling, 'authenticity' suggested 'a more strenuous moral experience than "sincerity" does, a more exigent conception of the self and of what being true to it consists in, a wider reference to the universe and man's place in it, and a less acceptant and genial view of the social circumstances of life'.[100] If one literary work exemplified this concern with authenticity, it was Joseph Conrad's *Heart of Darkness*, particularly in its characterization of Mr Kurtz. The megalomanic agent of European colonialism who directs the base-level pathology of that enterprise towards new and almost inexpressible extremes, Kurtz nevertheless attains the status of hero, for – as Trilling comments – he had 'sinned for all mankind. By his regression to savagery Kurtz had reached as far beneath the constructs of civilization as it was possible to go, to the irreducible truth of man, the inner-most core of his nature, his heart of darkness.'[101]

Kurtz, of course, was later to receive American citizenship and a commission in the Green Berets, as Francis Ford Coppola's *Apocalypse Now* transposed Conrad's story onto the tableau of Vietnam, and re-evoked the existential truths apparently offered by the experience of ethical transgression.[102] Coppola has been criticized for the lack of moral centre in his film, but he was hardly alone in his selection of theme.[103] By the end of the 1960s, 'authenticity' was on offer almost everywhere in the culture. In popular music, it was the season of Johnny Cash, with a million-selling single and two hit albums (all recorded live, before audiences of convicts), as well as a profile in *Life*, published just as the revelations about My Lai began to emerge.[104] What the magazine presented was an artist with intimate experience of the 'hard times' of which he sang: poverty, addiction and at least one night spent in a Georgia jail. 'Convicts,' Cash declared, 'feel that I am one of their own.' He was popular amongst the young 'because he has the ring of authenticity'. *Life* quoted a friend: 'Last year it was soul. This year everybody is scratching in the soil. That's why

[100] L. Trilling, *Sincerity and Authenticity* (Cambridge: Harvard University Press, 1972), p. 9.

[101] *Ibid.*, p. 108.

[102] *Apocalypse Now*, dir. Francis Ford Coppola (1979).

[103] Marin, 'Coming to terms with Vietnam', pp. 41–56.

[104] Johnny Cash, 'A Boy Named Sue' (Columbia, 1969); Johnny Cash, *At Folsom Prison* (Columbia, 1968); Johnny Cash, *At San Quentin* (Columbia, 1969); *Life* (21 November 1969), pp. 44–5.

Johnny works. He's got soil.' In one of the images accompanying the article, Cash's 'ruined' features were exhibited in close-up, craggy and lined, his gaze directed inwards; in another, he strode down a railroad track towards the camera, his eyes challenging the lens, guitar like a rifle slung across his back. William Calley later recalled a lieutenant-colonel who had been rejected for service on his court-martial jury, because he had admitted that he was prejudiced against the prosecution. The officer's face, Calley said, was 'hard, tired, weary, worn: I thought of Johnny Cash.'[105]

If Cash had a standard, it was 'Folsom Prison Blues', a song that contains perhaps the most economical account of what violence may owe to the desire for experience: 'I shot a man in Reno just to watch him die.' Hearing Cash sing that line, the convicts in the audience applauded and cheered. CBS correspondent John Laurence recalled listening to a tape of the song as he flew back to Vietnam in March 1970 after nearly two years away from the war. He found it 'repulsive and attractive at the same time. The idea of absolute evil touched a part of me I didn't want to know. Random anger and violence made me uncomfortable, driving me away and drawing me close, offering clues to an unknown self. The thoughts it brought up were too confusing, too frightening, too close to a deeper mystery to want to know more.'[106] Later that same trip, as he covered the invasion of Cambodia, Laurence alerted the crew of the armoured personnel carrier in which he was travelling to a North Vietnamese soldier preparing to shoot from behind a nearby tree. The soldier was quickly dispatched with machine-gun fire, leaving Laurence feeling shaken, as if he had encountered the 'unknown self' that he had shrunk from on the plane: 'The killing had let loose, if only for an instant, the darkest part of me, a part I hated, a killer-beast I did not want to accept.'[107]

Claims of authenticity were also claims to authority, demands, in a sense, for deference within the culture. For many veterans of Vietnam, such claims were not easily made (they had every reason, after all, to be suspicious of power), and nor, in the early 1970s, were they always readily met. Yet, even as their mobilizations ebbed and flowed, failing for the most part to achieve any real influence over administration policy, the veterans were accorded a certain special status, largely because of their experience of extremity. The significance of the Vietnam Veterans Against the War, asserted *Life* magazine in July 1971, 'derives not from their numbers but from their authenticity: they were there'.[108]

The 'authority' of the veterans was a particular issue for non-veterans who became involved with their community. A number of psychiatrists, for example, discovered they could not rely upon their professional credentials

[105] 'The Concluding Confessions of Lieutenant Calley', *Esquire* (September 1971), p. 226.
[106] Laurence, p. 529.
[107] *Ibid.*, p. 794.
[108] *Life* (9 July 1971), p. 25.

to secure the cooperation and trust of veterans who elicited their help. Rather, some suspension – perhaps even reversal – of conventional clinical hierarchies was required, reflected in the model of the veterans 'rap group'. These groups usually convened, not in a psychiatrist's office or clinical facility, but at a venue where the veterans felt more at ease – the New York City office of the VVAW. The therapist, meanwhile, was expected to contribute only as one amongst equals, and to speak as openly and honestly about his or her own life as the veterans did about theirs. On occasion, the judgements of the therapist would be challenged by members of the group.[109] For Robert Lifton, the encounter with the veterans stimulated a radical critique of the psychiatric profession, especially its insistence that what it practised was a technical form of expertise, ideologically neutral in both its theories and effects – an insistence, Lifton argued, which had left it susceptible to cooption by the state and its associated institutions. 'We professionals,' he wrote, 'came to the rap groups with our own need for a transformation in many ways parallel to that we sought to enhance in veterans. We too, sometimes with less awareness than they, were in the midst of struggles around living and working that had to do with intactness and wholeness, with what we have been calling integrity.'[110]

It was not just the desire for a new kind of psychiatry that the veterans awakened in Lifton, but also, he believed, a deeper apprehension of man's relationship with violence. What the veterans were offering were stories of war, which were set in Vietnam and expressive of that conflict's peculiar shape and form, but which Lifton also considered consistent with other examples of human response to 'immersion in death'.[111] Like some of the victims of Hiroshima (the subject of his earlier research), the veterans had taken on a 'survivor mission', an attempt to explore the meaning of their experience in a way that contributed not just to their own 'healing', but also potentially to a wider process of enlightenment. In Lifton's view, this had always been in part the social function of the warrior. There had long existed in human culture a myth of the 'warrior-hero', he asserted, according to which each soldier would follow 'the heroic life-trajectory of the call of adventure, the crossing of the threshold into another realm of action and experience, the road of trials, and eventually the return to his people to whom he can convey a new dimension of wisdom and of "freedom to live"'.[112] For the modern American fighting man, however, the conflict in Vietnam afforded few such satisfactions, due to the uncertain allegiance of those he was supposed to be protecting, the elusiveness of his enemy, the reliance of his peers upon technology-intensive

---

[109] Lifton, pp. 75–95.
[110] *Ibid.*, p. 412.
[111] *Ibid.*, p. 16.
[112] *Ibid.*, p. 26.

forms of war-fighting, the ultimate failure of the enterprise and, not least, his knowledge of the atrocities committed in its name.

Nevertheless, veterans of Vietnam retained some of the mystique of the 'warrior-hero', perceiving themselves certainly to be 'a victimized group unrecognized and rejected by existing society', yet also as 'a special elite who alone can lay claim to a unique experience of considerable value in its very extremity and evil'.[113] For a minority of veterans, their own particular 'immersion in death' had assumed 'an ultimate (virtually sacred) quality that carries them into a realm of death-linked experience never before known or comprehended by man. Their experience parallels that of priests and shaman, the predecessors of biblical prophets, who ventured into the "land of death" and then "returned" to bring to their people deepened knowledge of the mysteries of death and life.'[114] In Lifton's formulation, the promise of authenticity lay not so much in the encounter with death but in its use by the veteran to construct a new consciousness of himself and of the world in which he lived, and in doing so to seed a broader social transformation. It was a promise that he saw in Michael Bernhardt, after an intensive series of interviews about the massacre at My Lai (4): 'he had touched a certain level of truth, an interface of personal experience (self) and larger forces (world), around which he could build and grow'.[115]

That the vicissitudes of the Vietnam war could yield to the men who fought it – especially those most intimate with the mortal waste that it caused – a kind of unique personal insight into the human condition had been an emergent theme in national discourse in the months preceding the revelations about the massacre, not least because virtually all of the other cultural logics through which military service could be ascribed value – participation in a successful endeavour, the preservation of democracy and freedom – had by then been exhausted. It was a theme evident especially in visual representations of the US soldier. In June 1969, *Life* published photographs of all but 25 of the 242 Americans who had died in the war during the week 28 May to 3 June, noting: 'More than we must know *how many*, we must know *who*.'[116] Most of the images depicted young men posing happily in civilian clothes or earnestly in full military dress. Printed on the cover of the issue, however, was a picture of William C. Gearing, Jr, apparently taken in Vietnam, in which the troubled, reflective face of the subject suggested a story of loss more complex than that of a single human life. To the editors, his face may have expressed something of the impact of war upon the innocence of youth; it was the same face, perhaps, that Michael Herr reported having seen 'at least a thousand times' during the conflict – 'of boys whose whole lives seemed

[113] *Ibid.*, p. 68.
[114] *Ibid.*, p. 318.
[115] *Ibid.*, p. 316.
[116] *Life* (27 June 1969), p. 20.

to have backed up on them, they'd be a few feet away but they'd be looking back at you over a distance you knew you'd never really cross'.[117]

With greater resonance for the cultural conceptualization of atrocity, however, was another photo-story in *Life*, published just before the allegations about My Lai were disclosed to the American public. The magazine reported on the case of Colonel Robert Rheault, who had led the Special Forces team accused of shooting in cold blood a Vietnamese man thought to have been an enemy double agent.[118] The charges against Rheault had recently been dismissed, but only because the Central Intelligence Agency (on the orders of the White House) had refused to let any of its personnel testify in court.[119] Therefore, Rheault still resided, *Life* asserted, 'in a moral twilight somewhere between guilt and exoneration'. His career was over, a victim of the disparity between the ethical standards of the civilian world and 'the aberrant, equivocal principles of war as it is waged in the shadows'. Rheault had met a similar fate, the article suggested, to 'les soldat perdus' – the 'lost soldiers' – who had returned to France in the 1950s following the wars in Indochina and Algeria, 'too early hardened and too early disaffected'. Rheault was pictured on the cover of the issue inhaling a cigarette, his weathered skin and cool narrow gaze communicating a difficult, hard-boiled kind of glamour: a poster-boy for authenticity.

Thankfully, however, most of those who commented on the massacre at My Lai stopped short of according special existential status to its perpetrators, of ascribing to them any intimacy of communion with the deeper currents of the human psyche or any profound new awareness of man's capacity for violence. It was not a quality of authenticity that commended William Calley to his defenders, but a belief in his sincerity, which, according to John Sack, was 'crystal clear to anyone who is talking with him'.[120] Following his conviction, many Americans were prepared to describe the lieutenant as a hero, but this sentiment reflected, it seems, either the mistaken conviction that it was in the heat of battle that his killings had occurred or an empathetic response to the dignity and stoicism with which he had borne his ordeal at the hands of an apparently arbitrary justice, not a fascination with his passage to the depths. Over the course of his court martial, the mainstream media had received too comprehensive an education in the damning details of Calley's conduct in My Lai (4) to afford any space to a romanticized reappraisal. Moreover, Calley's own physical attributes offered little scope for the successful visual signification of authenticity; boyish when news of the massacre broke, he had become rather plump and prone to hair-line recession by the time the case came to court. Only very rarely did photographs of Calley exhibit a comparable

[117] Herr, p. 21.
[118] *Life* (14 November 1969), pp. 34–9.
[119] Haldeman, diary entries, 25, 29 September 1969, in Haldeman, pp. 90–1.
[120] Sack, p. viii.

iconic grammar to that used in the images of Robert Rheault and Johnny Cash, as in *Life* in March 1971, when he was shown sitting on his couch, cigarette in hand, gazing into the middle distance.[121]

In the view of a number of commentators, however, the model of massacre as catharsis – as a rite of passage into self-knowledge and maturity – did have resonance for the American nation as a whole. In the *New York Times*, Anthony Lewis asserted: 'To recognize the bad in ourselves with the good, to see ourselves honestly, would be healthy for the United States in the end. Only children and stunted adults live in fairy tales. Growing up is good for countries as well as individuals.'[122] *Time* magazine agreed: 'only the nation that has faced up to its own failings and acknowledged its capacities for evil and ill-doing has any real claim to greatness'.[123] On occasion, however, the massacre was assigned a meaning which moved beyond simply the potential it presented for collective enlightenment. As Jonathan Schell observed, the My Lai revelations tempted some 'toward a touch of actual pride . . . as if we had gone through an initiation ceremony into adulthood as a nation, or as if committing great crimes were part of being a great nation, like having a huge gross national product, or going to the moon'.[124]

In the pages of *Time* in mid-December 1969, an advertisement appeared with no obvious commercial purpose and no acknowledged sponsor besides the name of the advertising agency. Exhibiting a handwritten text on the right side of the spread, and a pair of eyes pictured at the top, cast partly in shadow, the layout of the advertisement implicated the reader in its production. The text incorporated a series of statements of experience and responsibility, in which the pronoun 'I' stood for every American. These statements juxtaposed achievements with transgressions: thus, 'I have died in Vietnam. But I have walked the face of the moon.' Similarly: 'I have beat down my enemies with clubs. But I have built courtrooms to keep them free'; 'I have watched children starve from my golden towers. But I have fed half of the earth.' Expressing a more complex collective self-image than that prevailing in the years before the Vietnam war threw narratives of national success and moral leadership into doubt, this advertisement nevertheless seemed to propose that a country's journey into greatness was inevitably marked by the contemporaneous performance of ethical extremes, that there was an essential duality between acts of generosity, intelligence and technical innovation and ones of violence, despoliation and neglect. As the text concluded: 'I am ashamed. But I am proud. I am an American.'[125]

[121] *Life* (5 March 1971), p. 26.
[122] *New York Times* (29 November 1969), p. 32.
[123] *Time* (5 December 1969), p. 27.
[124] Schell, 'Notes and comments: Talk of the town', *New Yorker* (20 December 1969), p. 28.
[125] *Time* (19 December 1969), pp. 70–1.

The massacre at My Lai (4) presented a challenge to the moral dimension of American exceptionalism, precipitating a defection from the notion that, uniquely amongst nations, the United States had been able to transcend the ruinous effects of war upon ethics and to arrest the broader operations of nature that drew men towards violence. More seriously still, the massacre provoked a search for an alternative source of national gratification, which did not depend upon the now suspect supposition of superior collective virtue; the commission of atrocities, perhaps, was a burden that great nations had to bear as they exercised power across a world stage. Sacvan Bercovitch's model of the American jeremiad no longer fully held. Although acts of negligence and delinquency continued to prompt expressions of regret, there was less assurance that they would induce a culture-wide effort of ethical regeneration; the dialectical dynamic between the real and the ideal seemed to have stalled. Violence and corruption were elementary facts of human existence from which there was no hope of escape. America might continue to do good, but only as a by-product of the otherwise amoral pursuit of the satisfactions of national power.

It was rare for Americans to agree on anything as much as they did on the outcome of William Calley's court martial. Yet that coalition of sentiment excluded important elements of national opinion (for example, many professional army officers and members of the mainstream press) and was unified only in its reaction, not in its reasons. On the most critical issue of all – responsibility for the massacre – the culture was unable to return a final verdict. Americans brought to the discussion divergent understandings of what had actually happened in My Lai (4) as well as sharply conflicting attitudes towards the Vietnam war as a whole. Public responses were also refracted through millions of personal histories, influenced in particular by experiences of combat and encounters with authority. This was a time, moreover, when the traditional arbiters of national controversy – the institutions of government and the media – found it difficult to reach consensus on very much at all, let alone act cooperatively to shape popular debate. The White House might get its way, but it could not always propagate its thoughts, and so with regard to My Lai, it never really tried. Having declared that he would review the Calley case at the end of the appellate process, President Nixon also asserted that, at the same time, he would make a statement 'setting the whole thing into perspective', and letting 'the American people know, and the world know, why such a prosecution did take place and why it was upheld, or why it is not upheld'.[126]

It was a commitment, however, that Nixon did not keep; indeed, after May 1971, he never spoke about the massacre in public again. In 1974,

[126] 'Panel interview at the Annual Convention of the American Society of Newspaper Editors', 16 April 1971, *Public Papers of the Presidents: Richard Nixon, 1971*, p. 539.

following affirmation of Calley's conviction by the Court of Military Appeals and its subsequent denial of a petition for reconsideration, the Secretary of the Army, Howard Callaway, reviewed the trial record and reduced the lieutenant's sentence from twenty to ten years, issuing a statement explaining his decision.[127] Callaway also dispatched the trial record to the White House, but his accompanying memorandum did not encourage another presidential intervention.[128] Nixon responded simply that 'no further action by me in this matter is necessary or appropriate'.[129] By that time, of course, Nixon's thoughts about the massacre would have carried little more authority than his views on political ethics, but it was also the case that the massacre was no longer an item of immediate national concern. Within the United States, there were now few individuals and institutions with any consistent interest in returning the country's attention to what had been done in My Lai (4). Only the victims had such an interest, but they were almost entirely without influence, for, in American tellings at least, they had already long been displaced from the story of their own desolation.

[127] Memorandum for Record: 'The Secretary of the Army Announces His Decision on LT William Calley', 16 April 1974, folder: 'Case Folder – 1LT William L. Calley, Jr [Part 2 of 4]', Box 6, Records Pertaining to the My Lai Massacre, 1969–74, Records of the Vietnam War Crimes Working Group, Office of the Deputy Chief of Staff for Personnel, RAS, RG319, NACP.

[128] Callaway to Nixon, 'General Court-Martial Case of *United States versus Calley*', 15 April 1974, folder: 'Presidential/SA Review of Calley Appeal, Apr–Nov 1974', Box 1, Records of the Calley General Court Martial, 1969–1974, Office of the Clerk of Court, Records of the Judge Advocate General (Army), RG153, NACP.

[129] Nixon to Callaway, 'General Court-Martial Case: United States vs. Calley', 3 May 1974, folder: 'Presidential/SA Review of Calley Appeal, Apr–Nov 1974', Box 1, Records of the Calley General Court Martial, 1969–1974, Office of the Clerk of Court, Records of the Judge Advocate General (Army), RG153, NACP.

5

Displacing the victims

Though unable to agree upon an answer, the question at least was not in doubt: whether they attributed the massacre at My Lai (4) to an aberrant company of soldiers, a criminal war, or man's natural propensity for violence, Americans were interested in the issue of causation and blame. After witnesses had confirmed that civilians had died, after images of the dead had been displayed across the national media, what more was there to be said about the immediate effects of the killing? Death was incommunicable, whilst the bereaved were unlikely to be consoled by any words of sympathy that Americans could offer. The destruction wrought upon My Lai (4) and its neighbouring settlements in the village of Son My was left for the most part to speak for itself, as Americans moved on quickly to the problem of why it had occurred: an enquiry, at least, which might yield a functional knowledge, a resource for reform.

To enquire into cause, however, was to enquire into America, and thus to contribute to a process by which the story of My Lai progressively evolved into a story about Americans – American soldiers, American institutions, American national life. Discussion of the massacre within the United States came to be dominated by the perspectives of the perpetrators, not those of the victims. It was a skewed, deformed discourse about which the surviving inhabitants of Son My could do little, for – left to their own devices – they had no channels of access into American politics and culture. When their voices were heard, it was at the discretion of the US media and the US military, institutions which did not always find their stories easy to incorporate into the effort to account for the crime, or consider them essential to that effort's eventual success.

In the attitudes of these institutions, there was undoubtedly a measure of racism at work (the army, after all, had charged Calley with the murder of 'Oriental human beings'), but their interventions in the transmission of victims' perspectives most usually expressed the more prosaic varieties of ethnocentricity, as well as the conventional stigmas attached to enemy allegiance or association during a time of war.[1] Reflecting, perhaps, upon

[1] Hammer, *The Court-Martial of Lt Calley*, pp. 46–7.

the failure of the wider American programme to 'capture Vietnamese hearts and minds', those investigating the massacre gazed across the chasm of language and culture dividing them from the survivors of Son My and decided that the substantive testimony of the latter could not readily be translated into a usable and authoritative record of the killings. These were residents, moreover, of what was regarded still as a Vietcong village, and some of the most cooperative witnesses among them had prior – possibly continuing – connections with local revolutionary forces. In a US court of law, their accounts would be vulnerable to aggressive cross-examination: potentially damaging to a prosecution which was confident that conclusive evidence for its case could be established from American testimony alone. The scene of the crime itself, meanwhile, was inaccessible to US correspondents and cameramen without a military escort. The court-house at Fort Benning emerged instead as the primary location of the story, and it was the image of William Calley entering and leaving that building – a little man in uniform accompanied by his lawyers – which came to engage the attention and emotions of the American audience, not the landscape of My Lai (4) and Son My and the physical legacies of massacre.

To effectively communicate the victims' experience of massacre to the American people would have been an exacting task, exorbitant in both resources and time, and unpredictable in its effects upon the pursuit of justice. It was an effort which may have encountered the resistance of the survivors themselves, for many had more pressing and immediate priorities than guiding America back through the ruin that it had made of their recent past: finding food, staying safe, tending to family, making a future. It was an effort, moreover, which had no ultimate prospect of success: one person's suffering cannot be fathomed by another, a culture cannot be compassed in all its diversity and depth. Yet it was a necessary effort if the massacre were to exert a proper claim upon the conscience of Americans, if their reflections were not to lapse into solipsism and thereafter succumb to the machinations of national politics and the discretions of official memory. That the inhabitants of Son My lived under the governance of the Vietcong did not inevitably place them beyond the reach of American sympathy: some served the revolution, others merely serviced its needs, others still had family members fighting with the ARVN, and all were persistently involved in a complex negotiation with ideology and power. To enquire into the pre-massacre history of the village would have been to reveal a tenacious human community in difficult conditions practising politics in most of its primary forms – autonomy, compliance and commitment.[2]

***

[2] For a valuable history of Son My village, based upon interviews with its inhabitants, see Hammer, *One Morning in the War*, pp. 24–60.

Only through a dialogue with the survivors, meanwhile, could that village history be disclosed, and a measure be taken of the full dimensions of its loss; and only through such dialogue could the US narrative of massacre, as played out within Son My, move beyond the apparent finality of bodies lying in a road, to incorporate accounts of burial and bereavement, departure and return, the slow resumption of domestic routine, the adaptation to a sudden, radical change in circumstance and prospects. In addition, for many survivors of catastrophe, the communication of experience is an important means by which they can recover a sense of agency and meaning. In the case of catastrophes authored by human hand, there is a particular wish to hear a recurring echo of their stories in the culture of the perpetrator. With respect to the villagers of Son My, therefore, America probably had an obligation to listen. Perhaps, moreover, it is only those who have suffered who can effect a full accounting, by flinging the visceral experience of atrocity and loss in the path of casual sentiment and inadequate justice; by insisting that the wounds they bear are not wounds that can heal; by making the memory of those responsible truly traumatic. It is only those who have suffered who can remind their audience whom the real victims are, and prevent the appropriation of their status by men like William Calley. Yet, none of this happened with Son My. Even as the massacre dominated public discourse in the United States, the people of the village were given little opportunity to graft their stories into the national memory: they remained either a petrified presence within American culture, images on a page, or an alien one: strange Oriental figures, infrequently glimpsed, ghosts inhabiting a faraway land.

Reflecting a broader cultural turn in historical studies, the problem of miscommunication and misunderstanding between the Americans and Vietnamese has become a familiar theme in accounts of the Vietnam war.[3] It is a theme which has also appeared in the highly conditional apologias offered by Robert McNamara, US Secretary of Defense throughout the escalatory phase of the war. For virtually all of the senior American officials who made the decisions to dispatch troops to its shores, McNamara asserts, Vietnam represented 'terra incognita', and the same was broadly true, he thinks, of policy-makers in Hanoi with respect to the United States.[4] In McNamara's view, indeed, the 'root cause' of the conflict was 'mutual ignorance, the inability of Washington and Hanoi to penetrate the outlook of the other side'.[5] Of course, an alternative interpretation is

[3] See, for example, Baritz, pp. 19–34; M. Bradley, *Imagining Vietnam and America: The Making of Postcolonial Vietnam, 1919–1950* (Chapel Hill: University of North Carolina Press, 2000); and Fitzgerald, pp. 3–31.

[4] R. McNamara with B. VanDeMark, *In Retrospect: the Tragedy and Lessons of Vietnam* (New York: Random House, 1995), p. xvi; R. McNamara, J. Blight and R. Brigham with T. Biersteker and H. Schandler, *Argument Without End: In Search of Answers to the Vietnam Tragedy* (New York: Public Affairs, 1999), p. 25.

[5] McNamara *et al.*, *Argument Without End*, p. 381.

available: that McNamara and his colleagues did not know very much about Vietnam because they did not think they needed to, because their purpose in escalating the war was to impress not the north Vietnamese, but the Chinese and the Soviets. Vietnam was primarily a site upon which American leaders could perform their credibility, their commitment to other, more important Cold War partners; in and of itself, Vietnam interested them little.[6]

It was the calculus of credibility, therefore, which structured Americans' ignorance of Vietnam and which also exacerbated many of the difficulties that they subsequently encountered in their relations with the Vietnamese. Repeatedly throughout the course of the war, American officials expressed frustration at the failure of the people of the south to commit themselves completely to the campaign against the Vietcong, at the unreliable, mercenary quality of their allegiance to the US-backed regime in Saigon, and at their apparent lack of gratitude for all the aid and assistance that Washington was sending their way. As Frances Fitzgerald observed, however, many South Vietnamese took the view that no greater enthusiasm, loyalty or gratitude should have been expected: 'on the contrary, the Americans owed them something for the use of their soil to fight a war that was really directed against China and the Soviet Union'.[7] Because the principal objectives of the conflict resided within a geopolitical realm ulterior to the actual theatre of combat, there existed no authoritative framework by which American commanders in Vietnam could precisely connect military means to ends, tactics to strategy, or calibrate their firepower against a clear calculation of likely benefits and costs.[8] The result was not just a quagmire, into which men and resources disappeared to no discernible strategic effect, but also a pattern of civilian exposure to harm which further undermined the political effort to bind the South Vietnamese to the American cause.

By rationalizing the war primarily in terms of national reputation, instead of the welfare of the people of South Vietnam, US policy-makers also reduced the ironic force of critiques which pointed to the civilian casualties generated by American military operations: in the United States, outside of the college-based anti-war movement, the quantum of suffering

[6] In July 1965, John McNaughton, Assistant Secretary of Defense, composed a now famous memorandum in which he expressed US objectives in Vietnam in the following terms: '70 per cent – to preserve our national honor as a guarantor (and the reciprocal: to avoid a show-case success for Communist "wars of liberation"); 20 per cent – to keep SVN (and then adjacent) territory from hostile expansive hands; 10 per cent "answer the call of a friend", to help him enjoy a better life. Also – to emerge from crisis without unacceptable taint from the methods used.' L. Berman, *Planning a Tragedy: The Americanization of the War in Vietnam* (New York: Norton, 1982), p. 140.

[7] Fitzgerald, p. 359.

[8] In a subsequent survey, almost 70 per cent of US Army generals involved in the management of the war asserted that national objectives in Vietnam had been insufficiently clear. Kinnard, pp. 447, 449.

endured by the Vietnamese hardly registered at all in public attitudes towards the conflict.[9] National reputation, moreover, was not quite as compelling a motive for military intervention as national survival: this was a war, therefore, that was not really being fought for South Vietnam or for the United States. The conditional nature of the country's investment in the conflict and in the fate of the South Vietnamese found expression in the operational convention that American servicemen were not to be risked if munitions could do the job, even though this sometimes resulted in the aerial destruction of entire hamlets in order to eliminate the nuisance of a single enemy sniper.

Similar imperatives were reflected elsewhere in military practice. The standard tour of duty was limited to a year. Officers, meanwhile, rotated every six months in and out of field commands and staff and advisory positions, and in and out of Vietnam itself. By maximizing experience of a variety of assignments and thus allowing its officers to enhance their prospects for promotion, the army hoped to keep their morale high and to season as many as possible in readiness for the real challenge which lay ahead: war with the Soviet Union, whenever it came.[10] Yet the practice of rotation, as Neil Sheehan has noted, 'provided for the unlearning rather than the learning of lessons'; in particular, it prevented American military personnel from accumulating anything but the most superficial understanding of Vietnam and the Vietnamese.[11] In the view of Frances Fitzgerald, many army officers assigned as advisers to the ARVN 'simply did not know enough, and with only a year or a year and a half in Vietnam, could not know enough, even to interpret what was happening. An experienced Vietnamese officer on his fifth or sixth American adviser probably had excellent reasons for disregarding all advice. Neither incompetent nor cowardly, he might be simply trying to deal with things as they were.'[12]

To conceive of the challenge to the regime in Saigon principally as a test of America's Cold War credibility – that is, as a struggle umbilically connected to the geopolitical aspirations of the Soviet Union and China – was effectively to discount the proposition that this genuinely was a revolutionary war, originating in and sustained by an authentic coalescence of the values and objectives of the Vietcong and those of the South Vietnamese people. The American soldiers sent to South Vietnam to contain and suppress the Vietcong were, however, often very swiftly made aware of the facts of the matter. The enemy guerrillas, they discovered, were resilient and committed, and usually impossible to distinguish from the civilian population except when encountered with a weapon in their hands, which did not happen very often. The indeterminate contours of the revolution

[9] Schuman, pp. 521, 524–5.
[10] Sheehan, *A Bright Shining Lie*, p. 650.
[11] *Ibid.*
[12] Fitzgerald, pp. 315–16.

encouraged the US military command to establish a system of secure compounds and bases throughout the country, to provide a measure of protection along with many of the comforts of home to American service personnel when they weren't out on patrol.

However, these compounds tended to conform to the model of a colonial outpost, their fences and walls communicating ambivalence about the surrounding culture and limiting contact between those who lived and worked within and those who dwelled outside to a few unlovely forms of mutual exploitation. In Gosney Compound at Phu Loi, just north of Saigon, there was a 'wholly American atmosphere', according to Jonathan Schell. Vietnamese were not permitted to enter after 10 p.m., except in an emergency, while the soldiers and officers inside enjoyed 'three solid American meals a day and a movie at night'. One evening when Schell was there, the movie was *Beau Geste*.[13] The concern of US commanders that operational plans shared with local officials might subsequently be shared also with the local Vietcong frequently led to the underplanning of operational elements for which the government authorities were formally responsible, such as the protection, housing and care of displaced civilians.[14] The hazards of ambush, sniper fire and mines, meanwhile, informed the strategy of air mobility, so that, as Schell once again observed, Americans travelling into or across the Vietnamese countryside only saw it from above, from their helicopters and planes, or else, when out on patrol, through the sights of their rifles.[15] Indeed, it was often on a hunt for the enemy that American soldiers had their first encounter with a Vietnamese village.

If the US and South Vietnamese armies were to fight effectively together, despite the asymmetrical strategic priorities that had produced their alliance, and if US commanders and their soldiers were to become more confident and precise in their judgements about who was an enemy and who was not (thus minimizing excesses of segregation and suspicion), there was a practical pressing need for American proficiency in the Vietnamese language. In itself, ease of communication could not have eradicated all of America's difficulties in Vietnam, which issued more directly from a particular set of ideological convictions and a particular perception of the US national interest, as well as from the political illegitimacy of the regime in Saigon and the commitment and resourcefulness of its revolutionary foe. At the local level, however, a capacity to talk and be understood (and to listen and understand), might have enabled the Americans to conduct themselves in a manner that inflicted less unnecessary harm upon the people of South Vietnam and their own efforts to win the war.

Such a capacity, however, was not readily achieved, partly, no doubt, because teaching a generation of soldiers to speak fluent Vietnamese did

---

[13] Schell, *The Real War*, pp. 116–18.
[14] *Ibid.*, pp. 100–4, 181.
[15] *Ibid.*, p. 67.

not seem the soundest investment of time and money to an army command still looking towards Europe as its primary theatre. Vietnamese, moreover, is especially difficult to learn; the vocabulary shares no common root with English and the language itself is 'tonal', so that the meaning of words can change quite radically depending upon inflection and pitch. Regional dialects and accents also affect pronunciation. Even those Americans who underwent intensive language tuition tended to emerge from their courses with only the most rudimentary powers of communication. Jonathan Schell reported: 'Every once in a while, with a display of uneasy shyness, an officer brings out a few words of Vietnamese, but if these ask a question, he more often than not listens to the answer in blank incomprehension.'[16] Americans, therefore, were often dependent upon ARVN interpreters for communication with the Vietnamese people and also upon ARVN soldiers for the implementation of civil affairs policy, but it was rare that they could be confident that their intentions and purposes had been fully understood and faithfully translated. Nor were they competent to determine all reactions and effects.

Outside the major cities, then, political and cultural transactions between US armed forces and South Vietnamese civilians either proceeded through intermediaries, or else took a form that expressed, even as it sought to overcome, a wider failure of communication. A group of local women and children followed Tim O'Brien's infantry company around as it patrolled near Chu Lai, selling Coke to the soldiers and performing chores in return for rations. 'Lying in the shade with the children, we learned a Little Vietnamese,' O'Brien later recalled, 'and they overheard words like "motherfucker" and "gook" and "dink" and "tit". Like going to school.'[17]

The sort of Vietnamese expressions generally used by American soldiers were terse and functional, consisting of no more than one or two words, and intended to command immediate action, not to persuade or to elicit a reflective response. An army veteran interviewed by Christian Appy realized some years after his service that he had probably never learnt the Vietnamese word for 'hello'. What he knew instead was 'how to tell someone to "get the fuck away from me", how to negotiate prices with peddlers and whores, and how to give instructions to the Vietnamese woman who shined his boots'.[18] In a search operation covered by NBC correspondent Robert Hager in the wake of the My Lai disclosures, US troops ordered the residents of a village out of their homes, shouting 'Di-di!' This was a phrase, Hager noted, 'ordinarily used to shoo off children or beggars. It means 'Get away! Get going!'[19]

[16] *Ibid.*, p. 77.
[17] O'Brien, *If I Die in a Combat Zone*, pp. 76–9.
[18] Appy, pp. 256–7.
[19] *NBC Nightly News*, 1 December 1969, VTNA.

Uncertain that any but the most simple Vietnamese words would carry the intended meanings when spoken by their forces, US psychological warfare officers frequently used taped loudspeaker announcements as well as leaflets and pamphlets to communicate with civilians, encouraging them to betray the Vietcong and to leave their villages for government camps. Once again, these methods did not invite dialogue, nor were they especially effective. Even if those who came across the leaflets (which were dropped from aircraft) were ready to be persuaded, they usually could not read.[20] Whether delivered in oral or written form, words alone failed the Americans. The available alternatives offered no greater promise of success. Having determined from 'research' that the sound of the flute caused the Vietnamese to feel nostalgic, psychological warfare units broadcast music into the countryside surrounding US military bases, hoping – as one officer informed Schell – 'to make the VC feel lonesome and want to go back home'.[21] In villages and refugee camps, Hollywood movies were screened, Westerns mostly, with the aim of portraying 'the American way of life'. Science fiction films, the officer noted, didn't really work, and nor did *The Swinger*, a sex comedy in which Ann-Margret plays a magazine writer who joins the 'swinging' underground to prove her worldliness to a sceptical publisher: 'That wasn't too good. That was a mistake. They won't show that one again.'[22] Propaganda leaflets and posters often illustrated their texts with photographs and cartoons, depicting, for example, the scene of an enemy atrocity or the consequences for a village if it harboured the Vietcong.[23] In the very common event, however, that their viewer was illiterate, the source of the violence might not have been clear; even if it was, the conclusions he or she reached about whom to resist and with whom to comply might frequently confound American intentions. As Schell's officer observed: 'the distribution of atrocity posters has to be limited. Sometimes they influence the people the wrong way, and help out the VC. Sometimes it is just what the VC want.'[24]

Even for those Americans who made a honest and determined effort to comprehend the experience and attitudes of Vietnamese civilians, communication did not come easy. These exchanges, of course, were vexed by the problem of language, but often also by the wariness that previous interactions with Americans had caused to be implanted in Vietnamese minds. With no history of regular dialogue, moreover, it was in the nature of such conversations that initially they disclosed mostly the amplitudes of the cultural divide, and not the narrow channels across which bridges could be built. When he visited the government camps, Schell was accompanied by an interpreter, but even then some of the civilians that he spoke to –

---

[20] Schell, *The Real War*, pp. 154–5.
[21] *Ibid.*, p. 255.
[22] *Ibid.*, p. 256.
[23] *Ibid.*, pp. 147–55, 252–5.
[24] *Ibid.*, p. 255.

doubtful, perhaps, that their words would be accurately translated – chose to communicate through pantomime instead: 'They stretched out empty palms to show that they had nothing, pointed to dirty children or pointed to their stomachs, and made theatrically exaggerated piteous faces, mimicking their own suffering.'

Schell also found it difficult to convince these civilians that he was only a reporter, having to repeatedly explain that he exercised no authority over their situation: 'They would nevertheless ask several more times for food or privileges, as though my claim to be a journalist were part of a game they had played with many interrogators before me.'[25] In Saigon, Michael Herr and a Vietnamese student conversed a few times, 'but we couldn't really communicate, all I understood was his obsessive comparison between Rome and Washington, and that he seemed to believe that Poe had been a French writer'.[26]

Alert though they were to the damage being inflicted upon the landscape of Vietnam and the bodies of its people, these Americans found it difficult to achieve any purchase upon what the Vietnamese themselves thought of it all. Conversations, when they were possible, were often unrevealing, and there was a limit to what one could learn simply by looking. To read the faces of the Vietnamese, according to Herr, 'was like trying to read the wind'.[27] Jonathan Schell refers to the 'sullen, cold masks' of the male inhabitants of Ben Suc, a village north-west of Saigon, after their families had been assembled together for the purpose of resettlement.[28] At another village nearby, the residents were congregated in the centre as US soldiers burned down and bulldozed their homes: 'Standing or crouching without speaking, their faces drawn tight in dead masks, the people seemed not to see or hear what was happening around them.'[29] As the Ben Suc villagers were evacuated, Schell thought he saw a new 'deadness and discouragement' seep into their expressions, but he wondered 'whether it was just that any crowd of people removed from the dignifying context of their homes and places of labour, learning, and worship, and dropped, tired and coated with dust, in a bare field would appear broken-spirited to an outsider'.[30] Whilst patrolling near Son My, Tim O'Brien shot an enemy soldier, and in a subsequent short story, 'The Man I Killed', he describes gazing at the corpse and trying to imagine the life that he had just brought to an end.[31] The most that he could manage,

[25] *Ibid.*, pp. 127, 265.
[26] Herr, p. 39.
[27] *Ibid.*, p. 11.
[28] Schell, *The Real War*, p. 78.
[29] *Ibid.*, p. 94.
[30] *Ibid.*, p. 99.
[31] O'Brien, 'The Man I Killed', in O'Brien, *The Things They Carried* (London: Flamingo, 1991), pp. 121–5. In O'Brien's memoir of the war, he states that he refused to look at the corpse (O'Brien, *If I Die in a Combat Zone*, p. 92).

however, was an ersatz Vietnamization of his own passage into war: the dead man as intellectual, physically unimpressive and fearful of war, but compelled to enlist by the power of local and familial expectation. All O'Brien could really know for certain was the body that lay before him, the punctured and bloody leavings of a life, nothing of its history and individual human worth.

For many Americans in South Vietnam, it simply seemed like hard, unrewarding labour to try to establish what its inhabitants thought and felt, what forces acted upon their behaviour and determined their loyalties. In the absence of that knowledge – or, perhaps more importantly, in the absence of a learning process constantly restimulated by the new information that regular dialogue provides – perceptions could quickly ossify into stereotypes, into the assumption that behind the fragile commitment and fitful prowess of the ARVN lay an elemental ethno-cultural inferiority; or that behind those unreadable civilian faces lay an inhuman indifference to any fate that might befall them as well as a common desire to see Americans killed. When Philip Caputo's company of Marines passed through Giao-Tri, a hamlet to the west of Danang which it had destroyed only a day or so before, the remaining inhabitants hardly responded at all: 'They just stood there, silent and still, showing neither grief nor anger nor fear.' For Caputo, pity and guilt turned swiftly to contempt. 'Why feel compassion for people who seem to feel nothing for themselves?'[32] Violence, then, could issue from a failure of communication. Yet it also, in a way, carried a message, like the other forms of exaggerated physicality – cartoons, pantomime – that the Americans and Vietnamese used to speak with each other when words did not work. In some zones of the war, the message of American violence, written in Vietnamese blood, was this: 'Do not trust us to grant you the benefit of doubt. If your loyalty to our cause is not conspicious, this may happen to you.'

Unless they lived in a government camp or joined the ARVN (and sometimes not even then), most Vietnamese could supply no proof of their allegiance that was likely to satisfy every American they might encounter during the course of the war. As Jonathan Schell observed, the criteria used by US soldiers to assess whether a particular individual was or was not an enemy, and should or should not die, were inconsistent and often arbitrary and ill-informed. During the operation in Ben Suc, he was told by an American officer that it was the black pyjamas of the Vietcong that distinguished them from the genuine peasant: 'They're no good for working in the fields. Black absorbs heat. This is a hot country. It doesn't make any sense.' A moment later, however, the officer reflected, 'What're you going to do? We've got people in the kitchen at the base wearing those black pajamas.'[33] In the officers' club at Chu Lai, a reconnaissance pilot

[32] Caputo, pp. 125–6.
[33] Schell, *The Real War*, pp. 90–1.

described how he had spotted an enemy soldier and directed an air strike down upon his position. When Schell asked how he could tell that the man was Vietcong, the pilot answered: 'Well, he walked real proud, with a kind of bounce in his gait, like a soldier, instead of just shuffling along, like the farmers do.'[34] One of his colleagues declared: 'I guess you can call it a kind of intuition. I think I can just about *smell* a VC from five thousand feet by now. Like everything else, some people have got the knack and some people don't. Some people wouldn't be able to tell a VC no matter *how* long they tried.'[35] If there was a standard protocol for determining the status of those spotted from the air, it was to fire in their direction and see if they ran for cover. If they did, they were classed as enemy and regarded as fair game.[36] That it was not judged the natural reaction of any rational human being to run from the source of gunfire indicates how, in some corners of the American war, the Vietnamese had been placed almost entirely beyond the reach of empathetic consideration.

The problems of miscommunication and ignorance, mistrust and military excess which characterized relations between the American military and the people of South Vietnam were especially aggravated in the province of Quang Ngai and in the area around Son My village. After the country had been partitioned in the Geneva settlement of 1954, many southern revolutionaries relocated to the north. In Quang Ngai, however, the revolution maintained a continuous presence, and thus, following the resumption of armed struggle, it was able steadily to dissolve any meaningful political authority exercised over the province by the government in Saigon, at least outside the major towns.[37] According to Richard Hammer, Son My came under Vietcong control early in 1964, when floods cut off the village from the province capital, Quang Ngai City, thus creating an opportunity for revolutionary consolidation.[38] By May 1965, the government's position in the province had become so weak that it contemplated abandoning Quang Ngai City itself.[39] When American ground troops arrived on the central coast of South Vietnam, therefore, they confronted an enemy that was battle-hardened and effective, committed to the defence of the balance of power in one of its principal political strongholds, and supported by much of the local population.

[34] *Ibid.*, p. 217.
[35] *Ibid.*, p. 225.
[36] C. Powell (with J. Persico), *A Soldier's Way: An Autobiography* (London: Hutchinson, 1995), p. 144.
[37] Schell, *The Real War*, p. 141. The Peers commission seems to have borrowed its own assessment of the revolutionary history of Quang Ngai from Schell's account (Goldstein *et al.*, pp. 59–60). For a discussion of the deterioration of the security situation in Quang Ngai, see also G. Allen, *None So Blind: A Personal Account of the Intelligence Failure in Vietnam* (Chicago: Ivan R. Dee, 2001), pp. 175–7.
[38] Hammer, *One Morning in the War*, pp. 41–5.
[39] Sheehan, *A Bright Shining Lie*, p. 523.

Perhaps inevitably, the subsequent war in Quang Ngai was more than usually brutal. In August 1965, US Marines fought a fierce battle with a Vietcong force that was attempting to prevent the establishment of an American military base at Chu Lai, about twenty miles north in the province of Quang Tin.[40] Over the next few months, the coast of Quang Ngai was pummelled by naval artillery and aerial strikes. In November, Neil Sheehan travelled to the area and discovered, just beyond a beach, five hamlets which had been almost totally obliterated – and hundreds of their inhabitants killed – after the Americans had decided that they constituted an enemy base. He was told that at least ten other hamlets in the area had suffered the similar fate.[41]

Throughout 1966, the Marine Corps implemented a pacification strategy in Quang Ngai, endeavouring in each operation to bring more territory and more people under American and government control.[42] During the following spring, however, the Marines were redeployed, and responsibility for military operations in the province passed to the army, supplemented by one brigade each of ARVN troops and Republic of Korea Marines.[43] Around this time, in Sheehan's view, the military effort in Quang Ngai became 'freed of all restraint'.[44] The military assistance command in Saigon established Task Force Oregon, and commissioned it not so much to extend and consolidate the effective jurisdiction of non-communist authority in the province as simply, outside of that jurisdiction, to hunt down and kill as many enemy as it could.[45]

In Quang Ngai, as in the rest of South Vietnam, there was no easy way to tell who was a guerrilla and who was not; perhaps more markedly than elsewhere, however, the presumption of civilian innocence dwindled and lapsed, due to the stimulus of these new command imperatives towards attrition as well as the local revolution's reputation for peasant mobilization.

It was in the summer of 1967 that Jonathan Schell accompanied American reconnaissance pilots on their flights over the province and observed how, with the exception of settlements close to Highway One (the main north–south thoroughfare), virtually all centres of habitation between the mountains and the sea had been destroyed, and how, on almost every occasion that they spotted Vietnamese below, the pilots claimed to find evidence of enemy allegiance.[46] It was around the same time that a platoon of Tiger Force soldiers from the 101st Airborne Division were out on

[40] *Ibid.*, pp. 536–7.
[41] *Ibid.*, pp. 570–1. See also Sheehan, 'Not a dove, but no longer a hawk', *New York Times Magazine* (9 October 1966), pp. 135, 137; and Sheehan, 'Should we have war crimes trials?', p. 2.
[42] Sheehan, *A Bright Shining Lie*, p. 686.
[43] Schell, *The Real War*, pp. 138–9.
[44] Sheehan, *A Bright Shining Lie*, p. 686.
[45] Schell, *The Real War*, p. 139.
[46] *Ibid.*, pp. 142–7, 275–6.

patrol in the Song Ve Valley, south of Quang Ngai City, shooting civilians on sight.[47] Later that year, according to an article written by an American intelligence officer assigned to the advisory team in the province, the Korean Marines swept through the Batangan Peninsula, where Son My was located, claiming subsequently to have killed over 700 enemy personnel – approximately 250 more than the total estimated number of Vietcong soldiers in the area. After the operation, the American officer queried the reported body-count with one of his Korean counterparts and was told that 'there is no such thing in Vietnam as an innocent civilian'.[48]

Whoever it was that the allies were killing in Quang Ngai, their deaths were having little discernible effect upon the ability of the Vietcong to prosecute the war. The aggressive pursuit of the enemy directed by the strategy of attrition inevitably exposed many more US soldiers to the hazards of mines, booby traps, sniper fire and ambush. In the southern part of the province, an American brigade of 800 combat troops suffered over 600 casualties between mid-April and mid-August 1967, with 120 killed in action. Set against those losses was an official enemy body-count of nearly 1900, with more than 500 weapons captured.[49] For all of Task Force Oregon's efforts, however, local revolutionary forces were still able to plan and prepare for their own contribution to the forthcoming nation-wide offensive. When the Tet offensive began, at the end of January 1968, those forces attacked the airfield and the ARVN headquarters in Quang Ngai City.[50] The provincial jail was opened and its prisoners set free.[51] To the south of the capital, the Vietcong seized control of the districts of Duc Pho and Nghia Hanh, and to the west and north, it established a formidable presence in both Tu Nghia and Son Tinh – the district to which Son My village belonged.[52]

Because of the security threat presented by local revolutionary forces and the shift in strategic emphasis away from pacification, US personnel in Quang Ngai tended to live and work in a condition of isolation from the civilian population that was unusual even in Vietnam. The high command of the Americal Division, which had taken over responsibility for the war in the province from Task Force Oregon in the autumn of 1967 and which was based at Chu Lai, enjoyed a gracious existence; their dinners were

[47] *Toledo Blade* (19 October 2003).

[48] J. Frosch, 'Anatomy of a massacre', *Playboy* (July 1970), p. 185. According to local villagers interviewed by the British writer Justin Wintle in 1989, the Koreans had conducted an operation in their area in December 1966, massacring hundreds. It is conceivable that there had been a slippage of dates, with Frosch and the villagers describing the same operation. It is equally conceivable, however, that there were two different Korean operations, a year apart, both devastating in their effects upon the civilian population. The Koreans had been stationed in the province since the summer of 1966 (Wintle, pp. 265, 269–78); Schell, *The Real War*, p. 139.

[49] Schell, *The Real War*, p. 155.

[50] Belknap, p. 53.

[51] Fitzgerald, p. 389.

[52] Goldstein *et al.*, p. 63.

served on fine china by GIs clad in white waiters' jackets, and were followed each night by a movie.[53] When Norman Schwarzkopf – then a lieutenant-colonel – visited the base in December 1969, he was invited to attend a tea dance. 'The place was almost worthy of a Club Med', he commented in his memoirs.[54]

It was a culture replicated in Duc Pho, at the headquarters of the 11th Brigade, to which senior officers would make a point of returning each day in time for a 'happy hour' in their mess. 'They would talk about promotions and all that stuff,' Colonel Barker's driver recalled, 'just like a cocktail party back in the world.'[55] At the US advisory compound in Quang Ngai City, Jonathan Schell recorded, 'all was American, and there was nothing to indicate that I had not magically been set down within the United States itself'.[56]

The closeted, familiar, congenial social environments of US compounds and bases in and around Quang Ngai were expressive of the polarities that were increasingly defining the American war in the province. The local divisional and brigade commands were exposed more consistently to the imperatives towards body-count (the principal index of success when the goal is attrition) than to sensitive assessments of the gradations of civilian-guerrilla association. The original function of government camps had been to enforce the distinction between combatant and non-combatant through the simple means of geographical separation, thus making it easier to exploit the advantages of superior American firepower in unpacified areas. However, as the camps became overcrowded and conditions within them deteriorated, many of their inhabitants elected to return to their original villages, whilst the Americans themselves began to reassess the desirability of additional evacuations.[57] What they generally did not reassess was the application of firepower that had previously only been judged acceptable once civilians had been removed from the target area.

Task Force Oregon started to burn down villages without making provision for the inhabitants, and to bomb them from the air without first issuing a warning to leave.[58] The Americal Division was no more conscientious: according to the Peers report, there was 'minimal coordination' between those planning tactical operations and the psychological warfare officers responsible for communications with the local civilian population.[59] Government authorities in the province, meanwhile, offered little resistance to these evolving American practices. They were almost as much an alien presence in Quang Ngai as the US forces were themselves, and adhered,

[53] Hersh, *Cover-Up*, p. 31.
[54] Schwarzkopf, pp. 150–1.
[55] Hersh, *Cover-Up*, p. 52.
[56] Schell, *The Real War*, p. 175.
[57] *Ibid.*, pp. 156, 162, 257–9.
[58] *Ibid.*, pp. 150, 259.
[59] Goldstein *et al.*, pp. 64–6.

if anything, even more insistently to the view that those not allied with Saigon were really loyal to the Vietcong. After American operations had laid waste to the southern districts of Duc Pho and Mo Duc, General Hoang Xuan Lam, the senior ARVN commander in I Corps (which stretched north from Quang Ngai up to the demilitarized zone), inspected the area and declared, 'Good! Good! They are all VC. Kill them!'[60]

The vitality of the local revolution, the remoteness of American commanders from the complex realities of civilian existence, the strategic pressures towards attrition and body-count, the inadequate resourcing of civil affairs programmes, and the failure of the South Vietnamese authorities to function as a mediating presence between the population and the US military: all these factors contributed to a situation in which it simply became expedient for US forces in Quang Ngai to think and to act as if everyone who chose to live outside government-controlled areas was a supporter of the Vietcong, probably even for those Americans who knew this not to be the case. 'If you let him in your village, you're an accomplice, aren't you?' asserted James May, the senior civilian adviser in the province.[61]

The officer whom Colonel Henderson had replaced as commander of the 11th Brigade, Brigadier General Andy Lipscomb, told the Peers Inquiry that 'the general feeling' of his troops was that 'anything that was shot was a VC. I'm speaking bluntly here now, but I think that generally was the accepted *modus operandi* over there . . . I don't think that they went to a great deal of trouble to distinguish between men and women.' A senior non-commissioned officer in the brigade's tactical operations centre testified that the people of Quang Ngai 'were not sympathizers, they were active supporters. Anybody. If you say innocent civilians killed, nobody could determine if he was an innocent civilian, because nine out of ten cases he was an active hamlet village guerrilla. A farmer in the daytime, and at night he carried his rifle. So you cannot use the term in this area saying he was an innocent civilian, because the VC ran this area and everybody was a VC.'[62] Interviewed in 2003 about an incident in which he ordered his Tiger Force platoon to shoot ten unarmed farmers in the Song Ve Valley, James Hawkins – a lieutenant at the time of the killings – asserted that the victims should have been in a relocation camp: 'Anything in [that area] was game. If it was living, it was subject to be eliminated.'[63] Former Private Douglas Teeters agreed: 'We didn't think twice about it. If they were civilians, what can you do? They shouldn't have been out there.'[64]

In Son My village itself, dominant political power was indeed exercised by the Vietcong. This did not mean, however, that every resident of the

[60] Schell, *The Real War*, p. 156.
[61] *Ibid.*, pp. 295–6.
[62] Hersh, *Cover-Up*, p. 47.
[63] *Toledo Blade* (20 October 2003).
[64] *Toledo Blade* (21 October 2003).

village wholeheartedly enlisted in the revolutionary struggle, though some undoubtedly did. After all, it was not necessarily personal commitment to the revolution that motivated a decision to remain: there was a natural reluctance to abandon homes and ancestral lands, and no assurance that life would be better in areas subject to government control. A number of families in the village had relatives serving with the ARVN. Routine cooperation with the guerrillas – constructing tunnels and bunkers, carrying weapons and supplies – was the price many villagers paid in order to be otherwise left alone: it constituted an acknowledgement of the local constellation of power at least as often as it did an expression of real allegiance.[65] In most of the sub-hamlets of Son My, the permanent Vietcong presence tended to be limited to senior officials responsible for security, administration and propaganda, and a handful of active guerrillas, cadres and supporters.[66] It was in My Khe sub-hamlet (marked on American maps as My Lai (1)), My Lai hamlet, that the largest concentrations of guerrilla personnel would usually reside: this sub-hamlet served as a key strategic base for the 48th Vietcong local force battalion, which harassed US, Korean and South Vietnamese forces in the eastern parts of the province throughout 1967.[67] After the Tet offensive, however, the battalion retreated to the mountains west of Quang Ngai City: having suffered substantial losses when the tide of the offensive turned in favour of the Americans, its surviving elements needed time to recover and regroup.[68]

To American military planners in early 1968, the nature of the revolution in Son My was even more of a mystery than it was in the rest of the province. For much of the previous year, the village had lain within the operational area of the Korean Marines and then, after the Koreans had been redeployed, the 2nd ARVN Division.[69] Neither of these forces were able to create the sort of secure environment in Son My that would allow government officials to operate there, nor – protective of their own prerogatives and prestige – were they especially receptive to offers of assistance from the Americans.[70] In the wake of Tet, however, the ARVN – fearing a second enemy offensive – became principally concerned with defensive duties in and around Quang Ngai City, and so it passed much of the responsibility for military operations in the east of Son Tinh district, including Son My, to the Americal Division – and, specifically, to the recently formed Task Force Barker.[71] Around the same time, there were

[65] Hammer, *One Morning in the War*, pp. 48–53.

[66] See, for example, the description of the Vietcong government apparatus in Xom Lang sub-hamlet, Tu Cung hamlet, provided to American interrogators by Do Vien, the sub-hamlet's propaganda chief at the time of the massacre. Moses, 'Witness Statement [Do Vien]', 4 January 1970, folder: My Lai 8/80, Papers of *Four Hours in My Lai*, LHCMA, KCL.

[67] Hammer, *One Morning in the War*, p. 49; Frosch, pp. 139, 184.

[68] Goldstein *et al.*, p. 58; Hersh, *Cover-Up*, pp. 96–7.

[69] Frosch, pp. 184–5.

[70] *Ibid.*, p. 185; Hammer, *One Morning in the War*, pp. 57–8.

[71] Goldstein *et al.*, pp. 63–4, 67–8.

personnel changes occurring within the US intelligence apparatus in Quang Ngai, with Captain Eugene Kotouc assigned to the position of intelligence officer to the task force, and Robert Ramsdell – a CIA operative with no previous experience in Vietnam – appointed to manage the Phoenix programme.[72] During its first incursions into Son My in February, Task Force Barker encountered only light enemy resistance (though it claimed to have achieved a high body-count); evidence available to the provincial advisory group, meanwhile, continued to indicate that the 48th battalion remained in the mountains. Nevertheless, Ramsdell and Kotouc seemed to have become convinced, and to have persuaded Colonel Barker, that the village was functioning as a major Vietcong base.[73] Barker began to plan another operation in Son My, to take place in mid-March.

The decision to return to the village was, therefore, based upon questionable intelligence. The same confusion and error was evident in almost everything else that the task force command thought it knew about Son My. Given the likelihood that the 48th battalion was somewhere else entirely, it is not surprising that Barker and Kotouc failed to resolve the issue of exactly where its headquarters were located within the village. Kotouc took the view, he later testified, that the enemy force was principally concentrated in and around My Lai (4) – Xom Lang sub-hamlet of Tu Cung hamlet – which was where Charlie Company was to be inserted. According to other officers, however, the assumption of the command was that My Lai (1), also known to them as Pinkville, was the site of the headquarters, as indeed it had been for much of the war. Bravo Company was given the task of assaulting this sub-hamlet. Both companies were told to expect heavy enemy resistance, consistent with the defence of a key tactical base.[74]

Barker and Kotouc also told the task force that any civilians encountered during the course of the operation could be classed as sympathetic to the Vietcong. It was an assessment informed by three assumptions, all of them mistaken: that the main motivation for continuing to live in Son My was to aid the guerrillas, that virtually everyone who lacked such motivation had already left the village for the government camps, and that the few genuine non-combatants who remained would in any case have departed for market by the time that the troops arrived on the morning of the assault.[75] In fact, as the task force discovered during the operation itself – and as subsequent refugee relocations also revealed – the civilian population of Son My was significantly higher than intelligence had suggested.[76] Moreover, although some villagers could have been expected to

---

[72] Hersh, *Cover-Up*, pp. 69, 85.
[73] *Ibid.*, pp. 61–5, 93–7; Frosch, pp. 189–90.
[74] Goldstein *et al.*, pp. 90–8; Hersh, *Cover-Up*, p. 10.
[75] Goldstein *et al.*, p. 90.
[76] Hersh, *Cover-Up*, p. 73.

go to market, it was also to be expected that many others would stay behind, especially the very young and old, the pregnant and infirm.[77] As it was, no warning was issued prior to the assault urging local inhabitants to leave, nor was any provision made for their evacuation. After all, as General Koster subsequently observed, the task force had nowhere to take them: the government camps were already full.[78]

The Task Force Barker operation of 16 March, therefore, was an outcome of the failure of the US military authorities in Quang Ngai to achieve a sympathetic comprehension of the people of Son My, and the complexities of their relationships with the Vietnamese revolution. They did not even know what to call the places where the people lived, a deficit of intelligence that was not just symbolic, for – as Richard Hammer has suggested – it may have been in part the conflation of My Lai (1) with My Lai (4) that sent Charlie Company to the latter expecting a battle.[79] Son My village (sometimes called Tinh Khe by revolutionary forces) was not a single, continuous settlement, but an administrative unit that incorporated four smaller administrative units, known as hamlets: My Lai, Co Luy (which the Americans spelled Co Lay), My Khe and Tu Cung. Within each of these hamlets were the settlements – sub-hamlets – in which the inhabitants of the village actually lived. Thus, Tu Cung hamlet contained five sub-hamlets, and one of them was Xom Lang (also known to its residents as Thuan Yen), the site where Charlie Company did most of its killing. Every sub-hamlet in Son My, and there were twenty in all, had its own specific name (although there was both a hamlet and a sub-hamlet, located in My Lai hamlet, known as My Khe). Unfortunately, the Vietnamese nomenclature did not coincide with that used by the Americans, who allocated each sub-hamlet a number according to the hamlet in which it was thought to be located: My Khe sub-hamlet in My Lai hamlet, for example, was identified on US maps as My Lai (1). These allocations, however, were often incorrect. Thus, the principal site of the Bravo Company massacre – My Hoi sub-hamlet in Co Luy hamlet – was judged to belong to My Khe hamlet and marked on the maps as My Khe (4). In addition, the US military seems not to have registered the existence of Tu Cung hamlet, which is why Xom Lang came to be known as My Lai (4).[80]

---

[77] *Ibid.*, pp. 70–1.

[78] *Ibid.*, p. 69.

[79] Hammer, *One Morning in the War*, p. 10.

[80] The fullest explanation of the Son My sub-hamlets' nomenclature, and the differences between the names by which they were known by local residents and those which appear on American maps, is provided by Richard Hammer (see *ibid.*, pp. 31–4). See also Hersh, *Cover-Up*, p. 181. However, even across those analyses most concerned to clarify the topography of Son My, inconsistencies remain. Hammer and Hersh differ in the way that they spell the names of some sub-hamlets. Hammer places the sub-hamlet known to the Americans as My Lai (6) in Tu Cung hamlet; Hersh allocates it to My Lai hamlet. Both were agreed that the subhamlet of My Hoi (My Khe (4)) was part of Co Luy hamlet, but the Peers commission was not, concluding instead that it belonged to My Lai hamlet. Peers, p. 184.

This, then, was the environment that Charlie Company entered when it arrived in Quang Ngai in December 1967: an environment in which the revolution was hardened, experienced and very soon to show its real teeth, and continuous in most localities with elements of the civilian population. The disposition of revolutionary allegiance, however, was often more complex and conditional than those directing the American war in the province, who established the standard of conduct and thought for ordinary soldiers in the field, were willing and able to admit. These commanders tended to operate according to a binary code, mentally ordering the people of the province into the categories of civilian or guerrilla, then creating a system of camps to give that order physical form, thereafter targeting massive levels of firepower upon the areas that the civilians were supposed to have left. No one who remained behind could be confident that they would be the object of discrimination or mercy. Indeed, it was the logic of the war that Charlie Company now joined that communities like that in My Lai (4) actually did not exist; though the people looked like defenceless civilians, they could not be so, not even the babies.

Over time, Charlie Company came to adopt the same binary codes. William Calley was not the sort of officer likely to achieve a nuanced understanding of the Vietnamese people and to offer a positive example of cross-cultural contact to his men, even had such a sensibility been encouraged by his superiors. In Hawaii, the day before leaving for Vietnam, he was given three minutes to brief the company about 'Vietnam Our Host', providing guidance in particular on the proper treatment of civilians. 'I did a very *very* poor job of it,' he subsequently recalled.[81] Calley also admitted that from the moment he had arrived in Vietnam, he had been afraid of its people – 'I had promised myself, *I'll act as if I'm never secure here.*'[82] He also found it almost impossible to communicate with them. A conversation about communism with the mamasan of a mobile caravan of prostitutes ended in mutual incomprehension.[83] In the field, Calley had access to a GI interpreter, Ronald Grzesik, who had received 360 hours of Vietnamese language tuition during the company's sojourn in Hawaii. Grzesik, however, had been taught only the Saigonese dialect, and was often at a loss when conducting interrogations in Quang Ngai – not that many of the villagers he spoke to would have been willing in any case to disclose the identity and location of the local Vietcong. Unable to distinguish where the revolution ended and civilian society began, Calley chose not to bother: 'I was there, I had to make decisions, I had to have answers, and I had no other logical one. If these people weren't all VC, prove it to me.' He reflected later on the relationship between the Americans and the people of South Vietnam: 'We didn't have the common

[81] 'The Confessions of Lieutenant Calley', *Esquire* (November 1970), p. 117.
[82] *Ibid.*, p. 118 (italics in original).
[83] *Ibid.*, p. 227.

courtesy to talk their language or learn of their customs: we scorned them. And killed them.'[84]

For the rest of the company, it was in the weeks immediately following their assignment to Task Force Barker that the real attrition of sympathy for the Vietnamese seemed to occur. In January, on their first serious combat patrols in the southern district of Duc Pho, the company's soldiers were eager to play with the children in the villages they entered.[85] Charles West recalled how, when he returned from the field, he would often visit a local orphanage: 'I'd go down there and the people would try to teach me more of the Vietnamese language and they would explain a lot of customs that I wanted to know something about.'[86] In February, however, after the company joined the task force and started to operate around Son My, its mood abruptly turned, influenced in part by command imperatives towards the aggressive pursuit of an enemy weakened by the battles of Tet, and in part by the fact that, though the enemy remained elusive, members of the company were now being wounded and killed. All but three of the forty-two casualties it suffered before mid-March were caused by booby traps and mines, for which the company held the inhabitants of nearby settlements responsible.[87] Its soldiers began to mistreat the Vietnamese that it encountered: children were kicked, women sexually assaulted, prisoners beaten and shot, and no effort was made by the company's officers to stop the abuse.[88] 'I didn't punish the GIs for it,' Calley remembered. 'Someday, I knew, those hordes of VC would be coming at us with sticks and stones and frying pans and weapons: someday soon, and I would need a platoon with a high fighting spirit.'[89]

By 16 March, the category of non-combatant had been erased almost entirely from the company's lexicon of war, and it was not likely to have been restored by the news that they were about to assault a Vietcong stronghold. The inhabitants of My Lai (4) 'were VC sympathizers,' Varnado Simpson told *Life*. 'You don't call them civilians. To us they were VC. They showed no ways or means that they wasn't.'[90] Testifying at Calley's court martial, Paul Meadlo described how he had stood guard over a group of seven or eight women, children and babies, sitting on the ground, close to the trail where they were soon to be killed. 'I assumed at every minute,' he said, 'that they would counterbalance. I thought they had some sort of chain or a little string they had to give a little pull and they

[84] 'The Continuing Confessions of Lieutenant Calley', *Esquire* (February 1971), pp. 59, 114.

[85] *Ibid.*, p. 59.

[86] *Life* (5 December 1969), p. 41.

[87] Goldstein *et al.*, p. 82.

[88] *Ibid.*, p. 206; Bilton and Sim, pp. 77–82.

[89] 'The Continuing Confessions of Lieutenant Calley', *Esquire* (February 1971), p. 59.

[90] *Life* (5 December 1969), p. 41.

blow us up, things like that.'[91] 'I only saw, *They're enemy*,' Calley himself declared.[92]

Yet to catalogue all of the practical and cultural impediments to empathy, to register the genuine problems of discrimination and proportionality with which revolutionary environments confront any counter-revolutionary force, and to record the manner in which the policies of the local command licensed and indeed encouraged excessive acts of violence by American troops in Quang Ngai, may be to light a path to an unwarranted forgiveness. These were not reasons enough for massacre. In My Lai (4), it was not just those who refused to kill who recognized that the people of the sub-hamlet did not conform to the standard definition of enemy combatant, but also some of those who did the killing, as they revealed in their actions at the time. According to Varnado Simpson, he fired upon a woman running into the settlement only because he was ordered to do so by his platoon sergeant: 'I didn't want to shoot no lady.'[93] Paul Meadlo began to weep as he emptied his rifle into the group at the trail.[94] Captain Medina remained on the north-western outskirts of My Lai (4) for over an hour before moving into the settlement with his command group and issuing an order to cease fire (though sporadic killings continued for some time thereafter).[95] In view of Medina's well-documented lack of confidence in the abilities of Lieutenant Calley as well as the obvious aural indications that the operation was uncontested (he would have heard only American rifles being fired), he might have been expected to be anxious to find out for himself what was going on. Instead, as Mary McCarthy observed, he evinced 'a morbid incuriosity. It is as if Capt. Medina desired to know as little as possible about this "combat assault", as if his main wish was to stay on the perimeter of it, while not actually running away.'[96]

Medina's keen appreciation of what it was and was not prudent to know and to have seen – and it was not prudent to have witnessed large numbers of old men, women and children being slaughtered or to have later observed too many of their bodies on the ground – was shared by his superiors. At times during the operation, the site of the massacre seemed to become virtually invisible to senior commanders, and after it was over, they regarded with no great enthusiasm the proposition that troops return to the settlement to confirm the count of civilian dead whilst the evidence was still fresh. Colonel Henderson and General Koster both denied seeing My Lai (4) in flames as they circled above the area in their helicopters,

[91] Hammer, *The Court-Martial of Lt Calley*, p. 160 (italics in original).
[92] 'The Concluding Confessions of Lieutenant Calley', *Esquire* (September 1971), p. 87 (italics in original).
[93] *Interviews with My Lai Veterans*, dir. Joseph Strick (1970).
[94] Belknap, p. 71.
[95] Goldstein *et al.*, pp. 130–8.
[96] McCarthy, p. 39.

although the smoke could be clearly viewed, ten kilometres away, in Quang Ngai City.[97] Henderson also testified that he had only noticed six to eight bodies during the course of his flights that day; his radio operator, in contrast, claimed to have observed a great many more.[98]

However, around three o'clock in the afternoon, perturbed by Hugh Thompson's report of atrocities, Henderson did instruct Medina to take his company back to My Lai (4), to conduct a precise census of the dead. Medina was reluctant, noting later that 'I was afraid of what I would find', and he was no doubt relieved when, following a complaint from Colonel Barker, General Koster intervened and rescinded the order. Koster was content simply to ask Medina how many civilian casualties he had himself seen. Medina replied that he had seen twenty to twenty-eight. 'Well, that sounds about right,' the general said.[99] Intelligence officers in the 11th Brigade also made no attempt to visit the scene, although it was standard procedure to do so when the enemy body-count was as high as that reported by the task force: a search of the bodies could usually be expected to yield valuable documentation. Incompetence may explain the oversight; or possibly these officers had learnt the real status of those who had been killed.[100]

Thompson's allegations placed the senior commanders in an uncomfortable position. Although they were probably unaware of the true scale of the atrocities committed, they seem to have recognized that excessive force had been used by their ground troops and that many non-combatants had died as a result. They certainly knew enough not to want the allegations to be brought to the attention of outside authorities, but – in view of the possibility that word of the incident might reach those authorities through some other channel – they took the precaution of contriving evidence of investigative activity. There was no motivation within the command to find out what had really happened. If there had been, Colonel Henderson would not have been instructed to investigate his own men; at the very least, Henderson would have done much more than he did. On 18 March, the day that his initial enquiries began (and came to an end), he might have travelled to My Lai (4) to inspect the site of the alleged atrocities; there, he would have discovered the mass graves – only a day or so old – in which the victims had been buried, and perhaps also some bodies still awaiting interment. He might have travelled to Quang Ngai City to interview survivors.[101]

Many of the inhabitants of Son My had immediately fled in the direction of Quang Ngai City on the morning of the assault (as they did so, some of them were fired upon and killed by American helicopter gunships); others

[97] Hersh, *Cover-Up*, pp. 101–2.
[98] *Ibid.*, p. 105.
[99] *Ibid.*, pp. 121–2.
[100] *Ibid.*, pp. 145–6.
[101] Goldstein *et al.*, pp. 259–64.

set out in the days that followed, having first returned to the village to bury relatives and neighbours and to recover what they could from the smoking ruins of their homes.[102] It was only a few hours after the assault, indeed, that the first survivors of My Lai (4) (Xom Lang sub-hamlet) reached the province capital, where they recounted their ordeal to Do Dinh Luyen, the government official responsible for Son My. Luyen also quickly learnt of the massacre in My Khe (4) (My Hoi sub-hamlet).[103] On 18 March, a field worker for the province census grievance committee submitted a report asserting that a large number of civilians as well as guerrillas had died during a 'fierce battle' in the vicinity of the hamlet of Tu Cung.[104] The revolution was also collecting information about the American atrocities. Nguyen Co – then the Vietcong sub-hamlet administration chief – was instructed to calculate the death toll in Xom Lang, a task he accomplished by asking the head of each household how many of its members had been killed, and by surveying nearby settlements to find out if any of their residents had been visiting Xom Lang on the day of the massacre and had not returned.[105] His labours – in consort with those of a fellow cadre who compiled a list of the names of the dead in My Hoi – was probably reflected in a National Liberation Front leaflet dated 28 March, which accused the Americans of murdering over 500 civilians in two sub-hamlets of the village of Tinh Khe (Son My).[106] In early April, allied forces discovered the script for a Vietcong broadcast, entitled 'American Evil Appears', which also described the killings in Son My.[107]

In the month following the operation, word of what the men of Task Force Barker had perpetrated in Son My started to reach local South Vietnamese officials and ARVN commanders. Do Dinh Luyen, the government village chief, passed on what he had heard to his immediate superior, Lieutenant Tran Ngoc Tan, chief of Son Tinh District, who dispatched the information in turn to Lieutenant Colonel Ton That Khien, chief of Quang Ngai Province, and to Colonel Nguyen Van Toan, commander of the 2nd ARVN Division.[108] In his report, Tan noted that the loyalties of the village had been with the Vietcong and asserted (erroneously) that the Americans

[102] Hersh, *Cover-Up*, pp. 100–1; Hammer, *One Morning in the War*, pp. 149–53.

[103] Hersh, *Cover-Up*, pp. 180–1.

[104] *Ibid.*, pp. 182–3; Goldstein *et al.*, pp. 270–1.

[105] Kirk, 'Witness Statement [Nguyen Co]', 15 January 1970, folder: My Lai 8/35, Papers of *Four Hours in My Lai*, LHCMA, KCL; Moses, 'Witness Statement [Do Vien]', 4 January 1970, folder: My Lai 8/80, Papers of *Four Hours in My Lai*, LHCMA, KCL.

[106] National Liberation Front Committee of Quang Ngai Province, 'Concerning the Crimes Committed by US Imperialists and Their Lackeys Who Killed More then 500 Civilians of Tinh Khe (V), Son Tinh (D)', 28 March 1968, folder: My Lai 8/59, Papers of *Four Hours in My Lai*, LHCMA, KCL. The Peers commission noted that US forces had only come across a copy of this leaflet in mid-December 1969, and that it may have been backdated and published 'in order to capitalize on the widespread publicity at that time concerning the Son My incident' (Goldstein *et al.*, pp. 274–5).

[107] Goldstein *et al.*, p. 275.

[108] *Ibid.*, pp. 271–3; Hersh, *Cover-Up*, pp. 181–2, 184.

had received sniper fire during the course of their assault; he nevertheless concluded that the result of the operation – 400 people killed in Tu Cung hamlet, 90 more in Co Luy – revealed 'an atrocious attitude if it cannot be called an act of insane violence. Request you intervene on behalf of the people.'[109] A number of officials at the province headquarters were aware of the census grievance report.[110] A copy of the Vietcong script alleging an American massacre in Son My was submitted to Colonel Toan.[111]

Both Toan and Khien, however, seem to have been reluctant to pursue the matter any further, to either investigate the allegations themselves or demand that the Americans conduct a proper inquiry. General Peers attributed their reticence in part to a distaste – common amongst Asians, he suggested – for causing offence to others.[112] Khien was also notoriously corrupt, and probably anxious, therefore, to avoid any action that might distract him from the accumulation of wealth and complicate his relations with the Americans in the province.[113] In the aftermath of Tet, moreover, the priority of the local authorities was the restoration of military security; for the national authorities, it was to keep the United States in the war. Neither of these purposes would have been served by the diversion of resources and public attention to the investigation of charges that American soldiers had massacred hundreds of civilians. In November 1969, Toan and Khien told US army investigators that, although they had believed that there was substance to the atrocity reports, 'they officially reported the incident as Viet Cong propaganda because of the injurious effect the incident would have on national policy'.[114]

It was only in mid-April that the commanders of the 11th Brigade and the Americal Division became aware of just how much the South Vietnamese authorities knew about what had happened in Son My. Around that time, Toan called Koster and informed him of the allegations; meanwhile, the Vietcong script and a written evaluation of Tan's report were passed to Koster and Henderson, apparently by an American adviser working in the province headquarters.[115] A round of contacts followed thereafter. With the probable intention of determining the level of their concern about the matter, Koster visited Toan and Khien; he seems to have come away confident that they would not make trouble.[116] All that was needed was that the paper trail of allegations which was now in existence – in the form, for example, of the broadcast script – be brought to a tidy close.

[109] Tan to Khien, 'Allied operation at Son My assembled and killed civilians', 11 April 1968, folder: My Lai 8/13, Papers of *Four Hours in My Lai*, LHCMA, KCL.

[110] Hersh, *Cover-Up*, pp. 182–3.

[111] Goldstein *et al.*, p. 273.

[112] Peers, p. 135, fn. 1.

[113] Frosch, p. 192; Hersh, *Cover-Up*, pp. 188–9.

[114] Gustafson to Westmoreland, 'My Lai Investigation', 20 November 1969, folder: 'Master File [Copy 1]', Box 15, RCCPI, RPI, RAS, RG319, NACP.

[115] Hersh, *Cover-Up*, pp. 194, 196.

[116] *Ibid.*, p. 197; Goldstein *et al.*, pp. 289–91.

Koster instructed Henderson to submit a written version of his earlier report on the Son My operation, but one which addressed in addition the documents that had since emerged from Vietnamese channels.[117] Henderson also visited Toan and Khien, asserting later that both men had taken the view that the charges of massacre simply constituted enemy propaganda – a conclusion that he was happy to reprise in his subsequent report.[118] That those charges had first been brought to the attention of the South Vietnamese authorities by their own village chief – whose relationship with the Vietcong was such that it was not safe for him to live in Son My itself – was conveniently overlooked.[119]

According to the operational records of the US military, as they stood from May 1968 through to April 1969 and the receipt of Ronald Ridenhour's letter, there had been no atrocities in Son My, and assertions to the contrary were the work of the enemy. At no time during the compilation of those records had any American officer revealed an inclination to find out from the villagers themselves whether the charges were true. While preparing the last report to be written on the incident before the operational files were closed, Colonel Barker apparently did not even bother talking to the American soldiers involved – he just made up their statements – let alone attempt to incorporate survivor accounts.[120] Colonel Khien later testified that, in June 1968, he had taken a South Vietnamese force into Son My in order to conduct an investigation of the alleged massacre site. Enemy resistance caused the investigation to be curtailed before it could enter Xom Lang, though Khien said that he had been able to speak to one or two of its residents. They apparently informed him that a hundred people had been killed in the American assault, thirty of them civilians, the rest Vietcong.[121] Khien's account, however, was contradicted by William Ford, an American adviser, who had accompanied the South Vietnamese force into the village and who told the Peers Commission that, if the mission had an investigative purpose, he had known nothing about it. Ford recalled that Khien had actually entered Xom Lang, which was overgrown with tropical vegetation and basically deserted but for a handful of old men, women and children who were 'scared to death'.[122]

[117] Hersh, *Cover-Up*, p. 198; Goldstein *et al.*, pp. 284, 291.

[118] Hersh, *Cover-Up*, pp. 201–2; Goldstein *et al.*, pp. 281–3; Henderson to Koster, 'Report of Investigation', 24 April 1968, folder: 'Master File [Copy 2]', Box 16, RCCPI, RPI, RAS, RG319, NACP. Henderson testified that he had visited Toan and Khien on his own initiative, before Koster requested the written report: the meeting had been prompted, he said, by his receipt of the Vietcong propaganda materials (Hersh, *Cover-Up*, pp. 200–1). The Peers Inquiry was unable to reconstruct the precise sequence of events on this point, although it did observe that Henderson's account was 'confused, contradictory, and belied by other testimony and the documentary record' (Goldstein *et al.*, p. 281).

[119] Hersh, *Cover-Up*, pp. 180–1.

[120] *Ibid.*, pp. 209–11.

[121] *Ibid.*, pp. 213–14; Khien, 'Results of the Investigation of the Case of the American Operation in the Son My Area (East of Son Tinh)', 30 November 1969, folder: My Lai 8/77, Papers of *Four Hours in My Lai*, LHCMA, KCL.

[122] Peers, pp. 159–60; Goldstein *et al.*, p. 265; Hersh, *Cover-Up*, pp. 213–14.

In early 1969, as part of Operation Russell Beach, the soldiers of the Americal Division returned to Son My village, seeking to relocate its remaining population (which was more than twice the size estimated by the authorities in Saigon) to a government pacification camp.[123] By that time, the Vietcong had returned to the area in earnest, and – through the use of booby traps and mines – resumed its harvest of American lives and limbs.[124] In May, Tim O'Brien's infantry company was sent to Son My and immediately wandered into an ambush – with the people of a nearby sub-hamlet offering no prior warning. Over the next few days, harassed by sniper-fire and mortars, the company started to beat up prisoners; a farmer was shot as he worked in a rice field; napalm was called in to level a hamlet. 'There were Viet Cong in that hamlet,' O'Brien wrote later. 'And there were babies and children and people who just didn't give a damn in there, too. But Chip and Tom were on the way to Graves Registration in Chu Lai, and they were dead, and it was hard to be filled with pity.'[125]

Throughout 1969, Son My remained under the control of the revolution, whilst even the government hamlet to which many of its inhabitants had been moved was officially rated as insecure.[126] In November, after the charges against Calley had finally become news, many correspondents seeking to travel to My Lai (4) passed through LZ Gator, a fire base located between Chu Lai and Quang Ngai City, and the headquarters of the 5th Battalion, 46th Infantry, which had taken over responsibility for the Son My area from the 11th Brigade. According to O'Brien, who was now stationed at the base, the executive officer of the battalion sought to familiarize these reporters with the realities of the war as it was fought in the vicinity of the village: 'You ever been to My Lai? Well, I'll tell you, those *civilians* – *you* call them civilians – they kill American GIs. They plant mines and spy and snipe and kill us. Sure, you all print colour pictures of dead little boys, but the live ones – take pictures of the live ones digging holes for mines.'[127]

It was inevitable, therefore, that the criminal investigation into the massacre allegations would not be particularly welcomed by either the American or South Vietnamese authorities in Quang Ngai. Although commanders of the Americal Division and the 11th Brigade performed the necessary public rituals of cooperation with the inquiry, they were privately purging their files of important materials pertinent to the operation of 16 March and subsequent 'investigative' activities. In the time that had passed since the actual massacre, many of the soldiers involved had been rotated

[123] Bond, 'Pacification History of My Lai Hamlet, Quang Ngai Province', 8 September 1969, folder: 'My Lai Allegations', Box 16, RCCPI, RPI, RAS, RG319, NACP.

[124] O'Brien, *If I Die in a Combat Zone*, pp. 109–10.

[125] *Ibid.*, pp. 110–13.

[126] Bond, 'Pacification History of My Lai Hamlet, Quang Ngai Province', 8 September 1969, folder: 'My Lai Allegations', Box 16, RCCPI, RPI, RAS, RG319, NACP.

[127] O'Brien, *If I Die in a Combat Zone*, pp. 173–7 (italics in original).

back to domestic bases or discharged from military service altogether, and thus it was in the United States that army detectives initially concentrated their efforts. Following receipt of Ridenhour's letter, a preliminary survey of the documentation held at Chu Lai was undertaken in April 1969, by a colonel from the Inspector General's office in Saigon, but he found no evidence either of atrocity or allegations of atrocity.[128] For the next five months, until André Feher arrived in South Vietnam in September, those in control of the divisional and brigade files were left to their own devices, and they took the opportunity to remove everything related to the original charges of massacre, with the exception of Henderson's written report. Colonel Barker's final report, for example, had entirely disappeared.[129] Fortunately, the South Vietnamese district and provincial authorities had conducted no similar purge; from their files, in Son Tinh and Quang Ngai City, investigators eventually obtained the reports from Do Dinh Luyen and Lieutenant Tan, as well as the evaluation of Tan's report and the Vietcong script.[130]

It was only in mid-December, however, that local government officials became so cooperative. Feher had first reached Quang Ngai a month before, just as the revelations about the massacre were beginning to break, and on 16 November he travelled to a relocation camp in Son My to try to find witnesses. There, in the presence of Do Dinh Luyen, Feher spoke to Do Tan Nhon, the chief of Tu Cung hamlet, who related what survivors had told him about the incident: that the villagers had been gathered together in three large groups in three different places and shot, with a total of 370 killed. Nhon said that there were ten survivors of the massacre currently living in the camp, as well as five other people who had helped to bury the dead. Feher briefly interviewed two of the survivors, Do Chuc and Do Hoai. Do Chuc's account matched that of Nhon: three groups, 370 killed.[131] American reporters followed Feher to the camp, and on 18 November, Do Chuc appeared on the evening news broadcasts of both CBS and NBC.[132] In the CBS report, he described the way in which the inhabitants of My Lai (4) had been lined up and shot, imitating with his hands how the soldiers of Charlie Company had held their rifles, then dramatically rocking and twisting his body to demonstrate what had happened to the victims when the soldiers opened fire.

[128] Whitaker, 'Preliminary Inquiry Concerning Alleged Massacre of All Vietnamese Residents of My Lai (BS 728795) by US Soldiers', 17 April 1969, folder: My Lai 8/40, Papers of *Four Hours in My Lai*, LHCMA, KCL.

[129] Hersh, *Cover-Up*, pp. 218–26.

[130] Peers, pp. 137–40.

[131] Feher, 'Witness Statement', 16 November 1969, folder: My Lai 8/35, Papers of *Four Hours in My Lai*, LHCMA, KCL; Feher, 'Statement [Do Dinh Luyen, unsworn]', 25 November 1969, folder: My Lai 8/35, Papers of *Four Hours in My Lai*, LHCMA, KCL.

[132] *CBS Evening News*, 18 November 1969, VTNA; *NBC Nightly News*, 18 November 1969, VTNA.

No doubt sensitive to the possible impact of the massacre upon political opinion in both the United States and South Vietnam itself – and probably conscious in addition that they were implicated in the initial failure to investigate – the provincial authorities sought to cast doubt upon the accounts provided by survivors and to prevent them from speaking again to the press. Colonel Khien told *CBS Evening News* that many of the inhabitants of Son My belonged to the Vietcong, who tended to exaggerate casualty figures.[133] In a memorandum to President Thieu, he stated that the villagers were hoping for compensation from the Americans 'so they stated that many houses were burned and civilians killed'.[134] Two days later, on 22 November, the South Vietnamese Ministry of Defence released a communiqué in which it asserted that Task Force Barker had encountered 'strong communist resistance' when entering My Lai (4). One hundred and twenty-five Vietcong guerrillas had been killed in the battle, along with about 20 civilians who were forced by the enemy to remain in the settlement, and who met their deaths during American aerial attacks. Reports that hundreds of civilians had died were 'absolutely untrue', the ministry declared.[135]

By the time that André Feher came to take formal statements from Do Tan Nhon, the Tu Cung hamlet chief, and Do Dinh Luyen, the Son My village chief, the two officials had both clearly been persuaded to conform their stories to the government line. Nhon now asserted that the villagers who had told him of a massacre were members of the Vietcong; since he had last spoken to Feher, he had conducted another investigation and learnt that in fact it had been the enemy guerrillas who had gathered together the civilians, using them as a shield from behind which they could throw grenades at the Americans. Fifteen to twenty villagers were killed in the resulting crossfire, and others died as a result of artillery and aerial bombardment. Nhon also testified that there were actually only three witnesses to the incident residing in the camp, not ten as he had previously believed. He told Feher: 'Do not continue to investigate about this, because the farmers know that the Americans like them, and the farmers only want the Americans to help them.'[136] Do Dinh Luyen, meanwhile, disavowed what he had reported to the district chief in the days following the massacre, like Nhon declaring that the villagers had been killed in a crossfire between the Americans and Vietcong.[137]

[133] *CBS Evening News*, 18 November 1969, VTNA.
[134] Khien to Thieu, 'Concerning the military operation on 16/2/68 at Tu Cung (H), Son My (V) belonging to Task Force Barker 11th Bde Americal Division', 20 November 1969, folder: My Lai 8/77, Papers of *Four Hours in My Lai*, LHCMA, KCL.
[135] Bunker to Rogers, US Embassy (Saigon) telegram 23612, 25 November 1969, folder: 'Department of State', Box 2, Administrative and Background Materials Files – Open Inventory, 1967–1970, RPI, RAS, RG319, NACP.
[136] Feher, 'Statement [Do Tan Nhon, unsworn]', 25 November 1969, folder: My Lai 8/35, Papers of *Four Hours in My Lai*, LHCMA, KCL.
[137] Feher, 'Statement [Do Dinh Luyen, unsworn]', 25 November 1969, folder: My Lai 8/35, Papers of *Four Hours in My Lai*, LHCMA, KCL.

By late November, media access to the massacre survivors was regularly obstructed by the local authorities. When ABC's Don Baker visited the relocation camp, he interviewed Ha Thi Quy, wife of Do Chuc, who had been shot in the hip during the massacre. Baker reported, however, that her story was 'cut short by village officials. The villagers were ordered to shut up. ABC was told to stop filming. Two weeks ago none cared, but that was before the Vietnamese government announced that civilians were not killed by Americans at My Lai.'[138]

Do Tan Nhon informed Richard Hammer that he could not enter the camp without a letter of permission from Colonel Khien, relenting only when the American officer accompanying Hammer said he had never heard of such a requirement: 'For another moment he tries to block the way and then, reluctantly, steps aside.' Once inside the camp, Hammer discovered that its residents all had been warned not to talk to Americans and that seven survivors of the massacre who already had done so had been taken away. When Nhon came across his sister, Nguyen Chi, speaking to Hammer in Quang Ngai City, he was angry, 'telling her not to say anymore, not to talk, that she was asking for trouble.'[139]

As compelling evidence of the massacre – in the form of perpetrator testimony and images of the dead – started to accumulate within the public realm, and as senior US officials, including the President himself, acknowledged the likelihood that a serious crime had indeed been committed in My Lai (4), the position adopted by the South Vietnamese government – that no such crime had occurred – appeared increasingly gratuitous and wilful, which were not quite the qualities that the Nixon administration wanted its ally to present to the world.[140] Moreover, under pressure to expedite both the criminal investigation and that of the Peers Commission, US authorities were anxious to secure – if not the active cooperation of the Saigon authorities – then at least an end to their interference and obstruction. In a meeting with the MACV Provost Marshall on 10 December, André Feher warned that interviews with Vietnamese witnesses in Quang Ngai would continue to be 'unproductive unless the GVN position on the facts of the My Lai (4) incident is substantially changed'.[141] The MACV Staff Judge Advocate agreed to discuss the problem with officials from the Vietnamese Ministry of Defence, and also to furnish them with the issue of *Life* containing photographs of the massacre and a number of CID statements, including those of Ronald Haeberle and Do Chuc.[142]

[138] *ABC News*, 1 December 1969, VTNA.

[139] Hammer, *One Morning in the War*, pp. 20–2.

[140] 'The President's news conference of *December* 8, 1969' *Public Papers of the Presidents: Richard Nixon, 1969*, pp. 1003–5.

[141] McGreevy, CID Task Force daily journal entry, 10 December 1969, folder: My Lai 8/36, Papers of *Four Hours in My Lai*, LHCMA, KCL.

[142] McGreevy, CID Task Force daily journal entry, 11 December 1969, folder: My Lai 8/36, Papers of *Four Hours in My Lai*, LHCMA, KCL.

As a result of these efforts, the government promised to permit a full investigation and directed Colonel Toan, the ARVN commander in Quang Ngai, to make massacre survivors available to the American authorities.[143] Colonel Khien was transferred to another province.[144] Nhon and Luyen, however, both remained in post, which probably informed the decision – on Feher's advice – to interview the survivors in Quang Ngai City, not at the relocation camp in Son My.[145] CID investigators, moreover, continued to complain about the sluggishness with which province officials furnished subjects for questioning.[146] The national government, meanwhile, still remained obstinate in its contention that there had been no massacre, prompting Secretary of the Army Stanley Resor and General Westmoreland to suggest that the US ambassador in Saigon make a presentation of evidence direct to President Thieu.[147]

As US army investigators endeavoured to find a way for the surviving residents of My Lai (4) to tell their stories without official interference or fear of reprisal, they were also making plans for a thorough forensic examination of the massacre site itself. André Feher briefly visited the settlement on 17 November, accompanied by Do Chuc, Do Hoai and Dennis Conti, a former member of Charlie Company who was still serving in Vietnam. Because the Vietcong continued to operate within the area, the party travelled in a convoy of armoured personnel carriers, under the protection of soldiers from the Americal Division. Photographs were taken of the ditch and the trail where much of the killing occurred, and of the unmarked graves of the victims, pointed out by the two survivors.[148] Feher believed, however, that a more intensive inspection of the site was required. Having expanded its remit to include an investigation of the massacre as well as the cover-up, the Peers Commission also wished to visit My Lai (4), as did both the defence and prosecution counsel in the Calley court martial. It was agreed, therefore, that these inspections would be integrated into a single operation, with logistical support and a security task force to be provided by the Americal Division.[149]

---

[143] McGreevy, CID Task Force daily journal entries, 14, 19 December 1969, folder: My Lai 8/36, Papers of *Four Hours in My Lai*, LHCMA, KCL.

[144] McGreevy, CID Task Force daily journal entry, 19 December 1969, folder: My Lai 8/36, Papers of *Four Hours in My Lai*, LHCMA, KCL; Peers, p. 139.

[145] McGreevy, CID Task Force daily journal entry, 14 December 1969, folder: My Lai 8/36, Papers of *Four Hours in My Lai*, LHCMA, KCL.

[146] Wells, CID Task Force daily journal entry, 24 December 1969 and 6 January 1970, folder: My Lai 8/36, Papers of *Four Hours in My Lai*, LHCMA, KCL.

[147] Resor and Westmoreland to Peers, 2 January 1970, folder: '"Top Secret" Messages, January to December, 1970s', Box 35, William C. Westmoreland papers, USAMHI.

[148] Feher, 'Witness Statement', 24 November 1969, folder: My Lai 8/34, Papers of *Four Hours in My Lai*, LHCMA, KCL; Gustafson to Westmoreland, 'My Lai Investigation', 20 November 1969, folder: 'Master File [Copy 1]', Box 15, RCCPI, RPI, RAS, RG319, NACP.

[149] McGreevy, CID Task Force daily journal entry, 17 December 1969, folder: My Lai 8/36, Papers of *Four Hours in My Lai*, LHCMA, KCL.

The security task force, in its practices and dimensions, communicated all the wariness and dread with which the Americal Division regarded Son My. Conceivably, it was intended to: the task force was commanded by the same officer who, at LZ Gator, had berated correspondents for assuming the village contained any such thing as a genuine non-combatant.[150] On 30 December, the force – consisting of an infantry company, a reconnaissance platoon and a platoon of engineers – moved into My Lai (4) to secure the settlement. It was augmented by combat tracker teams and mine and tunnel dogs. South Vietnamese popular forces and national policemen were directed to establish checkpoints on roads leading to and from My Lai (4), around which the task force constructed a security perimeter of wire and bunkers with overhead cover. Similar bunkers were constructed throughout the sub-hamlet for the protection of the investigative teams. Tents were also erected, equipped with electric lights. Visitors were permitted to enter the site only by helicopter, for which a steel landing pad was built. Upon arrival, their identities were checked against an access roster, and they were issued with steel helmets and armoured vests, and briefed as to the location of security forces in the sub-hamlet, and the trails (marked with white tape) which had been cleared of booby traps and mines. If they wished to venture beyond these trails, the investigators had first to ask for the area to be swept by mine detection personnel. During their visits, they were kept dispersed and in small groups, and were always accompanied by a security force. When the most important visitors – such as General Peers – were present on the ground, air cover was provided, and when the general conducted an aerial reconnaissance of the area, his helicopter was escorted by two gunships and an armed Huey with an infantry security team aboard. General Ramsey, the commander of the Americal Division, provided control from another helicopter. Having removed all sandbags and filled in the bunkers (leaving nothing that might be of use to the enemy), the task force finally departed My Lai (4) on 12 January. Contact with the enemy had been negligible.[151]

Undoubtedly, both the Peers Commission and CID investigators derived some benefit from their visit to the massacre site, primarily in the form of topographical orientation. On his reconnaissance flight over the area, Peers was accompanied by Hugh Thompson; on the ground, his party included two ARVN interpreters – Sergeant Nguyen Donh Phu and Sergeant Duong Minh – who had been attached to Task Force Barker during the 16 March operation, and Pham Chot, a former Vietcong cadre and resident of My Lai (4), who had observed the massacre from a nearby hill. All these witnesses

---

[150] O'Brien, *If I Die in a Combat Zone*, p. 177.

[151] For descriptions of the task force operation, see Ramsey to Mickerson, 'My Lai (4)', undated, folder: My Lai 8/64, Papers of *Four Hours in My Lai*, LHCMA, KCL; Abrams to McCain and Wheeler, 15 January 1970, folder: My Lai 8/64, Papers of *Four Hours in My Lai*, LHCMA, KCL; Feher to Bilton, 20 August 1990, folder: My Lai 8/35, Papers of *Four Hours in My Lai*, LHCMA, KCL; Peers, pp. 135–7.

assisted the commission team in identifying many of the sites where killing had occurred.[152]

CID investigators also made use of Vietnamese witnesses: when the task force entered My Lai (4) on 30 December, it captured two Vietcong operatives, Truong Ngu and Do Vien, who had both lived in the settlement at the time of the massacre. During interrogation, it became evident that Ngu and Vien, having helped to bury many of the victims (including members of their own families), were extremely well-informed about which residents had been killed by the Americans – and where and how they had died. They were subsequently taken back to the settlement and asked to identify the principal killing and burial sites.[153] A team of army engineers also spent four days in My Lai (4) conducting field work for a master drawing of the area, which was anticipated, upon completion, to be 10–12 feet long and 6–8 feet wide.[154]

Although it offered an opportunity for illustrated witness testimony and for the various investigative teams to become more familiar with the broad physical environment in which the atrocities had occurred, the onsite inspection of My Lai (4) did not produce much in the way of fresh forensic evidence. The settlement itself had changed considerably in appearance since the morning of the massacre, nearly two years before: many of its structures had been destroyed, either by Charlie Company or in subsequent military operations, and – with its inhabitants either departed or dead – nature had reclaimed most of what was left. According to General Peers, the frondescence of the jungle vegetation was such that visibility was often no more than 5 to 20 feet. The ditch into which scores of villagers had been pushed, to be thereafter shot, was so overgrown that it was difficult to judge its actual size; no American bullets were found there, even when a metal-detector was used.[155] It was also the rainy season on the central coast, and the heavy track vehicles driven by the security task force further obscured sections of the terrain, including the location of paddy dikes.[156] Despite extensive efforts, CID detectives were unable to positively match any of the remaining structures or parts of structures to those that appeared in Haeberle's photographs, although they did identify

[152] Peers, pp. 135–7; Kirk, 'Witness Statement [Pham Chot]'. 4 January 1970, folder: My Lai 8/35, Papers of *Four Hours in My Lai*, LHCMA, KCL.

[153] McGreevy, 'Witness Statement', 10 January 1970, folder: My Lai 8/34, Papers of *Four Hours in My Lai*, LHCMA, KCL; McLellan, 'Witness Statement [Truong Ngu]', 4 January 1970, folder: My Lai 8/80, Papers of *Four Hours in My Lai*, LHCMA, KCL; Moses, 'Witness Statement [Do Vien]', 4 January 1970, folder: My Lai 8/80, Papers of *Four Hours in My Lai*, LHCMA, KCL.

[154] Ramsey to Mickerson, 'My Lai (4)', undated, folder: My Lai 8/64, Papers of *Four Hours in My Lai*, LHCMA, KCL; Wells, CID Task Force daily journal entry, 6 January 1970, folder: My Lai 8/36, Papers of *Four Hours in My Lai*, LHCMA, KCL.

[155] Peers, p. 136; McGreevy, 'Witness Statement', 10 January 1970, folder: My Lai 8/34, Papers of *Four Hours in My Lai*, LHCMA, KCL.

[156] Melner to McCate, 'My Lai Investigation', undated, folder: My Lai 8/34, Papers of *Four Hours in My Lai*, LHCMA, KCL.

a tree seen in the image of the terrified group of women and children, moments before they were gunned down. Two pieces of the tree were mailed to an army laboratory for analysis.[157]

Overall, the investigative teams may have been disappointed with the results of their visit to the massacre site, yet the parameters of their efforts there had been narrowly defined from the very start. With the security task force commissioned only to provide access to My Lai (4), they were unable to extend their ground inspections to the neighbouring sub-hamlet of Binh Tay, where members of Charlie Company had also killed non-combatants, or to My Khe (4), the scene of atrocities by Bravo Company – about which the investigators were just beginning to learn.[158] Indeed, after the end of their investigation in My Lai (4), General Ramsey, commander of the Americal Division, prohibited the CID team from visiting anywhere in the eastern portion of the district of Son Tinh, asserting that it was not secure.[159] In My Lai (4) itself, the detectives made no attempt to exhume any of the bodies of those who had died in the massacre. Most of the graves were unmarked, and only in a small number of cases could survivors identify for certain who had been interred within. In the light of Buddhist tradition, disturbance of the dead would have piled offence upon offence; and in any case, given the local climate, there may not have been very much left to examine.[160] Probably, the returns would not have seemed likely to merit all the bother: there was no assurance that autopsy evidence would connect the fate of particular victims to the actions of any particular perpetrator, and even if it did, it would not necessarily dispose of the latter's defence. Through wholesale exhumation, the investigators may have been able to obtain an accurate tally of the dead, but it would have been a contentious and grisly process, and the count conceivably could be accomplished by some other means.

It was an impression of the settlement's utter desolation that many of the investigators took away from their visits. André Feher recalled that, when he had first entered My Lai (4) in mid-November, he had found it 'completely overgrown and deserted. There was very little to see inside of

[157] McGreevy, 'Witness Statement', 10 January 1970, folder: My Lai 8/34, Papers of *Four Hours in My Lai*, LHCMA, KCL; Wells, CID Task Force daily journal entry, 6 January 1970, folder: My Lai 8/36, Papers of *Four Hours in My Lai*, LHCMA, KCL.

[158] McGreevy, 'Witness Statement', 10 January 1970, folder: My Lai 8/34, Papers of *Four Hours in My Lai*, LHCMA, KCL. André Feher first heard of the massacre at My Khe (4) when interviewing a resident of the sub-hamlet on 15 December. McGreevy, CID Task Force daily journal entry, 15 December 1969, folder: My Lai 8/36, Papers of *Four Hours in My Lai*, LHCMA, KCL.

[159] McGreevy, 'Witness Statement', 20 January 1970, folder: My Lai 8/35, Papers of *Four Hours in My Lai*, LHCMA, KCL.

[160] Zara, 'Witness Statement', 20 July 1970, folder: My Lai 8/33, Papers of *Four Hours in My Lai*, LHCMA, KCL. Note, however, that the Saigon authorities were only too happy to dig up and display the bodies of those that they claimed to be the victims of the enemy occupation of Hué: T. Van Dinh, 'Fear of a bloodbath', *New Republic* (6 December 1969), pp. 11–14.

the village.'[161] General Peers noted: 'For all practical purposes, it was a dead village.'[162] My Khe (4), which he viewed from his helicopter, looked even worse, with 'little semblance of any life or previous habitation. A combination of the shifting sands from the ocean winds and the growth of grasses and jungle had all but obliterated it.'[163] Of course, the investigators tended to travel in the company of American soldiers, which may have encouraged any Vietnamese who did remain in these settlements to stay out of sight. Seasonal mist and rain, meanwhile, seemed to offer further confirmation of the local landscape's morbidity. Viewed from the air, there was a 'dank, evil-looking' quality to My Lai (4), Tim O'Brien observed. 'Even in stark, mid-morning daylight the place looks a monotonous grey from the air. Your eyes can stay on the place for only seconds; then you look away to the east, where the sea is so much more appealing.'[164]

American reporters would also commonly comment upon the desolation of the massacre site: that is, when they were able to visit it, which was not very often. As it was to investigators, My Lai (4) remained off-limits to journalists without a military escort. Thus, for the first week following the initial revelations, their coverage was confined to the relocation camp nearby and to shaky aerial footage of the actual settlement in which the killings had occurred.[165] Americans having recently landed on the moon for a second time, this footage implied a remoteness more profound than even that of outer space. 'This is as close as anyone can get safely to My Lai,' observed ABC's Roger Peterson on 26 November. 'A quick low pass in a helicopter.'[166]

He was not entirely accurate. A day or so before, Don Webster of CBS had accompanied a force of US soldiers into the settlement. He had discovered a bottle of warm tea there, presumably left by a Vietcong guerrilla in a hurry to get away.[167] Eventually, reporters from both ABC and NBC did make it into My Lai (4), but – though the story of the massacre continued to unfold for another year and a half – media access to the scene of the crime remained extremely limited.[168] In early January – after the Peers and CID investigative teams had completed their onsite inspection, but before the security task force departed – seven members of the press were permitted to visit the settlement, but only for an hour.[169] In

[161] Feher to Bilton, 20 August 1990, folder: My Lai 8/35, Papers of *Four Hours in My Lai*, LHCMA, KCL.

[162] Peers, p. 136.

[163] *Ibid.*, pp. 185–6.

[164] O'Brien, *If I Die in a Combat Zone*, p. 177.

[165] *CBS Evening News*, 18 November 1969, VTNA; *NBC Nightly News*, 18 November 1969, VTNA.

[166] *ABC News*, 26 November 1969, VTNA.

[167] *CBS Evening News*, 25 November 1969, VTNA.

[168] See, for example, *ABC News*, 1 December 1969, VTNA; *NBC Nightly News*, 5 December 1969, VTNA.

[169] Ramsey to Mickerson, 'My Lai (4)', undated, folder: My Lai 8/64, Papers of *Four Hours in My Lai*, LHCMA, KCL.

April, reporting from the relocation camp nearby, CBS correspondent Richard Threlkeld reprised Peterson's words: 'Now, two years after the massacre, this is about as close as anyone can safely get.'[170] As the Calley court martial drew to a close in March 1971, Tom Streithorst and an NBC camera crew did venture into My Lai (4), but without military protection, which the Americal Division had refused to provide. The village of Son My, Streithorst asserted, was 'now officially listed as pacified, but it's ranked in the lowest category of pacification. You still hear firing, there are mines and booby-traps reported; it's not advised for outsiders to remain here at night.'[171]

In his book *One Morning in the War*, Richard Hammer describes a journey by jeep from Quang Ngai City to Son My, heading north across the Tra Khuc River, and once over the bridge, turning right towards the coast. For the first few miles along the road, everything was familiar: there were Vietnamese riding bicycles and motorbikes, farmers working in their rice fields, one or two markets, the occasional camp for refugees. Then, suddenly, the scene was transformed:

> It takes the eye a moment to adjust, to accept the change. The carefully cultivated paddies are gone. Except for an occasional solitary quickly moving walker at the side of the road, there is no one. To the north and south of the road there is desolation, a wilderness overgrown, new trees beginning to push their way through the soft green turf, old palm trees, some fallen, some with the tops blasted away so that they stand naked and forelorn, making one somehow abashed and wanting to avert ones eyes. What must once have been paddies are now filled with weeds, laying fallow.

Hammer had arrived, he noted, at the western boundary of 'what used to be the village of Son My', from which it was a very short walk north 'toward what used to be Xom Lang'. The sub-hamlet was now 'a rubble of bricks and cinders, covered over by rampant growth'. Shell-holes pockmarked the landscape, filled with mud and water and the debris left by recent American visitors – probably the security task force and the investigative teams. 'And over everything,' Hammer observed, 'there is silence, a stillness so strange that one talks only in whispers.'[172]

That the entire community had been killed along with many of its people was a common theme in the handful of news reports made from the actual site of the massacre. Don Webster, glancing around him, described his location as 'what used to be My Lai'.[173] The settlement, said Richard Threlkeld, was 'not much of a place anymore, just a few ruined huts and at night it's the home of a few Vietcong'. The massacre's survivors, he suggested, 'will probably never return to their old homes.

[170] *CBS Evening News*, 24 April 1970, VTNA.
[171] *NBC Nightly News*, 19 March 1971, VTNA.
[172] Hammer, *One Morning in the War*, pp. 13–19.
[173] *CBS Evening News*, 25 November 1969, VTNA.

My Lai is a place of bad luck and bad memories.'[174] Yet, as one or two of the reports acknowledged, a return of sorts was already under way, at least to the fields surrounding Xom Lang. In early December 1969, *ABC News* showed a former resident of the sub-hamlet, Truong Thi Tung, planting rice close to 'the ruins of her home' and to the graves of her family.[175] Inhabitants of the refugee camp nearby, noted Hammer, had tentatively started to venture back to Xom Lang to try to reclaim the rice paddies and vegetable gardens abandoned in the wake of the massacre.[176] Tom Streithorst filmed survivors tending cattle in and around the settlement.[177]

To television audiences in the United States, watching recurring images of Fort Benning, where Calley and his defence team were based prior to his trial, and of its courthouse, where the trial was eventually to be held, the landscape of My Lai (4) itself and the physical legacies of the massacre there were to remain largely unwitnessed and obscure. They saw images of My Khe (4) hardly at all.[178] It was difficult for these audiences, therefore, to conceive of what had been perpetrated in Son My, in terms less abrupt than the frozen tableau of terror and death supplied by Ronald Haeberle: in terms of a vital and tenacious human community, with its own complex patterns of culture, politics and commerce, brought to the edge of extinction by American arms; but which nevertheless was not quite extinct, which was returning to the ruins and fashioning a future for itself, offering to American conscience the opportunity of work beyond simply the effort to call William Calley to account. Americans did not speak of making reparations, perhaps, because they did not know there was anything left that could be repaired.

Writing in the *New Yorker* in December 1969, Jonathan Schell observed that the victims of the massacre appeared 'indistinct – almost invisible. A death close to us personally seems unfathomably large, but their deaths dwindle in our eyes to mere abstractions. We don't know what kind of lives they led or what kind of things they said to each other. We are even uncertain of the right name of the village we are said to have annihilated.'[179] In the wake of the initial disclosures, US media renditions of the village, hamlet and sub-hamlet nomenclature in the vicinity of the massacre site were hopelessly confused, as reporters travelled to Quang Ngai and tried to reconcile the names used by American forces in the province with those used by its inhabitants. Inconsistencies, misdesignations, mis-spellings and mispronunciations proliferated. According to early coverage in the *New*

---

[174] *CBS Evening News*, 24 April 1970, VTNA.

[175] *ABC News*, 1 December 1969, VTNA.

[176] Hammer, *One Morning in the War*, p. 23.

[177] *NBC Nightly News*, 19 March 1971, VTNA.

[178] In one of the few substantial reports on the massacre at My Khe (4), *NBC Nightly News* presented an aerial view of the sub-hamlet and interviewed survivors residing in another part of Co Luy hamlet. *NBC Nightly News*, 18 February 1970, VTNA.

[179] Schell, 'Notes and comments: Talk of the town', *New Yorker* (20 December 1969), p. 27.

York Times, the massacre had occurred in the hamlet of 'Mylai' within 'Songmy' village.[180] *Life* magazine attempted a clarification: 'Mylai 4 was one of nine hamlets, each designated by a number, which were clustered near the village of Songmy, a name sometimes used also for the hamlets.'[181] Television newscasters explored every possible phrasing: Mee Lie, My Lay, May Lie. However it was written, however it was spoken, 'My Lai' (usually without the (4), and often still asserted to be a village) evolved over time into the default appellation of the place where the killings had occurred; indeed, it effectively became the name of the crime: 'The furor over the Calley verdict,' editorialized *Life* in April 1971, 'was in its way almost as appalling as Mylai itself.'[182] Only very rarely was it noted that, according to the local Vietnamese nomenclature, the massacre had not happened in 'My Lai' at all, but in Xom Lang sub-hamlet, Tu Cung hamlet, Son My village.[183] That a *nom de guerre* assigned to the settlement by the US military became the principal signifier of the suffering of its inhabitants exemplifies the capacity for displacement that existed as soon as the massacre was exposed to the operations of American culture: Americans had the power to call the massacre what they wanted.

By the end of December 1969, US investigators were finally in a position to proceed with systematic interviews of Vietnamese witnesses to the massacre. Having secured at least a modicum of cooperation from the provincial authorities, a team of six CID investigators arrived in Quang Ngai City on 22 December.[184] The following day, five witnesses were provided for them to interview.[185] Over the next few weeks, they took statements from around 70 witnesses, a total that included local officials as well as survivors.[186] The Peers Commission also conducted interviews with about twenty-five inhabitants of Son My.[187]

Some of the witness testimony proved extremely valuable. Whilst waiting in Chu Lai for the attitude of the Quang Ngai authorities to change, André Feher had interviewed Nguyen Thi Bay, a patient in an evacuation hospital at the base, and learnt for the first time about the Bravo Company killings in My Hoi (My Khe (4)).[188] The Peers Commission only realized that Charlie Company had also committed atrocities in Binh Tay, just to

[180] *New York Times* (20 November 1969), pp. 1, 14.

[181] *Life* (5 December 1969), p. 39.

[182] *Life* (16 April 1971), p. 40.

[183] Hammer, *One Morning in the War*, pp. 31–4.

[184] McGreevy, CID Task Force daily journal entry, 22 December 1969, folder: My Lai 8/36, Papers of *Four Hours in My Lai*, LHCMA, KCL.

[185] McGreevy, CID Task Force daily journal entry, 23 December 1969, folder: My Lai 8/36, Papers of *Four Hours in My Lai*, LHCMA, KCL.

[186] Wells, CID Task Force daily journal entry, 14 January 1969, folder: My Lai 8/36, Papers of *Four Hours in My Lai*, LHCMA, KCL.

[187] Peers, p. 141.

[188] McGreevy, CID Task Force daily journal entry, 15 December 1969, folder: My Lai 8/36, Papers of *Four Hours in My Lai*, LHCMA, KCL; Van Paulen, 'Combined Interrogation Report', 16 December 1969, folder: My Lai 8/36, Papers of *Four Hours in My Lai*, LHCMA, KCL.

the north of Xom Lang, when they questioned one of its residents, who described how he had hidden in bushes and watched as his mother had been raped and killed.[189] Nevertheless, as with the inspection of the massacre site, the results of the interviews disappointed the investigators. Not for the first time in the war, Americans confronted the dialect of central South Vietnam and were left at a loss. One US interpreter had to be replaced because the task of translation was beyond him and progress overall, as Major Thomas McGreevy, the chief CID investigator, observed, was 'very slow and difficult'.[190] The tortuous, often repetitive nature of the interviews may have been reflected in the evidential outcomes: summary statements of the witness testimony rather than verbatim transcripts. These statements were prepared in English, and signed by the investigators, not the interviewees (many of whom could not read even Vietnamese).[191] In addition, the instruments by which the investigators calculated relations of time and space – aspiring as they did to the collection of hard, empirical data about what happened where and when – were incommensurate with the devices used by most of the people of Son My. When asked at what time of day a particular incident had occurred, Nguyen Thi Doc held her hands approximately two feet apart to indicate the position of the sun in the sky.[192] A number of those interviewed were totally nonplussed when invited to identify locations on a sketch map of Xom Lang or on an aerial image, or to estimate distance in terms of western units of measurement, or to indicate direction by reference to the points of a compass.[193]

For the investigators, of course, this was all immensely frustrating, because the inability of the witnesses to convey their experiences in the conventional grammar of criminal evidence not only complicated the task of constructing a coherent, verifiable narrative of events in Son My but also reduced the likelihood that their testimony, which took such effort to obtain, would ever be used in court. These were, moreover, military men, their lives ordered by (and often dependent upon) objective measures of time and space. Clocks, calendars, cartography, metres and miles, north and south: this seemed like the basic stuff of sentient existence, and confronted with its absence from the culture of Son My, the investigators clearly had doubts about the worth of whatever was left. In his witness statement summarizing an interview with Ha Thi Quy on 23 December,

[189] Peers, p. 141.

[190] McGreevy, CID Task Force daily journal entry, 23 December 1969, folder: My Lai 8/36, Papers of *Four Hours in My Lai*, LHCMA, KCL; Wells, CID Task Force daily journal entry, 24 December 1969, folder: My Lai 8/36, Papers of *Four Hours in My Lai*, LHCMA, KCL.

[191] See, for example, Moses, 'Witness Statement [Do Vien]', 4 January 1970, folder: My Lai 8/80, Papers of *Four Hours in My Lai*, LHCMA, KCL.

[192] McGreevy, CID Task Force daily journal entry, 23 December 1969, folder: My Lai 8/36, Papers of *Four Hours in My Lai*, LHCMA, KCL.

[193] See, for example, Kirk, 'Witness Statement [Nguyen Thi Hoa]', 30 December 1969, folder: My Lai 6/1, Papers of *Four Hours in My Lai*, LHCMA, KCL; McGreevy, 'Investigator's Statement', 3 April 1970, folder: My Lai 8/35, Papers of *Four Hours in My Lai*, LHCMA, KCL.

André Feher concluded that the subject was 'a very primitive person, confused, having a wandering mind and being illiterate. She had no conception of numbers, distances and or directions. Her personal data was obtained with considerable difficulty.'[194] Another of the investigators, Juel Moses, borrowed from this template to describe almost all the Vietnamese witnesses that he interviewed.[195] In some instances, relations between the interviewer and the interviewee seem to have broken down almost entirely. Of Truong Thi Tung, agent Kenneth McLellan declared: 'She refused to furnish any names of persons she knew were killed by the soldiers or name any witnesses to the incident. She appeared to take little interest in the interview and was very reluctant to answer questions.'[196]

The same political conditions that had caused Son My to become a target of US military operations – a well-entrenched revolutionary infrastructure to which many residents were loyal or, at the very least, with which they were obliged to cooperate – also shaped the response of investigators to much of the testimony subsequently offered by survivors of the massacres in the village. North Vietnamese propagandists had been quick to exploit the atrocity revelations, describing them as evidence of an American policy of genocide.[197] Two young survivors of the massacre, Pham Thi Lien and Vo Thi Lien, were invited to Hanoi and, in early 1970, despatched to Europe, where they spoke at press conferences and public meetings in a number of national capitals.[198] The investigative team had also received intelligence that Vietcong political cadres were enjoining their disabled supporters in the province to travel to Quang Ngai City to carry out propaganda activities connected to the massacre.[199] The local authorities would sometimes inform the investigators when the witnesses they made available had connections with the enemy – noting, for example, that Ha Thi Quy's son belonged to the Vietcong.[200] At other times, the

[194] Feher, 'Witness Statement [Ha Thi Quy]', 23 December 1969, folder: My Lai 8/35, Papers of *Four Hours in My Lai*, LHCMA, KCL.

[195] See, for example, Moses, 'Witness Statement [Nguyen Thi Doc]', 23 December 1969, folder: My Lai 8/35, Papers of *Four Hours in My Lai*, LHCMA, KCL; Moses, 'Witness Statement [Pham Thi Tuu]', 25 December 1969, folder: My Lai 6/1, Papers of *Four Hours in My Lai*, LHCMA, KCL; Moses, 'Witness Statement [Pham Thi Don]', 29 December 1969, folder: My Lai 6/1, Papers of *Four Hours in My Lai*, LHCMA, KCL.

[196] McLellan, 'Witness Statement [Truong Thi Tung]', 25 December 1969, folder: My Lai 6/1, Papers of *Four Hours in My Lai*, LHCMA, KCL.

[197] *New York Times* (26 November 1969), p. 10.

[198] Dudley to Rogers, US Embassy (Copenhagen) telegram 285, 28 January 1970, folder: 'Miscellaneous Maltreatment', Box 16, RCCPI, RPI, RAS, RG319, NACP; Shullaw to Rogers, US Embassy (Helsinki) telegram 187, 27 February 1970, folder: 'Department of State', Box 2, Administrative and Background Materials Files – Open Inventory, 1967–1970, RPI, RAS, RG319, NACP; Transcripts of filmed interviews with Vietnamese survivors [Vo Thi Lien, roll 46, w/t int, pp. 36–43], folder: My Lai 3/1, Papers of *Four Hours in My Lai*, LHCMA, KCL.

[199] Extract from Quang Ngai Daily Intelligence Summary, 5 December 1969, folder: My Lai 8/36, Papers of *Four Hours in My Lai*, LHCMA, KCL.

[200] McGreevy, CID Task Force daily journal entry, 23 December 1969, folder: My Lai 8/36, Papers of *Four Hours in My Lai*, LHCMA, KCL.

investigators themselves detected external influences at play in the content of witness testimony. Told by Nguyen Ky that he had seen 'a tragic aray [*sic*] of death on the dirt road leading to his village', agent Moses observed: 'this phrase is pretty good from an individual that states he has no education, cannot read or write.'[201]

It was from witnesses with the most conspicuous connections to the revolution, however, that investigators obtained the most lucid and detailed accounts of what had happened in Son My. Revolutionary cadres, after all, had long represented the de facto government in the village, maintaining a roster of inhabitants and, in the wake of the massacre, making it their business to find out who had been killed. These cadres also may have embodied the brightest and the best of the village population. Some – such as Nguyen Co, Do Gien and Pham Chot – had formally transferred their allegiance to the Saigon regime by the time that they were interviewed.[202] Co, indeed, had surrendered to the provincial authorities only a few weeks before, in December 1969. Three others – Do Vien, the sub-hamlet propaganda chief, Truong Qui, the sub-hamlet security chief, and Truong Ngu, the security agent for Tu Cung hamlet – were captured when the security task force arrived in Xom Lang to prepare it for inspection by the CID investigators and the Peers Commission.[203] This all could have been perceived, perhaps, as just a little too fortuitous, but the investigators, it seems, were more interested in the plenitude of information provided by these witnesses than in the possibility that the Vietcong was making a coordinated attempt to influence their inquiries. Vien and Ngu were both taken back to Xom Lang where they pointed out to the investigators the locations in which many of the victims had been killed and then buried; they identified a number of the villagers, dead and alive, who appeared in Ronald Haeberle's photographs; and they also summoned from their memories extensive lists of the residents of the settlement at the time of the massacre, indicating on a sketch map the site of each household and recording what they knew about the fate of its members.

Indeed, it was probably from these two witnesses that investigators obtained their clearest information about the identities of those who had been killed in Xom Lang. A record of civilian casualties which had apparently been compiled in the wake of the massacre by Do Dinh Luyen,

[201] Moses, 'Witness Statement [Nguyen Ky]', 27 December 1969, folder: My Lai 8/35, Papers of *Four Hours in My Lai*, LHCMA, KCL.

[202] Kirk, 'Witness Statement [Nguyen Co]', 15 January 1970, folder: My Lai 8/35, Papers of *Four Hours in My Lai*, LHCMA, KCL; Feher, 'Witness Statement [Do Gien]', 26 December 1969, folder: My Lai 8/35, Papers of *Four Hours in My Lai*, LHCMA, KCL; Kirk, 'Witness Statement [Pham Chot]', 4 January 1970, folder: My Lai 8/35, Papers of *Four Hours in My Lai*, LHCMA, KCL; Peers, pp. 136–7.

[203] Moses, 'Witness Statement [Do Vien]', 4 January 1970, folder: My Lai 8/80, Papers of *Four Hours in My Lai*, LHCMA, KCL; Kirk, 'Witness Statement [Truong Qui]', 3 January 1970, folder: My Lai 6/1, Papers of *Four Hours in My Lai*, LHCMA, KCL. McLellan, 'Witness Statement [Truong Ngu]', 4 January 1970, folder: My Lai 8/80, Papers of *Four Hours in My Lai*, LHCMA, KCL.

the government village chief, could not be located in the district files.[204] Nguyen Co, who was the Vietcong's sub-hamlet chief of administration, had no copy of the post-massacre census of the dead conducted by his comrade in My Hoi and said that his own roster of the inhabitants of the settlement had been buried in the ground and destroyed by US shelling.[205] The provincial government itself maintained no register of the local population.[206] Even if a record of the population at the time of the massacre had been available, it still would have been difficult to confirm – for example, through another census – who had been killed and who had survived, because a number of the survivors were reported no longer to be living in Son My, with at least forty having apparently moved away to Saigon.[207] As most of the victims' graves were unmarked, the investigators, therefore, depended on witness testimony in attempting to reconstruct a record of the dead.

In cases where individual witnesses testified to the loss of close family members, or where a series of witnesses, asked to examine the Haeberle photographs, independently agreed on the identity of those featured, the investigators could confidently add another name to their official list of massacre victims. They were able to identify every member of the terrified group of women and children photographed by Haeberle moments before they were shot.[208] Do Vien identified his sister, Do Thi Can, in the group. She was holding his six-year-old son, Do Hat, in her arms. Do Vien buried both.[209] In the image of twenty or so bodies lying in the road, Truong Ngu recognized his daughter, Truong Thi Thu, as well as his niece, Truong Thi Bi.[210] By mid-January, thirty-five witnesses had provided identifications based on the photographs.[211] With regard to most of the dead, however, no such visual aide-memoire existed, and identifications were usually much more provisional.

Many of the families in the settlement, investigators concluded, were quite insular in character, their members knowing little about other inhabitants except those who lived in their immediate vicinity. When the investigators asked for information about who had been killed by the

[204] Goldstein *et al.*, p. 272.

[205] Kirk, 'Witness Statement [Nguyen Co]', 15 January 1970, folder: My Lai 8/35, Papers of *Four Hours in My Lai*, LHCMA, KCL.

[206] McGreevy, CID Task Force daily journal entry, 23 December 1969, folder: My Lai 8/36, Papers of *Four Hours in My Lai*, LHCMA, KCL.

[207] Wells, CID Task Force daily journal entry, 19 January 1970, folder: My Lai 8/36, Papers of *Four Hours in My Lai*, LHCMA, KCL.

[208] See the key to the pictures which was produced by the investigators: folder: My Lai 8/34, Papers of *Four Hours in My Lai*, LHCMA, KCL.

[209] Moses, 'Witness Statement [Do Vien]', 4 January 1970, folder: My Lai 8/80, Papers of *Four Hours in My Lai*, LHCMA, KCL.

[210] McLellan, 'Witness Statement [Truong Ngu]', 4 January 1970, folder: My Lai 8/80, Papers of *Four Hours in My Lai*, LHCMA, KCL.

[211] Wells, CID Task Force daily journal entry, 14 January 1970, folder: My Lai 8/36, Papers of *Four Hours in My Lai*, LHCMA, KCL.

Americans, the answers they received from the survivors were often limited or else could not be relied upon without rigorous cross-checking. Because a number of survivors were illiterate and could offer no assistance with the transcription of names, and because some victims had been known by a variety of names, it was possible, across the file of witness statements, for the same individual to be recorded as dead under a range of different identities. In many cases, estimates of age were approximate at best, as were readings of domestic status: a young woman said by some witnesses to have been the daughter of the head of the household might be known by others to have been his second wife.[212] The danger that victims might be registered more than once probably made the testimony of Do Vien particularly valuable to the investigators. Though as a Vietcong cadre, he may have had an incentive to inflate the count of the dead, he was also in a position to provide a single, integrated account of precisely who in each household had met their end in the massacre, and where and how they had been killed.[213] In September 1970, a CID investigative report specified the name, age and gender of 61 individuals who had died at the trail and 110 who had died at the ditch.[214]

In later reflections upon the investigation, two of the agents involved, André Feher and Wayne Thorn, suggested that the eventual CID estimate of the death toll in Xom Lang – the agency concluded that 347 residents of the sub-hamlet had died – had resulted either from the cumulative infelicities of identification contained in the witness statements or from the belief of the witnesses, who were paid for their time, that the investigators desired a high count of the dead.[215] 'I always had the feeling,' Feher recalled, 'that some of the survivors thought that we wanted to hear that so many people were killed.'

Such suspicions are probably unwarranted, not least because the investigators seemed to have been more troubled at the time by the reluctance of witnesses to cooperate with their enquiries and to make specific assertions about the massacre than by problems of over-compliance and suggestibility. Moreover, judgements that the soldiers of Task Force Barker had been responsible for many hundreds of deaths originated well before the investigators started making payments to survivors. In the immediate wake of the massacre, both local government officials and Vietcong propaganda

212 McGreevy, 'Investigator's Statement', 3 April 1970, folder: My Lai 8/35, Papers of *Four Hours in My Lai*, LHCMA, KCL.

213 Moses, 'Witness Statement [Do Vien]', 4 January 1970, folder: My Lai 8/80, Papers of *Four Hours in My Lai*, LHCMA, KCL.

214 Zaza, 'CID Report of Investigation', 25 September 1970, folder: 'Case Folder – 1LT William L. Calley, Jr [Part 4 of 4]', Box 6, Records Pertaining to the My Lai Massacre, 1969–74, Records of the Vietnam War Crimes Working Group, Office of the Deputy Chief of Staff for Personnel, RAS, RG319, NACP.

215 Thorn to Feher, 10 August 1990, folder: My Lai 8/35, Papers of *Four Hours in My Lai*, LHCMA, KCL; Feher to Bilton, 20 August 1990, folder: My Lai 8/35, Papers of *Four Hours in My Lai*, LHCMA, KCL; Goldstein *et al.*, p. 144.

had declared that around 500 civilians had been killed in Son My as a whole, including My Hoi sub-hamlet as well as Xom Lang and Binh Tay.[216] In his letter requesting an investigation, Ronald Ridenhour had cited the recollection of Charles Gruver, a member of Charlie Company, that the settlement attacked by the company had contained between 300 and 400 people and that 'very few, if any, escaped'.[217] When Feher himself arrived in Son My in November 1969 to investigate the massacre, the first two witnesses he interviewed, neither of whom he paid, had both volunteered the figure of 370 dead for the area of Xom Lang.[218] Thus, the CID estimate – produced through analysis and cross-referencing of witness accounts of how many members of each household in the settlement had been killed, and which therefore did not include the numbers dead in Binh Tay or My Hoi, or of visitors to Xom Lang who also became victims – was broadly consistent with previous calculations.[219]

It was the Peers Commission which offered the most conservative assessment of the scale of the slaughter, concluding that no less that 175– 200 people had been killed in Xom Lang and Binh Tay, including visitors to the two settlements. This figure, however, took into account only those deaths testified to and corroborated by American witnesses; it did not include, as the commission acknowledged, the many additional killings that were likely to have occurred out of general sight, inside bunkers and houses.[220] With regard to the actions of Bravo Company in My Hoi, about which those US soldiers most directly involved refused to testify, the commission gave credence to the claim made by one of the survivors, Nguyen Thi Bay, that 90 non-combatants had been killed.[221] The commission also accepted that the death toll for Son My village as a whole may have exceeded 400.[222]

As soon as the massacre story broke, US military authorities asserted that they would not comment on the number of civilians killed in Son My, though they did declare, long before they could be sure, that the figure of 567 mentioned by some survivors was exaggerated.[223] The policy continued even after the conclusion of the various massacre courts martial.[224] Yet greater official candour with regard to the reckoning of the dead may not have done much to change the pattern of domestic reaction to the atrocity.

[216] Tan to Khien, 'Allied operation at Son My assembled and killed civilians', 11 April 1968, folder: My Lai 8/13, Papers of *Four Hours in My Lai*, LHCMA, KCL; Goldstein *et al.*, p. 275.
[217] Goldstein *et al.*, p. 35.
[218] Feher, 'Witness Statement', 16 November 1969, folder: My Lai 8/35, Papers of *Four Hours in My Lai*, LHCMA, KCL.
[219] Peers, p. 180.
[220] Goldstein *et al.*, p. 144.
[221] *Ibid.*, pp. 174–6.
[222] *Ibid.*, p. 46, fn.
[223] *New York Times* (17 November 1969), p. 1; Sidle to Woolnough *et al.*, 'Public Affairs Guidance – My Lai Case', 18 November 1969, folder: 'Master File [Copy 2]', Box 16, RCCPI, RPI, RAS, RG319, NACP.
[224] Hersh, *Cover-Up*, p. 7.

Such statistics record only the termination of lives, not the social and emotional investments that produced and nurtured them, nor the social value that they produced themselves, nor their potential to produce more – the wasting of all of which marks the true dimensions of the crime. As *Life* magazine said about the American dead in Vietnam: 'More than we must know *how many*, we must know *who*.'[225]

Without this kind of knowledge of what had really been lost, even the visceral visual spectacle of the massacre could have only the most fleeting of impacts, receding thereafter into the numbing mix of images of hurt ambient within American culture at the turn of the 1960s, dissolving any specific challenge to the conscience of the viewer. An air stewardess in Oakland, shown the photographs taken by Haeberle, started to tremble: 'her chin dropped to her chest. Her eyes closed to shut the pictures out. For several seconds she seemed unable to move.' Then she recovered. '[W]hen people are taught to hate,' she said, 'it doesn't surprise me how they react, particularly when they are given a weapon; it just seems to be one of the outcomes of war.'[226] A few months after he had helped to arrange the publication of the pictures, Joseph Eszterhas was attending an Iron Butterfly concert at the Whiskey A Go-Go in Los Angeles: 'There was a light show. Slides: of John and Yoko; a Chicago cop wielding a billy club; Bonnie and Clyde. And then against a wall and over the ceiling, a slide of the clump of bodies at Mylai. And the band played on.'[227]

The principal account of the massacre published in *Life* alongside the photographs was constructed solely from the testimony of American participants and witnesses. The survivors of the massacre received only cursory attention, in a short two-column story from the relocation camp in Son My. Nguyen Thi Doc recalled how her family had been ordered out of their home into a field, whereupon the soldiers opened fire. She was pictured squatting in the doorway of her hut with two of her grand-children, the only other members of the family to survive. None of the victims who appeared in the massacre images was identified.[228] They remained anonymous, indeed, throughout the media's long coverage of the story, though many of their names – as army investigators discovered – could have been elicited from survivors.

Some media outlets and some correspondents did make a concerted effort to incorporate survivor narratives into their reporting. The most assiduous was Richard Hammer, who took a leave of absence from cover-ing domestic crime cases for the *New York Times* to visit Vietnam and research the killings at Son My. In his subsequent study, *One Morning in the War*, Hammer provided a valuable account of the history of the village,

[225] *Life* (27 June 1969), p. 20.
[226] Opton, in Sanford *et al.*, p. 61.
[227] Eszterhas, p. 471.
[228] *Life* (5 December 1969), pp. 36–45.

drawn from conversations with local elders.[229] He also constructed much of his narrative of the massacre from the testimony of the villagers themselves, occasionally indeed seeking to collapse the distance between readers and the victims: 'It was imperative not to run, either toward the Americans or away from them. If you ran, the Americans would think that you were VC, running away from them or running toward them with a grenade, and they would shoot.'[230]

Hammer went on to write a second book on the massacre, covering the court martial of William Calley, which he described as 'a show for the world conducted by Americans, with Americans, white Americans, as the principal spectators, actors, and participants'.[231] Hammer reminded his readers of what had been missing from the show – what indeed the show should have really been about – closing his volume with the story he had been told by Ngo Ngo Trininh, eighteen years old at the time of the massacre. When the soldiers arrived in Xom Lang and started shooting, Trininh crept through rice paddies to escape, returning to her home in the evening to find the bodies of her three brothers and two sisters. With her father and father-in-law, she searched for other members of her family. Four more lay dead in the ditch, alongside her husband's badly wounded brother. (Her husband was serving with the ARVN.) They found the body of her mother near by. After burying the dead, Trininh and the two men made a stretcher out of bamboo and cloth. By this time, it was dark. Carrying her husband's brother, who was to die the next day, they set out for Quang Ngai City.[232]

For the most part, however, correspondents seem to have been unable to use testimonies of this kind effectively to convey the human dimensions of what had happened in Son My to their audiences at home. There was an incidental quality to most of the survivor accounts that appeared in the American media: a face on a screen, personal horrors briskly summarized, the camera moves on, never to return. In an ABC report from Xom Lang in early December 1969, a young boy was filmed in close-up. 'There's really no way to repay Truong Thon', noted the correspondent, Don Baker. 'Truong Thon is 12 years old. In March 1968 he was at the market. He came home to find his entire family – mother, father, and two brothers – had been killed. He ran away. Neighbours buried the bodies.'[233] That was as much as anyone in America would ever probably learn about Truong Thon, as Baker turned away to another victim of the massacre, to another vignette of loss. The people of Son My had no power to claim any more attention than this: their stories in the end were always to be controlled

[229] Hammer, *One Morning in the War*, pp. 24–60.
[230] *Ibid.*, p. 123.
[231] Hammer, *The Court-Martial of Lt Calley*, p. 73.
[232] *Ibid.*, pp. 395–8.
[233] *ABC News*, 1 December 1969, VTNA.

and mediated by Americans, selected, abbreviated, summarized and conveyed to the audience complete with editorial annotations.

Though it resisted the temptation to rationalize the massacre by describing its victims as Vietcong sympathizers, and though its tone for the most part was sensitive to the losses endured by those who survived, US media reporting from the village was not entirely free from ambivalence – exhibiting some of the traditional tropes of western Orientalism – and its concerns were perhaps inevitably the concerns of Americans, dwelling, in particular, upon the problem of reparation and punishment. When describing adult survivors of the massacre, American reporters frequently observed that they appeared older than their years. 'Ha Thi Quy is 44,' said Don Baker. 'She looks 64.'[234] The perception that the inhabitants of Son My had been prematurely aged by experience could coalesce easily with received cultural notions of 'Oriental' society as peculiarly canted towards the passive acceptance of fate, an acceptance expressed in gnomic utterances about the human condition. In the epilogue to their account of William Calley's life and trial, Arthur Everett, Kathryn Johnson and Harry Rosenthal – three correspondents for *Associated Press* – describe an encounter close to the massacre site between an old man and a convoy comprising Tran Van Don, a member of the South Vietnamese Senate, and an American television crew. Dressed in tattered black pyjamas, rocking back and forth on his haunches, the old man told the convoy that the area had once been prosperous. Asked what had happened, he said: 'We had death here. But then death is as much a part of the day here as the rising sun.' Having inspected the ruins of Xom Lang, the convoy passed by the 'old man' again: 'His conical hat was pulled over his eyes, and he did not seem to see the group pass. He was still quietly rocking when they all drove away.'[235] With that final ambiguous image, the book concludes.

Reporters in Son My also informed their audiences that many survivors of the massacre held no animus against Americans, even those Americans actually participant in the killing: the immediate needs of the village would not be served by seeing William Calley in jail. According to Don Baker, Truong Thi Tung – interviewed whilst she was trying to reclaim the rice fields close to her former home – 'doesn't want to see anyone punished, but she does think the village should be repaid somehow'.[236] CBS newsman Richard Threlkeld asserted that the inhabitants of Son My were 'tired of talking to reporters and investigators and they really cannot understand what all the fuss is about'.

Accompanying Threlkeld's commentary were images of life inside the relocation camp close to the site of the massacre: a boy with a wooden

[234] *ABC News*, 1 December 1969, VTNA. For other examples, see *Life* (5 December 1969), p. 45; and Hammer, *One Morning in the War*, p. 20.
[235] Everett *et al.*, pp. 301–6.
[236] *ABC News*, 1 December 1969, VTNA.

leg, a girl, smiling, with a wounded right eye, a street with people working, someone carrying wood. He interviewed a member of the small squad
of US Marines responsible for protecting the camp, who said that some of
the residents remained hostile and suspicious: 'they think you're trying to
hurt them in one way or another'. Yet, Threlkeld noted, the marines 'have
won a few friends here'. One was Truong Thi Phon, who was twelve when
her mother and father were killed in the massacre. '[T]he war has made
her a woman with a wisdom beyond her years. Why should I hate these
Americans, she says. They did not kill my parents. They were killed in the
war. I cannot blame these men for it. Nor am I the only orphan here. What
is the use of weeping?' Amongst the survivors, Threlkeld concluded, 'there
is no concern any more with reliving the past. There is a new crop of rice
to be harvested, and a new generation to be raised. Recriminations, trials,
investigations are for those who have time for them.'[237]

Those who did have time for investigative and prosecutorial responses
– most obviously, the US military and the news media – progressively
came, however, to have less and less time for the villagers of Son My.
After the initial influx of reporters to the vicinity of the massacre, after the
completion of the onsite investigation and witness interviews, most of the
major new developments in the case occurred elsewhere, at the Pentagon
or in the military courthouse at Fort Benning. Attention drifted away from
the massacre site and from the survivors, and as it did so, perhaps, the
motivation to expose the full dimensions of the crime clearly to public
view may have ebbed away, to be replaced by priorities originating in
institutional and procedural logics: in the case of investigators, to contain
the harm that was being done to the army's reputation; in the case of
prosecutors, to indict individual soldiers for their actions and successfully
secure their conviction; in the case of the US media, to tell the story of the
massacre in the manner most consistent with the interests of its audience,
in terms of the fate of the Americans involved, not the Vietnamese.

For all the apparent integrity of its senior personnel and for all the
dismay with which the army's leaders greeted its report, the Peers investigation was an exercise in institutional damage limitation, not independent historical enquiry. Its principal purpose – albeit one which was not
specified in formal directives – was to demonstrate that the army did in
fact have standards of conduct, that its command did not take the view
that massacre was an allowable excess. Peers was not instructed to make
recommendations for reform with respect to the actual events in Son My
and indeed he made very few, though his commission identified a multitude of factors that had contributed to the massacre.[238] It was the afterlife of the massacre within the US military with which he was primarily

[237] *CBS Evening News*, 24 April 1970, VTNA.
[238] Resor and Westmoreland to Peers, 'Directive for Investigation', 26 November 1969, in
Goldstein *et al.*, p. 33; Goldstein *et al.*, pp. 192–206, 320.

concerned. The commission interviewed survivors and visited Xom Lang, but it generally took the massacre's legacies for the victims and their communities to be a given, unlikely to reward sustained inquiry or reflection. 'Once having recognized the extent of the tragedy,' Peers recalled, 'I became somewhat numb to the details given by subsequent witnesses. From that point on, the Inquiry was just plain hard work.'[239]

After reading a short preliminary version of the commission's report, Secretary of the Army Resor asked Peers to avoid 'overemotionalism' by substituting wherever possible identifications of the victims as women, children, old men and babies with the term 'non-combatant casualties' and tempering the vividness with which some of the rapes had been described.[240] Peers agreed, as he also did – rather more reluctantly – when the army's Chief of Information requested that he not use the word 'massacre' in relation to the events in Son My when speaking to a news conference at the conclusion of his inquiry.[241] In the final report, meanwhile, the testimony of survivors was referred to hardly at all. In constructing its narrative of the massacre (just as it had in calculating the number of dead), the commission displayed a clear preference for the testimony provided by American witnesses, although – probably predictably – a number of those witnesses were far from reliable, either refusing to testify or offering accounts of their actions that were self-interested and misleading.[242]

The subsequent efforts of army lawyers to secure the conviction of culpable individuals also did little to open the national debate to the voices of survivors or to make their lives and losses more comprehensible and meaningful to the American public. Aubrey Daniel, counsel for the prosecution in the Calley trial, wishing to familiarize the jury with the topography of My Lai (4), used Haeberle's image of the bodies at the trail to prove that the lieutenant's actions in that place had resulted in many Vietnamese deaths.[243] He made no effort, however, to identify for the court any of the people with whose murder Calley was charged, declaring in his opening remarks: 'The victims are unnamed, and the government cannot give their names. The victims' ages are not given, and the government does not know their ages. The victims' sexes are not delineated, and the government cannot delineate their sexes.'[244] As Daniel was no doubt aware from reading the army CID investigative reports, the identities of many of those killed in the course of the massacre had actually been established, though some of the spellings were uncertain and the ages approximate. It was much more difficult, however, to specify the victims murdered by William

239 Peers, p. 105.
240 *Ibid.*, pp. 210–11.
241 *Ibid.*, pp. 216–17.
242 For examples, see *ibid.*, pp. 106, 153–4, 160–4, 169.
243 Hammer, *The Court-Martial of Lt Calley*, pp. 75–6, 86.
244 *Ibid.*, p. 75.

Calley himself, and Daniel was probably anxious that any effort to do so might simply complicate his case. He was on safer ground with numbers than he was with names, and it was by their body-count, therefore, that the victims continued to be known.

Although Daniel travelled to Quang Ngai during the CID investigation with the intention of interviewing massacre survivors, he quickly came to the conclusion that none of them would be of use to his case.[245] No survivors, indeed, testified at any of the massacre courts martial.[246] Possibly, prosecutors were deterred by the same impediments to communication that the army investigators had encountered in their own series of interviews. Most of the witnesses who were cooperative and well informed, meanwhile, had a record of service with the enemy, a record upon which the defence could be expected to dwell, both to discredit their evidence and to imply that many of those killed at Son My may not have been quite so innocent after all.[247] The main reason for not presenting survivor testimony to the court, however, may simply have been its likely low evidential value. Asked to explain the omission, a senior Pentagon official asserted that few of the people living in the vicinity of the massacre 'could contribute anything that would have qualified as relevant evidence'.[248] It was doubtful, two or more years later, that any of the survivors would have been able to identify the soldiers involved.[249] In any event, that Calley had killed non-combatants could be amply revealed by the court testimonies of his men, and on the issue perhaps most pertinent to his legal guilt – whether he had been ordered to engage in mass slayings and whether he should have known that such orders, if given, were wrong – witnesses from Son My had nothing to contribute.

The courts martial were rarely anything other than lily-white affairs. Richard Hammer observed that few black Americans had attended the Calley trial except as witnesses, and that no Vietnamese had ever been present, even as spectators. The defence team had taken depositions from

[245] Davis, 'Coordination for the Visit of the Counsel in the Case of US v. Calley to the Americal Division', 4 January 1970, folder: My Lai 8/28, Papers of *Four Hours in My Lai*, LHCMA, KCL; Wells, CID Task Force daily journal entry, 13 January 1970, folder: My Lai 8/36, Papers of *Four Hours in My Lai*, LHCMA, KCL.

[246] Wallace to Hughes, 'Vietnamese Witnesses in My Lai Prosecutions', 17 September 1971, folder: 'My Lai Cases – General', Box 15, John Dean Subject Files, Staff Members and Office Files, White House Special Files, NPM, NACP.

[247] In one of the Son Thang courts martial, the prosecutor had introduced a witness from the hamlet simply in order to confirm the identity of the victims. However, the defence counsel used the opportunity of cross-examination to force an admission that a number of the hamlet's residents, including the witness's son, had connections with the Vietcong (Solis, pp. 163–4).

[248] Wallace to Hughes, 'Vietnamese Witnesses in My Lai Prosecutions', 17 September 1971, folder: 'My Lai Cases – General', Box 15, John Dean Subject Files, Staff Members and Office Files, White House Special Files, NPM, NACP.

[249] Feher to Bilton, 20 August 1990, folder: My Lai 8/35, Papers of *Four Hours in My Lai*, LHCMA, KCL.

four Vietnamese witnesses, including Toan and the two interpreters, Sergeant Phu and Sergeant Minh, and these were read out in court by Kenneth Raby, Calley's military counsel, 'complete,' noted Hammer, 'to the use of broken, halting, falsetto pidgin English'.[250] In Medina's court martial, it was the prosecution which submitted depositions from Phu and Minh (the South Vietnamese authorities had refused them permission to travel to the United States to testify in person). The defence attempted to have them declared inadmissible, arguing that it was uncertain whether either of the men understood English. According to Mary McCarthy, the deposition (which had been recorded on tape) also revealed the defence's view that 'Minh, being Vietnamese, would not know the truth from a lie'.[251]

The peculiar needs and logics of the massacre prosecutions, combined most probably with a measure of ethnocentricity and a fear of the unknown (how would survivors from Son My, usually illiterate, speaking only Vietnamese, conceivably with past revolutionary connections, be received and conduct themselves in an American courtroom?), served therefore to quarantine the massacre victims from the effort to secure justice for the crimes committed against them. Possibly, however, it is the nature of such proceedings that, in concentrating upon questions of causation and culpability, they direct attention away from those who have suffered to those who inflicted the suffering.

Contrary to popular belief, the war-crimes trials in post-war Germany did not in fact play a particularly effective role in revealing the scale and nature of Jewish mortality at the hands of the Nazis. As Donald Bloxham has established, the principal purpose of the trials was to achieve a German national reformation: to educate the German people about the criminal workings of the Nazi regime, not about the lives and deaths of its victims. The prosecution case, therefore, was constructed primarily from captured Nazi documents, with Jewish witnesses to the crimes contributing little. Reservations concerning the likely objectivity of their testimony and fears of an anti-Semitic backlash as well as ethnic prejudice on the part of one or two trial-planners also operated to limit the use of Jewish testimony.[252] Even the trial of Adolf Eichmann – explicitly intended by the government of Israel to make good the inattentions of the Nuremberg tribunals by informing the world about the fate of the Jews in the Holocaust – ended with the perpetrator, rather than the victims, dominant in its audience's mind. For most commentators – whether they regarded him as a sadistic brute or as a banal bureaucrat who had supervised mass murder, simply because he had believed that to be his job – it was Eichmann, encased in a bullet-proof glass box to the left side of the stage in the court

[250] Hammer, *The Court-Martial of Lt Calley*, pp. 181–2.

[251] McCarthy, pp. 28–9.

[252] D. Bloxham, *Genocide on Trial: War Crimes Trials and the Formation of Holocaust History and Memory* (Oxford: Oxford University Press, 2001), pp. 63–9; Bloxham, 'The missing camps of *Aktion Reinhard*: the judicial displacement of a mass murder', in Gray and Oliver, pp. 118–31.

auditorium, who became the main object of attention, not the lives and losses of those who testified against him. Outside Israel, the trial undoubtedly contributed to the movement of Jewish suffering towards the centre of Holocaust memory, but other developments – non-judicial in character – were ultimately more decisive in ensuring its arrival.[253]

Overall, therefore, a sad irony pertained: the judicial process intended at least in part to achieve an accounting for the crimes committed in Son My provided the people of that village with minimal opportunity to weave their stories into American narratives of the massacre or the wider war. In diverting public attention to the fate of the perpetrators, moreover, the massacre prosecutions may even have been instrumental in effacing victim perspectives from American cultural discourse. In the immediate wake of the Calley verdict, when all the action was at home – at Fort Benning, in Washington, throughout the south, and at every Veterans of Foreign Wars (VFW) post in the nation – few US news organizations, it seems, elected to send correspondents back to the site of the massacre. Morley Safer did travel there, reporting for the CBS documentary series *60 Minutes*, filming graves at Xom Lang as well as some of the survivors, and asking: 'Do they forgive? Do they understand the justice of Fort Benning? Do they even remember which one was Calley?'[254] For most Americans, however, the essential story of the massacre was now located elsewhere, not with the immutable reality of the dead and the distant ongoing struggles of those who had survived.

This is not to assert that American culture entirely lacked the knowledge and imaginative resources with which to facilitate an empathetic projection into the condition of the people of Son My. Many in the anti-war movement already claimed to have experienced for themselves some of the violent excesses of the American state, at Chicago, for example, or during the battle in May 1969 to reclaim the People's Park in Berkeley from the University of California and the Californian national guard. Of the latter confrontation, the poet Denise Levertov wrote:

Everyone knows (yet no one yet
believes it) what all shall know
this day, and the days that follow:
now, the clubs, the gas,
bayonets, bullets. The War

comes home to us . . .[255]

[253] Arendt, pp. 4–10; J. Shandler, *While America Watches: Televising the Holocaust* (Oxford: Oxford University Press, 1999), pp. 83–132; P. Novick, *The Holocaust and Collective Memory: The American Experience* (London: Bloomsbury, 2000), p. 134.

[254] Safer's report for *60 Minutes* was broadcast on 13 April 1971. Fourteen years later, an extract from the broadcast was included in a special series of *CBS Evening News* reports entitled 'Vietnam Remembered' (*CBS Evening News*, 29 April 1985, VTNA).

[255] D. Levertov, 'Excerpt from "Staying Alive"', in W.D. Ehrhart (ed.), *Carrying the Darkness: The Poetry of the Vietnam War* (Lubbock: Texas Tech University Press, 1989), pp. 169–71.

After the Son My revelations, elements of the movement – particularly the anti-war veterans – sought to overcome the apparent indifference of the American public by confronting them with the spectacle of massacre at home. In September 1970, the VVAW staged a series of 'guerrilla theater' incidents along the route of a four-day march – entitled Operation Rapid American Withdrawal – from Morristown, New Jersey, to Valley Forge, Pennsylvania, simulating 'search and destroy' exercises in local towns, including the abuse of (willing) civilians. In Flemington, New Jersey, they handed out a leaflet which read: 'A US infantry company has just passed through here. If you had been Vietnamese, we might have burned your house, shot you and your dog, raped your wife and daughter, burned the town, and tortured its citizens.' In Washington, DC, during Operation Dewey Canyon III, similar re-enactments were performed. Plastic bags of red paint were burst all over the steps of the Capitol by three girls in coolie hats after they had been 'fired' upon by an imitation infantry squad armed with toy rifles.[256]

Those who witnessed these theatrics, however, were often more mortified by the display of dissent than by the intended lesson: the experience of their country's violence projected back upon themselves. It seems to have been difficult for Americans to feel genuine pity – whatever that may have felt like – for the Vietnamese victims of the war. Some may have adhered to the view that the inhabitants of Son My were members of an inferior race, though probably not that many: only one person surveyed by the Wright Institute sought to justify the massacre in such terms.[257] Others were defeated, just as Charlie Company had been, by the challenge of fathoming the diverse, fluctuating relations between the civilian population and the revolutionary enemy in South Vietnam. In the opinion of another poll respondent: 'there are no civilians in Vietnam. They're either for you or against you. They all have killing in their minds.'[258] Many Americans were unwilling to invest their compassion in a constituency of such apparently indeterminate allegiances, no matter what it may have suffered.

For others still – more troubled by the effects of the war upon the Vietnamese, more ready to try to apprehend those effects – the problem of knowledge remained: it was easy to succumb to Orientalist cliché. There was also the hazard that, in gazing at the wreckage, one would see only wreckage, effacing the agency of the living, dwindling the promise of their future. In another of her poems, 'What Were They Like?', Denise Levertov discussed the people of Vietnam as if they belonged to a dead civilization, as if all enquiries about their society and culture could be answered only with speculation. 'Did they hold ceremonies/ to reverence

[256] Scott, pp. 13–14, 21; Stacewitz, pp. 230–1; Hunt, pp. 50–1.
[257] Opton, in Sanford *et al.*, pp. 65–6.
[258] Kelman and Lawrence, 'American response to the trial of Lt William L. Calley', p. 45.

the opening of buds?' she asks. The reply: 'Perhaps they gathered once to delight in blossom/ but after the children were killed/ there were no more buds.'[259]

If empathetic identifications were made anywhere with respect to the massacre, then, it was generally not with those who had been exposed to the rawest end of the experience. It was easier for Americans to stick with what they knew, or what they thought they knew: William Calley; the other Americans in arms; America itself. All over the culture, victim status was being claimed. Sixty-nine per cent of poll respondents assigned it to William Calley, regarding him as the scapegoat of an army anxious to disassociate itself from the orders he had been given and from conduct that it had hitherto condoned.[260] After the nation had withdrawn from the war and its soldiers – including the men who had been held captive by Hanoi – returned home, Calley would refer to himself as the 'last POW'.[261] For those who believed that the massacre had been an aberration, the reputation of the army became the principal object of concern: 'These allegations,' General Westmoreland declared, 'must not desecrate the dedicated performance of thousands of soldiers who had served in Vietnam honorably and with distinction.'[262]

To the extent that professional soldiers were prepared to acknowledge that the integrity of the army had indeed been corroded, they chose to place the blame elsewhere, seeing the service as the victim of all the talented young Americans who had refused to take part in the war, who had secured deferments from the draft and thus left the junior officer corps in the hands of trash like William Calley.[263] For those who asserted still more forcefully that the war itself was an atrocity writ large, it was essential that the nation's sympathy extend to the veterans now dealing with the moral and psychological legacies of their participation in the enterprise. The theme of the discarded, traumatized Vietnam veteran began its journey through the culture. Robert Jay Lifton compared the 'immersion in death' experienced by these veterans to that undergone by the survivors of Hiroshima.[264]

In the view of Mrs Charles Smith of Memphis, interviewed by the *Wall Street Journal* in late November 1969, the press should not have reported the massacre. 'It upsets people,' she said.[265] What the people she spoke of generally found most upsetting about the story, however, was not the

[259] D. Levertov, 'What Were They Like?', in Levertov, *To Stay Alive* (New York: New Directions, 1971), p. 15.

[260] Gallup, p. 2296.

[261] Bond, 'Prisoner's Progress Summary Data', 31 July 1973, folder: My Lai 8/30, Papers of *Four Hours in My Lai*, LHCMA, KCL.

[262] Westmoreland, Address to Reserve Officers Association, Huntsville, Alabama', 16 January 1970, folder: My Lai 8/11, Papers of *Four Hours in My Lai*, LHCMA, KCL.

[263] W. Just, *Military Men* (London: Michael Joseph, 1972), pp. 228–9.

[264] Lifton, p. 16.

[265] *Wall Street Journal* (1 December 1969), p. 1.

thought that the lives of hundreds of Vietnamese civilians had been brought to a bloody end, but instead the revelation that the deed had been committed by American soldiers. This was a knowledge that they would rather not have had. They may well have been sorry, but it was, it seems, mostly for themselves. The *New York Times* called the killings 'An American Nightmare'; they represented 'An American Tragedy', according to *Time*.[266] Commentators frequently invoked the discourse of the tragic when reflecting upon the massacre, by implication attenuating the agency of the perpetrators and eliding their fate with that of the inhabitants of Son My, as if malignant fortune – in the form of a mutually ruinous war – had made victims of them all. The disclosures, concluded Frank Reynolds of *ABC News*, offered 'the most compelling argument yet advanced for America to end its involvement in Vietnam, not alone because of what the war is doing to the Vietnamese or to our reputation abroad, but because of what it is doing to us'.[267]

It had come to this in part because Vietnam had never really been that important to the United States. In time, many American veterans would come to that realization, and argue that their energies and promise – along with the lives of 55,000 of their comrades – had been wasted on a war that the country had neither needed to fight nor possessed the will to win. Yet they were not the primary victims in the matter. The disparity between the strategic rationale that informed the US intervention (that the challenge to the Saigon government was orchestrated from outside South Vietnam, in Hanoi, Beijing and Moscow), and the evidence encountered daily on the ground that the revolution had the consent and active support of much of the South Vietnamese population, left American soldiers morally disorientated and often angry and indignant. At the same time, the geo-strategic assumption that the real war lay in the future, to be fought most probably against the Soviet Union in Europe, retarded the development and implementation of effective counter-revolutionary doctrine and precluded the emergence of an officer cohort with the sort of sustained in-country experience and linguistic resources that might have encouraged the US Army to respond more creatively to the complex combat environment that it confronted in Vietnam. In many places, at many times, the Saigon authorities lacked both the competence and the inclination to function as a mediating force between their own citizens and the American military.

Almost by default, therefore, firepower became the principal instrument by which the Americans sought to impose order upon the nebulous geographies of South Vietnamese political allegiance and to limit their own exposure to the sudden, unpredictable ravages of revolutionary violence. Those South Vietnamese who did not conspicuously conform to the

---

[266] *New York Times* (22 November 1969), p. 36; *Time* (5 December 1969), p. 23.
[267] *ABC News*, 29 November 1969, VTNA.

definition of friend – because they worked in a rice paddy close to the placement of a mine, or tried to run away from American troops, or resided within an unpacified village – could be classed as foe and subjected to the use of force. It was a definition to which many in the rural population may well have not conformed at one time or another; if their timing was poor, the outcome was often fatal. In the province of Quang Ngai, it was fatal more often than probably anywhere else.

What happened in Son My, of course, travelled well beyond even the expansive latitudes of violence normally considered permissible in Quang Ngai. Operational commanders, upwards from Medina, may not have known the true dimensions of the slaughter, but they knew enough to seek to keep it under wraps. The deliberate circumspection with which they enquired into the initial allegations of massacre, together with the fabrications and evasions contained in their subsequent reports, revealed the extent to which these commanders (much like the soldiers of Charlie Company who had strolled through Xom Lang shooting women and children on sight) were able only to identify with themselves. Of those Americans who were aware of the killings, few besides Hugh Thompson and his crew seem to have registered them as a challenge to their conscience, as such an affront to the moral logic of a shared humanity that they compelled personal intervention and protest. Similarly, senior South Vietnamese officials had no real moral interest in the fate of the residents of Son My, and did little to bring the matter to account.

The cover-up itself made it exceptionally difficult for later investigators to find out what had really happened in the village. In the twenty or so months that passed before army detectives made their way to the site of the killings, Xom Lang had been reclaimed by jungle vegetation, many witnesses had moved (or had been moved) away, and the provincial government – as the record of its inaction lengthened – had developed a considerable stake in upholding the position that no massacre had occurred. In December 1969 it was impossible to replicate the censuses of the dead conducted by both local Vietcong cadres and the government village chief in the days and weeks immediately after the massacre. Radical asymmetries of language and culture also blighted the investigation just as it had the wider prosecution of the war; in their interviews with survivors, detectives invested considerable labour and time for what were often marginal evidential returns. The revolution, meanwhile, maintained a formidable presence in Quang Ngai: even the fullest survivor accounts, therefore, could not be entirely trusted, whilst ground-level forensic surveys had to be confined to Xom Lang.

For the media, meanwhile, the restrictions upon access to the actual site of the massacre, the efforts of the provincial authorities to keep witnesses quiet, and the apparent opacity of local culture resulted in reporting from Son My that was incoherent and superficial: survivors spoke to the cameras, then mysteriously disappeared; their settlement was a desolation, yet some were returning to its ruins; their response to the massacre was either gnomic and unfathomable, or else pragmatic and forward-looking, unburdened by the past. The terse, disjointed distillations of survivor narratives offered by reporters also perhaps reflected an intuition that these narratives were not really news: most major developments in the story seemed to be occurring back in the United States. If intimate, detailed knowledge of loss is a prerequisite for empathy, then with respect to the people of Son My, the media did not give its audiences very much to go on. Nor did the courts, for prosecutors took the view that few certain benefits would accrue from placing massacre survivors on the stand. The perpetrators had little competition in their quest for public sympathy. Americans may have glanced at magazine images of anonymous bodies on a trail; they may have seen one or two survivors on the television news pointing to the ditch where their families had been killed; but the decisive spectacle was that of William Calley, small in stature, attired in full military dress, entering the Fort Benning courthouse and asserting that he had little control over the conduct of his work. Although that work had been bloody, Calley's claim was one with which many Americans identified, more readily than they did with the experience of those orphaned and widowed by the lieutenant and his men one morning two years before, half a world away.

To feel sympathy for others, Susan Sontag has suggested, expresses a belief that we are free from guilt: 'Our sympathy proclaims our innocence as well as our impotence.'[268] In reality, however, sympathy and empathy are consanguineous with guilt. Just as an empathetic insight into suffering can be a resource for effective violence (we know that this will hurt), so guilt is only animated by an affective knowledge of the damage that has been done, by us personally or by those commissioned to act on our behalf. Where there is no empathy for the victims, there will be no sense of guilt, and where there is neither, or where they have only a tenuous hold upon public sentiment, the memory of the crime is likely to quickly fade. So it was that the reception of the massacre in My Lai (4) established the conditions for the forgetting that was soon to come.

[268] Sontag, *Regarding the Pain of Others*, p. 102.

6

Remembering atrocity

As the court martial of William Calley was drawing to a close in mid-March 1971, *NBC Nightly News* anchorman Frank McGee declared that My Lai was a name 'now seared into the American consciousness'.[1] On 1 April, after the lieutenant had been found guilty and sentenced to life imprisonment, CBS correspondent Dan Rather seemed to confirm the point, reporting that the number of telegrams and telephone calls received by the White House on the subject of the court martial already represented an 'all-time Washington record', surpassing even the influx of communications provoked by the invasion of Cambodia eleven months before.[2] In the week immediately following the conclusion of the trial, indeed, an estimated 230,000 letters, cards and telegrams arrived at the White House offering views about its outcome.[3] That same week, over a million Americans purchased copies of 'The Battle Hymn of Lt Calley' by Terry Nelson and 'C' Company, an opportunistic recording which defended Calley as a patriot and the massacre as a battle ('we responded to their rifle fire with everything we had'), sung to the accompaniment of 'The Battle Hymn of the Republic'.[4] According to a survey commissioned by the White House, the level of public awareness of the verdict against the lieutenant was 96 per cent: 'the highest we've gotten on any subject in any of our polls', commented Chief of Staff Bob Haldeman.[5]

Americans, however, would never again be as interested and engaged in the massacre story as they were that first week in April 1971. The Calley case had many more years to run, concluding only in 1976 when the US

[1] *NBC Nightly News*, 19 March 1971, VTNA.
[2] *CBS Evening News*, 1 April 1971, VTNA.
[3] Melencamp to Price, 'Acknowledgment of Communications about the Calley Case', 7 April 1971, folder: 'Calley Correspondence', Box 14, John Dean Subject Files, Staff Members and Office Files, White House Special Files, NPM, NACP.
[4] Terry Nelson and 'C' Company, 'The Battle Hymn of Lt Calley' (Wilson/Smith), in *Feel Like I'm Fixin' to Die* NME NAM 1 (1988); *ABC News*, 6 April 1971, VTNA.
[5] Haldeman, diary entry, 2 April 1971, Audio Cassette No. 6, Part 2, Diaries of Harry R. Haldeman, NPM, NACP.

Supreme Court refused to review the judgment of the US Court of Appeals that the original trial had been fair, but its cathartic moment had passed in the public's response to the conviction, and there would not be another. Whatever one thought of its implied commentary upon the massacre and the conduct and outcome of the trial, President Nixon's decision to release the lieutenant from the Fort Benning stockade into house arrest and to announce that he would personally review the case at the end of the appellate process undoubtedly served to ease public concern that Calley would simply be surrendered into the hands of a hypocritical and unsympathetic military establishment and left to rot in one of its jails. That much of the mainstream news media, meanwhile, endorsed the court's verdict may have helped to persuade some Americans that Calley was not in fact quite as undeserving of his fate as they had initially assumed. Into early May, the White House was still receiving over 15,000 items of mail a week on the subject of the trial, but this was the wash of an ebbing tide, reduced considerably in volume and intensity from the previous month.[6]

Both the President and the Pentagon were now anxious not to offer any new stimulus to the controversy: American war crimes were not what they wanted the public to be discussing whilst there remained an American war to be fought; and further intervention – whether verbal or procedural – would risk queering the pitch for other war crimes prosecutions, including those outstanding with respect to My Lai, as well as for Calley's appeal.[7] Members of the White House staff were instructed to say nothing, on or off the record, about the massacre cases.[8] Following a news conference on 1 May, Nixon himself never spoke publicly about the massacre again.[9] Calley too was silent, permitted no contact with the press nor with other officers.[10] Neither the court martial of Captain Medina nor that of Colonel Henderson later in 1971 could match the original drama and spectacle offered by the Calley proceedings, and neither therefore attracted the same level of attention. ('What did the press and public want,' asked Mary McCarthy, 'mint-fresh atrocities, in preference to stale ones?'[11]) These

[6] Smith to Wilson, 13 May 1971, folder: 'Calley Correspondence', Box 14, John Dean Subject Files, Staff Members and Office Files, White House Special Files, NPM, NACP.

[7] Attachment: Haig to Ehrlichman, 'My Lai', 7 April 1971, folder: 'Calley – April–May 1971', Box 14, John Dean Subject Files, Staff Members and Office Files, White House Special Files, NPM, NACP; Dean to Ehrlichman, Haig and Krogh, 'Discussion Memorandum Re War Crimes Cases', 14 May 1971, folder: 'War Crimes Study', Box 15, John Dean Subject Files, Staff Members and Office Files, White House Special Files, NPM, NACP.

[8] Dean, 'White House Comments on Calley and Related Cases', 9 April 1971, folder: 'Calley – April–May 1971', Box 14, John Dean Subject Files, Staff Members and Office Files, White House Special Files, NPM, NACP.

[9] 'The President's news conference of *May* 1, 1971', *Public Papers of the Presidents: Richard Nixon, 1971*, pp. 610–11.

[10] 'Extract of Telephone Conversation – M.G. Talbott, CG, USAIC, and B.G. Parker, Deputy TJAG', 1 April 1971, folder: My Lai 8/83, Papers of *Four Hours in My Lai*, LHCMA, KCL; Bilton and Sim, p. 353.

[11] McCarthy, p. 19.

trials, moreover, both resulted in acquittals: the 'scapegoats' escaped, and thus excited no tumult of popular sympathy comparable to that which had followed the conviction of Calley. Thereafter, with the courts making no further claims upon their time, most of the men involved in the massacre retreated from the limelight (itself already dimming), hoping to dissolve their notoriety by embracing the rituals and routines of everyday American life. By the end of 1971, periodic developments in the Calley case apart, the massacre was no longer making history; for Americans at least, it could be consigned to the past.

With the prosecutions over, and the US involvement in south-east Asia drawing to a close, the massacre was unlikely to maintain its hold upon the attention of the nation. In the early 1970s, after all, a multitude of other, more urgent concerns – Watergate, inflation, conflict in the Middle East – would come to confront Americans and even those who had the inclination to reflect upon recent history would not necessarily have directed their thoughts to what happened in My Lai (4), over the riots, the assassinations, and the rest of the Vietnam war. As the years passed, the regression continued: there were new events and situations always crowding in, each commanding consideration, yielding status in their turn to some more immediate emergency, claiming a place thereafter in an ever-expanding canon of crisis and catastrophe. The Mayaguez incident, the hostages in Iran, the bombing of the US Marine Barracks in Beirut, the space shuttle disasters, the Iran-Contra scandal, the fall of the Berlin Wall, the wars in the Gulf and the former Yugoslavia, the genocide in Rwanda, the terrorist attacks of 9/11 and the subsequent conflicts in Afghanistan and Iraq: what country could keep all of this current within its culture, commemorating each according to its due, and still attend conscientiously to the atrocities at Son My? Some attrition of memory is inevitable, as is selection: the individual who remembers everything is likely to go insane; the country that falls too deeply into an enchantment with its past is a country that ceases to function effectively in the present.

The imperative towards selection may be natural, but the outcomes of the process are not. The memories that endure within American public culture tend to be more compatible with the interests of power than those of events, like My Lai, which disrupt the identification of the nation with perpetual historical virtue, and which recommend by implication that current purposes and policies remain the subject of moral scrutiny. Government officials had always been reluctant to speak about the massacre, not just because their words might prejudice prosecutions; and that reticence has persisted through to the present day. The army, meanwhile, embarked upon a series of reforms in response to the massacre, seeking to extend and improve troop instruction in the laws of war and, in its officer training programmes, to emphasize the ethical dimension of military leadership. For a number of years, the character and conduct of Medina, Calley and their men were recurring referents within internal army discourse. In its

conversations with the civilian world, however, the army had other priorities, not least of which was recruitment, and so it generally maintained
a public silence on the subject of My Lai: quotas would not be filled by
invoking a memory of American atrocities.

When Americans turned their thoughts back to the massacre in the
years that followed the end of the Calley trial, it was rarely, if ever,
because they had been encouraged to do so by the political or military
establishments. Nor, once the war was over, did the massacre constitute
much of a rhetorical resource for those still asserting their opposition
to power. Calley himself made a brief, lucrative foray into the public-
speaking circuit after he had been paroled, but then elected to shut his
mouth and get on with his life, subsequently refusing ever to discuss the
subject with reporters or historians.[12] A few members of Charlie Company
have been more willing to talk, but never on their own initiative: their
testimonies illuminate accounts that somebody else has decided to write.

If an awareness of American atrocities survives within the wider national
memory of the Vietnam war, it is in large measure because other veterans
of the conflict (though certainly not all) have insisted upon the centrality of
such incidents to their own experiences of combat and to their experiences
since: in oral histories, memoirs, novels and films, and also in exchanges
with therapists and researchers, which later percolate out through the
clinical literature into the public record. Aside from the mnemonic prompts
provided by veteran narratives, the killings at My Lai (4) have been the
object of only intermittent and usually partial public interest, awakened
briefly by television documentaries or by their depiction in a novel. The
news media has revisited the massacre on most of its major anniversaries,
or when fresh revelations of atrocities, in past or current conflicts, have
stimulated a search for analogies and precedents. Historical commemoration, however, is not the media's primary function and these reports have,
therefore, interrupted the silence rather than brought it to an end. Overall,
indeed, the massacre has lacked a constituency: individuals or associations
within the United States with a strong moral, political or professional
investment in curating its public memory.

Americans might have said more about the massacre if they had known
what to say, if its memory had lent clear authority to a particular agenda
for change, sustaining itself through the promise of constructive application. As it was, the controversy that lasted from the initial disclosures to
the conclusion of the Calley trial yielded no consensus about the principal
causes of the killings nor therefore about lessons and reforms. The army
quietly revised its training schedules, but for everybody else, there were
few obvious purposes to which the massacre could be turned, especially
after the end of the national intervention in Vietnam. Perhaps it reminded

---

[12] *Newsweek* (17 March 1975), p. 54; *Chicago Tribune* (31 May 1985) (Tempo) p. 1; Bilton
and Sim, p. 2; Belknap, p. xiv.

some Americans to light another candle against war, for whatever good that would do, but most people, most likely, simply gave a shrug of their shoulders and hoped it wouldn't happen again. Not that there was nothing else to be done: there were survivors in need of aid, settlements still to be repaired, and a proper memorial to the dead to be funded and built. The victims, however, had long since been displaced from the centre of American concern. Outside of investigative reports, there existed no consolidated archive of their voices which might have subsequently served as a challenge to memory and conscience.

After the fall of Saigon and the extension of US government restrictions on travel and assistance to the south of Vietnam as well as to the north, few opportunities existed for the people of Son My to direct American attention back to their sufferings or for conscientious Americans to make an effort at reparation. Moreover, with the victims of atrocity essentially excluded from the culture, there were no wounds on display or spectacles of bereavement and loss to chasten its inclination to incorporate such crimes into the standard *Bildungsroman* of the US soldier in Vietnam, to project the (rarely original) wisdom acquired as a result as an equitable return upon the killing of innocent life. Similarly, there was nothing to obstruct the allocation of victim status to American veterans of the war, a status that many of them claimed, even those – like the men of Charlie Company – who had enthusiastically made victims of others. In recent years, with the normalization of government relations, it has become possible for more and more US citizens to visit Son My and to speak to survivors of the massacre. Some of these visitors have recognized an obligation to offer aid to the inhabitants of the village. Ironically, how-ever, what most take away from Son My, as from other war-related sites in the rest of Vietnam, is a memory that is increasingly denuded of ethical challenge and critique. It is now the 'buying mood' of the American tourist that Vietnamese authorities really wish to cultivate and preserve, not a sense of shame nor a commitment to the clearance of still outstanding national moral accounts.

President Johnson and his advisers did not decide in early 1965 to escalate the American military commitment to South Vietnam because they were concerned in particular with the fate of the South Vietnamese. It was the credibility of the United States that they were most anxious to defend, and there were many other places where they might have chosen to make their stand. Partly as a consequence, the war was not fought as if the lives of the South Vietnamese were that relevant to its purpose; neither was it fought as if that purpose was so important that it was to be achieved at any cost. Across America, therefore, the costs fell unevenly: some paid the ultimate price, whilst others paid no price at all, for the sake of an objective that seemed less than indispensable. What happened to South Vietnam was not without strategic significance, however. What-ever measure of American credibility had been invested in the survival of a non-communist government in the south before 1965 had significantly increased by the end of that year, by which time US troops had become responsible for the prosecution of the war. From that point on, powerful disincentives operated to stall retreat, and the retreat when it eventually came, swiftly followed by the fall of Saigon, was difficult to distinguish from a serious strategic defeat.

It was probably inevitable, then, that contests would arise over the public memory of the war: there were good reasons to believe that it had been a mistake and perhaps immoral to send American forces to Vietnam, but also to believe that, once the commitment had been made, more should have been done to make it a success.[13] Former hawks and former doves drew different lessons from the conflict, their disputes working frequently to confound the efforts of those in power to construct a democratic foreign policy for the post-Vietnam world. What the hawks and doves agreed upon, however, was more problematic still: that America should not be in the business of fighting limited wars. National leaders rarely endeavoured to resolve these disputes, nor did they try very often to explain why it was that not every intermediate emergency met with a moderate application of American military force would necessarily descend into a repeat of Vietnam. What they suggested, instead, was that the war just be forgotten, disregarded as an aberration, and that debates about the nation's role in the world be reconfined within the parameters of the bipartisan consensus that had last obtained in the early 1960s. Speaking in New Orleans in April 1975, as North Vietnamese and Vietcong forces were preparing for their final assault upon Saigon, President Ford declared that the United States could now 'regain the sense of pride that existed before Vietnam. But it cannot be achieved by refighting a war that is finished as far as America is concerned. As I see it, the time has come to look forward to an agenda for the future, to unify, to bind up the Nation's wounds, and to restore its health and its optimistic self-confidence. I ask that we stop refighting the battles and the recriminations of the past.'[14]

The success of Ford's appeal may be measured in the fact that it had to be repeated, fourteen and twenty years later respectively, by two of his successors, George H.W. Bush and Bill Clinton. In his inaugural address in 1989, Bush called for an end to the polarization of national politics, which he judged to have originated in the debates about Vietnam: 'But, friends, that war began in earnest a quarter of a century ago, and surely the statute of limitations has been reached. This is a fact: The final lesson of Vietnam is that no great nation can afford to be sundered by a memory. A

---

[13] K. Oliver, 'Towards a new moral history of the Vietnam war?', *The Historical Journal* 47:3 (2004), pp. 757–74.

[14] 'Address at a Tulane University Convocation, April 23, 1975', *Public Papers of the Presidents: Gerald R. Ford, 1975* (Washington, DC: US Government Printing Office, 1977), vol. I, pp. 568–73.

new breeze is blowing, and the old bipartisanship must be made anew.'[15] In July 1995, announcing the normalization of relations with Vietnam, Clinton asserted similarly that Americans should now 'move forward' beyond the divisions produced by the war: 'This moment offers us the opportunity to bind up our own wounds. They have resisted time for too long. We can now move on to common ground. Whatever divided us before let us consign to the past.'[16]

On occasion, however, national leaders have tried to do more with the Vietnam war than simply hasten it into the past. Speaking to a VFW convention during the presidential election of 1980, Ronald Reagan notoriously declared that the American intervention in Vietnam had been in the service of 'a noble cause', an early revisionist sally which resonated poorly with voters.[17] By 1985, however, the conservative campaign to rehabilitate the war had succeeded in dressing its ideological muscle in a more respectable intellectual cloth, and had also acquired a measure of political relevance as the Reagan administration sought to convince the nation of the need to combat the threat of left-wing insurgencies throughout Central America.[18] Thus, on the tenth anniversary of the fall of Saigon, Secretary of State George Shultz delivered a major address entitled 'The Meaning of Vietnam', asserting that there had been nothing immoral about US objectives in the war. Then, as now, policy-makers were justified in their efforts to contain the expansion of communism: 'Our goals in Central America *are* like those we had in Vietnam: democracy, economic progress and security against aggression.'[19]

Whether they were seeking to draw a line under the national debate about the war or to lend their authority to a favoured school of thought, these leaders for the most part maintained a studious silence on the subject of the material damage and suffering which the Vietnamese people had endured as a result of America's intervention and military policies.[20] Asked in 1977 whether the United States had a 'moral obligation' to help to rebuild Vietnam, Jimmy Carter responded that 'the destruction was mutual', which was certainly true but not quite the point.[21] George Shultz,

[15] 'Inaugural Address, January 20, 1989', *Public Papers of the Presidents: George H.W. Bush, 1989* (Washington, DC: US Government Printing Office, 1990), vol. I, pp. 1–4.

[16] 'Remarks announcing the normalization of diplomatic relations With Vietnam, July 11, 1995', *Public Papers of the Presidents: William J. Clinton, 1995* (Washington, DC: US Government Printing Office, 1996), vol. II, pp. 1073–4.

[17] L. Cannon, *Reagan* (New York: G.P. Putnam's Sons, 1982), pp. 271–2.

[18] For revisionist accounts of the war, see especially Lewy, *America in Vietnam*, and N. Podhoretz, *Why We Were in Vietnam* (New York: Simon & Schuster, 1982).

[19] G. Dionisopoulos and S. Goldzwig, '"The meaning of Vietnam": political rhetoric as revisionist cultural history', *Quarterly Journal of Speech*, 78 (1992), 61–79.

[20] McMahon, 'Contested Memory', p. 171.

[21] 'The President's news conference of March 24, 1977', *Public Papers of the Presidents: Jimmy Carter, 1977* (Washington, DC: US Government Printing Office, 1977), vol. I, pp. 496–504.

meanwhile, constructed his defence of the conflict on the ground of morality of intention, rather than means; and though he expressed sympathy for the inhabitants of South Vietnam, it was with respect to their ordeals after the imposition of communist rule, not those that had occurred during the era of American war.[22] Nobody was inclined to talk about My Lai. Indeed, as revealed in the rhetoric of Ford and Clinton, when wounds were discussed, they were usually American, usually metaphorical and usually the subject of an invitation to heal. These bromides, however, did not succeed in speeding public memory of the war into oblivion: there were simply too many bodies in the way – alive, dead and missing – making claims upon care, commemoration and a proper accounting. Almost exclusively, though, these were American bodies, not Vietnamese: further evidence, if it was needed, that memory is formed and persists only by means of forgetting.

In large measure, however, the images of American victimization which, at moments in the decades following the war, seemed to evacuate all other content from the nation's memories of Vietnam had been a deliberate creation of the federal government, which also played a role thereafter in keeping them current. It had been the administration of Richard Nixon, casting around for a means of mobilizing public support for the continued prosecution of the war, which first elected to emphasize the fate of American servicemen captured by the enemy. Nixon insisted that there could be no peace settlement in Vietnam until these prisoners were released: this was contrary to customary practice, which provided for such releases after a settlement had been negotiated, at the moment it came into force.[23] His administration also conflated its register of likely prisoners with those recorded as missing in action, presenting a combined list to the enemy delegations in Paris along with a demand that they account for the fate of all of the men that it named, fostering the popular perception that many of the missing were being held by Hanoi.[24] In the end, Nixon's manipulation of the POW/MIA issue was not enough by itself to keep the United States in the war, and he eventually conceded to a settlement providing for prisoner release simultaneous with American withdrawal.[25] To the post-Vietnam era, however, he had left a poisonous legacy, in the form of fuzzy government maths, families nurturing false hopes that their loved ones were still alive, a well-connected network of activists and racketeers with a range of emotional, political and economic investments in the continuation of the cause, and the rhetorical convention that there had been something unusual and vindictive about the position of the Vietnamese

[22] Dionisopoulos and Goldzwig, pp. 67–8.

[23] H. Franklin, *M.I.A., or Mythmaking in America* (Brooklyn: Lawrence Hill Books, 1992), p. 58.

[24] *Ibid.*, p. 68.

[25] *Ibid.*, p. 75.

communists with regard to the release of US prisoners of war, to which it was easy to append the proposition that they had not released them all.[26]

For twenty years thereafter, whatever the US government said and did with regard to Vietnam was conditioned by the fantasy of American service-men in chains. If officials did not subscribe to the fantasy themselves, they knew people who did: sixty-nine per cent of the population accord-ing to a poll in 1991.[27] Successive administrations insisted that the normalization of relations with Vietnam (ending restrictions upon trade, aid and travel) would occur only after that country had made the 'fullest possible accounting' for the US military personnel still listed as missing.[28] What was full, what was possible and, most of all, what was reasonable were subject, of course, to very different judgements in Washington and Hanoi, which remained unable to account for many hundreds of thou-sands of its own soldiers and civilians lost during the war.[29] Through the late 1970s and 1980s, the Vietnamese authorities cooperated only sporad-ically with American demands for information, although they continued to repatriate the remains of dead US servicemen.[30] Both the Reagan and Bush administrations declared their working assumption to be that Amer-ican personnel were still held captive in Indochina, whether in Laos, Cambodia or Vietnam.[31] Only in the early 1990s did this pernicious myth begin properly to be dispelled, in studies by H. Bruce Franklin and Susan Katz Keating, and in a report by the specially-convened US Senate Select Committee on POW/MIA Affairs, chaired by John Kerry. As the Vietnam-ese, meanwhile, looked to improve their economic ties with the West, there were new incentives accumulating on both sides towards the normalization of relations and thus, as a necessary first step, also towards cooperation on the issue of the American MIAs. Vietnam agreed to a rolling series of joint field operations and excavations which, over the course of the decade, resulted in the discovery of the remains of nearly 300 US servicemen.[32] Its reward was the lifting of the American trade embargo in 1994, normaliza-tion the next year, and a visit from President Clinton in November 2000; but not, it seems, an end to the solipsism of US official memory. Clinton travelled to a rice paddy close to Hanoi where, tears welling in his eyes, he watched as American forensic experts and Vietnamese labourers searched for the remains of a downed US pilot, later attending a ceremony

---

[26] For discussions of the afterlife of the POW/MIA issue, see Franklin; S. Keating, *Prisoners of Hope: Exploiting the POW/MIA Myth in America* (New York: Random House, 1994); and US Senate, *Report of the Select Committee on POW/MIA Affairs*, 13 January 1993, (Washington, DC: US Government Printing Office, 1993).

[27] Franklin, p. xi.

[28] *Ibid.*, p. 4.

[29] *Washington Post* (19 November 2000), p. A1.

[30] *Report of the Select Committee on POW/MIA Affairs*, pp. 371–6.

[31] Franklin, pp. 3–5.

[32] *Washington Post* (19 November 2000), p. A1.

to mark the repatriation of three sets of remains recovered earlier that year.[33] He did not visit Son My.

From the sphere of civilian authority, therefore, emerged no trace of a stimulus towards the fashioning of a conscientious and constructive national memory of the massacre at My Lai (4). The culture was left to do that for itself, as were other institutions, even the US Army, for all the recent evidence that its capacity for self-analysis and self-criticism tended to congeal into self-interest when not exposed to the discipline of external review. In the wake of the Calley trial, Nixon's White House counsel, John Dean, returned to the proposal for a commission of inquiry into the causes of the massacre, suggesting that such a commission might also be asked to examine other incidents of war crimes in Vietnam and to make recommendations with regard to the effectiveness of training in the laws of war, the recruitment and promotion of service personnel, the ethics of operational doctrine and practice, and the provisions and processes of military justice.[34] It was a suggestion made, however, at the end of a long memorandum, at a time when the massacre controversy was beginning to recede, and so it died there on the page, unheeded and possibly even unread. What the massacre would produce in the way of military reform was left very much for the military to decide.

The decisions it reached were, for the most part, logical and responsible. It was in the interest of the military that there should be no repeat of My Lai, and it was critical, furthermore, that its actions to that end be implemented swiftly and exposed to public view. The army may have tried to present the massacre as an aberration, but it was not so confident of its case that it would trust in the old routines to prevent such an atrocity from happening again. As one of its middle-ranking officers observed: 'The aftermath of My Lai has been too traumatic and erosive of public confidence in the Army to risk the recurrence of a similar incident.'[35] Not far in the future, moreover, lay the challenge of recruiting an all-volunteer force, a challenge that could only be met if the army proved to ordinary Americans that it was not still making murderers of its men.

That significant discrepancies existed between the formal content of the laws of war, the knowledge of those laws retained by US soldiers and officers upon the completion of their training, and the manner of their interpretation out in the field in Vietnam had been registered by the army high command well before March 1968 and the moment of their most grotesque inversion that morning in Son My. Instructors were only required to offer one hour of tuition on the Geneva Conventions during basic combat

[33] *Ibid.*

[34] Dean to Ehrlichman, Haig and Krogh, 'Discussion Memorandum Re War Crimes Cases', 14 May 1971, folder: 'War Crimes Study', Box 15, John Dean Subject Files, Staff Members and Office Files, White House Special Files, NPM, NACP.

[35] Schopper, 'Lessons From My Lai', 14 April 1973, folder: 'Schopper, Jared B.', Army War College Student Papers: NR 1972/73, USAMHI, p. 18.

training. They were provided with a detailed lesson outline, scheduling precisely how many minutes of that hour should be allocated to each element of the curriculum (with four minutes, for example, devoted to the right of prisoners of war to be treated humanely). A lecture script was also supplied, offering the instructor an easy means of keeping to time, albeit at the expense of actually engaging the class. Questions were invited only at the end. There was no reference in the script to the reporting of war crimes, nor to illustrative examples drawn from the war in Vietnam (or, for that matter, from any other conflict).[36] Rarely, it seems, was application of the conventions integrated into the field exercise scenarios used to train and test troops outside of the classroom.[37]

In the summer of 1967, investigators from the army's Office of the Inspector General concluded that, though formal tuition on the conventions faithfully reflected their content, 'the sum effect of all training' – which included the informal accounts of combat offered by instructors with experience in Vietnam – had been to leave many enlisted men and junior officers with the impression that, in the conditions of combat, other imperatives might override the word of the law. During the course of their inspection of the Officer Candidate School at Fort Benning (William Calley was in attendance around the same time), the investigators asked students who had already received their scheduled instruction on the conventions and who were within two weeks of graduation whether, in circumstances where they needed information quickly, they would seek to obtain it by mistreating prisoners of war. In one class, 50 per cent of students replied that they would.[38] That the training was not always having its intended effect was also evident to the military authorities in Vietnam itself: prompted by reports of non-combatant casualties, mistreatment of prisoners, and excessive and indiscriminate applications of firepower, General Westmoreland periodically issued directives urging his field commanders to reiterate to their men the need to comply with the laws of war and the rules of engagement.[39]

Sixty minutes of arid legal discourse, almost entirely abstracted from the real conditions of war, together with occasional exhortations to more righteous conduct handed down from on high could not really be said to amount to an ethical education. In the wake of the revelations about My Lai, the army could reasonably assert that the soldiers of Charlie

[36] Army Subject Schedule No. 21–18: 'The Geneva Conventions', 20 April 1967, folder: 'Laws of War Reference File, 1975 – Folder #1', Box 14, RCCPI, RPI, RAS, RG319, NACP.

[37] Schopper, 'Lessons From My Lai', 14 April 1973, folder: 'Schopper, Jared B.', Army War College Student Papers: NR 1972/73, USAMHI, p. 3.

[38] 'Resume of Report on Inspection of Geneva Convention and Handling of POW at Fort Benning', attached to: Horwitz to Resor, 'Alleged Atrocities by US Military Forces in South Vietnam', 5 July 1967, folder: My Lai 8/21, Papers of *Four Hours in My Lai*, LHCMA, KCL. See also Seymour Hersh, 'My Lai, and its omens', *New York Times* (16 March 1998), p. 25.

[39] 'Summary of Remarks by COMUSMACV Emphasizing Troop Conduct', 23 December 1969, folder: My Lai 8/11, Papers of *Four Hours in My Lai*, LHCMA, KCL.

Company should still have known better, but not that it had done everything it could to ensure that better knowledge had endured. In mid-
December 1969, Stanley Resor, the Secretary of the Army, asked General
Westmoreland – who was, by that time, the Army Chief of Staff – to
determine whether those receiving instruction in the Geneva Conventions
'really understand what their obligations are'. In particular, he wanted
a survey to be conducted of enlisted men and officers, eliciting their
responses 'to hypothetical but concrete situations in which the teach-
ings of the Conventions would be relevant'.[40] Four thousand soldiers were
interviewed for the study, with an additional 18,000 completing a questionnaire. By April 1970, the initial results were in, and indicated that
14.6 per cent of army personnel did not comprehend what was required of
them under the conventions. Thirty per cent of officers as well as enlisted
men gave incorrect answers to over half of the questions. Many did not understand that they could be court-martialled if they carried out an illegal
order; many also considered it permissible to mistreat or kill prisoners
of war. These findings, moreover, had yet to incorporate responses from
US soldiers stationed in Vietnam.[41]

It was evident, therefore, that the existing regime of instruction in the
laws of war had to be reformed. A recommendation to that effect, contained in a report otherwise rather light on specific proposals, had also
recently been made by the Peers Commission.[42] The army swiftly revised
its regulations, requiring that instruction in the conventions during basic
combat training be extended from one to at least two hours, with similar
classes to be included in the curricula of all officer-training programmes
and service schools courses, as well as that of the Command and General
Staff College (CGSC). When they first arrived in a theatre of operations,
army personnel were to receive orientation in both the conventions
and the local rules of engagement, as well as a further two-hour refresher
class every calendar year. The classes were to be taught jointly by a judge
advocate and an officer with experience of combat and command, preferably one who had fought in counter-insurgency conditions.[43] The army
was now anxious not just that its soldiers should be well-versed in the
letter of the laws of war, but that they also should have registered the
compatibility of such laws with the effective, disciplined use of force and

[40] Resor to Westmoreland, 'Training Concerning the Geneva Conventions', 17 December
1969, folder: 'My Lai Incident – Answer to 8 Feb 72 Ltr from Cong. Stratton from SA, 7 Apr
72', Box 16, RCCPI, RPI, RAS, RG319, NACP.

[41] Westmoreland to Resor, 'Training Concerning the Geneva Conventions', 8 April 1970,
folder: 'My Lai Incident – Answer to 8 Feb 72 Ltr from Cong. Stratton from SA, 7 Apr 72',
Box 16, RCCPI, RPI, RAS, RG319, NACP.

[42] Goldstein *et al.*, pp. 319–20.

[43] Army Regulation No. 350–215: 'Training: The Geneva Conventions of 1949 and Hague
Convention No. IV of 1907', 28 May 1970, folder: 'Laws of War Reference File, 1975 – Folder
#1', Box 14, RCCPI, RPI, RAS, RG319, NACP.

know how to apply them in particular combat situations.[44] Three new films were produced to support and illustrate elements of the instruction, all of which presented scenarios set in an Asian counter-insurgency environment, as well as examples of illegal orders and guidance on how they could be resisted and reported.[45] Where possible, application of the conventions was to be integrated into 'tactical training and related subjects'; the army staff was preparing scenarios involving civilian detainees and enemy prisoners which could be introduced into field exercise play.[46]

In March 1970, a few days after he had submitted his commission's report on the Son My massacre, General Peers sent a memorandum to General Westmoreland describing the ethical standards that he believed an army commander had to embody and maintain, particularly when leading combat units in a counter-insurgency environment. It was incumbent upon commanders to take an active interest in the conduct and welfare of their men, monitoring their mood for signs of the 'frustrations and bitterness' which could often be generated by contexts of counter-insurgency, and moving quickly to arrest the development of such attitudes before they became manifest in violent excesses. They had a responsibility to ensure that firepower was used in a controlled and discriminate manner, and that their soldiers treated enemy prisoners humanely and safeguarded the lives and property of non-combatants. If a commander had knowledge that a crime had been committed, he was required to take immediate remedial action, 'regardless of the personal consequences'. Where these standards were not maintained, Peers concluded, there was a potential for disaster, similar to that which had occurred at Son My.[47]

Peers's memorandum prompted Westmoreland to commission a study into the attitudes and values of the army's officer corps.[48] The conclusions

[44] W. Hays Park, 'The United States military and the law of war: inculcating an ethos – international justice, war crimes, and terrorism: the US record', *Social Research*, 69 (Winter 2002); *Washington Post* (14 February 1971), p. A14.

[45] Department of the Army Instructors Film Reference: 'The Geneva Conventions and the Soldier', 21 January 1971, folder: 'Laws of War Reference File, 1975 – Folder #1', Box 14, RCCPI, RPI, RAS, RG319, NACP; Department of the Army Instructor's Film Reference, 'When the Enemy is My Prisoner', 19 October 1971, folder: 'My Lai Incident – Answer to 8 Feb 72 Ltr from Cong. Stratton from SA, 7 Apr 72', Box 16, RCCPI, RPI, RAS, RG319, NACP; Department of the Army Instructor's Film Reference: 'The Geneva Conventions and the Military Policeman', folder: 'My Lai Incident – Answer to 8 Feb 72 Ltr from Cong. Stratton from SA, 7 Apr 72', Box 16, RCCPI, RPI, RAS, RG319, NACP; Kerwin to Palmer, 'Training Film Illustrating Extreme Examples of Illegal Orders', 17 June 1970, folder: 'References for Reply to Rep. Stratton's 8 Feb 1972 Letter re: Lessons Learned by Army from Son My Incident [2 of 2]', Box 24, RCCPI, RPI, RAS, RG319, NACP; Schopper, 'Lessons From My Lai', 14 April 1973, folder: 'Schopper, Jared B.', Army War College Student Papers: NR 1972/73, USAMHI, p. 9.

[46] Army Regulation No. 350–215: 'Training: The Geneva Conventions of 1949 and Hague Convention No. IV of 1907', 28 May 1970, folder: 'Laws of War Reference File, 1975 – Folder #1', Box 14, RCCPI, RPI, RAS, RG319, NACP; Schopper, 'Lessons From My Lai', 14 April 1973, folder: 'Schopper, Jared B.', Army War College Student Papers: NR 1972/73, USAMHI, p. 10.

[47] Peers, pp. 246–9.

[48] Zaffiri, p. 344.

of this study, conducted by the Army War College and submitted in late June 1970, did not make for cheerful reading, nor did those of a second, much larger study completed the following year. Apparently, many senior officers did not aspire to offer ethical leadership to their men, seeking only to serve the interests of their own careers. There were Hendersons and Kosters almost everywhere one looked.[49] These studies did not inspire the wholesale reformation of institutional values – their dissemination within the wider army community remained too limited for that, whilst the promise of career advancement was seen as critical to the success of recruitment and retention efforts in the approaching era of the all-volunteer force.[50]

On one important point, however, the army command was persuaded: that the attrition of service integrity revealed most starkly by the massacre at My Lai (4) and by the subsequent attempts to void it from history could not be redressed simply through improvements in instruction on the laws of war. There was a need, the command now recognized, to remind American soldiers – and officers, in particular – that the army was a calling as well as a career. Throughout the service school system, curricula were revised to incorporate classes on the ethics of leadership. In some cases, extracts from the Army War College studies and the memorandum that Peers had submitted to Westmoreland were used as student texts.[51] This was not a wholly momentary fad. In 1990, a twenty-hour module for the US Army Command and General Staff College (CGSC) on the *Fundamentals of Senior-Level Leadership in Peace and War* was still devoting three of those hours to the subject of 'Ethics and the Senior Leader', and requiring that its students be able 'to explain the source and components of the professional Army ethic and the ethical responsibilities of senior-level leaders'.[52]

It was a measure, perhaps, of the advances that the army perceived itself to have made since the time of the massacre that, in May 1974, it proposed that the Department of Defense issue a directive establishing a uniform protocol for implementation of the laws of war across all the military services, offering the assistance of its own staff in the drafting of that directive.[53] Six months later, the directive was published, clarifying

[49] Kitfield, pp. 109–10; Cincinnatus, pp. 130–4; US Army War College, *Leadership for the 1970's: USAWC Study of Leadership for the Professional Soldier*, 20 October 1971.

[50] Kitfield, p. 112; Cincinnatus, pp. 130, 167; Peers, p. 251.

[51] Cincinnatus, p. 175. At the US Military Academy at West Point, cadets taking courses in Military Psychology and Leadership were also required to read sections of the second Army War College study, as well as Michael Walzer's *Just and Unjust Wars: A Moral Argument with Historical Illustrations* (New York: Basic Books, 1977). Dr Conrad Crane, interview with author, Carlisle, PA, 27 August 2003.

[52] Advance Sheet Booklet: *Fundamentals of Senior Level Leadership in Peace and War (P913)*, 1 May 1990. Courtesy of Dr Conrad Crane.

[53] Callaway to Schlesinger, 'Draft Directive on the Implementation of the Law of War', 29 May 1974, folder: 'Laws of War Reference File, 1975 – Folder #1', Box 14, RCCPI, RPI, RAS, RG319, NACP.

the allocation of responsibility within the Pentagon itself, the military departments and local commands for coordinating, monitoring, developing and implementing policies and procedures with respect to the laws of war.[54] There now existed an integrated framework within which the army – or, more specifically, its corps of judge advocates – could work to disseminate its experiences and practices across the rest of the military: for example, through the preparation of class materials that could be used by instructors in the other services.[55] In addition, the directive advertised the view of senior military officers and civilian defence officials that everything reasonable should be done to ensure national compliance with the laws of war, fostering an environment sympathetic to procedural innovations consistent with that goal.

So it was that, from the 1983 intervention in Grenada onwards, judge advocates functioned ever more frequently as inhouse consultants to combat commanders, who wanted to ensure that their operational concepts and plans would not violate the laws of war and that they had ready access to expert guidance in the event that the operation wandered into uncertain legal ground. During the first Gulf War, for example, the commanders of VII Corps found that their troops had captured so many Iraqi prisoners of war that they could not sustain the pace of their advance. A staff judge advocate assigned to the VII Corps tactical operations centre was asked whether the prisoners could simply be given food and water and instructed to walk south, allowing the advance to continue unhindered. He replied that this would be illegal: VII Corps was now responsible for the safety of the prisoners, and would have to provide them with protection and escort them to the rear.[56] In 1998, the operational role of judge advocates had become so much the convention that it was written into a revised version of the original laws of war directive.[57]

In their preparations for the court martial of William Calley, information officers at Fort Benning anticipated that, with the trial proceedings unlikely to produce compelling news every single day, correspondents might sometimes turn their attention away from the judicial content of the massacre story, and seek to examine its wider institutional effects. It was predicted, in particular, that they would be interested in covering lessons in which enlisted men and officer candidates were taught the laws

[54] Department of Defense Directive No. 5100.77, 'DoD Program for the Implementation of the Law of War', 5 November 1974, folder: 'Laws of War Reference File, 1975 – Folder #1', Box 14, RCCPI, RPI, RAS, RG319, NACP.

[55] F. Borch, *Judge Advocates in Combat: Army Lawyers in Military Operations from Vietnam to Haiti* (Washington, DC: Office of the Judge Advocate General and Center of Military History, United States Army, 2001), p. 31; J. Addicott and W. Hudson, 'The twenty-fifth anniversary of My Lai: a time to inculcate the lessons', *Military Law Review*, 139 (1993), p. 182.

[56] Borch, p. 324.

[57] Department of Defense Directive No. 5100.77, 'DoD Law of War Program', 9 December 1998: www.dtic.mil/whs/directives/ (accessed August 2004).

of war. Guidance was passed to instructors indicating how best to conduct these lessons when members of the press were present. If the resulting coverage was positive – and a subsequent internal assessment reported that it was – it would complement the efforts of the army in the Calley court martial itself to prove to the American people that it viewed its values as incompatible with acts of atrocity.[58]

This was all very well for as long as the Calley case served to keep the massacre in the news. By the end of 1971, however, public interest in the case had markedly declined, and the army no longer felt so obliged to speak the name of My Lai. It preferred not to do so, not even in the cause of assuring Americans how much it had changed. Internally, the army may have been making constructive and instructive use of the massacre, but as it prepared for the challenge of enlisting only volunteers, it was happy to let the controversy without subside into silence. In February 1972, Winant Sidle, the army's Chief of Information, queried the wisdom of a decision to discharge Kenneth Hodges from the service against his will and to exclude him from future enlistment. Hodges, a sergeant with Charlie Company, had been charged with rape and assault with intent to murder, though the charges were later dropped. 'In media coverage,' Sidle warned, 'he can be portrayed as another scapegoat and score points in his behalf with public and press while the Army is again placed at a disadvantage through prolonged media interest in a most unfavourable story.'[59]

In September 1972, a fact sheet on the massacre was prepared for General Creighton Abrams, the incoming Chief of Staff, and then with-drawn on the advice of the Army General Counsel. If the existence of the fact sheet became known to outside parties, one officer noted, it could 'pose a problem with proliferating requests for information'.[60] The army, meanwhile, said nothing to the press about its four-year investigation into multiple atrocities committed by the 101st Airborne Division's Tiger Force platoon, nor did it file charges against any of the soldiers involved. Lieuten-ant James Hawkins, who had commanded the platoon, later recalled that in November 1975 he had been summoned to the Pentagon and told that the case was closed: 'This was a hot potato. See, this was after [My Lai], and the Army certainly didn't want to go through the publicity thing.'[61]

The army was concerned, it seems, to tend only its own memories of the massacre. In that regard, at least, its efforts were generally consci-entious, though not necessarily conclusive or compelling. Schedules for

[58] Office of the Information Officer, Headquarters US Army Infantry Center, Fort Benning, 'Public Affairs Aspects of Calley Court-Martial', *c.* April 1971, folder: My Lai 8/31, Papers of *Four Hours in My Lai*, LHCMA, KCL.

[59] Sidle to Seitz, 'Administrative Review of Son My Cases', 14 February 1972, folder: My Lai 8/30, Papers of *Four Hours in My Lai*, LHCMA, KCL.

[60] Dyke, 'Preparation of a Fact Sheet for General Abrams, Subject: Overview of Son My Incident', 14 September 1972, folder: 'LTC Dyke Chron. File #1, 3 Aug–28 Sep 72', Box 15, RCCPI, RPI, RAS, RG319, NACP.

[61] *Toledo Blade* (20 October 2003).

instruction in the laws of war may have been expanded, but the basic constitution of behavioural and attitudinal influences to which young servicemen were exposed stayed largely the same. During the court martial of William Calley, a correspondent from the *Washington Post* attended a lesson on the laws of war taught at the Officer Candidate School, Fort Benning. 'The lesson doesn't go over easily,' he observed. 'In tone and emphasis, it seems to conflict with so much of the other training.' The students were asked what they would do if, following a firefight in which US casualties had been incurred, an enemy soldier armed with a machine gun had kept their forces pinned down until his comrades had withdrawn and he had run out of ammunition, whereupon he attempted to surrender. 'In loud unison, the 200 students instantly chorused their response: "Shoot him! Shoot him!"' [62]

Whilst soldiers might expect to receive further training on the laws of war throughout their service in the army, initial classes were often taught as if they were entirely self-contained. In 1988, during the course of a single lesson, officer candidates at Fort Benning were instructed in the formal provisions of the law and asked to reflect on the reasons why their violation was undesirable, not just from the perspective of ethics, but also in terms of utility and unit discipline. They were offered illustrative examples from the Second World War, the Falklands War and the intervention in Grenada. The instructor discussed the massacre at My Lai, with reference to the photographs taken by Ronald Haeberle and an extract from the Peers Commission report. The students were also shown excerpts from the film *Breaker Morant*, an account of three Australian officers court-martialled for shooting prisoners during the Boer War. The transcript of the lesson was forty-one pages long. Though honest and innovative in his efforts to communicate a difficult subject, the instructor was simply asking his students to process too much material far too quickly, and so it was impossible to be certain what they had, or had not, taken in. [63]

Nor was the army's commitment to the effective inculcation of the lessons of My Lai so complete that it became invulnerable to all competing imperatives. In the early 1970s, severe budgetary constraints, combined with increasing internal dissatisfaction with a training regime that was highly centralized and prescriptive, resulted in reforms which devolved responsibility for unit instruction down to the level of the individual company. [64] Thus, a year or so after it had first been introduced in response to the massacre revelations, the requirement that all personnel receive an

---

[62] *Washington Post* (14 February 1971), p. A14.

[63] Transcript of lecture on the law of land warfare by JAG Captain Jack Sheen to young infantry officers at Fort Benning, 30 September 1988, folder: My Lai 12/12, Papers of *Four Hours in My Lai*, LHCMA, KCL.

[64] R. Brownlee and W. Mullen, *Changing an Army: An Oral History of General William E. Depuy, USA Retired* (Carlisle Barracks, PA: United States Military History Institute, 1986), pp. 183–4.

annual refresher lesson on the laws of war was effectively eliminated.[65] For many soldiers, the experience of formal lessons in the subject, presented by qualified instructors, came to an end once basic training had been completed: whatever classes they received thereafter would occur at the discretion of their unit commander, and would be taught by their own officers or senior NCOs, guided by lesson plans contained in army training circulars.[66]

The memory of the massacre, moreover, could only continue to be instructive as long as the army itself remained interested in Vietnam and in the tactical, as well as ethical, problems that were involved in the fighting of a counter-insurgency war. As it turned out, the army was not that interested. By the early 1970s, it was turning its attention – with a degree of relief – back to what it had long believed to be its principal mission: the conventional defence of Europe against an assault by the forces of the Soviet Union and the Warsaw Pact.[67] If the memory of any conflict was stimulating doctrinal innovation in this period, it was not Vietnam, but the Yom Kippur war of 1973, which was judged to have demonstrated both the importance of winning the first battle and the role to be played by high-technology weapons systems and concentrations of firepower in the achievement of that objective. Although a series of official monographs assessing aspects of the army's performance in Vietnam had been commissioned in the final years of the war, most seem to have passed their intended audiences by. In the course of its structural reorganization from 1972 to 1974, moreover, the army allowed its 'lessons learned' system for the analysis and subsequent dissemination of recent experience to lose its institutional home and thereafter to lapse.[68]

In so far as its senior commanders sponsored any particular interpretation of the army's conduct of the Vietnam war, it was that contained in Harry Summers' *On Strategy*, which argued that it had not been flaws in the practice of counter-insurgency which condemned the military intervention to failure, but rather the decision to practise counter-insurgency at all. Summers took the (highly questionable) view that the difficulties which confronted the regime in Saigon originated in Hanoi, and that they would have been decisively eased by the early application of conventional,

[65] Gard to Bennett, 'Lessons Learned From the Son My Incident', 15 June 1972, folder: My Lai 8/30, Papers of *Four Hours in My Lai*, LHCMA, KCL.

[66] See, for example, Department of the Army, 'Training Circular No. 22-9-1: Leader Development Program: *Military Professionalism* (Platoon/Squad Instruction)', 5 May 1986. Courtesy of Dr. Conrad Crane.

[67] C. Crane, *Avoiding Vietnam: The US Army's Response to Defeat in Southeast Asia* (Carlisle, PA: Strategic Studies Institute, US Army War College, 2002), pp. 4–5; R. Cassidy, 'Prophets or Praetorians? The Uptonian Paradox and the Powell Corollary', *Parameters*, 33:3 (2003), 137–8; R. Lock-Pullan, '"An inward-looking time": the United States Army, 1973–1976', *Journal of Military History*, 67 (2003), 483–511.

[68] D. Vetock, *Lessons Learned: A History of US Army Lesson Learning* (Carlisle Barracks, PA: US Army Military History Institute, 1988), pp. 119–20.

defensive force along the demilitarized zone in order to isolate the revolution in the south from its principal source of support.[69]

Within the army, therefore, the construction of a usable past from the operational history of the Vietnam conflict constituted, at best, a distinctly minority enterprise. It was not necessary to extract lessons from specific incidents in that history – like the massacre at My Lai (4) – as long as military and civilian leaders continued to keep in mind the most important lesson of all: that American soldiers should only fight in conventional wars. Just prior to his retirement as Chief of Staff, General Westmoreland did order the compilation of a 'lessons learned' study describing the various changes made to army policies in response to the massacre.[70] This study, however, was to be restrictive in scope, concentrating, for example, upon problems encountered in the recruitment of capable junior officers and upon recent improvements in training, but not upon the failure of some senior army commanders in Vietnam to adequately monitor and control the behaviour of their men.[71] Yet, if written in accordance with such a covenant, the study was likely to appear defensive, evasive and possibly also complacent, and so eventually the project was placed on indefinite hold.[72]

What the army valued most in its soldiers in the mid- to late 1970s, therefore, was not the ability to walk into a Vietnamese village and by lawful means determine who was a guerrilla and who was not. The army expected to fight its next war in central Europe: a confrontation between predominantly conventional (and uniformed) formations, in which American hopes for victory rested on its forces' effective use of a new generation of advanced weapons systems. As a first priority, the army sought to nurture functional proficiencies in its recruits, who would often be serving in quite specialized technical roles. That these soldiers should comprehend the ethical contexts to which their proficiencies were to be applied was desirable, but not essential. 'I think you should train a man for the job he

[69] H. Summers, *On Strategy: A Critical Analysis of the Vietnam War* (Novato: Presidio Press, 1982).

[70] Bennett, 'Lessons Learned from the Son My Incident', 17 May 1972, folder: 'Lessons Learned from the Son My Incident – Chron. File #1', Box 14, RCCPI, RPI, RAS, RG319, NACP.

[71] Johns, 'Memorandum for Record', 26 May 1972, folder: 'My Lai Lessons Learned Reports [Drafts and Working Papers]', Box 6, Records Pertaining to the My Lai Massacre, 1969–1974, Records of the Vietnam War Crimes Working Group, Office of the Deputy Chief of Staff for Personnel, RAS, RG319, NACP.

[72] General Charles Dyke, interview with author, Washington, DC, 5 September 2003; Dyke to Patchell and Fulwyler, '"Lessons Learned" Document Concerning the Son My Incident', 16 November 1972, folder: 'Lessons Learned – My Lai. (Input from Agencies and COL Schopper's Compilation – 1972 [1 of 2]', Box 14, RCCPI, RPI, RAS, RG319, NACP. Colonel Jared Schopper, the officer originally responsible for compiling the 'lessons learned' document, later wrote a paper on the subject whilst studying at the Army War College. See Schopper, 'Lessons From My Lai', 14 April 1973, folder: 'Schopper, Jared B.', Army War College Student Papers: NR 1972/73, USAMHI.

is going to perform,' asserted General William Depuy, who headed the army's Training and Doctrine Command from 1973 to 1977, 'and then you can educate him so that the intellectual and moral environment in which he pursues his particular job will be enhanced.'[73] Although there have been significant changes in doctrine since the immediate post-Vietnam era, the army has continued to regard the exploitation of advanced technology systems as critical to its mission, whilst the prospect of operating those systems has encouraged many young Americans to enlist in the service over the last three decades.[74]

If there was a danger in all this, of course, it was that the instrumentalist logics which already pervaded army culture – most routinely in its insistence upon obedience and discipline – would become ever more dominant as computerized weapons magnified both the physical and experiential distance separating soldiers from the end results of their actions. On the electronic battlefield, formal ethics could still hold, but their application only rarely expressed empathetic intelligence. In this kind of combat, soldiers could have no more knowledge about the lives and deaths of the people they were killing than they could in conditions of a computer simulation. In a conventional campaign, that perhaps did not matter, but conventional campaigns often seem now to be a prelude to counter-insurgency wars, which generally present soldiers with a more exacting ethical challenge and, for their effective prosecution, require the patient accumulation of first-hand knowledge of local communities and their culture. Recent innovations in military doctrine, favouring rapid force deployment and leaner, lighter combat formations, make the task of counter-insurgency more challenging still, compressing the time available for orientation and training, disrupting systems of command and control designed to ensure that soldiers comply with the laws of war.[75] Although some active force elements might be well-prepared for such environments – having conducted, for example, exercises at training centres first established in the mid-1990s to condition troops to the rigours of what was then an equally unfamiliar peace-keeping mandate – others may not.[76]

'We were supposed to be the experts on this, but all we knew is what we learned in our summer camp,' recalled Scott McKenzie, a member of the military police reserve despatched at a few weeks' notice to run detention facilities in Iraq.[77] At one such facility, the Abu Ghraib jail in

---

[73] Brownlee and Mullen, p. 186.

[74] Crane, pp. 8–9, 12; D. King and Z. Karabell, *The Generation of Trust: How the US Military has Regained the Public's Confidence since Vietnam* (Washington, DC: The AEI Press, 2003), pp. 71–4.

[75] B. Knickerbocker, 'War boosts Rumsfeld's vision of an agile military', *Christian Science Monitor* (11 April 2003).

[76] D. Isenberg, 'Confronting the demons of urban warfare', *Asia Times* (5 May 2004): www.atimes.com (accessed August 2004).

[77] D. Jehl and E. Schmitt, 'In abuse, a picture of GIs ill prepared and overwhelmed', *New York Times* (9 May 2004).

Baghdad, inadequacies of troop preparation, a permissive culture of command, shifting lines of authority, as well as the apparent exclusion of judge advocates from oversight of interrogation practices combined to produce not just multiple instances of prisoner abuse but also probably the worst crisis of moral legitimacy that the army had experienced since the massacre at My Lai (4).[78]

Out of the massacre disclosures, the army laboured constructively to create a legacy of reform. A number of those reforms continue to affect the training and conduct of army personnel today, though others have not endured. Whilst it may have institutionalized some of the lessons, the army remains a rather ambivalent guardian of the memory of the massacre itself, and of other American atrocities committed in Vietnam. In the late 1990s, the massacre was still used as an example in officer instruction and at West Point, but it seems rarely to have been mentioned to ordinary recruits.[79] Visiting Fort Benning in March 1998, a CNN reporter asked one young soldier what he knew about My Lai. 'Never heard of it, sir,' came the answer.[80]

Earlier that same month, in a public ceremony at the Vietnam Veterans Memorial in Washington, the army awarded the Soldier's Medal to Hugh Thompson and his helicopter crew in recognition of their efforts to rescue some of the inhabitants of My Lai (4).[81] Thompson was also invited to address cadets at the service academies at West Point, Annapolis and Colorado Springs.[82] Yet it had taken several years for the army to respond positively to the suggestion – first made by a college professor in 1991 – that Thompson's actions at My Lai (4) merited a medal. 'We would be putting an ugly, controversial, and horrible story on the media's table,' observed one officer in the Pentagon who reviewed the proposal.[83] Army leaders were conscious, however, that, as its thirtieth anniversary approached, the massacre would attract media attention whatever they did. If silence was impossible, then the next best thing would be acts of commemoration that cast the massacre as aberrance. To award medals to Hugh Thompson and his crew was to emphasize that good people did serve in Vietnam, even at My Lai (4), and that the army had changed and learned lessons from its past.

'The details of the events of that day were thoroughly investigated,' asserted Major General Michael Ackerman in his speech at the ceremony,

[78] *Ibid.*; S. Hersh, 'Torture at Abu Ghraib', *New Yorker* (10 May 2004); J. Tapper and C. Sandell, 'Advice rejected: JAG lawyers say political appointees ignored their warnings on prisoner treatment', *ABC News*, 16 May 2004: http://abcnews.go.com (accessed August 2004).

[79] Dr Conrad Crane, interview with author, Carlisle, PA, 27 August 2003; C. Carter, 'Memories of My Lai all but forgotten in Calley's hometown', *Associated Press* (13 March 1998).

[80] *CNN Worldview*, 16 March 1998, VTNA.

[81] Angers, p. 32.

[82] *Ibid.*, p. 205.

[83] *Ibid.*, pp. 15–16, 24.

'and from those recommendations the Army was able to look at itself and take corrective action to ensure My Lai would never happen again. And it has not happened again.'[84] Of course, what the army was seeking to redress by means of the medals was an injustice done to Americans. The time for redressing those perpetrated upon the villagers of Son My, and upon the many other victims of US atrocities in Vietnam, seemed to have passed, if indeed there had ever really existed such a time. 'The case is more than 30 years old,' observed an army spokesman in 2003, announcing that the original investigation into the serial crimes committed by Tiger Force platoon in Quang Ngai and Quang Nam would not be reopened.[85]

Neither the government nor the military, then, cared much to remind the American public of what had happened in Son My, or more broadly of the torments suffered by the people of South Vietnam as a result of the war the US had chosen to fight on their land. Indeed, there were very few institutions or caucuses in the United States that maintained a commitment to those particular memories of the war. With the fall of Saigon, the anti-war movement, already much depleted in numbers and in influence, found its purpose finally exhausted, and whatever affects of solidarity its residual enclaves still nurtured with respect to the Vietnamese became in time somewhat chastened, because the post-war regime in Vietnam was not that easy to love.[86] For as long as travel and communication between the two countries remained subject to restrictions by both governments, the Vietnamese voices heard most often in the United States were those of exiles and refugees, victims of the revolution, not the American war.[87] The survivors of Son My lacked biographers in 1969, and they have not acquired any since, unlike – for example – Kim Phuc, the girl famously photographed running down a road after the South Vietnamese air force discharged napalm on her village, whose story – physically and ideologically – became more accessible to Americans when she left behind her life as a symbol of revolutionary martyrdom and defected to Canada.[88]

---

[84] *Ibid.*, pp. 46–7.

[85] *New York Times* (28 December 2003), p. 18.

[86] DeBenedetti, pp. 380–3; P. Collier and D. Horowitz, *Destructive Generation: Second Thoughts about the '60s* (New York: Summit Books, 1990), pp. 174–6.

[87] See, for example, A. Santoli, *To Bear Any Burden: The Vietnam War and Its Aftermath in the Words of Americans and Southeast Asians* (Bloomington: Indiana University Press, 1999); and D. Chanoff and D. Van Toai, *'Vietnam': A Portrait of its People at War* (New York: I.B. Tauris, 1996). These books were first published, respectively, in 1985 and 1987. If one Vietnamese figure has featured prominently in American culture since 1975, it is Le Ly Hayslip, author of two autobiographies which describe her vicissitudinous existence in war-time Vietnam (including her rape by Vietcong guerrillas) and, from 1970 onwards, in the United States. L. Hayslip (with J. Wurts), *When Heaven and Earth Changed Places* (London: Pan Books, 1991); L. Hayslip (with J. Hayslip), *Child of War, Woman of Peace* (London: Pan Books, 1994). In 1993, Hayslip's life became the subject of a major Hollywood motion picture. *Heaven & Earth* dir. Oliver Stone (1993).

[88] D. Chong, *The Girl in the Picture: The Story of Kim Phuc, the Photograph, and the Vietnam War* (London: Scribner, 2001).

.

If Americans were to be reminded about the atrocities committed by their soldiers in Vietnam, it would probably have to be by the soldiers themselves. For veterans to speak such a memory would have been consistent, after all, with the initiatives that some of them had taken at the time of the massacre controversy, believing that, when properly informed about what was happening in Vietnam, the American people would bring the national intervention immediately to a close, and hoping also that, by offering their own experiences to that end, they could salvage some measure of personal meaning from their participation in what they now regarded as a morally indefensible war. It has become part of American folklore that the veterans succeeded too well, not so much in their efforts to mobilize public sentiment in favour of withdrawal, but rather in the validation that they gave to the political and cultural conflation of military service in Vietnam with an intimate knowledge of the very worst that man can do. Hence the regular invocation of what sociologist Jerry Lembcke has termed 'the spitting image': usually apocryphal accounts of returning veterans greeted by volleys of saliva and cries of 'babykiller' from radical anti-war activists.[89]

That those who served in Vietnam could not escape popular association with atrocity seemed to be confirmed in the mid-1970s, when motion picture producers and audiences alike briefly developed a taste for the character of the psychotic veteran, intent now on perpetrating massacres back home.[90] Clinical discussions about Vietnam veterans, meanwhile, still continue to reflect the two propositions originally advanced by Robert Jay Lifton in the last few years of the war: that these veterans had found it more difficult to readjust to civilian existence than had soldiers returning from earlier American wars, and that often the origin of their difficulties lay in the experience of atrocity. According to one extensive investigation, a 'substantial minority' of Vietnam veterans reported psychological symptoms 'severe enough to be called a disorder', whilst almost two million suffered from 'less acute forms of distress'.[91]

In 1980, as a result of concerted campaigning by Lifton and other veterans advocates, post-traumatic stress disorder (PTSD) was incorporated into the diagnostic manual of the American Psychiatric Association, and thereafter a series of clinical studies indicated that (self-reported) participation in atrocity was the 'combat stressor' that correlated most commonly with diagnosis of the disorder in Vietnam veterans.[92] Although the image

---

[89] J. Lembcke, *The Spitting Image: Myth, Memory, and the Legacy of Vietnam* (New York: New York University Press, 1998).

[90] *Tracks*, dir. Henry Jaglom (1976); *Taxi Driver*, dir. Martin Scorsese (1976); *Black Sunday*, dir. John Frankenheimer (1977).

[91] Egendorf, p. 2.

[92] N. Breslau and G. Davis, 'Posttraumatic stress disorder: the etiologic specificity of wartime stressors', *American Journal of Psychiatry*, 144 (1987), pp. 578–83. See also R. Yeruda, S. Southwich and E. Giller, 'Exposure to atrocities and severity of chronic posttraumatic stress disorder in Vietnam combat veterans', *American Journal of Psychiatry*, 149 (1992), pp. 333–6.

of the psychotic (as opposed to merely troubled) veteran faded rather quickly from the national culture, atrocity narratives did not, featuring prominently in oral history collections like Mark Baker's *Nam*, in popular studies of the war's emotional legacies like Myra McPherson's *Long Time Passing*, and also in veterans' memoirs, novels and films, most notably Philip Caputo's *A Rumor of War*, Tim O'Brien's *In the Lake of the Woods*, and Oliver Stone's *Platoon*.[93] For some veterans, indeed, the culture was talking too much of atrocity, at a cost of forgetting the many thousands of American soldiers who had fought conscientiously and with honour.[94] They found it impossible to forgive those of their comrades who had come home from the war and publicly condemned its conduct as immoral, as John Kerry – one-time VVAW spokesman – discovered when campaigning for the White House in autumn 2004.[95]

Once again, a marked failure of perspective is evident in the complaint that a persistent and exaggerated memory of wartime atrocities has worked to deprive Vietnam veterans of the recognition and appreciation that had previously accrued to Americans returning from active military service. Since at least the dedication of the Vietnam Veterans Memorial on the hallowed ground of the Washington Mall in November 1982, the words, images and rituals which have tended to be used to commemorate the conflict have attributed to those who fought it the same qualities of moral purpose, patriotic duty and selfless sacrifice conventionally attributed to the soldiers of earlier national campaigns. At one of the entrances to the memorial stands a 60-foot flagpole, ringed by the legend: 'THIS FLAG REPRESENTS THE SERVICE RENDERED TO OUR COUNTRY BY THE VETERANS OF THE VIETNAM WAR. THE FLAG AFFIRMS THE PRINCIPLES OF FREEDOM FOR WHICH THEY FOUGHT AND THEIR PRIDE IN HAVING SERVED UNDER DIFFICULT CIRCUMSTANCES.'[96]

The tone of the memorial may be mournful and subdued, but the knowledge that makes it so, inscribed 58,000 times, name by name, in reflective black granite, is a knowledge alone of American loss. That the veterans of the war, wittingly or unwittingly, had invested their labour and their promise in a cause that was only obliquely related to 'the principles of freedom', and which effected a waste of countless thousands of Vietnamese lives and millions of acres of Vietnamese land, was too insolent an assessment for so reverent a commemorative venture.[97] Accordingly, John Kerry – though not formally disavowing the sentiments he

[93] T. O'Brien, *In the Lake of the Woods* (New York: Penguin, 1995); *Platoon*, dir. Oliver Stone (1986).

[94] B. Burkett and G. Whitley, *Stolen Valor: How the Vietnam Generation Was Robbed of Its Heroes and Its History* (Dallas: Verity Press, Inc., 1998).

[95] J. O'Neill and J. Corsi, *Unfit for Command: Swift Boat Veterans Speak Out Against John Kerry* (Washington, DC: Regnery Publishing, 2004); M. Dobbs, 'Swift boats accounts incomplete', *Washington Post* (22 August 2004), p. A01.

[96] Turner, pp. 179–80.

[97] Sturken, pp. 82–3.

expressed during his time with the VVAW, just some of the words that he used – found it more convenient as a presidential candidate to emphasize the choice he made to serve in the war, rather than his public declaration upon return that veterans were 'ashamed of and hated what we were called to do in Southeast Asia'.[98]

Many American soldiers, of course, had never been much concerned by what they were called to do in south-east Asia, and following the US withdrawal, even those who were seemed to rechannel the flow of their pity away from the Vietnamese back to themselves, invoking an image of the veteran as a victim rather than agent of the war. Whether or not they judged the conflict to have been just, the veterans of Vietnam could find reason to consider themselves unfortunate: for not being furnished, as their fathers' generation had been in the Second World War, with a decent cause to fight, or for not being permitted to win and thereafter return home to the ticker-tape parades that, again, their fathers had enjoyed after the surrenders of Germany and Japan.[99] Whatever motivated public ambivalence towards the war in which they had served – the belief that it had been waged in error or disappointment at its outcome – the veterans felt it keenly. In 1984, Myra McPherson observed: 'In interviews with hundreds of veterans – from the most successful to the least well-adjusted – I have yet to find one who did not suffer rage, anger, and frustration at the way the country received them.'[100]

It was not difficult, moreover, for many veterans to start reading that ambivalence into what they perceived as institutional resistance to or chronic under-resourcing of programmes that might assist in alleviating their post-war problems of adjustment. There were undoubtedly imperfections in programme provision: in the late 1960s, the medical facilities operated by the Veterans Administration were organized primarily to meet the requirements – which were, by this time, mostly unconnected to military service – of those who had fought in the Second World War. For many years thereafter, the traditional veterans' associations obstructed the process of restructuring care by insisting that existing budgets were sacrosanct, and that the specific needs of Vietnam veterans had to be addressed through the allocation of additional funds or else not at all.[101] It was only in 1979 that Congress granted monies for the establishment of a network of centres in which veterans could receive psychological counselling – a particular priority for the men who had served in Vietnam,

[98] 'Statement of John Kerry, Vietnam Veterans Against the War', 22 April 1971, in US Congress, Senate, Committee on Foreign Relations, *Legislative Proposals Relating to the War in Southeast Asia*, p. 181; 'Kerry's 1971 testimony on Vietnam reverberates', *CNN.com* (23 April 2004): www.cnn.com (accessed August 2004); 'Text of John Kerry's acceptance speech at the Democratic National Convention', *washingtonpost.com* (29 July 2004): www.washingtonpost.com (accessed August 2004).
[99] McPherson, pp. 57–8.
[100] *Ibid.*, pp. 54–5.
[101] Scott, pp. 8, 39.

according to the programme's advocates.[102] Yet the package of benefits and care made available to these veterans was far more generous and extensive than that offered to most ordinary Americans, whilst also exceeding by several degrees anything that inhabitants of post-war Vietnam could hope ever to receive.[103] For example, following a long and aggressive campaign by the Vietnam Veterans of America (VVA), the Veterans Administration agreed to pay service-related disability benefits to over 10,000 former military personnel on the presumption that their illnesses were connected to war-time exposure to Agent Orange, though the scientific evidence informing that presumption remains fairly fragmentary and inconclusive. On much the same basis, of course, there is a case for awarding compensation to hundreds of thousands of Vietnamese citizens, but few American veterans, it seems, have bothered to make it.[104]

It is the attribution of post-traumatic stress disorder to veterans who committed atrocities in Vietnam, however, which establishes the ground for potentially the most treacherous inversion of moral logic and identity. The clinical ideologies which informed the passage of the disorder into the formal medical literature, and which continue to be reflected in diagnostic practice, have been criticized for the licence they offer to psychiatric professionals to identify veterans, and to veterans to identify themselves, as the victims of trauma.[105] To improvise still further, as some therapists do, by asserting an equivalence between the perpetrators of combat atrocities and those, for example, who may have suffered childhood abuse (an analogy enforced in part by the increasingly contested notion of repressed traumatic memory) is not only to displace the actual victims of atrocity from the primary locus of concern, but also to imply that the perpetrators' memories of what they had done, like any other kind of pathogen, could and should be treated and cured.[106] Writing about their work with Vietnam veterans, therapists have insisted that, if the traumas of the war are to be 'healed', they must first be communalized, a process which can only begin when the veteran possesses the confidence that he can tell his story without

---

[102] *Ibid.*, p. 69.

[103] E. Dean, *Shook Over Hell: Post-Traumatic Stress, Vietnam, and the Civil War* (Cambridge: Harvard University Press, 1997), p. 185.

[104] Scott, pp. 120, 207–9, 222–3; T. Fawthrop, 'Vietnam's war against Agent Orange', *BBC News: World Edition*, 14 June 2004: http://news.bbc.co.uk (accessed August 2004); Institute of Medicine: Committee to Review the Health Effects in Vietnam Veterans of Exposure to Herbicides, *Veterans and Agent Orange: Update 2000* (Washington, DC: National Academy Press, 2001), pp. 6–12.

[105] Dean, pp. 180–209; A. Young, *The Harmony of Illusions: Inventing Post-Traumatic Stress Disorder* (Princeton: Princeton University Press, 1995).

[106] J. Herman, *Trauma and Recovery: from Domestic Abuse to Political Terror* (London: Pandora, 2001). For critiques of the notion of repressed memory, see E. Showalter, *Hystories: Hysterical Epidemics and Modern Culture* (London: Picador, 1997), pp. 144–58; and S. Brandon, J. Boakes, D. Glaser and R. Green, 'Recovered memories of childhood sexual abuse: implications for clinical practice', *British Journal of Psychiatry*, 172 (1998), pp. 296–307.

fear of being judged.[107] Yet there are surely some stories – such as those told by the soldiers who killed the inhabitants of My Lai (4) – that must require even therapists to offer a moral judgement, to inform the veteran in question that it is entirely appropriate that he should feel pain and distress when reflecting upon his deeds: that it is not a cure that he must seek, but an opportunity to make reparation to his victims.[108]

Not all Vietnam veterans implicated in atrocities subsequently found it difficult to live with the memory of their actions.[109] In the years following the massacre at My Lai (4), the soldiers of Charlie Company experienced remorse and distress in very different measures: some affected insouciance, others were rendered infirm. 'I have regrets for it,' Ernest Medina told a journalist in 1988, 'but I have no guilt over it because I didn't cause it.'[110] Kenneth Hodges also seemed utterly unrepentant. Interviewed on the British television documentary, *Four Hours In My Lai*, he declared: 'I feel we did not violate any moral standards.'[111] According to a report in *People* magazine, however, Hodges was a recovering alcoholic and slept with the lights on.[112] 'It's just something you've got to live with,' commented Paul Meadlo, who lost his right foot to a mine the day after the massacre. 'It's rough. Eventually you just got to cross it out of your mind and go on with your life.'[113] On occasion, reporters visiting Columbus, Georgia – William Calley's home town – would be told by Calley's friends that he was still troubled by his experiences in Vietnam and later during his trial, but also that he had come to terms with his conscience and now lived for the most part a contented, comfortable life: indeed, if he appeared tormented by anything, it was the knowledge that, as every significant anniversary approached, reporters like themselves would venture into his jewellery store and attempt to ask him questions about the massacre.[114]

'I'm told that Calley has the American dream,' asserted James Bergthold in 1989. 'What makes him different than me?' Bergthold claimed to have committed only mercy killings in My Lai (4), but his life since the massacre had been punctuated by addictions to drink and drugs, flashbacks and nightmares, long periods of unemployment, marital problems and thoughts

[107] Shay, pp. 188–9; Egendorf, pp. 51–2.

[108] For a similar argument, see P. Marin, 'Living in moral pain', in W. Capps (ed.), *The Vietnam Reader* (New York: Routledge, 1991), pp. 40–53.

[109] R. Laufer, E. Brett and M. Gallops, 'Symptom patterns associated with posttraumatic stress disorder among Vietnam veterans exposed to war trauma', *American Journal of Psychiatry*, 142 (1985), 1304–11; R. McNally, *Remembering Trauma* (Cambridge, MA: The Belknap Press of Harvard University Press, 2003), p. 87.

[110] G. Esper, 'Soldiers look back at My Lai 20 years later', *Associated Press* (13 March 1988).

[111] *Four Hours in My Lai*, dir. Kevin Sim (1989).

[112] C. Unger and B. Hewitt, 'William Calley: convicted of the My Lai slaughter of innocents, he lives a middle-class life, far from Vietnam', *People* (20 November 1989).

[113] Esper, 'Soldiers look back . . .', *Associated Press* (13 March 1988).

[114] Unger and Hewitt, 'William Calley: convicted of the My Lai slaughter . . .', *People* (20 November 1989).

of suicide. He admitted that he was overprotective of his children: 'You think about what you did, and here you've got kids of your own. The wondering puts a lot of mental strain on you. Maybe God isn't finished punishing me yet.'[115]

The previous year, Robert T'Souvas – responsible for the deaths of at least five women and children in My Lai (4) – had been shot and killed by his wife. Both homeless alcoholics, the couple had been living in a make-shift shelter under a bridge in Pittsburgh. T'Souvas's father explained to reporters that his son 'had problems with Vietnam over and over. He didn't talk about it much. But he had problems with body counts, things like that. He lasted 20 years, but he was walking a tight line.'[116] Around the same time, Varnado Simpson was interviewed by the makers of *Four Hours in My Lai* at his home in Jackson, Mississippi. Diagnosed with post-traumatic stress disorder, with several bottles of powerful medication lying on a table closeby, Simpson seemed to be a man entirely trapped by his past, by the knowledge that the massacre had provided of his own capacity for violence: 'There's more destructiveness in my mind than goodness. There's more wanting to kill or to hurt than to love or to care.' Simpson, however, was as fearful of others as he was of himself: 'I have burglar bars all over my house, on my doors and my windows and I still put furniture behind the door because I think someone is trying to get in to get me, or they're trying to get in to get me – the people from Vietnam.' He could not escape his condition even through suicide, having tried three times and failed. 'Maybe the man, the good Lord, is not ready for me to go,' he said.[117]

Whatever it was that his doctors had tried to do for Varnado Simpson, it seemed not to have worked, probably in part because their diagnosis of trauma, allied with the insistence of veterans and their advocates that civilian America had not fulfilled its responsibilities to those who served in Vietnam, had left him profoundly confused about his own moral identity. ('They use you, and once they're through with you, you're cast to the side,' he complained.)[118] Simpson judged himself to be both a perpetrator and a victim, and in the conflicting moral logics of those two identifications lay the likely source of his paralysis. Grievance obscured the obligations of guilt. Just as the veterans of Vietnam never really became the agents of the wider social changes predicted by some of their advocates, because the imperatives of 'healing' were too amorphous to apply to any programme of reform beyond the service of their own immediate interests, so Simpson was denuded of the means with which to compass the true dimensions of

[115] *Ibid.*

[116] *New York Times* (14 September 1988), p. A22.

[117] Bilton and Sim, pp. 5–8; *Four Hours in My Lai*, dir. Kevin Sim (1989); Transcript of filmed interview with Varnado Simpson, 26 September 1988, folder: My Lai 2/9, Papers of *Four Hours in My Lai*, LHCMA, KCL.

[118] Transcript of filmed interview with Varnado Simpson, 26 September 1988, folder: My Lai 2/9, Papers of *Four Hours in My Lai*, LHCMA, KCL.

his guilt, and unable as a result to restore purpose and meaning to his life by converting his memories of the massacre into a resource for constructive penance.[119]

Because they have not felt the need, or because they have not recognized the need for what it really was, the former soldiers of Charlie Company have, it seems, made no attempt to offer redress for the harm they inflicted upon the people of Son My village. Of course, it would not have been easy, given the restrictions that the US government imposed upon the provision of assistance to Vietnam. Still, a number of their countrymen, including some who served in the war, have since the end of the conflict registered an obligation to aid the survivors of the massacre. In the late 1970s, private contributions from nearly 13,000 Americans funded the construction of a 100-bed hospital close to the site of the massacre.[120] Ten years later, a new clinic was built by a charity called the International Mission of Hope, led by Cherie Clark, who had worked as a paediatric nurse in Vietnam during the final years of the war.[121] Visiting Son My to lay the foundation stone of the clinic, one of Clark's associates, a former Marine, told the British writer Justin Wintle that he had been 'overwhelmed by the forgiveness' that he had encountered in Vietnam.[122]

In 1992, a group of California veterans travelled to Son My to instal a solar-powered generator at the hospital.[123] Money to finance its day-to-day functions as well as its maintenance, however, arrived only irregularly, and many of the clinic's rooms remained empty or short of basic equipment.[124] Backed by a group of Quakers from Madison, Wisconsin, another US veteran, Mike Boehm, raised $15,000 to establish a revolving loan scheme, which has provided over 400 of the village's women with the capital they needed to start and operate their own small businesses. Boehm and the Quakers have also funded extensions to the existing school facilities in Son My, including a new twenty-room primary school, as well as a local 'peace park' where children could play and where others could 'meditate over the past with its suffering and losses and also to hope for a better future'.[125] The International Mission of Hope, accompanied by teams from Veterans for Peace and the Medics of Illinois, visited Son My again in June 2001 to deliver medical supplies to the clinic, build a kitchen and replace its window shutters with glass.[126] Unfortunately, less than two

[119] Lifton, pp. 381–408; Egendorf, pp. 249–95.

[120] *Associated Press* (16 March 1978); e-mail from Cora Weiss to author, 2 December 2004.

[121] *United Press International* (30 April 1990).

[122] Wintle, p. 266.

[123] Veterans Vietnam Restoration Project, 'Team VI, 1992: My Lai': www.vvrp.org/ (accessed August 2004).

[124] H. Kamm, *Dragon Ascending: Vietnam and the Vietnamese* (New York: Arcade Publishing, 1996), pp. 9–10.

[125] For details of these projects, see: www.mylaipeacepark.org/ (accessed August 2004).

[126] T. Gale, 'A returning veteran to Viet Nam says "It is great to be alive"', 4 July 2001: www.veteransforpeace.org/vietnamreturn.htm (accessed August 2004).

years later, the charity closed down all of its operations in Vietnam, and ended its sponsorship of the clinic, following a dispute with the US Immigration and Naturalization Service over its adoption programme in the country.[127]

Although the attempts of these veterans, and the organizations to which they belong, to make amends for the wreckage caused by the war have occasionally attracted the attention of the national media back home, it has not been the Vietnamese experience of American violence that has primarily interested American culture, but rather the meaning of that violence for its immediate agents and authors: that is, American soldiers.[128] The same preoccupation is evident in many of the contributions made by veterans themselves to cultural production on the war.

Veterans' narratives have frequently conformed to the model of the *Bildungsroman*: the soldier enters the war in a state of innocence, encounters its violence and is changed by it, eventually to return to 'the world' with a more profound understanding of himself and his comrades, and of human nature in general. In these narratives, it is often an instance of atrocity that initiates the conversion of experience into wisdom. 'I turned the crank a couple of times myself,' one veteran told Mark Baker, describing the use of a field telephone to deliver an electric shock to a Vietnamese prisoner. 'I feel bad about that. The thing that I feel the worst about was that my own humanity was called into question, my own values, my own sense of myself as a moral, righteous person. I was defrocked. I was exposed as a barbarian along with all the rest.'[129] *Nam*, Baker's anthology of interviews with veterans (none of them identified), is structured as if it is a collective memoir, in four quasi-chronological sections, beginning with 'Initiation' (accounts of enlistment, training and arrival in Vietnam), and followed by 'Operations' (accounts of day-to-day existence in the combat zone), 'War Stories' (accounts of atrocities committed against the Vietnamese and of the death and wounding of comrades), and finally 'The World' (accounts of return and readjustment). Baker thus inscribes the commission of atrocity into the default narrative of military service in Vietnam, presenting it almost as a normative stage in what he asserts to have been 'the ritual passage to adulthood for a generation of Americans'.[130]

In his best-selling memoir *A Rumor of War*, Philip Caputo recalls how, as a young officer in Vietnam in 1966, his anger and frustration accumulated to the point that he ordered a patrol to capture or kill two Vietcong suspects in a local village, making it clear that he would feel no personal regret if capture proved not to be an option. When the patrol shot the wrong men, Caputo was charged with murder, though the charges were

[127] C. Clark, 'Viet Nam Update', 16 April 2002: www.imh-vn.org; 'Viet Nam Update', 6 January 2003: www.imh-vn.org (accessed August 2004).
[128] See, for example, *ABC News*, 10 June 1990, VTNA.
[129] Baker, pp. 152–3.
[130] *Ibid.*, p. xiv.

eventually dropped. Convinced that the conflict was unwinnable, he nevertheless also considered it to have been an instructive experience, for others as well as for himself. What he and his fellow soldiers had come to understand, he said, was that 'war, by its nature, can arouse a psychopathic violence in men of seemingly normal impulses'.[131] That lesson learnt, they returned home from Vietnam as 'peculiar creatures, with young shoulders that bore rather old heads'.[132]

Chris Taylor, the principal character in Oliver Stone's *Platoon*, receives much the same kind of moral education. It is an utterly unfamiliar, treacherous world that he enters upon arrival in Vietnam: the heat is oppressive and the jungle foliage lacerating; snakes sidle around his feet; men attempt to climb a ridge, then tumble back down. His training seems useless, his equipment a burden. It is not an officer who offers leadership to Taylor's platoon, but two sergeants, Elias and Barnes, who are engaged in their own war of personality and purpose. Soldiers are lost to booby traps; another is captured and killed, and his mutilated corpse is later discovered close to a village reportedly used as a base by the North Vietnamese. Internal and external restraints upon the behaviour of the platoon begin to disintegrate. Entering the village, Barnes shoots a man seen running away in the distance. He tosses a grenade into a still-occupied bunker. Taylor finds a woman and her one-legged son hiding underneath a hooch. Frustrated and resentful because he cannot make himself understood, he fires his gun repeatedly at the young man's foot, forcing him to hop up and down: 'Dance, motherfucker!' It is an important scene, for it implicates the audience in Taylor's violence by extension of the empathetic identification they have made with him hitherto.[133] After a few seconds, however, Taylor stops firing, and starts to weep in horror at what he has done. Another soldier, Bunny – who declares later that he is enjoying the war because it gives him the freedom to do whatever he wants – steps forward and clubs the man to death with the butt of his rifle. They move outside, to where Barnes is interrogating a village elder. He shoots the man's wife, irritated at her protests, and threatens to kill his daughter. Taylor watches, appalled, but cannot will himself to intervene. Much of the platoon has become impatient for massacre. 'Let's go for it,' one soldier cries. 'Let's do the whole fucking village!'[134]

Atrocity is averted, indeed, only by the intervention of Elias, also critical to the narrative, because it reminds both Taylor and the film's audience

[131] Caputo, pp. xvii–iii.

[132] *Ibid.*, p. xv.

[133] For useful discussions of this scene, see M. Taylor, *The Vietnam War in History, Literature and Film* (Edinburgh: Edinburgh University Press, 2003), pp. 119–21; and M. Hammond, 'Some smothering dreams: the combat film in contemporary Hollywood', in S. Neale (ed.), *Genre and Contemporary Hollywood* (London: British Film Institute, 2002), pp. 67–8.

[134] *Platoon*, dir. Oliver Stone (1986).

that it is possible to act morally even in the conditions of war. As the platoon prepares to depart the village, Taylor himself assumes a measure of moral agency, as he was not able to earlier, rescuing a girl from a group of soldiers bent on her rape. When Elias is killed by Barnes, it is Taylor who becomes the instrument of justice, killing Barnes in turn, and restoring balance thereby to the moral order that prevails in what is left of the platoon. In a retrospective peroration, delivered over the image of him leaving the war, the veteran Chris Taylor asserts that 'those of us who did make it have an obligation to build again, to teach to others what we know, and to try with what's left of our lives to find a goodness and a meaning to this life'. The knowledge he has acquired, however, is a knowledge so hard-won that it cannot admit it is not enough. It is a knowledge only of America, as if – for all the atrocities in the village, for all the incredible violence of the encounter between Taylor's platoon and the North Vietnamese at the conclusion of the film – it was only the outcome of the struggle between good and evil for his own and his nation's soul that really mattered in Vietnam, with every other consequence reduced to the status of collateral damage. 'I think now, looking back, we did not fight the enemy. We fought ourselves, and the enemy was in us.'

In stark contrast, the only novel by a veteran to deal explicitly and substantially with the My Lai massacre itself – Tim O'Brien's *In the Lake of the Woods* – resists both the model of the *Bildungsroman* and the sententious metaphysics that structure *Platoon*. It features a search for knowledge, but not much can be learnt; nor can the mysteries be safely contained by reference to a transcendent discourse. During the Minnesota Democratic primary race for the US Senate in 1986, John Wade – a hitherto successful state politician – is revealed to have been involved in the killings at My Lai (4). He loses the race, and retreats with his wife Kathy to a remote cabin in the Lake of the Woods, in the north of the state. Kathy disappears, and an investigation ensues. Probably Wade has killed her, possibly he has not. He himself does not seem to know. A month or so later, Wade also disappears, although for a few days thereafter he continues to broadcast 'rambling incantations' over the radio of his boat, somewhere on the lake.[135]

The novel has a narrator, also a veteran, who shares much of his biography with O'Brien the author, and who 'craves to know what cannot be known': what John Wade did and why he did it.[136] He compiles and presents (complete with footnoted references) evidence documenting Wade's life, including extracts from the report of the Peers commission and Richard Hammer's chronicle of the Calley court martial, though elements of this material – for example, quotations from histories of the Indian wars or from clinical discussions of trauma – also seem to imply a broader set of

---

135 O'Brien, *In the Lake of the Woods*, p. 302.
136 *Ibid.*, p. 295, fn. 124.

explanations and contexts. He constructs a series of hypotheses about Kathy's disappearance, some of which progressively shed the conditional idiom of speculation ('Maybe . . .') until they read like the work of an omniscient narrator. There are also chapters of apparently conventional narration, providing an account of Wade's life from childhood, through college and his early romance with Kathy, through his service in Vietnam and the killings at My Lai (4), through his return from war, his marriage and his political career, that must themselves be hypotheses. The narrator is not omniscient: there are many details of the story he is telling that he could not have known.

What the reader can salvage from these reconstructions is probably not knowledge, but certain elements of the narrative seem more reliable than others: that Wade was damaged before he went to Vietnam by an alcoholic father who had shown him no love, who had also committed suicide when his son was fourteen; that he was damaged by the massacre, by his experience of shooting an old man carrying a wooden hoe and, later, of somehow coming to stand in the killing ditch, knee-deep in slime, from where he also shot one of his fellow soldiers; that he was further damaged in the years following the massacre by the strain of secrecy, guilt and repression; and that finally he was damaged, upon the public disclosure of his involvement, by the realization that his efforts to disguise (or defer) the moral wreckage of his life with a political career had all been for naught.

The novel thus invites empathy for John Wade – it would not work without it – but it does not ask for forgiveness or pity. The narrator, who had also served in Quang Ngai, admits that – knowing local people were complicit in the loss of his friends to booby traps and mines – he had personally felt 'the butchery sizzling like grease just under my eyeballs'. Yet he does not seek to justify the actions of Charlie Company, 'for in my view such justifications are both futile and outrageous'.[137] As Tim O'Brien himself has declared elsewhere: 'There were no mitigating circumstances. It was mass murder.'[138] John Wade never really attempts to atone for his behaviour in My Lai (4). Occasionally, he had thought of politics 'as a medium of apology, a way of salvaging something in himself and in the world', but that was not the primary motive behind his venture into politics, which was instead his need for love.[139] Later, if Wade displays any sorrow, it is only because Kathy, his one remaining source of love, is gone. There is no justice or redemption in his story, no healing, transcendence or closure. The novel concludes with the image of Wade heading north in his boat, across the endless horizon of the Lake of the Woods, 'weaving from island to island, skimming fast between water and sky'.[140]

---

137 *Ibid.*, p. 199.
138 O'Brien, 'The mystery of My Lai', in Anderson, p. 173.
139 O'Brien, *In the Lake of the Woods*, p. 152.
140 *Ibid.*, p. 303.

Like most of the contributions made by American veterans to the national memory of the Vietnam war, *In the Lake of the Woods* does not dwell upon its legacies for the Vietnamese.[141] O'Brien is unusual and conscientious, however, in his resistance to the lachrymose revisionism that converts Americans into the principal victims of their own atrocities; or the claim that there was a higher human wisdom to be extracted from an encounter with atrocity that somehow compensated for all the harm that had been done; or the proposition that atrocity represented the sort of experience of moral challenge that was essential if Americans were to make their way to a mature state of national virtue. For the most part, Vietnam veterans have not functioned as custodians of the conflict's moral memory; they have tended to seek the redemption only of the moral debts that were owed to themselves.

The record of academic historians and other writers on the conflict in recommending the subject of atrocity, and the killings in Son My in particular, to the attention of the American public, and in offering a model of analysis that does not invite too easy a resolution, has been similarly rather mixed. The conflict, of course, did not begin in Son My, nor did it end there, and those attempting to reconstruct the broad course of its history, therefore, confront the formidable task of measuring the massacre's significance, in itself and as an example of wider trends and themes, relative to all the countless other items of available narrative content. In such general histories, the massacre only rarely compels more than a paragraph or two, presented as evidence of the brutality of the fighting after the Tet offensive, or of the moral degeneration that could occur in conditions of counter-insurgency.[142] Assessing its consequence thus, historians become prone to the errors of inattention. Robert Schulzinger, for example, places Quang Ngai province to the north, not the south, of Danang, and asserts that the troops under Lieutenant Calley's immediate command were responsible for the deaths of over five hundred civilians and that the story was eventually broken by Seymour Hersh in the *New York Times*.[143]

More assiduous efforts to explore the lessons and meanings of what happened in Son My have been made by a number of scholars and commentators, but few have managed to move much beyond the ethnocentricity that has conventionally characterized American discussions of the massacre. In 1994, for example, Tulane University hosted a conference on My Lai, organized in an innovative round-table format to permit

---

[141] O'Brien does, however, discuss those legacies, and criticize his nation's solipsism, in an article describing his visit to Vietnam (including the site of the My Lai massacre) in 1994: O'Brien, 'The Vietnam in me', *New York Times Magazine* (2 October 1994).

[142] See, for example, G. Herring, *America's Longest War: The United States and Vietnam 1950–1975* (New York: Alfred A. Knopf, 1986), p. 215; R. Schulzinger, *A Time for War: The United States and Vietnam, 1941–1975* (New York: Oxford University Press, 1997), p. 262; G. DeGroot, *A Noble Cause? America and the Vietnam War* (Harlow: Longman, 2000), pp. 295–6.

[143] Schulzinger, pp. 262, 283.

free-flowing exchanges between invited speakers, who included Hugh
Thompson, Ronald Ridenhour, Seymour Hersh, Robert Lifton and Tim
O'Brien. It was a format that was evocative of the early veteran rap groups,
as was the stated aim of the conference: that participants should 'openly
confront and analyze harsh facts about their society in a shared effort to
heal both personal and national trauma'.[144] As some speakers pointed out,
however, there was something evasive and self-absorbed about the efforts
of Americans to 'heal' their own 'wounds' from the massacre when they had
so conspicuously failed to secure justice for the principal victims – the
villagers of Son My – and to make proper reparation for their suffering. 'I
don't think that the wounds should be healed,' Tim O'Brien declared. 'We
live in this weird culture where we think everything can be helped and
healed, even if somebody goes out and shoots someone. I think we've
healed the wounds too well, if anything. The country has obliterated the
horror that was Vietnam. To the Vietnamese people who lost whole families or lost legs and arms, we've healed it too damn well.'[145]

Perhaps the most significant contribution to American popular memory
of the massacre, indeed, has been made by two British writers and broadcasters, Michael Bilton and Kevin Sim, initially in their 1989 television
documentary *Four Hours in My Lai*, retitled *Remember My Lai* for its
showing on the PBS network in the United States, and subsequently, three
years later, in a book, *Four Hours in My Lai*, published by Penguin.
Bilton had first become interested in the massacre when he lighted upon
a copy of the Peers commission report.[146] A consultant hired to assess the
feasibility of making a film on the subject advised him that, since the
publication of that report, nothing very much had been written about
the massacre: as a result, 'many people today either don't know the full
story, or have forgotten it'.[147]

From the documentary itself, two main themes emerge: the 'psychology
of slaughter' (how it was that the massacre occurred) and the inability of
most of those involved, victims and perpetrators alike, to come to terms
with what they had experienced that March morning in My Lai (4).[148]
The origins of the massacre, the film suggests, lay in the training that had
been received by the soldiers of Charlie Company. Contemporary images
of troop instruction at Fort Benning, presenting young recruits practising
thrusts of their bayonets and shouting 'Kill!' as they did so, illustrate the
assertion of Kenneth Hodges, recorded in voice-over, that the purpose of
military training is to convert civilians into killers.[149] Hodges, who had

[144] Anderson, p. xii.
[145] *Ibid.*, pp. 176–7.
[146] Angers, p. 193.
[147] Himelfarb, 'The My Lai Massacre: Preliminary Report', undated, folder: My Lai 8/73,
Papers of *Four Hours in My Lai*, LHCMA, KCL.
[148] *Ibid.*
[149] *Four Hours in My Lai*, dir. Kevin Sim (1989).

assisted in the training of Charlie Company, says he was 'very pleased with the way they turned out. They turned out to be very good soldiers.' It was the training, Varnado Simpson declares, to which he surrendered when he entered My Lai (4): 'I just blinked. I just went. The training came to me, programming to kill. I just started killing.'

Although it is clear that this explanation has failed to appease Simpson's own conscience – after all, if being trained how to kill entirely determined one's conduct, Hugh Thompson and Michael Bernhardt would not have acted in the way that they did in My Lai (4), and there would have been massacres every day, all over Vietnam – such complexities exceed the film's aspirations. When it was first broadcast in Britain, as part of the documentary series *First Tuesday*, the series presenter Olivia O'Leary informed the audience (erroneously) that the soldiers of Charlie Company had been in Vietnam for only seven weeks at the time of the massacre: 'It didn't take long to change them from supposedly civilized people to barbarians – only some months of military training and the pressures of war. The training hasn't changed perceptibly. Given another war, it could all happen again.'

A number of the interviews that Bilton and Sim conducted with former soldiers who had witnessed or participated in the massacre, Bilton later recorded, 'bordered on the confessional at one extreem [sic.] and almost personal counselling on the other'. Wives of the interviewees would sit in on the sessions, in some cases hearing for the first time 'the background behind their loved-ones nightmares. They told us that often their husbands would wake up screaming in the night in a blind panic, sweating profusely, shaking, crying.'[150]

In the film, Fred Widmer wipes away his tears as he recalls killing a young boy who was walking around with his arm shot off and a bewildered look on his face: 'This is what haunts me from the whole ordeal down there.' Varnado Simpson, meanwhile, clasps a handkerchief to his nose, with an album of newspaper and magazine clippings about the massacre resting on his lap. 'This is my life,' he says, tapping the album. 'This is my past. This is my present. This is my future.' On the table next to his chair stands a photograph of his infant son, who was shot whilst playing outside his grandmother's home in Jackson. By the time Simpson arrived at the scene, the boy was already close to death. 'So when I looked at him, his face looked like the same face of a child that I had killed. And I said: "This is the punishment for me killing the people that I killed."' When Simpson returned from the funeral, he discovered that the photograph had been cracked, and cracked it remained, to serve as one more symbol of a life frozen in time and purpose by morbidity and guilt.

---

[150] Bilton to Wilson, 31 July 1990, folder: My Lai 8/40, Papers of *Four Hours in My Lai*, LHCMA, KCL.

Aside from Kenneth Hodges (whose apparent conviction that the actions of Charlie Company in My Lai (4) had been consistent with the finest traditions of the US Army signifies a different kind of damage), the only soldier implicated in the killings who seems to have escaped the burden of guilt is William Calley himself. Unwilling to grant any interviews, Calley is filmed walking to his car outside the jewellery store he manages in Columbus, Georgia. After his trial, the narrator notes, he was released into house arrest and paroled three years later, 'a free man'. Calley drives off into traffic, disappearing from view.

The images of Widmer and Simpson, made miserable by memory, are intercut with film of the survivors of the massacre, wind rustling in the trees around them like the spirits of the dead. 'It's why I'm old before my time,' declares Truong Thi Le. 'I remember it all the time. I'm all alone and life is hard. Thinking about it has made me old.' Pham Thi Trinh says that, when she is sad, she often thinks 'of starting a new life somewhere else. But it would be the same anywhere in my country. Here is where I belong. The grave of my mother and loved ones is my consolation. That's why I can never leave.'

Bilton and Sim also interviewed Vo Thi Lien, who described her visits to Europe after the massacre revelations, and her education at a school for southern students in Hanoi. She now resided in Danang with her husband, where she worked at the Ho Chi Minh Museum.[151] Lien was pregnant at the time of the interview, an indication that she at least had managed to construct a life for herself beyond the memory of the massacre. 'Meeting her informally, away from My Lai, is somehow cleansing,' recorded Justin Wintle, who visited Lien at her home a year or so later. 'Her capacity for ordinary happiness is what has survived.'[152] She does not appear in the film.

Between the making of the film and publication of the book, the first Gulf War occurred, a short, conventional conflict which produced no account of American atrocities to match those, like My Lai, that had emerged out of Vietnam. Although they were aware, quite early on in the project, that US military training had been reformed in the wake of the massacre, Bilton and Sim had chosen not to incorporate that knowledge into their film, which constructed a claim for relevance around the implication that few lessons had been learnt.[153] The war in the Gulf further complicated that claim, and so they presented in the book a set of more conditional judgements about the causes and legacies of the massacre, invoking the same triad of explanations that had structured the public response when word of the killings was still new: that all wars create the potential for atrocity; that, in Vietnam and Quang Ngai in particular, US military

[151] Transcripts of filmed interviews with Vietnamese survivors [Vo Thi Lien, rolls 45, 46, pp. 36–44], folder: My Lai 3/1, Papers of *Four Hours in My Lai*, LHCMA, KCL.

[152] Wintle, pp. 258–60.

[153] Himelfarb to Bilton and Sim, 'My Lai Project', undated, folder: My Lai 8/73, Papers of *Four Hours in My Lai*, LHCMA, KCL.

commanders were derelict in their duty to limit that potential by ensuring that their men continued to observe the rules of engagement; that, whatever the quality of their leadership, the soldiers in My Lai (4) retained the power of moral choice. Bilton and Sim concluded their reflections, moreover, with the (now familiar) image of the perpetrator as victim (the survivors of the massacre disappear from the written account as soon as they have been interviewed by US Army CID). Varnado Simpson sat shaking in his chair, the authors asserted, not just because of what he had done, but because the rest of America had left him to bear the burden of responsibility and memory all on his own.[154]

Once the Calley court martial was over, and the country had vented its spleen, the story of the massacre began its long retreat back into the twilight of media attention. Newsmen failed to turn up in anything like their expected numbers at the trial of Ernest Medina.[155] When the Department of the Army finally released the report of the Peers commission in November 1974, the *New York Times* buried its notice deep in its inside pages.[156] News agencies were left to keep half an eye on the tortuous progress of the Calley appeal. From the mid-1970s on, whatever the press would say about the massacre would be either analogy or epilogue: the story of My Lai no longer had much of a life of its own.

Every few years – on a massacre anniversary or as part of a project to commemorate the Vietnam war as a whole – media outlets would tell the story again, commissioning retrospectives from Seymour Hersh or Ronald Ridenhour (now a writer himself), or dispatching their reporters to solicit recollections from the American soldiers involved, sometimes even sending them to the scene of the slaughter.[157] In these accounts of American return, reminders of the devastation that US forces had left behind in My Lai (4) (the massacre in My Khe (4) was hardly ever mentioned), competed for attention with evidence that, after the war, people had moved back into the settlement and were busily reconstructing their community, restoring the land to productive use, raising a new generation. 'They're not forgetting [the massacre],' Ronald Ridenhour told *CBS Evening News* in 1977 following a visit to Son My, 'but it is certainly not their primary focus. I was frankly amazed at their capacity to deal with the business of getting on with life and to understand or to just take the war as something that's happened, that's over with, and is something that won't be forgotten but can't be dwelled on forever.'[158]

[154] Bilton and Sim, p. 378.

[155] McCarthy, pp. 17–18.

[156] *New York Times* (14 November 1974), p. 16.

[157] For examples, see Unger and Hewitt, 'William Calley: convicted of the My Lai slaughter of innocents . . .', *People* (20 November 1989); Hersh, 'My Lai, and its omens', *New York Times* (16 March 1998), p. A25; Ridenhour, 'Perspective on My Lai', *Los Angeles Times* (16 March 1993), p. B7; G. Esper, 'A picture in my mind I cannot forget', *Associated Press* (2 January 1985).

[158] *CBS Evening News*, 8 May 1977, VTNA.

In 1985, George Esper – Saigon bureau chief for *Associated Press* during the final days of the war – travelled back to Vietnam and visited My Lai (4). 'The rice and vegetables grow in the lush green fields, the flowers are in bloom and the trees are tall', his report began. Children 'walk laughing' through the settlement. 'Cows graze, dogs bark, chickens cackle. Just as the rice harvest comes up every spring, life goes on . . .'

These images of fertility, vitality and continuity, however, quickly gave way to memento mori, to descriptions of the museum and the memorial to the dead built on the site of the massacre, and to an account of an interview with Pham Thi Trinh, who wept as she recalled the murder of her family. With her words, the article concluded: 'In my heart I still hate very much the American soldiers because the picture is still in my mind. I cannot forget.'[159] Weeping survivors, asserting that they could never forgive America, were also a feature of an *ABC News* report from Son My in 1990, but this time only as a preface to a story of 'hope and reconciliation', relating the efforts of Cherie Clark and the International Mission of Hope to build a hospital in the village. Said to be as welcome in Son My 'as a member of the family', Clark was shown with her arm around one of the women who had declared that she was unable to forgive. The ceremonies to dedicate the hospital, the correspondent concluded, had provided local people with an image of Americans very different to those 'burned into memories here, but then again Cherie Clark and a few others have succeeded where an entire war failed: winning the hearts and minds of the Vietnamese'.[160]

In March 1998, the American news media returned in some force both to the subject of the massacre and to the place where it had occurred, prompted by the army's award of medals to Hugh Thompson and the two members of his crew, Larry Colburn and (posthumously) Glenn Andreotta, in recognition of their efforts to save some of the inhabitants of My Lai (4), and by the thirtieth anniversary ceremonies held in Son My, which Thompson and Colburn attended. For the media, here was something that could be salvaged from the memory of the massacre: a tale of American heroism, and the promise of a poignant encounter between Americans and the survivors that would not revive discomfiting questions about responsibility and guilt. 'Out of America's most shameful moment in Vietnam, a single shining act of courage,' opined NBC's Robert Hager, who had reported on the original massacre story.[161] So had CNN's Bruce Morton, who reflected that the medal ceremony, conducted as it was at the Vietnam Veterans Memorial in Washington DC, offered Thompson and Colburn 'a kind of closure'. Most of the men who had served in Vietnam had done so with honour, Morton observed. 'Most have come home. And in My Lai, the dead rest, thirty years on.'[162]

[159] Esper, 'A picture in my mind I cannot forget', *Associated Press* (2 January 1985).
[160] *ABC News*, 10 June 1990, VTNA.
[161] *NBC Nightly News*, 6 March 1998, VTNA.
[162] *CNN Worldview*, 6 March 1998, VTNA.

At the site of the massacre, there was evidence enough – for those who wanted to find it – that the memory of the past, just like the dead, might now also be allowed to rest. In the view of Tim Larimer from *Time* magazine, 'it is strange to come to this place, 30 years later, and find it so beautiful, and so serene. A gentle breeze from the nearby seashore brings relief from the penetrating sun, and carries the sounds of life: a baby crying, the hum of a rice thresher.'[163]

'I'm very busy, so I don't think of the massacre often,' Do Tan Dung, the son of Truong Thi Le, told a reporter from the *Dallas Morning News*. He had been protected from American gunfire by the bodies of other villagers fallen around him. Now he was 'a handsome farmer with a shy smile and four children', wearing a Pepsi cap on his head.[164] On their visit to Son My, Thompson and Colburn were accompanied by Mike Wallace, who was filming a report for CBS's *Sixty Minutes*. Wallace commented later that they had been 'able to see a My Lai restored to a bucolic, serene peace'.[165] They were also able to meet two of the villagers they had saved. 'I will say thank you to him,' declared one, Pham Thi Nhanh, before Thompson arrived. 'If he did not rescue us, we would have died, because there was another American soldier who would have shot us.'[166]

Many survivors of the massacre had good reason to be grateful to Thompson – aside from carrying a number of them to safety, he had also complained fiercely about the killing to his superiors, prompting them to issue an order to cease fire – yet there was also a limit to the solace and the 'closure' that his visit could bring. Hundreds had still been butchered, and they still lay in the ground, and, after Thompson returned home, the villagers would still have to live with that knowledge and that loss. 'If there wasn't a massacre, I would have a wife and all my children today,' asserted Pham Dat, another survivor, 'and I wouldn't be standing in front of an altar praying and burning incense.'[167] Thompson himself was unable to provide the people of Son My with an explanation for what had occurred. 'Why your police kill my people?' a young boy asked him, as he toured the local grammar school. Thompson struggled to respond: 'It's a question that can never be answered. They just went crazy that day.'[168] *Time* found a surface serenity in the village, but also inhabitants who suffered frequently from nightmares.[169] *ABC News* filmed a woman touching Ronald Haeberle's photographs of the massacre – which were displayed in the museum – then breaking down in tears.[170] Americans may have sought to

---

[163] Tim Larimer, 'Echoes of My Lai', *Time* (16 March 1998).
[164] *Dallas Morning News* (16 March 1998), p. 1A.
[165] M. Wallace, 'Introduction', in Angers, p. 6.
[166] *CNN Worldview*, 14 March 1998, VTNA.
[167] *Dallas Morning News* (16 March 1998), p. 1A.
[168] Angers, p. 75.
[169] Larimer, 'Echoes of My Lai', *Time* (16 March 1998).
[170] *ABC News*, 16 March 1998, VTNA.

put the massacre behind them, but they could not claim that the licence to do so wholly reflected the will of those who continued to live with the rawest of its legacies. 'Should My Lai be with us for time immemorial?' asked CNN anchor Bernard Shaw of Seymour Hersh, following a report on the anniversary ceremonies in Son My. 'I just think it is,' Hersh replied. 'We have no choice.'[171]

For the American news media – or, at least, for the generation of reporters schooled in the living history of the Vietnam war – the massacre was a story which warranted and rewarded occasional return, but only, perhaps, occasional return: it offered an affective drama of violence and suffering, as well as a menu of possible lessons and reflections responsive to the sonorous tones and thoughtful pauses of the journalist-performer, whilst presenting (so long as the return remained brief) not too profound a challenge to the world view of the audience. In addition, if there exists a fund of basic historical knowledge shared across the profession, the massacre is probably part of it, available for recall and reference whenever another incident of US military atrocity – past or present – arrives in the news. Its memory was invoked in reports and editorial comment about the shooting of civilians near the village of No Gun Ri during the Korean war, about the raid by Bob Kerrey and his team of Navy Seals upon the hamlet of Thanh Phong, about the killings perpetrated by Tiger Force platoon in Quang Ngai and Quang Nam, and about the torture of Iraqi prisoners in Abu Ghraib jail.[172]

Yet, with respect to their own practice, media institutions seemed to have learned less from the memory of My Lai than even the US military. As each of these recent atrocity stories made their way into the public domain, they encountered much the same caution and resistance on the part of the news establishment that Seymour Hersh had experienced in 1969 when trying to find an outlet for his revelations about the charges faced by William Calley. The *Associated Press* delayed publication of the story of the slaughter at No Gun Ri for over a year. Though the story had been confirmed by many witnesses, both American and Korean, the agency feared a political assault similar to that which had been recently provoked by a CNN report alleging that sarin nerve gas had been used by US troops during the Vietnam war (CNN had been forced to retract the report when flaws were revealed in the supporting evidence.)[173] *Newsweek* learnt about the raid on Thanh Phong in 1997, and by December the following year had Bob Kerrey's confirmation that innocent civilians had been killed. Around the same time, however, Kerrey announced that he would not be contesting

[171] *CNN Worldview*, 16 March 1998, VTNA.

[172] See, for example, *Washington Post* (30 September 1999), p. A1; G. Vistica, 'One awful night in Thanh Phong', *New York Times Magazine* (25 April 2001); *New York Times* (28 December 2003), p. 18; T. Karon, 'How American was Abu Ghraib?', *Time.com*, 11 May 2004: www.time.com (accessed August 2004).

[173] Hanley *et al.*, pp. 269–75.

the Democratic presidential nomination in 2000. *Newsweek* decided not to publish.[174] 'We just didn't want to do it to the guy when he wasn't running for president,' recalled Evan Thomas, its assistant managing editor.[175] The murder of twenty Vietnamese civilians was only to be counted as news if a candidate for the White House was implicated in the crime. Two years later, when the *New York Times* and CBS's *Sixty Minutes II* finally broke the story, most of the mainstream press seemed willing to forgive Kerrey not just for his actions in Thanh Phong (as if such forgiveness was in their gift), but also for his failure to admit or report them until compelled to do so, thirty years on, by the knowledge of imminent public disclosure.[176] Absent the involvement of a political celebrity, indeed, and past atrocities could not be assured of the status of news.

The revelations about those committed by Tiger Force platoon were totally ignored by many major news organizations in the United States, including the CBS, NBC and CNN networks, *Time*, *Newsweek* and the *Wall Street Journal*.[177] The *New York Times* published an account only belatedly, two months after the story had first appeared in the *Toledo Blade*.[178] In the case of Abu Ghraib, CBS acceded to a request from General Richard Myers, Chairman of the Joint Chiefs of Staff, that it delay the broadcast of a report on the abuses in the jail whilst American forces remained engaged in fierce battles around the Iraqi city of Fallujah. The report was eventually aired two weeks later when the network learnt that the *New Yorker* also had the story, researched and written – no doubt with a powerful sense of *déjà vu* – by Seymour Hersh.[179]

Sixty-six per cent of Americans polled in May 2004 asserted that the soldiers involved in the abuse of prisoners at Abu Ghraib should be charged with a crime.[180] With respect to older atrocities, however, moral judgement seemed to be subject to a statute of limitations. The stories about No Gun Ri and the actions of Tiger Force were both good for a Pulitzer, but they generated little in the way of public pressure for either prosecution of the perpetrators or payment of compensation to those who had been wounded or bereaved. Even had the Pentagon wished to place Bob Kerrey on trial for his role in the killings in Thanh Phong, it probably could not have

[174] Vistica, *The Education of Lieutenant Kerrey*, pp. 9–11, 194–207.

[175] *Washington Post* (27 April 2001), p. A4.

[176] See, for example, 'Bob Kerrey's war', *Washington Post* (30 April 2001), p. A16; W. Safire, 'Syndrome returns', *New York Times* (30 April 2001); and H. Hertzberg, 'Talk of the town: a military secret', *New Yorker* (7 May 2001), pp. 31–2. For more critical perspectives, see M. Kelly, 'The rush to avoid judging Kerrey', *Washington Post* (2 May 2001), p. A21; J. Schell, 'War and accountability', *Nation* (21 May 2001); and C. Hitchens, 'Leave no child behind?', *Nation* (28 May 2001), pp. 9, 24.

[177] S. Sherman, 'Press watch', *Nation* (1 March 2004).

[178] *New York Times* (28 December 2003), p. 18.

[179] *New York Times* (4 May 2004); Hersh, 'Torture at Abu Ghraib', *New Yorker* (10 May 2004).

[180] *Washington Post/ABC News* poll, 5–6 May 2004: www.washingtonpost.com (accessed August 2004).

done so: any such move – in the view of Gregory Vistica, the reporter who first revealed what had happened in the hamlet – would have 'cut directly against the political and cultural mood of the country'.[181] In the public's apparent ambivalence towards the prospect of prosecuting 30- to 50-year-old war crimes, there was an element of charity that was entirely defensible. During the decades that divided the original atrocities from their subsequent disclosure, the perpetrators in many cases might be predicted to have changed markedly in character, purpose and conscience, to the extent that their trial might seem almost to be judging one set of men for the deeds of another. The 'fog of war', moreover, was held to become increasingly impenetrable with age: the claim that only those who were there, immersed in the pressures and perils of combat, had the authority to offer a moral assessment of what occurred was not surrendered willingly to the countervailing appeals of historical evidence and perspective. Not there at the time, and now thirty or more years late: many Americans felt themselves unfit to demand that justice finally be done.

Yet this ambivalence cannot be explained simply by the passing of years. Americans disliked the spectacle of their own soldiers on trial even when the Vietnam war was at its height, even when the evidence of the crimes committed was compelling and conclusive; and they were inclined even then to empathize with those soldiers more than with their victims. In the opinion of some commentators, a sinew of ethical dissent has always been present in public memories of the war, resistant to the revisions and erasures of political and cultural elites.[182] Around 70 per cent of those polled from the late 1970s to mid-1980s agreed with the statement that the conflict in Vietnam 'was more than a mistake: it was fundamentally wrong and immoral'.[183] In most cases, however, what was recalled in this response was probably not an image of bodies lying on a road outside the settlement of My Lai (4), or of the other Vietnamese casualties of the war. The initial massacre revelations, after all, had made no discernible impact upon levels of public support for the war, which were driven downwards instead by frustration with its progress and the toll of American, rather than Vietnamese, lives.[184] Moreover, it was during the court martial of William Calley that opinion polls registered for the very first time a majority judgement that the military effort in Vietnam was morally wrong, with the proceedings persuading many of those who had hitherto taken hawkish positions on the conflict that national elites did not have the will to do whatever it took to win; indeed, that they would even go so far as to punish the soldiers who did.[185]

[181] Vistica, *The Education of Lieutenant Kerrey*, p. 267.
[182] Herman and Chomsky, pp. 238, 378, fn. 157; McMahon, p. 175.
[183] J. Rielly (ed.), *American Public Opinion and US Foreign Policy 1987* (Chicago: The Chicago Council on Foreign Relations, 1987), p. 33.
[184] Mueller, pp. 54–62; Schuman, pp. 524–6, 533–4.
[185] Harris poll data, folder: My Lai 8/83, Papers of *Four Hours in My Lai*, LHCMA, KCL.

This theme – of young Americans dispatched to a difficult war, denied the chance to prevail, victimized upon return – came to define much of what was written and said about Vietnam in the years that followed. Subsequent expressions of public contrition and moral censure with respect to the war, therefore, were most likely inspired by the fate of its American veterans, not the fate of the Vietnamese, about which the culture has remained largely incurious. *In the Lake of the Woods*, *Four Hours in My Lai*, reappraisals in the press every five or ten years: these have not been enough to make the massacre a canonical moment within the national memory, of the kind that each generation seeks to instil knowledge of in the next.[186] In 1983, Robert Muller, founder of the Vietnam Veterans of America, embarked on a speaking tour of American colleges: 'I swear, the first college I went to, they asked, "What's My Lai, and who is Lieutenant Calley?"'[187] A decade later, Tim O'Brien recalled much the same experience: 'In the colleges and high schools I sometimes visit, the mention of My Lai brings on null stares, a sort of puzzlement, disbelief mixed with utter ignorance.'[188]

Americans, of course, had only known so much about the massacre in the first place, and aside from periodic media updates about the lives of its perpetrators, that knowledge was not increasing. Well into the 1980s, the village of Son My remained as remote from and as alien to American culture as it had been in 1969 – more so, indeed, given the restrictions imposed by the governments of Vietnam and the United States upon travel and communication between the two countries after the end of the war. A handful of Americans – mostly those with an established record of sympathy for the revolutionary cause – were able to visit the site of the killings in the immediate post-war years, but in general foreign access was restricted to fraternal communist delegations from Eastern Europe and

---

[186] Other novels which incorporate accounts of the massacre and its aftermath include M. Busby, *Fort Benning Blues* (Fort Worth: Texas Christian University Press, 2001) and N. Church Mailer, *Windchill Summer* (London: Fourth Estate, 2001). Since the early 1970s, there have been occasional indications of interest in the subject on the part of Hollywood. Stanley Kramer – director of *Judgment at Nuremberg* – attended the Calley trial, subsequently producing a dramatization of the case for American television. See Hammer, *The Court-Martial of Lt Calley*, p. 172; *Judgement: The Court-Martial of Lieutenant William Calley*, dir. Stanley Kramer (1975). One veteran of Charlie Company, James Dursi, recalled that he had also been approached by Disney. Record of conversation with James Dursi, 26 June 1988, folder: My Lai 4/1, Papers of *Four Hours in My Lai*, LHCMA, KCL. Vietnam westerns and *Platoon* aside, Hollywood perhaps came closest to portraying the massacre and its aftermath in *Rules of Engagement*. The film presents an account of a siege at the US Embassy in Yemen, in the course of which a force of American marines open fire upon a crowd of demonstrators, killing sixty-three – women and children among them. The marines' commander is tried for murder, in what Mike Hammond describes as 'an exposition of the moral dilemma entailed in fighting a guerilla force that is making strategic use of innocent civilians'. Audiences in test screenings demanded that the film conclude with the officer's acquittal. *Rules of Engagement*, dir. William Friedkin (2000); Hammond, 'Some smothering dreams', pp. 62–3.

[187] McPherson, p. 726.

[188] O'Brien, 'The Vietnam in me'.

Cuba.[189] The socialist realist sculpture erected at the site – depicting a woman with one arm raised in defiance, the other clasping a dead child, with four wounded figures collapsed at her feet – reflected such an audience, as did the literature then available at the museum nearby. According to a leaflet handed to Justin Wintle when he visited the museum in 1989, the massacre evoked 'irresistibly the satanic profile of that monster called US imperialism.'[190]

By the late 1980s, however, the attitude of the Vietnamese authorities towards Western travellers was beginning to change. A stagnating economy combined with the transformation of Soviet attitudes towards the funding of distant allies prompted party leaders in Hanoi to seek sources of capital from outside the communist world.[191] This was also the period in which other Asian countries – Thailand especially – were experiencing a boom in Western tourism, and it was to that model that Vietnam referred when drafting the blueprint for its own economic renewal. Access restrictions were eased; the Vietnam National Administration of Tourism was created to coordinate the development of the tourist industry, along with an agency – Vietnamtourism – responsible for promoting travel to the country and organizing tours; the government declared 1990 to be 'Visit Vietnam Year'.[192] At this time, however, the efforts of Vietnamese officials to market their country to (preferably wealthy) Western tourists coexisted somewhat awkwardly with the categorical imperatives of a revolutionary tradition and with the nervous reflexes of an authoritarian power structure, which was unhabituated to accommodating the curiosity and will-to-roam of foreign visitors. Vietnamtourism produced brochures that emphasized the agency's service to the propaganda functions of the state.[193] Anyone who wished to journey to the interior had to apply for permission.[194] Justin Wintle was handed an official itinerary and accompanied almost everywhere he went by government minders.[195] Those who wished to visit the memorial in Son My required a permit from the local police.[196]

In time, most of the remaining restrictions on visitor access were rescinded, whilst the revolution learnt to reduce its own political conspicuousness. Obviously, revolutionary sites of memory such as Dien Bien Phu,

[189] *Associated Press* (16 March 1978); Kamm, *Dragon Ascending*, p. 3. Until 1986, the number of foreigners entering Vietnam averaged around 7,000 a year, nearly all from socialist countries: L. Kennedy and M. Williams, 'The past without the pain: the manufacture of nostalgia in Vietnam's tourist industry', in H. Ho Tai (ed.), *The Country of Memory: Remaking the Past in Late-Socialist Vietnam* (Berkeley: University of California Press, 2001), pp. 138–9.

[190] Wintle, p. 263.

[191] M. Ebashi, 'The economic take-off', in J. Morley and M. Nishihara (eds), *Vietnam Joins the World* (Armonk: M.E. Sharpe, 1997), pp. 37–65.

[192] Kennedy and Williams, p. 140.

[193] Vietnamtourism, *Vietnam: A Tourist Guide* (Hanoi: Vietnamtourism, 1991), p. 3.

[194] Kennedy and Williams, p. 139.

[195] Wintle, pp. xiii–iv.

[196] J. Jones, *Guide to Vietnam* (Chalfont St Peter: Bradt Publications, 1994), p. 212.

the Ho Chi Minh trail, and the Cu Chi tunnels, north-west of Saigon (now Ho Chi Minh City), continue to attract a great many foreign visitors, but the regime (and the international investors who have financed much of the country's tourist development) has been assiduous in denuding them of both ideological and ethical content.[197] What these sites present, as Laurel Kennedy and Mary Rose Williams have asserted, is a 'muted and angerless history', expressly designed to minimize any feelings of suspicion, anxiety and guilt that visitors (particularly American visitors) might have brought with them to Vietnam.[198] To a large extent, indeed, the attention of tourists is directed away from the war, towards attractions that pre-date the American presence – Buddhist pagodas, French colonial archi-tecture, remnants of the ancient Cham civilization, the imperial citadel at Hué – which imply by their very existence that, whatever the damage done during the course of hostilities, the country's heritage had survived: that continuities of culture were more significant than episodes of dis-ruption, however violent they had been.[199]

Inevitably, sites that commemorate American atrocities in the war, such as the Son My memorial or the War Crimes Museum in Saigon, sit rather uneasily with this new version of Vietnam offered to the world. The edu-cative purpose that they were previously held to serve, for Vietnamese and approved visitors alike (Wintle's minders insisted upon taking him to Son My), has been superseded in national priorities by avidity for the dollar, which is not judged to be compatible with summoning its bearers to an exhibition of their past collective sins.[200] The War Crimes (now War Remnants) Museum remains open, and continues to display photographs of American GIs posing with decapitated Vietnamese heads, scenes of torture, jars of malformed foetuses asserted to be the result of Agent Orange, as well as Ronald Haeberle's images of the massacre at My Lai (4). There is a section devoted to Bob Kerrey's raid upon Thanh Phong. No men-tion is made of revolutionary terror, the massacre in Hué, or post-war refugees. However, even as the museum continues to confront its visitors with evidence of the suffering inflicted upon the Vietnamese people by the armed forces of the United States and its 'puppet' ally in Saigon, its ration-ale for doing so is changing and so, ultimately, too is the story that it tells. Its displays now also incorporate evidence of national recovery – farms, orchards and rebuilt city streets where battles were once fought and bombs once fell – as well as perspectives offered by US veterans of the war, as if to suggest a narrative of the conflict as a tragedy for both sides, rather than as an outrage that one side endured at the hands of the other.[201] The objective of the museum, its own leaflet declares, is not to incite hatred,

[197] Kennedy and Williams, pp. 152–5.
[198] *Ibid.*, p. 136.
[199] *Ibid.*, pp. 148–9, 155–6.
[200] Wintle, pp. 258–9.
[201] Author's observations during visit to Vietnam, 14–22 February 2004.

but to allow lessons to be learnt from history: 'Human beings will not tolerate such a disaster happening again, neither in Vietnam nor anywhere on our planet.'[202]

Like the War Crimes Museum, the Son My memorial was not mentioned in the official guide to Vietnam published by Vietnamtourism in 1991, not even in the itineraries of organized tours scheduled to travel along Highway One, only a few miles to the west of the massacre site, as they made their way south from Danang or Hoi An, or north from Qui Nhon or Nha Trang.[203] Another travel guide, issued by the Vietnam National Administration of Tourism in 2001, also ignores the memorial, along with all the rest of Quang Ngai.[204] The province lags behind much of Vietnam in the development of tourist facilities and attractions. Coach parties pass through Quang Ngai, often breaking their journeys with a quick stop at the memorial and lunch at a local hotel; private tour companies in Hoi An, eighty or so miles to the north, also arrange day trips to Son My; but there are currently few obvious reasons to stay in the area for more than a day. This may change in the near future: on the beach at My Khe, close to the location of the Bravo Company massacre, a new luxury hotel is being built; and an hour's drive away, on the site of the old American military base of Chu Lai, an airport is under construction. The coastal stretches of Quang Ngai may soon become a tourist destination rather than an excursion, and if they do, the memorial at Son My will receive many more foreign visitors, and the settlements around it will be further transformed.[205]

In the act of communicating memory, there is the potential for the speaker to be changed as much as the listener. Audiences affect the stories they are told. Son My may have been rather isolated from the main currents of national economic development, but it is nevertheless much altered not just from how it was at the time of the massacre, and during the subsequent years of desolation, but also from the place that Western visitors encountered when first welcomed to Vietnam in the late 1980s. 'The growing prosperity is evident in many ways,' wrote an American correspondent in 1998: 'new motorcycles or scooters in front of most houses, radios and cassette players, even television sets in many homes.'[206] At the memorial itself, there is also a television set as well as a video player, showing an English-language version of the Vietnamese film, *The Sound of the Violin in My Lai* – a record of the visit of Hugh Thompson and Larry Colburn to Son My on the massacre's thirtieth anniversary.[207] In

---

[202] 'War Remnants in Vietnam', produced by the War Remnants Museum, Ho Chi Minh City.

[203] Vietnamtourism, *Vietnam: A Tourist Guide*.

[204] Vietnam National Administration of Tourism, *Vietnam Travel Guide 2001* (Hanoi: Vietnam National Administration of Tourism, 2001).

[205] Author's observations during visit to Vietnam, 14–22 February 2004.

[206] *Dallas Morning News* (16 March 1998), p. 1A.

[207] *The Sound of the Violin in My Lai*, dir. Tran Van Thuy (1999).

the same building stands a long dining table with a glass cover, under which many visitors have placed their business cards. At the entrance to the site, visitors can buy a T-shirt featuring the main memorial. If they arrange in advance and are willing to pay an additional fee, one of the massacre's survivors will act as their guide.[208]

As with the War Remnants Museum in Saigon, the Son My memorial's origins in an era of socialist piety and nationalist indignation remain evident even as its custodians seek to adapt to the expectations of a more ecumenical audience: close to the television set stands a bust of Ho Chi Minh; in the memorial garden, socialist realist sculptures continue to offer expressive gestures of suffering, pity and defiance, in contrast to the stillness and abstraction of much recent memorial art in the West; the exhibits in the museum could be more scrupulously curated. (One image of a Vietnamese woman, a rifle held to her head, is included in the display of photographs taken by Ronald Haeberle, as if it had been taken during the massacre. It is also displayed in the War Remnants Museum, there attributed to an episode that occurred at Tan Lap, in the province of Quang Tri.) Yet it is no longer the 'satanic profile' of American imperialism that the memorial seeks to evoke, but rather the virtues of peace and hope for the future.

From copies of Thompson's and Colburn's medal citations, visitors can learn that not all American soldiers participated or acquiesced in the project of slaughter. The remains of the homes from which the inhabitants of Xom Lang were taken to be killed, and some of their graves, are cradled now in a beautiful, fertile garden, shaded by trees, with butterflies flitting and drifting through the flowers. It was 'a hard resurrection', the current memorial leaflet declares, and the hurt is 'still smouldering', but the village 'is coming back to life day after day'. The leaflet presents photographs of the village's new school, fishermen and women on My Khe beach, and Vo Thi Lien with her four-year-old daughter. 'So people in Vietnam and all over the world,' the leaflet concludes, 'did not forget coming to Son My (Tinh Khe) to pray: "This will never happen again in the world."'[209]

The lessons that visitors are encouraged to take away from the massacre site are now more consistent with the conventions of Western liberal discourses than with the rhetoric of socialist solidarity and revolutionary martyrdom, and it is to the well-tested clichés of liberal internationalism – war is bad, peace is good – that many of them resort when trying to compose a response for the memorial's visitors' book. Yet the memorial (no doubt, in part, because the story of American violence and Vietnamese suffering that it tells is not as obviously freighted with ideological meaning as once it was), does have a capacity to provoke its American visitors

[208] Author's observations during visit to Vietnam, 14–22 February 2004; Kamm, pp. 3–4.
[209] Author's observations during visit to Vietnam, 14–22 February 2004; Son My memorial leaflet (2002).

into reflections that challenge the various strains of self-pity manifest in their own nation's public memory of the war, and to stimulate new circuits of empathetic identification. 'I can honestly say that I am 100 per cent ashamed to be an American,' one such visitor from New London, Connecticut, asserted in January 2004. 'It is beyond my comprehension how my country could partake in the massacre & not punish any of the men who took part in this.' In December 2003, another visitor, from Seattle, Washington, pasted a photograph of his two sleeping grandchildren into the book, and wrote: 'when I think of the atrocities that took place here, I think of them . . . Those who died here were the great future of this beautiful country . . . [W]hile it is said that we learn from history, I doubt – for once again we are in turmoil.'[210]

There are many now living in Son My who have no personal memories of the massacre; who are not perpetually enveloped by sorrow and grief: the children especially, who shout 'hello' in English to foreigners entering the memorial site and giggle with delight when the greeting is returned. For those who witnessed the killings, who had to bury their own mothers and fathers, brothers and sisters, sons and daughters, who decided to return to their former homes at the end of the war, the spectacle of Western visitors proceeding into and out of the memorial must excite some complex emotions. Before such visits became routine, it was common for survivors to express their loathing of Americans, not just because of the massacre, but because they had made no effort afterwards to atone for and repair the damage that was done. 'Now, my people hate the Americans,' said Ha Thi Quy in 1988. 'If they want some dealings with the Liberation, they must repent and accept their mistakes and then we would not hate them. But we can't forgive the stubborn ones. Those who repent and accept their mistakes, who listen to what we say and understand, then those Americans are all right.'[211] Five years later, Mrs Quy guided Tim O'Brien around the massacre site when he visited Quang Ngai. 'She's smiling, accommodating,' he noted. 'Impossible, but she seems to like us.'[212]

Perhaps these encounters were as instructive for the survivors as they were for Americans, and as likely to influence their attitudes as official injunctions to show their former enemy a welcoming face. Here at last there were Americans taking notice of what their soldiers had done; here at last they were expressing regret. 'If the Americans want to have normal relations we are very happy,' Mrs Quy informed Henry Kamm. 'I can draw the line between people. There are some bad Americans, but I respect the American people. If they admit their mistakes, I can forgive what happened

[210] Author's observations during visit to Vietnam, 14–22 February 2004; entries in Son My memorial visitors book, 11 December 2003 and 11 January 2004.
[211] Transcripts of filmed interviews with Vietnamese survivors [Ha Thi Quy, slates 427 and 430, pp. 56–9], folder: My Lai 3/1, Papers of *Four Hours in My Lai*, LHCMA, KCL.
[212] O'Brien, 'The Vietnam in me'.

in the past.'[213] Pham Thanh Cong, another survivor who was also chief attendant at the memorial, said: 'I think the people of the village know that what happened did not represent America. When Americans come here to pay their respects, they are received like all others. There is no anger against them.'[214]

That Americans should return to the site of the massacre, speak to its survivors, make an effort to imagine the terror, pain and grief that the soldiers of their country had visited upon Son My, and come finally to feel some of the moral weight of their own recent history: this was all very necessary, yet it was not a resolution, and could not be. Communication, tears of expiation, aid and assistance (if they are ever forthcoming): these might bring a measure of satisfaction and comfort to the inhabitants of Son My but they cannot restore the dead to life, or cause wounds to disappear, or somehow redistribute the primary burden of suffering and loss. Putting money, conscience and language to work in the village reflects a long-deferred obligation but it also represents an asymmetric response: the damage has been done and cannot be repaired. As they toured the memorial, Ha Thi Quy pulled down her trousers and showed Tim O'Brien and his companion, Kate, the scar that covered the bullet-hole in her hip: 'Kate nods and makes sounds of sympathy. What does one say? Bad day. World of hurt.'[215] Mrs Quy began to cry, as survivors often have when reprising their accounts of the killing for the edification of foreign visitors. They do not do so for effect. For the people of Son My, the massacre exceeds any use that can be made of its memory. 'I still feel frightened to tell the story,' Mrs Quy told a reporter in 1998.[216]

Americans, meanwhile, have not made use enough of the massacre. With the imperfect exception of the US army, their culture has largely failed to fashion a purpose from its memory. It was an aberration; it was Vietnam; it was the wages of war: whatever one believed, what more was there to say that had not already been said? The controversy could not be resolved, but it could slowly be eased towards the dimmer recesses of the past. Political elites led by example, remaining mute on the subject of American atrocities in Vietnam. Veterans talked a little more, but mostly about themselves. Absent cues from these sources, the media returned to the massacre story only every five or ten years, and then but briefly. All of this could happen because the victims of the crime had already been eased from the horizon of public concern, and the post-war years offered them few opportunities to work their way back. Now, perhaps, that opportunity does exist: now at last, ordinary Americans who want to can travel to the site of the killings, thereafter restoring to their own national

213 Kamm, p. 9.
214 *Ibid.*, p. 6
215 O'Brien, 'The Vietnam in me'.
216 *Associated Press* (4 March 1998).

culture some of the knowledge it has lost, exciting an empathetic imagination that it never really had. Yet it is probably too late: in the United States, such endeavours have long since ceased to seem socially imperative, if indeed they ever did; in Vietnam, meanwhile, the survivors of atrocity are ageing, and their own country's attention lies elsewhere, and even in Son My, at once bustling and tranquil, it is now difficult – perhaps also obscene – to make a reach of the mind to the reality of what happened that day when the Americans came to the village and dealt death to its people.

Conclusion

What happened in Son My was not the worst that man has done; it is probably not even the worst that Americans have done. That is irrelevant, however. What was done in Son My was the worst that could be done in Son My, and it merits attention for that fact alone. It was there that, for a few hours one morning, Charlie Company and Bravo Company plumbed the depths. There are other reasons for remembering the massacre. The victims – living and dead – deserve our regard, at least to the degree that we would hope and expect to be regarded if such a disaster was visited upon us. We certainly have a right, also an obligation, to attend to our own lives, to our families, friends and neighbours, but it is in the recognition that the same human talent for empathy which warms our experience of community at home has no essential, natural limits of application that much of the promise of a less violent, more conscientious world resides. It is hard work to try to fathom something of the sufferings of others, especially those who belong to a distant, foreign culture, but perhaps not quite as hard as, with respect to the inhabitants of My Lai (4), Americans made it seem. In time, of course, we must turn to questions of causation and responsibility, in an effort to ensure that the deed is not repeated and that the needs of justice are served; there may be the potential also to harvest a higher wisdom. Yet these efforts should come second, as for the most part they did not with My Lai, to the enquiry that allows us to learn and weigh what it was that was really done: Who are these people?

Finally, of course, our attention may be drawn to the killings in Son My because they were committed by US soldiers. More than with any other nation, it matters how the United States conducts itself abroad, and not just because, in comparison with other nations, it has the greatest capacity for the projection of its power, and thus the greatest capacity to do good and harm. It matters because Americans have usually expected the best of themselves, and have sought to encourage that expectation in others. When America disappoints – as it did in Vietnam, in Son My more precisely, and also in the way that it responded to the massacre – it does more than disappoint. It embarrasses the hope for a better world. It should not be a consolation to talk about revolutionary terror and the massacre at Hué, or Lidice and Oradour, for those do not set the standards by which Americans or anybody else should seek to be judged. In the wake of My Lai, many Americans claimed that their troops, their war in Vietnam, their country as a whole had been too harshly condemned. It would have been better to regard that condemnation as a tribute of a kind: to fear above all a situation in which condemnation does not come, in which no expectations of America are disappointed by such a crime, when the massacre at My Lai (4) is no longer discussed because it has ceased to seem so shocking and so strange.

Select bibliography

Manuscript sources and archive collections

America Since Hoover Collection, 1929–80, Gerald R. Ford Presidential Library, Ann Arbor, Michigan.
British Government (National Archives, Kew, UK)
    Prime Minister's Office
Papers of *Four Hours in My Lai*, Liddell Hart Centre for Military Archives, King's College London.
John B. Hightower Papers, Museum of Modern Art Archives, New York.
Lyndon B. Johnson (Lyndon Baines Johnson Presidential Library, Austin, Texas)
    National Security Files
    White House Central File
Richard M. Nixon (Richard M. Nixon Presidential Materials, National Archives, College Park, Maryland)
    National Security Council Files
    White House Special Files
    White House Tapes
    Diaries of Harry R. Haldeman
Records of the Army Staff, RG319, National Archives, College Park, Maryland.
    Records of the Peers Inquiry
    Records of the Vietnam War Crimes Working Group, Office of the Deputy Chief of Staff for Personnel (ODCSPER)
Records of the Judge Advocate General (Army), RG153, National Archives, College Park, Maryland.
    Records of the Calley General Court-Martial, 1969–1974, Office of the Clerk of the Court
US Army Military History Institute, Carlisle, Pennsylvania.
    William R. Peers Papers
    William C. Westmoreland Papers
Vanderbilt Television News Archive, Nashville, Tennessee.

Printed sources

Addicott, J. and W. Hudson, 'The twenty-fifth anniversary of My Lai: a time to inculcate the lessons', *Military Law Review*, 139 (1993).

Anderson, D. (ed.), *Facing My Lai: Moving Beyond the Massacre* (Lawrence: University Press of Kansas, 1998).

Angers, T., *The Forgotten Hero of My Lai: The Hugh Thompson Story* (Lafayette: Acadian House, 1999).

Appy, C., *Working Class War: American Combat Soldiers and Vietnam* (Chapel Hill: University of North Carolina Press, 1993).

Baker, M., *Nam: The Vietnam War in the Words of the Men and Women Who Fought There* (London: Abacus, 1982).

Baritz, L., *Backfire: A History of How American Culture Led Us into Vietnam and Made Us Fight the Way We Did* (New York: William Morrow & Co., 1985).

Belknap, M., *The Vietnam War on Trial: The My Lai Massacre and the Court-Martial of Lieutenant Calley* (Lawrence: University Press of Kansas, 2002).

Bilton, M. and K. Sim, *Four Hours at My Lai* (London: Penguin, 1992).

Bourke, J., *An Intimate History of Killing: Face-to-Face Killing in Twentieth Century Warfare* (London: Granta, 1999).

Braestrup, P., *Big Story: How the American Press and Television Reported and Interpreted the Crisis of Tet 1968 in Vietnam and Washington* (Boulder: Westview Press, 1977).

Browne, M., *The New Face of War* (New York: Bobbs-Merrill Co., 1965).

Burkett, B. and G. Whitley, *Stolen Valor: How the Vietnam Generation Was Robbed of Its Heroes and Its History* (Dallas: Verity Press, 1998).

Capps, W., *The Unfinished War: Vietnam and the American Conscience* (Boston: Beacon Press, 1990).

Caputo, P., *A Rumor of War* (New York: Ballantine Books, 1977).

Carson, M., 'F. Edward Hébert and the congressional investigation of the My Lai massacre', *Louisiana History*, 37 (1) (1996).

Chanoff, D. and D. Van Toai, *'Vietnam': A Portrait of its People at War* (New York: I.B. Tauris, 1996).

Chong, D., *The Girl in the Picture: The Story of Kim Phuc, the Photograph, and the Vietnam War*, (London: Scribner, 2001).

Cincinnatus, *Self-Destruction: The Disintegration and Decay of the United States Army During the Vietnam Era* (New York: Norton, 1981).

Crane, C., *Avoiding Vietnam: The US Army's Response to Defeat in Southeast Asia* (Carlisle, PA: Strategic Studies Institute, US Army War College, 2002).

Dean, E., *Shook Over Hell: Post-Traumatic Stress, Vietnam, and the Civil War* (Cambridge: Harvard University Press, 1997).

DeBenedetti, C. with C. Chatfield, *An American Ordeal: The Antiwar Movement of the Vietnam Era* (Syracuse: Syracuse University Press, 1990).

DeGroot, G., *A Noble Cause? America and the Vietnam War* (Harlow: Longman, 2000).

Dower, J., *War Without Mercy: Race and Power in the Pacific War* (New York: Pantheon, 1986).

Egendorf, A., *Healing from the War: Trauma and Transformation after Vietnam* (Boston: Shambhala, 1986).

Ehrhart, W. (ed.), *Carrying the Darkness: The Poetry of the Vietnam War* (Lubbock: Texas Tech University Press, 1989).

Englehardt, T., *The End of Victory Culture: Cold War America and the Disillusioning of a Generation* (New York: Basic Books, 1995).

Eszterhas, J., 'The selling of the Mylai massacre', in B. Rosset (ed.), *Evergreen Review Reader: An Anthology of Short Fiction, Plays, Poems, Essays, Cartoons,*

Photographs, and Graphics, 1967–1973 (London: Four Walls Eight Windows, 1998).

Everett, A., K. Johnson and H. Rosenthal, *Calley* (New York: Dell Publishing Co., 1971).

Faludi, S., *Stiffed: The Betrayal of Modern Man* (London: Vintage, 2000).

Fitzgerald, F., *Fire in the Lake: The Vietnamese and the Americans in Vietnam* (Boston: Little, Brown and Company, 1972).

Franklin, H., *M.I.A., or Mythmaking in America* (Brooklyn: Lawrence Hill Books, 1992).

Frascina, F., 'Meyer Schapiro's Choice: My Lai, Guernica, MOMA and the Art Left, 1969–70 [Parts 1 and 2]', *Journal of Contemporary History*, 30:3 and 4 (1995).

French, P. (ed.), *Individual and Collective Responsibility* (Rochester, VT: Schenkman Books, 1998).

Gellhorn, M., *The Face of War* (New York: Atlantic Monthly Press, 1988).

Gershen, M., *Destroy or Die: The True Story of My Lai* (New Rochelle: Arlington House, 1971).

Goldstein, J., B. Marshall and J. Schwartz, *The My Lai Massacre and Its Cover-up: Beyond the Reach of Law? The Peers Commission Report with a Supplement and Introductory Essay on the Limits of Law* (New York: The Free Press, 1976).

Gray, P. and K. Oliver, *The Memory of Catastrophe* (Manchester: Manchester University Press, 2004).

Greenhaw, W., *The Making of a Hero: A Behind-the-Scenes View of the Lt Calley Affair* (Louisville: Touchstone, 1971).

Haldeman, H., *The Haldeman Diaries: Inside the Nixon White House* (New York: Putnam, 1994).

Hallin, D., *The 'Uncensored War': The Media and Vietnam* (Berkeley: University of California Press, 1989).

Hammer, R., *One Morning in the War: The Tragedy at Son My* (New York: Coward-McCann, 1970).

Hammer, R., *The Court-Martial of Lt Calley* (New York: Coward, McCann & Geoghegan, 1971).

Hammond, W., *Public Affairs: The Military and the Media, 1962–1968* (Washington, DC: US Army Center for Military History, 1988).

Hammond, W., *Public Affairs: The Military and the Media, 1968–1973* (Washington, DC: US Army Center of Military History, 1996).

Hanley, C., S. Choe and M. Mendoza, *The Bridge at No Gun Ri: A Hidden Nightmare from the Korean War* (New York: Henry Holt, 2001).

Hellmann, J., *American Myth and the Legacy of Vietnam* (New York: Columbia University Press, 1986).

Herr, M., *Dispatches* (London: Picador, 1979).

Herring, G., *America's Longest War: The United States and Vietnam 1950–1975* (New York: Alfred A. Knopf, 1986).

Hersh, S., *Cover-Up: The Army's Secret Investigation of the Massacre at My Lai 4* (New York: Random House, 1972).

Hersh, S., *My Lai 4: A Report on the Massacre and Its Aftermath* (New York: Random House, 1970).

Hersh, S., *The Price of Power: Kissinger in the Nixon White House* (New York: Summit Books, 1983).

Herzog, T., *Vietnam War Stories: Innocence Lost* (London: Routledge, 1992).

Hunt, A., *The Turning: A History of Vietnam Veterans Against the War* (New York: New York University Press, 1999).

Kamm, H., *Dragon Ascending: Vietnam and the Vietnamese* (New York: Arcade Publishing, 1996).

Keating, S., *Prisoners of Hope: Exploiting the POW/MIA Myth in America* (New York: Random House, 1994).

Kelman, H. and L. Lawrence, 'Assignment of responsibility in the case of Lt Calley: preliminary report on a national survey', *Journal of Social Issues*, 28 (1) (1972).

Kelman, H. and L. Lawrence, 'American response to the trial of Lt William L. Calley', *Psychology Today*, 6 (June 1972).

Kennedy, L. and M. Williams, 'The past without the pain: the manufacture of nostalgia in Vietnam's tourist industry', in H. Ho Tai (ed.), *The Country of Memory: Remaking the Past in Late-Socialist Vietnam* (Berkeley: University of California Press, 2001).

Kimball, J., *Nixon's Vietnam War* (Lawrence: University Press of Kansas, 1998).

Kitfield, J., *Prodigal Soldiers: How the Generation of Officers Born of Vietnam Revolutionized the American Style of War* (New York: Simon & Schuster, 1995).

Knightley, P., *The First Casualty: The War Correspondent as Hero and Myth-Maker from the Crimea to Kosovo* (London: Prion, 2000).

Lang, D., *Casualties of War* (New York: McGraw-Hill, 1969).

Laurence, J., *The Cat From Hué: A Vietnam War Story* (New York: Public Affairs, 2002).

Lembcke, J., *The Spitting Image: Myth, Memory, and the Legacy of Vietnam* (New York: New York University Press, 1998).

Lewy, G., *America in Vietnam* (Oxford: Oxford University Press, 1980).

Lifton, R., *Home From the War: Vietnam Veterans: Neither Victims nor Executioners* (London: Wildwood House, 1974).

Limqueco, P. and P. Weiss (eds), *Prevent the Crime of Silence* (London: Allen Lane, 1971).

Lind, M., *Vietnam: The Necessary War: A Reinterpretation of America's Most Disastrous Military Conflict* (New York: The Free Press, 1999).

Lippard, L., *A Different War: Vietnam in Art* (Seattle: The Real Comet Press, 1990).

Logevall, F., *Choosing War: The Lost Chance for Peace and the Escalation of the War in Vietnam* (Berkeley: University of California Press, 1999).

Marin, P., 'Coming to terms with Vietnam: settling our moral debts', *Harper's* (December 1980).

Marin, P., 'Living in moral pain', in W. Capps (ed.), *The Vietnam Reader* (New York: Routledge, 1991).

Martin, A., *Receptions of War: Vietnam in American Culture* (London: University of Oklahoma Press, 1993).

McCarthy, M., *Medina* (London: Wildwood House, 1973).

McCrisken, T., *American Exceptionalism and the Legacy of Vietnam: US Foreign Policy Since 1974* (Basingstoke: Palgrave Macmillan, 2003).

McMahon, R., 'Contested memory: the Vietnam war and American society, 1975–2001', *Diplomatic History*, 26:2 (2002).

McNamara, R. with B. VanDeMark, *In Retrospect: the Tragedy and Lessons of Vietnam* (New York: Random House, 1995).

McNamara, R., J. Blight and R. Brigham with T. Biersteker and H. Schandler, *Argument Without End: In Search of Answers to the Vietnam Tragedy* (New York: Public Affairs, 1999).

McPherson, M., *Long Time Passing: Vietnam and the Haunted Generation* (London: Sceptre, 1988).

McWilliams, W., *Military Honor After Mylai* (New York: Council on Religion and International Affairs, 1972).

Melling, P., *Vietnam in American Literature* (Boston: Twayne Publishers, 1990).

Milgram, S., *Obedience to Authority: An Experimental View* (New York: Harper & Row, 1975).

Mueller, J., *War, Presidents and Public Opinion* (New York: John Wiley & Sons, 1973).

Myers, T., *Walking Point: American Narratives of Vietnam* (New York: Oxford University Press, 1988).

Neilson, J., *Warring Fictions: Cultural Politics and the Vietnam War Narrative* (Jackson: University Press of Mississippi, 1998).

O'Brien, T., *Going After Cacciato* (London: Flamingo, 1988).

O'Brien, T., *If I Die in a Combat Zone* (London: Granada, 1980).

O'Brien, T., *In the Lake of the Woods* (New York: Penguin, 1995).

O'Brien, T., *The Things They Carried* (London: Flamingo, 1991).

Obst, D., *Too Good To Be Forgotten: Changing America in the '60s and '70s* (New York: John Wiley & Sons, 1988).

Oliver, K., 'Atrocity, authenticity and American exceptionalism: (ir)rationalizing the massacre at My Lai', *Journal of American Studies*, 37:2 (2003).

Oliver, K., 'Towards a new moral history of the Vietnam war?', *The Historical Journal*, 47:3 (2004).

Olson, J. and R. Roberts, *My Lai: A Brief History with Documents* (Boston: Bedford Books, 1998).

Peers, W., *The My Lai Inquiry* (New York: Norton, 1979).

Polsgrove, C., *It Wasn't Pretty, Folks, But Didn't We Have Fun? Esquire in the Sixties* (New York: Norton, 1995).

Powell, C. with J. Persico, *A Soldier's Way: An Autobiography* (London: Hutchinson, 1995).

Prochnau, W., *Once Upon a Distant War: Reporting from Vietnam* (Edinburgh, Mainstream Publishing, 1996).

Sack, J., *Lieutenant Calley: His Own Story* (New York: Viking Press, 1971).

Sanford, N., C. Comstock *et al.*, *Sanctions for Evil* (San Francisco: Jossey-Bass, Inc., 1971).

Santoli, A., *To Bear Any Burden: The Vietnam War and Its Aftermath in the Words of Americans and Southeast Asians* (Bloomington: Indiana University Press, 1999).

Schell, J., *The Real War* (London: Corgi, 1989).

Schuman, H., 'Two sources of antiwar aentiment in America', *American Journal of Sociology*, 78 (3) (1972).

Schwarzkopf, H., *It Doesn't Take a Hero: the Autobiography* (London: Bantam Press, 1992).

Scott, W., *The Politics of Readjustment: Vietnam Veterans Since the War* (New York: Aldine De Gruyter, 1993).

Shay, J., *Achilles in Vietnam: Combat Trauma and the Undoing of Character* (New York: Atheneum, 1994).

Sheehan, N., *A Bright Shining Lie: John Paul Vann and America in Vietnam* (London: Picador, 1990).

Solis, G., *Son Thang: An American War Crime* (New York: Bantam Books, 1998).

Sontag, S., *On Photography* (New York: Dell Publishing, 1978).

Sontag, S., *Regarding the Pain of Others* (New York: Farrar, Straus and Giroux, 2003).

Stacewicz, R., *Winter Soldiers: An Oral History of the Vietnam Veterans Against the War* (New York: Twayne Publishers, 1997).

Steinman, R., *Inside Television's First War: A Saigon Journal* (Columbia: University of Missouri Press, 2002).

Sturken, M., *Tangled Memories: The Vietnam War, the Aids Epidemic, and the Politics of Remembering* (London: University of California Press, 1997).

Taylor, M., *The Vietnam War in History, Literature and Film* (Edinburgh: Edinburgh University Press, 2003).

Taylor, T., *Nuremberg and Vietnam: an American Tragedy* (Chicago: Quadrangle Books, 1970)

Thompson, K., A. Clarke and S. Dinitz, 'Reactions to My-Lai: a visual-verbal comparison', *Sociology and Social Research*, 58:2 (1974).

Tiede, T., *Calley: Soldier or Killer? (Your Decision)* (New York: Pinnacle Books, 1971).

Tritle, L., *From Melos to My Lai: War and Survival* (London: Routledge, 2000).

Turner, F., *Echoes of Combat: The Vietnam War in American Memory* (New York: Anchor Books, 1997).

Vistica, G., *The Education of Lieutenant Kerrey* (New York: St Martin's Press, 2003).

Walsh, J. and J. Aulich (eds), *Vietnam Images: War and Representation* (Basingstoke: Macmillan, 1989).

Wilson, W., 'I had prayed to God that this thing was fiction . . .', *American Heritage* (February 1990).

The Winter Soldier Investigation: An Inquiry into American War Crimes by the Vietnam Veterans Against the War (Boston: Beacon Press, 1972).

Wintle, J., *Romancing Vietnam: Inside the Boat Country* (London: Penguin, 1992).

Wyatt, C., *Paper Soldiers: The American Press and the Vietnam War* (New York: Norton, 1993).

Young, A., *The Harmony of Illusions: Inventing Post-Traumatic Stress Disorder* (Princeton: Princeton University Press, 1995).

Index

Note: page numbers in *italic* refer to illustrations